Navigating Opportunity:
Policy Debate in the 21st Century

Wake Forest National Debate Conference

Navigating Opportunity:
Policy Debate in the 21st Century

Wake Forest National Debate Conference

Allan D. Louden, editor

International Debate Education Association
New York & Amsterdam

Published by:
International Debate Education Association
400 West 59th Street
New York, NY 10019

Library of Congress Cataloging-in-Publication Data

National Developmental Debate Conference (2009 : Wake Forest University)
  Navigating opportunity : policy debate in the 21st century : Wake Forest
National Debate Conference / Allan D. Louden, editor.
     p. cm.
  Papers presented at the National Developmental Debate Conference held
June 5–7, 2009 at Wake Forest University; Allan D. Louden, conference
director.
  Includes bibliographical references and index.
  ISBN 978-1-932716-61-0
  1. Debates and debating--Congresses. 2. Debates and debating--Study and
teaching (Higher)--Congresses. I. Louden, Allan D. II.
International Debate Education Association. III. Title.
  PN4181.N38 2009
  808.53--dc22
                                    2010015216

Printed in the USA
IDEBATE Press

Conference Sponsors

American Debate Association (ADA)
American Forensics Association (AFA)
Cross Examination Debate Association (CEDA)
National Debate Tournament (NDT)
Wake Forest University—Office of the Provost

Conference Directors

Allan D. Louden, conference director, Wake Forest University
George Ziegelmueller, honorary codirector, Wayne State University

Special Thanks
Steering Committee

Timothy O'Donnell, University of Mary Washington
Robin Rowland, University of Kansas
Gordon Stables, University of Southern California

Distinguished Advisory Committee

Thomas Hollihan, University of Southern California
David Zarefsky, Northwestern University

Administrative Associates

Odile Hobeka, University of Pittsburgh
Will Sears, Wake Forest University

Special Recognition

Jeffrey Jarman, Wichita State University—CEDA Web Presence
Seth Gannon, Wake Forest University—Hospitality/Transcription
Alex Lamballe, Wake Forest University—Local Logistics
Ananda Mitra, Wake Forest University Communication Department—Chair

Dedication

Several giants of the debate community have passed away since the conception of the National Developmental Conference and the publication of this work.

This book is dedicated to their decades of loyal service as debate educators.

Scott Deatherage (47) (December 2009). Director of debate at Northwestern University (1990–2008). Scott Deatherage led the Northwestern University Debate Society to seven national championships as director from 1990 to 2008. "He believed very strongly in debate and what it could do for students—how valuable it was for their education," said David Zarefsky.

Douglas Duke (70) (March 2010). A teacher for 46 years, Douglas Duke spent much of his coaching time with the University of Central Oklahoma. His college coaching career began back in 1962 when he coached at Southeastern State College in Durant, Oklahoma.

John Gossett (57) (June 2009). Director at the University of Northern Iowa (1979–1981) and North Texas (1981–1991), department chair for 17 years. He was a member of the National Debate Tournament Board of Trustees from 1992 to 2002.

Frank Harrison (69) (June 2009). Director of debate at Trinity University for 20 years. At the 1961 National Debate Tournament, Frank was third speaker and final round participant for King's College. He served as a United States Representative for the state of Pennsylvania.

Scott Nobles (85) (December 2008). A longtime winning director at Oregon and Macalester, Scott Nobles will always be remembered for winning the first National Debate Tournament in 1947 with partner, Jerry Sanders. He consistently produced a nationally recognized program, leading one of his teams to win the national Cross Examination Debate Association tournament in two consecutive years.

Michael Pfau (63) (March 2009). A successful director of debate at Augustana College, SD in the 1970s–1980s. He was Communication Department chair at the University of Oklahoma for a decade, authoring and coauthoring more than 100 articles and book chapters.

Ross Smith (54) (July 2009). A conference participant, Ross was the longtime Wake Forest debate coach and director of debate (1985–2009) who led the squad to two national championships. He was the 2009 winner of the George Ziegelmueller Award.

James Unger (66) (April 2008). A highly successful debate coach at Georgetown and American universities who was also a past director of the National Forensics Institute and an innovative argument theorist. As one of his alumni wrote, "He lived it, breathed it, epitomized it, enjoyed it, perfected it, practiced it, and made it a permanent part of our lives." His "policymaking" approach to debate strategy became standard practice for debate teams at the high school and college levels.

Contents

Beginnings: The National Developmental Debate Conference

Allan D. Louden, Conference Director, Wake Forest University

Ideas grow from a mixture of motive and opportunity. For nearly a decade, policy debate professionals have had a sense that the debate community needed to draw a breath, discount busyness and inertia, and take the time to systematically assess the state of policy debate at the outset of the twenty-first century.

A more pressing motive presented itself in the summer of 2008 when an unbecoming YouTube video went viral, making public a post-debate confrontation at the Cross Examination Debate Association (CEDA) national debate tournament. CNN picked up the video, obliging nearly everyone associated with debate to explain to friends, colleagues, and reporters how otherwise committed coaches could trade invective and "physical display" before their students. Even the sympathetic were perplexed.

That an assessment of the role of debate was overdue, prompted by events, resulted in the National Developmental Debate Conference, hosted by Wake Forest University in Winston-Salem, North Carolina, June 5–7, 2009.

Debate leaders Timothy O'Donnell (University of Mary Washington), chairperson of the National Debate Tournament (NDT), and Gordon Stables (University of Southern California), president-elect of the CEDA, with the reliable encouragement of NDT board of trustees chair, Robin Rowland (University of Kansas), took up the challenge.

At the behest of what became the Conference Steering Committee, I was brought onboard. Over the period of a year, planning for the conference ensued. Themes facing the debate community were developed, resulting in ten areas of inquiry. Six months before the conference, debate leaders with relevant expertise were identified and invited to constitute working groups charged with investigation and development of recommendations. Members of the debate community were independently invited to participate in the conference.

Former Wayne State director, George Ziegelmueller, who chaired the first two developmental conferences, cautioned me in phone conversations that the meeting was not without risk. While a gathering of specialists skilled in argument and representing a continuum of strongly held opinion might appear ominous, the 90 professionals assembled in the spring warmth of Winston-Salem displayed a cooperative hardworking attitude that graced the three days. The conferees sacrificed time and resources to attend, largely because they believed deeply in the educational contributions of debate and wanted to be part of making it better.

CONFERENCE PHILOSOPHY—HISTORICAL ROOTS

The Wake Forest conference marks the third national development conference for intercollegiate debate. Previously, representatives of the collegiate debate community convened in Sedalia, Colorado, in 1974, and at Northwestern University in 1984.

This volume abounds with references to the previous developmental conferences, acknowledging discursively our collective historical debt to these prior efforts (and the larger-than-life coaches who oversaw the heyday of American forensics).

There is a continuity among the conferences that goes beyond problems and issues common across the generations. The shared themes have more to do with purpose: a life lived with bright students, curious and sometimes aggressive; a commitment to the future; and for many a calling.

Conferences can alter our thinking, often bring us to consensus, and potentially energize us, but they are also made up of distinct individuals who define the enterprise.

No individual made it to Winston-Salem who also traveled to Sedalia, Colorado. The long time span since the first conference and changing nature of debate meant that no individual attended all three conferences, although representatives of the Sedalia conference were present at Wake Forest. David Zarefsky provided continued guidance and, absent a prior commitment, would have bridged all three. As already acknowledged, George Ziegelmueller's voice is present in all three conferences.

A few attendees had participated at Northwestern: Fred Sternhagen (Concordia) and Dave Hingstman (Iowa, then Baylor). Ed Panetta (Georgia, then Wake) and I wrote a paper on summer workshops that *did not* make the published proceedings. A young Robin Rowland (Kansas, then Baylor) chaired the group on Topic Selection; and particularly salient now, Ross Smith (Wake Forest) served on the Ethics in Advocacy committee, primarily concerned with correct citations for debater's evidence. The scope of this previous work now looks antiquated in the Internet environment.

The advantage of setting aside time, absent the demands of tournament or academic conference, is obvious, yet we seldom make possible that luxury. The conference allowed discussion and reflection and occasional "out-of-the-box" thinking, challenges to standard practice that mark the essays in this work.

The range of topics considered at Winston-Salem is broader than that of the first two developmental conferences. Sedalia was primarily concerned with examining debate programs' residency in their academic homes. The resulting book, *Forensics as Communication* offered commissioned research, a Delphi protocol to assess opinion, and 63 formal recommendations (McBath 1975). *American Forensics in Perspective*, which grew out of the Northwestern conference, offered researched position papers largely addressing practice, from summer workshops to selecting a topic, producing 29 formal resolutions (Parson 1984).

The third developmental conference was by design more organic. The essays found in *Navigating Opportunity* avoid standardization. Their utility is reflected in different audiences and purposes. The chapter on tenure and promotion, for example, is designed as a stand-alone formal document, for sharing with administrators. Other sections are more for an internal audience and range from topics such as defining pedagogical goals to tournament practice. Other sections, such as those on innovations and nontournament practices, aim to stimulate thinking about what is possible in designing and conducting debate programs.

The Wake Forest conference was more open than Sedalia and more exclusive than Northwestern. Conferees were targeted for invitation based on both expertise and distinction, yet the working groups were not closed, as interested parties self-identified, enriching knowledge and range. The structure, less formal than either prior conference, intentionally assumed a more fluid blueprint.

The first two conferences did a commendable job—but for a different time.

A New World of Debate
After two years of planning and commissioned research, a handful of invited conferees met in Sedalia for six days. In Evanston, ten years later, the four-day

conference was the populist version of a developmental conference with 120 self-nominated participants.

The Wake Forest conference, by contrast met for three days, with two working days that included working group "hearings" and a "legislative session," covering a broad swatch of the core issues facing debate.

How is it possible to produce the quality reflected in this collection? The answer is that the world and the world of debate have dramatically changed since Sedalia and Northwestern. Working groups were able to communicate with ease, completing considerable work before gathering. The instantaneity cut months out of the process required in 1974. I mention this not to point out the obvious, that communication has quickened, but to offer the conference process as a metaphor for the revolution that is changing debate in ways of real consequence.

An example of this upheaval is the process of topic selection. Prior to the 2009 conference, the CEDA/NDT topic committee met for two days at the conference site. The topic proceedings were live-blogged, inviting the far-flung debate community to participate in real time.

Contrast this to Sedelia, which spoke generically of choosing topics, or Northwestern, which recommended "use caution when employing encompassing terms such as 'all,' 'every,' or 'any.'" Topic construction was not even on the radar for the third conference. Technology brought topic construction to anyone who wanted to participate, remote or in person. Topic debates are owned not by a removed conference but by the debate community as a whole with access via technology.

CONFERENCE MISSION

The undertaking of the third developmental conference was in some ways more complex than the first two conferences: issues were more far ranging, relationships with the academy more tenuous, and audiences more assorted.

In the first two published proceedings, recommendations were to directors on how to conduct a program, to the American Forensics Association about professional leadership, to departments on their responsibility to debate. The voices universally reflected the traditional paradigm of tournament-based programs, only recently removed from central roles in what were largely speech departments.

The tone was from a position of relative strength, dictating best practices for academic departments and debate teams. For example, a recommendation from Sedalia advised: "All institutions granting a doctoral degree in Speech Communication should have an active forensics program providing supervised instruction for future forensics directors."

While the recommendations were sound, many were not realized. One explanation for this is that the world surrounding debate was changing at an accelerated rate, and often debate was not a player in that evolution.

To explain the design of the Wake Forest conference, a quick look at a topic shared across conferences is illustrative. Diversity in debate—activities, participants, organizations—was a concern addressed at length in the first two conferences. Recommendations asked for more research on who participates and advised the community to be open to experimentation—suggestions that sound familiar.

The present conference took a more expansive view of diversity—ranging from the mission, to pedagogical assumptions, to manifestations of programs. For the earlier period "diversity in forensics" was largely addressed in terms of public debate vs. classroom vs. tournament and debate vs. individual events. The Sedalia conference, for example, advised that "Students should have the opportunity to participate in both debate and individual events."

The Northwestern conference attempted to corral the proliferation of debate organizations, proposing a Council of Forensics Organizations. Although a balkanized community was legitimately considered a problem in 1984, theirs was a world essentially before CEDA as we know it, before the National Parliamentary Debate Association, the internationalization of debate, before Urban Debate Leagues and online instructional resources. Appendix II, "Guide to Debate Organizations on the Web," provides a noninclusive list of nearly 100 debate organizations and educational outreach efforts.

Answering the simple question of what it means to engage in policy debate, itself a question of diversity, dictated that the Wake Forest conference adapt a more malleable structure, with multiple voices and audiences addressed.

The first two conferences also approached debate as if it were an identifiable practice. The Sedalia report, for example, noted "Conferees were sharply divided on how best to respond to controversial tournament practice . . . [such as] the spread, operational definitions and linguistic shorthand." They called for more research.

Today, debate, like the academy, occupies a post-deconstruction actuality that lacks a definable consensus. Sections of the Wake Forest conference proceedings approach these questions, but from a much enlarged frame.

The immense changes occurring in institutions of higher education are only accelerating. These realities dictated a less fixed design for the product of the conference working groups.

A renaissance within the academy and society is generally aimed at countering a political culture adrift in high-pitched pundits and seeking a more reasoned model of civic engagement. An apparent mass-culture version is Denzel Washington's movie *The Great Debaters*, but, more vitally, the academy is taking on (re)making the "world safe for democratic institutions," asking for the mode of engagement and civility contained in academic debate's very scaffolding.

A recent commentary published on insidehighered.com called for teaching debate across the curriculum, isolating the "very building blocks of civility, debate elements as a corrective to media excess. The basic elements are the same across formats: Argument, evidence, forced reciprocity and dialogue, equal time, and mandatory listening" (Herbst 2009).

Proceeding's Plan of Action
Those gathered at Wake Forest were under no illusion that conferences change the world or that this published work will remake debate or preserve an activity as we know it. Uncertainties abound surrounding academic debate.

A majority of those assembled grew up in the tournament tradition, with memories forged in competitive encounters, yet they recognize that the manner in which debate is practiced will undoubtedly change. In fact, the pace of change makes it plausible that our activity may be unrecognizable in the not-too-distant future. There are real questions as to whether tournament debate will survive when a turn to technology is easier and cheaper than getting past airport security.

Rather than becoming insular or suspicious of a changing activity, the emergent theme expressed in this collection is more one of adaptation and a renewed faith in the fundamental value of debate. Many of the essays properly discuss improving practice, but with each essay is a current of the future, openness to amendment, and confidence that debate as a process of knowing will survive and prosper.

We are cautioned in William Keith's provocative keynote address, "A New Golden Age: Intercollegiate Debate in the Twenty-first Century," that the union of academe and debate, while long in tradition, is always in transition. His essay evokes debate's past to explore its future. He argues not from an insider's defensive stance but rather from a critical perspective grounded in history.

The report of Timothy O'Donnell's group, "A Rationale for Intercollegiate Debate in the Twenty-first Century," summons substantial research in support of debate's participant outcomes. The essay is required reading for those seeking to position their program in the new academic environment. The report is bolstered by a review of research compiled by Sarah Spring, Joseph Packer, and Timothy O'Donnell (see Appendix I: Debate in Research, Practice, and History: A Selected Annotated Bibliography).

The essays negotiate the strains of both change and tradition. Robin Rowland, in "Status of Standards for Tenure and Promotion in Debate," and Dave Hingstman, in "Development and Advancement in the Coaching Profession," look at debate within educational institutions, through a lens informed by administrators, not solely by practitioners. Gordon Mitchell, in "Pathways to Innovation in Debate Scholarship," reinvents what scholarship and research mean in communicatively connected worlds.

The conference was also cognizant of reflecting on current practice and providing some practical suggestions. Gordon Stables's group, in "Consolidating Debate Governance: Working Group Recommendations," recognizes that debate is a larger community than it was when the first two developmental conferences met. There are multiple organizations, most of which did not exist in 1984. If anyone doubts the vitality of new debate organizations or the proliferation of governing bodies, they need only consult the appendix assembled by Anjali Vats, "Appendix II: Guide to Debate Organizations on the Web." The working group makes the case that it is time to rethink forensics governance.

The content of this work reflects the changing world that informs debate practice in ways not imaginable in the earlier eras. Rich Edwards's "Best Tournament Practices: Recommendations and Data" would not be fathomable to a 1984 tournament director. In an earlier era, Edward M. Panetta's "Controversies in Debate Pedagogy" would have been more about consensus than managing incommensurate worldviews. The recommendation of Scott Segal's group, in "Constructing Alumni Networks," to establish alumni social networking on a national scale could not have been imagined.

Many of the chapters chronicle paths toward new relationships between debate, departments, university directives, and curricular trends. Generally, the authors advance reasons for optimism, viewing contemporary debate not as alienated from core academic movements but rather as an enactment of them. Karla Leeper's "Innovation and Debate" argues for this integration as survival. Two essays—Theodore Albiniak's "Alternative Debate Models," and Anjali Vats's "Civic Engagement Through Policy Debate: Possibilities for Transformation"— find that nontraditional participation uniquely satisfies the academy's call. Finally, ten invited essays document many initiatives exemplifying ways to take debate programs into the future.

THE CHALLENGE

The developmental conference participants are hopeful that these essays can serve as a *beginning*, framing debate as a player in a changing environment. Adaptation is essential to survival, and innovation is crucial to leadership. Debate has the qualities that offer method to reason. Debate's distinctiveness is a precise way of knowing, which results in unmatched experiential learning. With anticipation, this book makes the Affirmative Case.

References

Herbst, S. 2009. "Change Through Debate." http://www.insidehighered.com/views/2009/10/05/herbst/ (accessed January 15, 2010).

McBath, J.H. 1975. *Forensics as Communication: The Argumentative Perspective.* Skokie, IL: National Textbook Company.

Parson, D.W., ed. 1984. *American Forensics in Perspective: Papers from the Second National Conference on Forensics.* Annandale, VA: Speech Communication Association.

Framing Policy Debate in the 21st Century

Keynote Address: A New Golden Age— Intercollegiate Debate in the Twenty-first Century

William Keith, University of Wisconsin–Milwaukee

INTRODUCTION: THE STATE OF DEBATE[1]

As intercollegiate debate looks toward its future in the twenty-first century, it must do so with a clear understanding of its past, and its present. What makes an episode of reason-giving a debate, rather than some other kind of argumentation? While argument can be both agonistic and irenic, debate is typically understood as an agonistic form of argument. An ancient image, the open hand and the closed fist (Corbett 1969), captures this distinction nicely: the open hand of cooperation and comity contrasted with the closed fist of conflict and domination. That is not a criticism of debate in itself, since this image suggests that each is appropriate at different times. We can still ask whether debate currently has too great an emphasis on contest and conflict. While conflict can surely go overboard, most contemporary debaters believe that since contest of ideas and arguments is the raison d'être of debate, one cannot have too much of that particular good thing.

Yet there are signs that as intercollegiate debate moves into the next century, it may need to evolve, once again, and specifically away from a model of debate that is excessively conflict driven. Has debate, in what I will call its "postmodern escalation," crossed the line? Obviously, opinions differ, sometimes sharply, within the debate community over whether lines have been crossed (Bilyeu 2004; Caldwell 2001; Cheshier 2002; Durkee 2005; Glass 2002; Heidt 2003; Schwartzman 2000). Let us consider an infamous incident and its implications. I have no doubt that Bill Shanahan and Sharnara Reid are smart people and good coaches. But their behavior in a famous clip, which (for unknown reasons) was posted to YouTube in August 2008, seems out of touch with the norms for any academic or civic activity—or intercollegiate sport, for that matter (InsideHigherEd 2008). The incident has to make one ask whether the culture of competition in intercollegiate debate has gotten out of control.

---

[1] The author would like to express his appreciation to Kathryn Olson, Steve Fuller, and Timothy O'Donnell for discussions that were helpful in writing this essay, and to Allan Louden for inviting it.

A response from the debate community *might* be: Well, not for us. But that raises a second question, one of accountability. Whose debate is it, anyway? Does intercollegiate debate have any accountability to audiences or communities outside itself, either in terms of behavior or intelligibility? Maybe not, in current practice. Here is some commentary posted (again on YouTube) about a clip of a recent National Debate Tournament (NDT) nationals that viewers found strange and unintelligible on several levels.

> For all of you who don't like this and are trashing it . . . just shut the f**k up. This debate ISN'T FOR YOU. It is for those select few of us who actually put all we have into this activity. The debate we do does not exist for anyone but those of us who actually participate and are a part of the debate community. F**k presidential debates. (www.youtube.com/user/Duke4667, accessed May 22, 2009)

Duke4667 colorfully and succinctly rejects any relationship between debate and those who are interested in civic discourse and the future of democracy; there might be one, but he just does not care. Flawed as presidential debates are, people expect they will have some family resemblance to intercollegiate debate, if only in terms of relevance.

I want to claim in this essay that whatever the virtues of this model of contemporary debate—and they are many—the attitudes and norms reflected in these two episodes are probably barriers to progress in the next century. I can say this with some confidence because the history of debate is also the history of American higher education; in each era, as colleges and universities have evolved, their new challenges for intercollegiate debate have been met. Based on where higher education is headed, the key issues for debate are likely to be

> **Debate as critical deliberation:** Debate will need to reassert its primacy as a form of argument that can enhance and embody public deliberation.
> **Accountability/transparency to publics and stakeholders:** Debate will need to become not only more transparent and less introverted but also more responsive to its publics.
> **Accessibility:** Debate will need to become (relatively) more accessible to students and others, in multiple ways that foster student involvement and public engagement.

To make this case, first, I will outline a parallel history between higher education and debate, aligning the history of intercollegiate debate with stages in the evolution of American colleges and universities. Second, I will indicate the relevant characteristics of higher education in the next few years, and how intercollegiate debate might adapt to them. Some will find these suggestions a bit radical, and so the third section outlines some temptations the debate community should avoid, while the fourth and final section will sketch what are, in my view, the choices that the community faces moving forward.

I write here as an official outsider to debate. I have never debated, but I have been a friendly observer of debate, debate coaches, and debaters for the past twenty-five years. There is no doubt that I will get some things wrong in the eyes of debate insiders, but I hope any such inaccuracies are more than balanced by the ability to bring an informed yet outside perspective to the crucial issues facing the future of debate. I am not taking a position on policy versus parliamentary versus public forum formats; this is an attempt to move the discussion to a place where reconsidering the current structures of debate makes sense.

1. THE AGES OF DEBATE: FROM THE LIBERAL ARTS COLLEGE TO THE POSTMODERN UNIVERSITY

Before launching into my version of the history of U.S. intercollegiate debate, a few words about history and historiography are in order. Obviously, we can tell a story in different ways that reflect different kinds of evidence and different "morals to the story." A couple of storylines that crop up commonly are probably not too helpful here. In particular, if we want the history to be instructive, we want to be careful of falling into a "Whig" history of intercollegiate debates. Whig histories are those that configure the past as an inevitable progression toward the glorious present; they tend to tell smooth stories that skim over the complexities and ambiguities of the actual history. So for our purposes, we should be suspicious of narratives that tell a triumphal story of debate that shows it as progressing from the simple to the complex, the easy to the difficult, the naive to the sophisticated. It is too easy to underestimate the things we are currently naive about; we may also fail to see the sophistication of the past, which can get hidden by the need of each generation (at least partially) to reject the one before. As great as current accomplishments may be, they should not blind us to how great—and how different in basic assumptions—things have been before. The past may not have been a rehearsal for the present, and may not have been an embryonic version of it.

Simply put, history is a resource; in its full complexity and ambiguity, it provides important clues to the present and the future. History is not determinative; nothing I will say here forces any particular choices, but it will put the status quo in a different frame, where it looks more contingent, more a result of choices that were made, and can be remade. History thus allows us to imagine alternate futures and to see the present in focus.

The Age of the Liberal Arts College: Debate as a Performative Art, 1840–1910

Nineteenth-century colleges in America still fit the mold of traditional liberal arts education; despite their religious origins, they provided education to people who had the "freedom" of time and income to get an education for no particular purpose. While some college students intended to go into the family business or the professions (as a minister or lawyer), the primary function of the liberal arts college was to reproduce a certain stratum of society by passing along a particular type of culture. In a sense, this type of liberal education focused on developing a certain kind of person. Debate, in this context, followed suit. Debate was intramural, consisting mainly in debating clubs modeled on the Oxford Debate Union. The emphasis was on a fairly casual style of debate (with little regard for research), and placed a premium on quality performance. The debates of the day were more like serial speeches, and this "public speaking" model dominated intercollegiate debate at its beginning. In the emphasis on performance, debate was integrated with other "speech" activities, from performing poetry or prose to declamation and oratory.

The college environment for debating was elitist, but only implicitly. All students could participate, and many did. Yet since schools only admitted certain types of people, for the most part only the elite were involved in debate. The benefits of debate at this point are vague. It ranked behind elocution as training for public life, and that life ("the platform") was clearly part of the aim for many college students. Oddly, though the movie is set in the 1930s, this is the style of debate mythologized in *The Great Debaters*. The polished speeches, written mostly by the coach and delivered skillfully by the students, hark back to the era of the liberal college, which is exactly what Wiley College was.

The Age of the Public University: Debate as a Civic Art, 1910–1945

In 1863, President Lincoln signed the Morrill Act, which provided for the establishment of "Land Grant" universities in each state. Over the next fifty years, the United States got many new states and many new universities, as most states added at least a normal school and sometimes other campuses. This expansion ushered in an era for new students in higher education; many more types of students, from different geographic, class, and ethnic backgrounds, found their way into higher education (though the diversity was certainly less than we currently see). Universities expanded, and they began, slowly, to adopt a more research-oriented approach to the training and hiring of faculty. Though the research model did not dominate universities as it would by the mid-twentieth century, as it took hold, debaters themselves began to integrate research into their practice.

Several factors helped produce the research climate. The development of debate from serial speeches between just two teams, into a tournament system similar to the one used now, happened during the Progressive Era. Progressive ideas included the belief that not only could government be reformed to serve common, public interests, but that increasing the degree of popular democracy was possible and desirable. The development of the referendum, the direct election of senators, the city-manager form of government, the "Wisconsin Idea" (that government and academia could partner to solve social problems) are just a few examples of Progressive Era developments (Mattson 1997). As college students from increasingly diverse backgrounds debated policy resolutions, they did increasing amounts of research to bolster their arguments.

The importance of research was also a consequence of the tournament system and professional coaching. With the tournament system, debaters would debate both sides of a resolution multiple times, as opposed to the original contract system where there was a different resolution each time two schools met. So the research got heavily used, and was worth the effort. As faculty members became both coaches and judges, the bar was raised for debating skill. In the long run, some thought this was a bad thing, since it also meant that debate could potentially be severed from its civic context, which was less likely when members of the community were judges. This was also the era when, despite debating concrete policy resolutions, judging shifted from judging the question to judging the debate, that is, from voting on whether the League of Nations was itself a good idea to voting on which side showed more skill on that day. Once the judging of the debate begins, the question itself might have only academic interest.

But the civic context of debating was still quite lively at this point in time. They did not call them debate "topics" yet, but "resolutions" in the sense of parliamentary procedure; the terminology of affirmative and negative, status quo, and so on was directly borrowed from the parliamentary procedure they thought they were imitating. At least in the imagination of those involved, debate was still tethered to, if not directly an imitation of, civic life and participation. Debate had become more accessible and more conversational, less oratorical and performative; it was more focused on research (a learned skill) than eloquence (increasingly perceived as a talent). Evidence of this can be found in the 1916–18 debates in the pages of the *Quarterly Journal of Speech* over the rules and spirit of debate, as well as in the "Nomenclature Report" of 1940 (Ross, Garland, and Sattler 1940). In this report, which takes into account the emergence of discussion and public forums, the authors try to divide up the different ways that people can interact over public and private decisions, and produce a comprehensive category system, based on the kind of decision-making process.

While debate was the competitive version of argument (as opposed to discussion, which is cooperative), it still prized sportsmanship; competition was a means to the civic end, not an end itself. The University of Southern California coach, Judge Hugh Wells, put the vision of debate as civic education movingly in 1918:

> I know of no miracle so wonderful as the sudden unfolding of a man's mind or the glorious blossoming of a womanly spirit, and I am filled with gratitude that I am permitted to behold these things, and with humility that I should be, in even so small a degree, a contributor to the awakening. With these rich gifts, we salute thee, O America! These are our offerings to the Democracy of the Future! Because democracy stands for the untrammelled right and opportunity to share in thought, the commingled ideas and propulsions, no other department of learning and instruction can rob us of our rich heritage. (Wells 1918, 172–73)

The Age of the Cold War University: Debate as a Puzzle-Solving Art, 1946–1985

Debate in the post–World War II era seemed to revolve around developing the virtuoso, the debater who had enormous mastery of information and argument, while her connection to her civic context became narrowed and indirect. The most important structural fact of the period from 1950 to 1980 was that the number of universities exploded, at first due to the GI bill, and later to the massive number of baby boomers who wanted to go to college. This was also the era of the cold war; international tensions and the background threat of nuclear annihilation structured America's approach to civic life, and resulted in research agendas and grant dollars that came from the U.S. government, many times directly from the Department of

Defense, the Office of Naval Research, and the Defense Advanced Research Projects Agency. Interestingly, of the many forms of debate that have flourished since 1950, the most popular one, National Debate Tournament, was born in the heart of the U.S. military, at West Point. NDT-style debate is intensely focused on competition, almost, one might say, in a warlike way. The heart of NDT style debating is a little bit like the "closed world assumption" of early wargame planners, or maybe game theory: Within a system that has a certain set of options, how can one side use those options in a creative way to triumph over the other side? (Edwards 1997).

Hence, I want to argue that this period is typified by a puzzle-solving focus, on the level of both policy resolutions and tournament practice. We can draw an analogy to Steve Fuller's argument that Thomas Kuhn's philosophy of science (famously based in the concept of a "paradigm") is a cold-war philosophy. Fuller argues that paradigms seal disciplines off from each other, ensuring that there is no general or public critique possible, and hence serving the purposes of the government funding the research (which can deflect criticism by claiming that only its paid experts can critique a given area). By focusing on research, debate became more professionalized, and hence isolated from the other features of rhetoric that made it traditionally a more public and civic activity, in terms of not only appeal but also potential impact. In that sense, it became less dangerous, less liable to have an impact outside of itself. (One might say that this is a microcosm of what happened more generally to the humanities as they became more professionalized.) Debate in the cold-war era worked from within a clear set of boundaries, but the boundaries were not, as in previous eras, provided by the civic character of debate. Rather, a kind of insularity set in. Increasingly, politics made the resolution's relevance recede into the background, while debaters devised ever more ingenious ways to evade and exploit the logic of stock-issue debate. Counterplans and other novelties reflected how debaters and coaches sought strategic advantage in the tournament setting. If people worried about whether or not counterplans were realistic to parliamentary politics, they did not let that get in the way of winning.

And, just like the cold war itself, debate became obsessed with nuclear war. To show that a policy, or the failure to adopt a policy, was bad, one had to argue that it led to bad consequences. The worst possible consequence was nuclear war, and hence, any topic or resolution at all turned out to be connected to nuclear war and the annihilation of the world. Nuclear consequences were more reasonable with some topics or resolutions, but the trope itself is interesting for the light it casts on both the topicality of debate and its concern with escalation. The amount of research escalated; for top programs, this might mean that senior teams might be spending thirty hours a week on research—almost a full-time job outside of being a student, and outside of the travel involved in debate.

Debate became, at this point, more elite, requiring more time and money (at least for the team and the school). Early in this era, the question of character—what kind of debaters are we creating?—reemerged, in much the same vein as in 1918. A series of articles in 1958 renews the controversy over debating both sides of the question. Does it produce sophistic students who are ill-prepared to take principled positions when they assume civic leadership roles? Of course, NDT debaters continued to debate both sides, but we should notice that there is still a tie to the civic character of debate, at least enough to raise the objection.

Debate, in the period, seems most civically relevant when it is aligned with "freedom of speech." A certain kind of free speech absolutism permeated debate culture in the late twentieth century; at times debaters resembled John Peters's "abyss artists" in their insistence that the liberal democratic character of speech must be proved, over and over again, by the evidence that debaters can and must argue anything—there there be no limits on debate (Peters 2005). Paradoxically, focusing on unlimited freedom of speech pushed debate away from civic life at the same time it professed to support it, since if there were no restrictions on debate, then it could become arcane, irrelevant, and uncivil. While political argument typically has many constraints, rhetorical and reasonable, these do not necessarily obtain in a debate round. After the idea of "debate as laboratory," was accepted (i.e., claiming that the advantage of debate is that it lacks realpolitik constraints, and hence is a laboratory for ideas and arguments that might not arise in the "real world"), this freedom was institutionalized. Yet debate harbored a deep ambivalence about its relation to the civic: Are relevance and realism to be feared or sought out? And which kind of realism would that be?

The Postmodern University: Debate as the Art of Deconstruction, 1985–Present

Starting in the late 1980s, debate, along with much of the humanities, begins to take a postmodern turn. Just as scholars in many fields began to imagine their arguments without foundations, debaters began to ponder the foundations of debate. In part, as universities begin to grapple with alternate epistemologies, radical feminism and multiculturalism, diversity and inclusiveness, these new options become part of the arguments, and in some cases the frameworks, debaters use in rounds—and they win. The postmodern version of the cold-war escalation is that instead of simply more research, faster talking, more arguments, now every assumption about debate is up for grabs. The essence of postmodernism is the reflexive moment, and debate achieves it.

Traditionally, NDT debate was synonymous with "policy debate" because debaters brought boxes of research to the debate to make arguments about a policy. Now it is called "policy debate" because of the research focus, but the debate is often about debate itself. For example, any case that debaters make relies on some notion of argument, of "making a case." So a team might attack the other side by attacking the idea of argument or reasoning itself. Or consider the assumption traditionally called "fiat": Debaters argue as if the results of their debate will actually be enacted, in order to prevent endless wrangling of the type "That's a great idea but you'll never get the legislature to accept it." To postmodern eyes, fiat is just one more assumption. Why should the other team get away with arguing under a pretense? What if you could make the case that pretend arguments have real consequences, and based on them the pretend arguments of the other team should be rejected? In some cases, postmodern debaters used alternative tactics to the high-speed recitation of arguments and evidence, including rapping in rounds (to illustrate the racial bias of debate), or disrobing (evidencing the "gender trouble" inherent in the activity). It is laudatory, of course, to recognize the various ways in which debate favors some participants over others. But spending the majority of rounds on debate theory and kritik does not solve the problem of social exclusion, and, of course, these strategies are not intended to; they are intended to help teams win.

Frameworks and performance might seem to be completely different from the cold war version of debate, but they are not. They flow from it naturally, and the connection is the pattern of escalation. These interesting new levels of argument, which often have little to do with the resolution, are possible because of two new features of debate tournaments. The first is the hashing out of the big-picture issues of intercollegiate debate in contest rounds; while it was always implicitly true that a good or relevant argument was whatever a judge would accept as one, in the postmodern period judges seem willing to assent to arguments and behavior in rounds that fundamentally challenge the traditional premises of debate. This is not the decision of the debate community in any corporate sense, but rather a pattern of debate being remade one round at a time, by five people in a room. This tendency is accelerated by the development of mutual-preference judging, which tends to allow debaters to argue to judges sympathetic to their paradigm.

At this point, debate has two opposing faces. One face says that debate has an important civic dimension because it focuses on debate theory and kritik; however, since the kritik is about inequities internal to debate, its public significance is dubious (we could, after all, just get rid of intercollegiate debate and get on to real social inequities). But debaters still, as they always have, display the inclination to valorize debate as having civic significance. The noncivic face of debate is that it is a sport that develops agile, muscular minds. The debate-as-sport analogy goes back to its very beginnings, as does the controversy over it. Can a characterization of debate as merely technique really justify its importance as the laboratory of democratic argument? Suppose that debaters really are unusually clever and agile researchers; are they any better wonks than people who are degreed experts in various fields? Will they really discover new and important arguments if their arguments are mostly not constrained by the resolution and instead concern debate theory?

2. The New Golden Age

According to I. Bernard Cohen (1987), the original metaphor of "revolution" referred to the idea of the "great wheel" of history, turning once again and bringing back the past. So "revolution" did not originally suggest complete overthrow and an utterly new regime, but rather the return, with changes, of previous forms and ideas. So even if there were a revolution in intercollegiate debate in the twenty-first century, it would not likely result in something entirely new, but in a return of some traditional ideas and practices in a new guise.

What I want to suggest is that universities are moving out of their postmodern period; they are not abandoning the lessons of critical theory, but moving past their aporetic moments of theory and incorporating its lessons into a new vision of higher education. I will argue that we have entered the Age of Service and Civic Participation. All types of institutions are now seeking to reassert and renew their role in the civic life of the United States. In little over a decade, service learning has become part of students' education across the country. The age of service and civic participation should present an incredible opportunity for debate, given its history of different modes of training for discursive civic participation; debate might return to its history, yet with the tools and concepts more recently developed.

The current situation is even more interesting. The commitment of colleges and universities to civic participation is part of an enormous movement toward democratic participation and deliberative democracy in and out of the academy.

The evidence is overwhelming that the interest group/power politics paradigm that dominated thinking in the postwar era is breaking up and being replaced by a multitude of practices that go under the titles of "participatory" and "deliberative" (Bessette 1994; Bohman and Rehg 1997; Dryzek 1990; Fishkin 1991, 1995; Ackerman and Fishkin 2005; Gastil 2000; Gastil and Levine 2005; Keith 2007; Zukin et al. 2006). Yet while the "deliberation train" is already leaving the station, intercollegiate debate is not on it. Its wonkiness, opacity, and focus on internal meta-issues leave it a bystander to the revolution in public discourse now taking place.

The new golden age for debate will arrive when it is reunited with deliberation, broadly understood. I am not claiming very many constraints on what the union will look like; just as deliberative opportunities and forms are diverse, so are the possibilities for debate to prefigure, influence, and educate toward them. But probably research will have a different role than it has in the past; debate in recent years has taken Walter Lippmann's side in the Dewey-Lippmann debates, and it will need to come to a more Deweyan understanding that there are different kinds of expertise needed in public debate, and not all of them can be found in a library. A model might be Steve Fuller's democratized conception of science and science policy, which (while he would not admit it) is thoroughly Deweyan in its argument that rather than requiring citizens to be PhD scientists before they participate in public debate about science and its funding, those in the science community have the requirement to make their work accessible, plausible, and relevant to people with different educational backgrounds (Fuller 2004). Stakeholders' educations may be a PhD in a different field or just a high school diploma; they all count as citizens in a democracy, and hence parties to the public discourse. I am not arguing that debaters should argue from ignorance, but that they go beyond a mere facility with information that can produce obscurantism and create an environment in which winning debaters also enlighten lay audiences, rather than just dazzling their peers.

This new vision of debate has other benefits. Curricular integration has become an increasing problem for intercollegiate debate as it is less at home in its historic location in departments of Communication. Deliberation, however, is a multidisciplinary field; its connections among departments and disciplines are not based on policy content, but on the ability to connect content with deliberation.

Martín Carcasson of Colorado State University has provided an excellent guide to potential interconnections between fields in the larger field of deliberation.

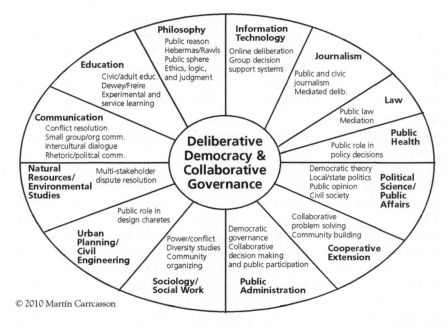

Philosophy
Public reason
Hebermas/Rawls
Public sphere
Ethics, logic,
and judgment

Information Technology
Online deliberation
Group decision
support systems

Journalism
Public and civic
journalism
Mediated delib.

Education
Civic/adult educ.
Dewey/Freire
Experimental and
service learning

Communication
Conflict resolution
Small group/org comm.
Intercultural dialogue
Rhetoric/politcal comm.

Law
Public law
Mediation

Deliberative Democracy & Collaborative Governance

Public Health
Public role in
policy decisions

Natural Resources/ Environmental Studies
Multi-stakeholder
dispute resolution

Political Science/ Public Affairs
Democratic theory
Local/state politics
Public opinion
Civil society

Public role in
design charetes

Urban Planning/ Civil Engineering

Power/conflict
Diversity studies
Community
organizing

Democratic
governance
Collaborative
decision making
and public participation

Collaborative
problem solving
Community building

Cooperative Extension

Sociology/ Social Work

Public Administration

© 2010 Martín Carrcasson

Carrcasson's diagram shows that there are many disciplinary, and even departmental, contexts for debate. It shows the many places where debate could be an important co-curricular activity, as well as places where debaters and their coaches might have research impact.

3. TEMPTATIONS: IT AIN'T NECESSARILY SO

Debaters, obviously, are a rowdy and disputatious bunch, which can be a strength or a weakness, depending on the situation. Most of what I have said here is debatable, and I hope it will be debated in the future. Nonetheless, I think there are temptations in responding to change that are not always productive. I recognize that debate, for many coaches and debaters, is a life-changing activity; it is so much more than just an extracurricular activity they did for a year or two in college. Naturally they are protective of themselves and the debate they love. Even so, I submit that the debate community should reject the following temptations as they refashion intercollegiate debate for the new century:

The status quo is a choice. Not really. Of course, the easiest thing to do is just go on as before, or decide that debate in the twenty-first century will be just like debate in the twentieth century, only more so. But this position flies in the face of history, which shows us that debate has always evolved as universities have evolved. We know where the universities are going, and the challenge is for debate not to follow, but to lead that change.

Any changes will destroy debate as we know it, or change is always change away from quality debate. Many things can make debate "high quality," and probably the sharpest disagreements within the debate community are over what the relevant qualities are, and who gets advantaged or disadvantaged by them. These disagreements are crucial, because they reveal the underlying values of debate and debaters. But claiming that all change would be detrimental is just a kind of conversation-stopper; it is just a reassertion of love for the status quo.

Debate made me such a smart person, and made all these ex-debaters such accomplished people. If debate is judged on its outcomes, many accomplished people can be brought forward as evidence. Yet does this mean debate cannot change for fear of losing this outcome? No. Calling for change or reform or renewal in intercollegiate debate in no way slights the abilities or accomplishments of debaters, past or present. Debate has contributed enormously to many people's education, and new forms of debate will contribute just as much.

There is always a zero-sum trade-off between time/energy spent in research and foregrounding other goals and formats in debate. I am neither qualified nor able to say exactly how to strike the right balance among the many elements of debate, but it is surely another conversation-stopper to imply that any and every change takes away from "research" or "information-processing," and therefore degrades the quality of debate. Debate was and is always more than research, and this framing of the issue bespeaks an unwillingness to have a serious discussion about the ends of intercollegiate debate and the means for achieving them.

4. AT THE CROSSROADS: CHOICES AND QUESTIONS

The future directions collegiate debate will take depend on decisions of the community; the debate community probably needs to create better spaces in which to deliberate that future. In light of this exigency, there are some crucial choices and questions that confront debate in the coming century—and the coming decade. How these choices are made and how questions are answered will largely shape debate.

Coach vs. independent judges. If debate is to remain a competitive practice, judging needs to evolve. Not only is debate poorly served by mutual-preference judging, it is a symptom of a larger problem. It is hard to imagine anyone taking a college sport seriously if the referees for it were coaches from opposing teams. Practical difficulties abound, but the exigency is real. The danger that debate will become more and more insular is directly related to using coach judges. Recent experiments with "lay" judges need to continue; many more possibilities for developing a cadre of judges exist. This will require coaches (and programs) to be willing to cede control of tournament outcomes and winning—so much the better for the larger social and cultural importance of debate.

Transparency and accountability. The other side of the coin from judging reforms is making debate open to public scrutiny and participation. It would be incredible if people cared about the outcome of debate tournaments or team styles the way they care about schools or teams in college football or basketball. But in those sports, there is a high level of transparency; these sports have "publics," groups of people that are not just theoretically fans, but who watch competitions closely, dissect results, discuss strategy, and so forth. For many reasons, debate is in no position to develop this kind of recognition and influence. During a discussion about the public image of debate, an anonymous poster posed this question:

> What percentage of DOF's [Director of Forensics], coaches, etc. would rather soil themselves than have a high ranking administrator from their institution spend a weekend with them at a tournament? (e-debate February 2004)

He received no response; in asking people this question since then, I have generally gotten some version of the response: "Why would you invite administrators to a tournament?" It is a shame that tournaments are inaccessible, and even worse if they are an embarrassment. The debate community needs to make itself part of some larger communities. This might happen in a variety of ways with a variety of communities, but tournaments need an audience and a public that goes beyond other debaters.

Tournaments matter for themselves vs. for something else. How can debate distinguish itself from the Chess Club or the video game World of Warcraft? Those are two activities that take intelligence and dedication to excel at, yet these things are just demonstrations of personal prowess, not the enactment of our deepest political values—which debate should be. "Winning" should be politically/morally meaningful vs. mere demonstration of (admittedly tremendous) skills. While there are certainly debaters who only compete for the personal satisfaction, the popularity of kritik shows that debaters may in fact be interested in the larger political meaning of debate, and willing to compete toward politically significant standards of argument.

Coarticulation of civic education and debate. Right now, debate, as a competitive activity, seems to be framed in terms of "Who's the smartest?" with "argument in a democratic society" as an afterthought. The renewal of debate will require subordinating the frame of debate as personal prowess to debate as a civic activity. There are many ways of understanding debate as civic, and many ways of changing the activity to enact civic ideals. It is not as if there is a single way to articulate civic discourse, and somehow debate must be adjusted to that. Debate and goals of civic education should be coarticulated, brought into alignment with each other through a thoughtful, deliberate process.

Debate, based on its history (Keith 2007), can become an important force in twenty-first-century universities and colleges, with schools ever more focused on public service and civic education. John Dewey was right, when he said, in *The Public and Its Problems,* that "the improvement of the methods and conditions of debate, discussion and persuasion . . . is the need of the public." Intercollegiate debate can, and should be, a leader in that change.

References

Ackerman, B., and J. Fishkin, 2005. *Deliberation Day.* New Haven: Yale University Press.
Bessette, Joseph, 1994. *The Mild Voice of Reason.* Chicago: University of Chicago Press.
Bilyeu, R. 2004. "An Army of One: A Challenge to Debate Coaches." *Rostrum* 78: 72–86.
Bohman, J., and W. Rehg, eds. 1997. *Deliberative Democracy: Essays on Reason and Politics.* Cambridge, MA: MIT Press.
Caldwell, J. 2001. "Answering Critiques." *Rostrum* 75: 9–13.
Cheshier, D. 2002. "Defending Pragmatism as an Alternative to Some Critiques." *Rostrum* 76: 1–5.
Cohen, I. B. 1987. *Revolutions in Science.* Cambridge, MA: Harvard University Press.
Corbett, E.P.J. 1969. "The Rhetoric of the Open Hand and the Rhetoric of the Closed Fist." *College Composition and Communication* 20, no. 5: 288–96.
Dryzek, J. 1990. *Discursive Democracy: Politics, Policy, and Political Science.* New York: Cambridge University Press.
Durkee, J. 2004. "Debating About Debating." *Rostrum* 78: 49–52.
Edwards, P. 1997. *The Closed World: Computers and the Politics of Discourse in Cold War America.* Cambridge, MA: MIT Press.
Fishkin, J.S. 1991. *Democracy and Deliberation: New Directions in Democratic Reform.* New Haven: Yale University Press.
———. 1995. *The Voice of the People: Public Opinion and Democracy.* New Haven: Yale University Press
Fuller, S. 2004. *Philosophy, Rhetoric and the End of Knowledge: A New Beginning for Science and Technology Studies.* Second edition. Mahwah, NJ: Lawrence Erlbaum.

Gastil, J. 2000. *By Popular Demand: Revitalizing Representative Democracy Through Deliberative Elections*. Berkeley: University of California Press.

Gastil, J., and P. Levine, eds. 2005. *The Deliberative Democracy Handbook*. San Francisco: Jossey-Bass.

Glass, D. 2002. "Post Modern Critiques in the Policy Debate Stratagem." *Rostrum* 76: 7–13.

Heidt, J. 2003. "Performance Debates: How to Defend Yourself." *Rostrum* 77: 5–9.

InsideHigherEd. 2008. "A Debate Performance Laid Bare." http://www.insidehighered.com/news/2008/08/14/debate/.

Keith, W. 2007. *Democracy as Discussion*. Lanham, MD: Lexington Books.

Mattson, K. 1997. *Creating a Democratic Public*. State College: Pennsylvania State University Press.

Peters, J.D. 2005. *Courting the Abyss: Free Speech and the Liberal Tradition*. Chicago: University of Chicago Press.

Ross, H.; J. Garland; and J. Sattler. 1940. "Report of the Committee on Nomenclature in the Field of Discussion." *Quarterly Journal of Speech* 26: 311–16.

Schwartzman, R. 2000. "Postmodernism and the Practice of Debate." *Rostrum* 75: 1–8.

Wells, H.N. 1918. "Comment on Professor O'Neill's Latest Mss." *Quarterly Journal of Speech* 4: 426–30.

Zukin, C.; S. Keeter; M. Andolina; K, Jenkins; and M.X. Delli Carpini. 2006. *A New Engagement: Political Participation, Civic Life and the Changing American Citizen*. Oxford: Oxford University Press.

A Rationale for Intercollegiate Debate in the Twenty-first Century

Chair
Timothy O'Donnell, University of Mary Washington

Members
Neil Butt, Wayne State University
Stefan Bauschard, Lakeland School District, New York
Joseph Bellon, Georgia State University
Warren Decker, George Mason University
John Kastulas, Boston College
William Keith, University of Wisconsin-Milwaukee
James Lyle, Clarion University
Danielle Verney O'Gorman, U.S. Naval Academy
Joseph Packer, University of Pittsburgh

INTRODUCTION

Democracy demands that people become citizens. It is a mandate that requires individuals to move from identities based in private interests to an engagement in civic life, speaking as members of a deliberative public. At the dawn of the twenty-first century, one of society's most pressing challenges lies in connecting public life to our various institutions, including those charged with cultivating an active and engaged citizenry.

Over the past ten years, a revolution has occurred, born of the realization that education alone is insufficient to produce capable citizens. These challenges are illustrated by recurrent calls for Americans to participate more consistently in the structures of public life. Predictably, in this environment, educators at all levels—irrespective of discipline or field—are increasingly concerned with creating and promoting programs that foster service learning, social responsibility, and civic engagement. A complex world inundated by instant communication and overwhelming information flows demands the acquisition of "technologies" to mediate the simultaneous explosion of political speech.

Intercollegiate debate, positioned at the nexus of liberal learning, is uniquely located to rejoin the call to renew the promise of the American experiment. Debate is a technology that connects the explosion of political speech with a civic-oriented vision for the future as well as a mode of speech and inquiry that is constitutive of citizenship; people (students) become citizens both in and through their participation in debate.

Citizenship is both an identity and a skill—qualities that are cultivated through a liberal education that prizes debate. More than any other activity, debate prepares students to speak as citizens. Students must view themselves as participating in and being implicated by the vast systems of discourse that comprise civil society while at the same time imaginatively engaging in institutional decision making. In addition, they must have the skills essential to effective participation—skills to both consume public discourse and take part in it. In the present moment we need to emphasize these prerequisite proficiencies of democracy.

Debate is training for citizenship. As an essential tradition of democracy in the Western world, it possesses a rich pedagogy focused on preparing for and investing in civic life. Such a conception of the role of argument in the civic imagination is both traditional and contemporary:

> We ought, therefore, to think of the art of discourse just as we think of the other arts, and not to form opposite judgments about similar things, nor show ourselves intolerant toward that power which, of all the faculties which belong to the nature of man, is the source of most of our blessings. For in the other powers which we possess . . . we are in no respect superior to other living creatures; nay, we are inferior to many in swiftness and in strength and in other resources; but, because there has been implanted in us the power to persuade each other and to make clear to each other whatever we desire, not only have we escaped the life of wild beasts, but we have come together and founded cities and made laws and invented arts; and, generally speaking, there is no institution devised by man which the power of speech has not helped us to establish. (Isocrates 1929, *Antidosis*, II, 327–28)

Isocrates's paean to the place of speech and argument in human life has stood for 2,500 years as a touchstone of liberal education. It is an approach that acknowledges the linkage between speech and reason as a distinctive human characteristic, essential for the organization of human life and society. Even in a world rich with information and digital technologies, speech—the basic face-to-face interaction where people trade reasons in order to generate knowledge or reach decisions—even when mediated, stands at the core of what makes us human.

For a variety of reasons, recent years have been witness to a resurgence of interest in public deliberation and participation—even to the point of radical democracy. Advocates for public deliberation assert that policy wonks and interest-group politics are insufficient on their own to completing democracy's vision. Rather than mediate power struggles among interest groups, such advocates seek means of communication that are adequate to the task of (re)introducing meaningful discussion and debate to the policy process while at the same time empowering mass participation. In such an environment, at the dawn of the twenty-first century, the tools of the fifth century BCE seem more relevant than ever.

More than language is required to make democracy work. As Tocqueville concluded, the success of American democracy rests on structures of civil society that support it; democratic institutions in the United States rest on a massive understructure of civil society, sustained by forms of communication. From the school board to the neighborhood watch, the Rotary Club to the PTA and the Red Cross, people come together in nongovernmental groups. In their communion, such groups allow for the realization of what John Dewey called "the public"—groups of people (often dispersed across society) who share common concerns. As Dewey described it, democracy was more than a set of governmental institutions (plus voting); it was a mode of associated living. Every social interaction is a chance to enact the democratic ideals of debate, discussion, and rational argument, noncoercively producing agreement on solutions to problems. More recently, deliberative democrats, such as Benjamin Barber (2004) and James Fishkin (2009), have sought to take seriously this legacy of democracy as reasoned decision making.

Yet, participants in the movement for a return to deliberation realize there will be no simple return to the idyll of Athenian democracy (if, indeed, it ever existed) nor can it be accomplished by nostalgia for the mystic chords of memory wrought from the American experience. The world has changed. But so has debate education. In writing a rationale for debate in the twenty-first century, our purpose is to articulate how and why intercollegiate debate prepares students for civic participation, while also serving as a tool of civic change itself.

Debate trains the mind the way sports train the body, making it more powerful and capable. In daily life, in situations large and small, we are called upon to receive arguments and invent our own, as part of a process of collective inquiry. Cultivating the habits of mind and skills to advance, defend, and judge claims is the essence of liberal learning and the staple of knowledge production in the academy and beyond. We can no longer take for granted that the only essential skill of democratic life is mere speaking. Though there are certainly many varieties of speaking, informed speakers advancing critical arguments over issues that matter is the standard of democratic life.

Liberal education is the education of the "free" (*liber*) citizen to make decisions and engage others. Debate as a mode of liberal learning is incredibly powerful. And debate, especially in its highly developed contemporary form, as practiced through intercollegiate debate, is a technology of liberal education without equal; it is intrinsically cross-disciplinary, applicable to any field and able to connect any field to public life.

Despite changes in form and function, a constellation of values has connected and distinguished intercollegiate debate for over a century.

> Debate is a cross-disciplinary method of collaborative inquiry and intentional learning, focused on the controversial public policy issues of the day, emphasizing the fundamentals of argument—reasoning, research, communication, and practical judgment—through the clash of competing ideas and the habits of mind that come from understanding others' arguments as well as one's own. Although intercollegiate debate is a highly competitive activity, it is profitably viewed from a pedagogical perspective as a leadership laboratory designed to prepare the next generation for entry into the public sphere and the process of lifelong learning. From public administration to community activism, from personal decision making to government policy, and across a wide variety of fields from business to education, intercollegiate debate provides a liberal education that is the foundation of civic engagement.

How does contemporary intercollegiate debate embody the values and goals of liberal education for a democratic society? At its core and from its earliest appearance in the American academy in the once wildly popular literary societies to its contemporary manifestation in national championship tournament competition, intercollegiate debate is a well-established and highly successful educational practice with substantial educational benefits for all students (O'Donnell 2008a). It is, in every sense, what George Kuh (2008) refers to as a "high-impact educational practice." The literature review that follows seeks to ground this claim in a body of research. In so doing, it identifies the essential skills, virtues, and modes of inquiry that participation in debate fosters: critical thinking, leadership training, academic achievement, and ethics of advocacy, community building, active, intentional and cooperative learning, and empowerment.[1] The literature selected for review focuses predominantly on research

---

[1] Although the review that follows is the product of many hands and has benefited from the efforts of many in the working group, a substantial portion of the research was contributed by John Katsulas, director of debate at Boston College, prior to the conference.

concerning intercollegiate debate. The body of work concerning classroom debating and other forms of noncompetitive debate have been intentionally excluded, although they are equally robust and provide additional testimony to the enduring value of debate education. Much of that literature has been collected in an annotated bibliography compiled by Sarah Spring, Joseph Packer, and Timothy O'Donnell (see Appendix 1).

1. Critical Thinking

Developing critical-thinking skills is one of the primary goals of American education. A survey by the Higher Education Research Institute (2009) of 22,562 full-time college and university faculty members reported that 99.6% of them viewed critical-thinking skills as paramount to undergraduate education. Several national reports (Association of American Colleges and Universities 1985; National Educational Goals Panel 1991; National Institute of Education Study Group 1984) have identified critical thinking as a major goal of higher education.

Many have written about the importance of critical thinking to achieving a free, safe, and prosperous society. Richard Franke, a fellow of the National Academy of Sciences, observes: "the value of critical thinking is incalculable. From assessing markets to identifying the salient features of a policy to decisions about life, liberty, and the pursuit of happiness, critical thinking clears a path for rational judgment" (2009, 22). Argumentation professors Douglas Ehninger and Wayne Brockriede recognize that in the nuclear age, it is imperative for society to develop leaders with strong critical-thinking skills: "in an age when a single bomb can wipe out a great city, critical thinking is not a luxury but a necessity" (1978, 3). Edward Panetta and Dale Herbeck argue that critical-thinking skills developed by policy-debate training "will help resolve impending geo-political crises" (1993, 25).

John Dewey considered critical-thinking skills to be an essential characteristic of good citizenship, and subsequent work has demonstrated this connection. Critical-thinking skills are a precondition for citizenship engagement and deliberation about public affairs (Owen 2004). For example, Jack Rogers (2005) shows that debaters are more likely than nondebaters to vote in elections and to participate in social and political campaigns.

Debate scholars claim that the teaching of critical-thinking skills is one of debate's greatest educational achievements. Enhancing critical thinking is "the most frequently cited educational merit of debate" (Omelicheva 2007, 163). Glenn Capp and Thelma Capp (1965) list critical thinking as one of the seven educational benefits to debate training. James McBath argues that debate provides an educational laboratory for training students in "critical thinking skills through the discovery of lines of argument and their probative value" (1984, 10). Edward Inch, Barbara Warnick, and Danielle Endres state "that intercollegiate debate provides students with an intensive and exciting method for developing their debating skills and critical thinking abilities" (2006, 354). Austin Freeley and David Steinberg contend, "since classical times, debate has been one of the best methods of learning and applying the principles of critical thinking" (2005, 2).

Lived experience is reflected in the opinion of former debaters' assessment of acquiring critical-thinking skills. Several demographic surveys (Katsulas and Bauschard 2000; Matlon and Keele 1984; Williams, McGee, and Worth 2001) reveal overwhelming support from former debaters that the activity sharpened their critical-thinking skills. In response to the survey by John Katsulas and Stefan Bauschard, Daniel Sutherland, the National Debate Tournament (NDT) winner in 1982, replied, "debate significantly enhanced my development as a lawyer. I think the major area is in critical thinking—understanding my own arguments, coming to grips with my opponents' arguments and forecasting how the judge might evaluate both positions" (Katsulas and Bauschard 2000, 7). Cynthia Leiferman, an NDT finalist in 1984, agreed, writing that debate training taught her how "to think 'outside the box.' Creative critical thinking is the lifeblood for a successful litigator" (ibid.).

Additionally, empirical research demonstrates that debate training increases critical-thinking skills. Several studies comparing debaters to nondebaters substantiate this link. Kent Colbert's (1987) study of NDT and Cross Examination Debate Association (CEDA) debaters found that they scored substantially higher than nondebaters on the Watson-Glaser Critical Thinking Appraisal (WGCTA). This research tool measures critical-thinking ability in five areas: "inference, recognition of assumptions, deduction, interpretation, and evaluation of arguments" (Colbert 1987, 199). Colbert's study validated the results of prior studies (Cross 1971; Howell 1943; Jackson 1961; Williams 1951) showing a link between debate participation and critical thinking.

Using a different measuring technique, studies by Kenny Barfield (1989) and Kip McKee (2003) also demonstrate a positive link between debate and critical thinking. Barfield and McKee found that high school debaters scored substantially higher than nondebaters in reading comprehension and thinking skills on the Stanford Achievement Test (SAT). Because research proves that higher reading comprehension scores on the SAT correlate well with higher critical-thinking skills on the WGCTA, Barfield and McKee's findings prove that debate participation enhances critical thinking.

The most definitive evidence comes from a meta analysis by Mike Allen et al. (1999), which examined data from 22 studies over 50 years that had explored the link between communication skills and critical thinking. Most of these studies used the WGCTA as their measurement instrument. The cumulative evidence indicated that communication skill instruction increased critical-thinking ability by 44%. However, "participation in forensics demonstrated the largest improvement in critical thinking whether considering longitudinal or cross-sectional designs" (Allen et al. 1999, 27). Allen et al. conclude that competitive debate enhances critical thinking more effectively than argumentation classes and public speaking. This study provides powerful support for the value of competitive debate to improve critical thinking.

Given all of the above evidence, Colbert's assessment that "the preponderance of defendable evidence suggests competitive debate experience can indeed improve critical thinking skills" is a valid conclusion (1995, 60). He also correctly points out that the few studies (e.g., Whalen 1991) not demonstrating a link suffer from flaws in "design limitations, instrument ceiling, sampling, teaching methods, or statistical procedures" (Colbert 1995, 60).

How does debate teach effective critical-thinking skills? There are numerous ways. Debate teaches analytical skills, whereby students practice identifying errors in reasoning and proof, recognizing inconsistencies in arguments, assessing the credibility of sources, challenging assumptions, and prioritizing the salience of points (Murphy and Samosky 1993). Critical thinking requires that decision makers arrive at conclusions based on a careful examination of the facts and reasons, which is the heart of the methodology taught by debate. Jeffrey Parcher (1998) argues that the devil's advocacy approach to debating, whereby students argue both sides of a controversy, improves critical thinking. Research also shows that critical-thinking skills are developed through consistent practice, which debate tournament competitions afford to students (McKee 2003)

.

2. Leadership Training and Career Advancement

Debate is a "premier training ground for the future leaders of this country" (O'Donnell 2008b, A38). The former debaters who occupy prestigious leadership positions in law, education, government, politics, and business have long constituted an illustrious club. Brilliant lawyers who were former debaters include Alan Dershowitz, famous criminal appellate attorney and Harvard law professor; Thomas Goldstein, cofounder of SCOTUSBLOG and a litigator who has argued over 20 cases before the U.S. Supreme Court; Laurence Tribe, preeminent constitutional law professor of Harvard; Erwin Chemerinsky, founding dean of the University of California, Irvine School of Law; and Neal Katyal, the deputy solicitor general of the United States. Prominent educators include three former college presidents: Alexander Meiklejohn of Amherst College, Lawrence Summers of Harvard, and David B. Henry of the University of Illinois. At least two active college presidents, David Boren of the University of Oklahoma and John Sexton of New York University, were debaters. Politicians include six U.S. presidents who served during the twentieth century, including John F. Kennedy Jr., and numerous U.S. senators and representatives. Titans from the world of business include Lee Iacocca, former CEO of Chrysler, Ted Turner, the media and entertainment mogul, and Ross Perot, billionaire businessman and former presidential candidate.

A plethora of evidence exists to support the claim that participation in debate facilitates the professional careers of students. Numerous surveys of former debaters have overwhelmingly found that debate participation was a positive influence in advancing their careers. Ronald Matlon and Lucy Keele's survey of 703 debaters who participated in the NDT found that "successful attorneys, educators, legislators, businesspersons, and consultants" stated unequivocally "that debate was as important as the total of the rest of their education, or more so" (1984, 205). A survey of former debaters by Jeffrey Hobbs and Robert Chandler (1991) arrived at similar findings, with 86% of the respondents recommending debate as beneficial training, including 75% of lawyers, 85% of managers, 97% of ministers, and 84% of teachers. David Zarefsky, a past president of the National Communication Association, a distinguished professor of communication at Northwestern, and an immensely successful debater and coach, says, "It's hard for me to imagine a profession for which debate is not a valuable kind of preparation" (Wade 2006).

Evidence from two longitudinal studies comparing the employment success of debaters and nondebaters provides empirical support for the claim that debate participation enhances career skills (Rogers 2002, 2005). In the first longitudinal study, Jack Rogers (2002) tracked the performance of 100 freshmen who were debaters versus 100 nondebaters over four years. The results showed that upon graduation, the debaters received job offers superior to those of the control group. Rogers concluded there is "a strong correlation between debate experience and involvement in professional internships," which resulted in the debaters receiving a higher rate of job offers upon graduation as compared with the nondebaters (2002, 16). In a follow-up study, Rogers (2005) examined the performance of this same group of students over four additional years. Once again, the results showed the debate group with superior career advancement. The study found that debaters received more job offers in their field, more positive evaluations from their supervisors, and slightly higher pay increments.

Especially in the field of law, debate training is overwhelmingly beneficial. A survey of 98 law school deans found that 70% of them recommended that students should participate in intercollegiate debate (Freeley and Steinberg 2005). Most prelaw academic counselors also advise undergraduates to take courses in argumentation and debate (Pfau, Thomas, and Ulrich 1987). A survey directed to 82 prominent lawyers who were former debaters asking about the benefits of collegiate debating revealed strong support for the belief that debate taught them skills in oral advocacy, critical thinking, brief writing, research, and listening (Katsulas and Bauschard 2000). Law school dean Erwin Chemerinsky credits his debate training for teaching him skills in analysis, research, and public speaking and he claims that "not a day goes by that I do not use the skills and lessons I learned in debate in my teaching, my writing, and my advocacy in courts" (2008, A11).

While the law remains the preferred career choice for many debaters, the skills taught by debate are just as necessary and useful for debaters who want to succeed in the world of business. Employers recognize this and perceive debating experience as a valuable asset. Bill Lawhorn, an economist with the Bureau of Labor Statistics, speaks about the value of debate training for employers: "Debaters must have strong research skills, be able to think quickly, and be able to communicate well. In addition, debaters must be comfortable performing in front of an audience—and having the confidence to do so is a valuable workplace skill, especially when it comes to making presentations to coworkers or superiors" (Lawhorn 2008, 19).

Several large companies have been established and are being operated by former debaters. For instance, Michael Beckley, a former Emory debater, and Marc Wilson, a former Dartmouth debater, cofounded Appian, a fast-growing software company. Beckley and Wilson credit their debate training for affording them the presentation skills to persuade clients such as Home Depot to use Appian's software instead of that of larger companies such as Oracle and IBM (D. Jones 2004). Beckley and Wilson go so far as to say that their company, which has grown to 190 employees, would never have existed without their debate background (D. Jones 2004). Other former debaters who are CEOs of successful companies include Lance Rosenzweig of PeopleSupport, Chuck Berger of Nuance Communications, Mark Astone of Panagraph, Tod Loofbourrow of Authoria, and Cynthia McKay of Le Gourmet Gift Basket (ibid.).

Management consulting firms also recognize the value of hiring debaters. A.T. Kearney, a global management firm with offices in 34 countries, has actively sought to hire former debaters after being highly impressed with the job skills brought by Leslie Mueller, a former Northwestern debater (Ross 2002). Mueller now attends debate tournaments to recruit prospective employees because she says debaters have superior analytic and communication skills (ibid.).

3. Academic Achievement in the Classroom
College educators overwhelmingly believe that participation in debate increases students' academic achievement. Melissa Wade, the director of forensics at Emory University, who has coached thousands of high school and college debaters over two decades, says that the value of debate training is well documented: "the effect on academic achievement has been measured and confirmed to improve critical thinking, research and communication and organization skills" (2006, 1). Kent Colbert and Thompson Biggers share this view: "the educational benefits of debate seem to be well documented: improved communication skills; exposure to important social issues of our time; improvement of critical thinking ability" (1985, 238).

In fact, there is considerable empirical evidence to prove that academic debate boosts academic achievement. Several studies show that debaters achieve higher average grade point averages than nondebaters (Barfield 1989; Collier 2004; Hunt, Garard, and Simerly 1997; K. Jones 1994). It is also the case that almost three-quarters of debaters believe that involvement in debate benefits them academically (Hunt, Garard, and Simerly 1997). Jack Rogers (2002) found that debaters maintained higher grade point averages than nondebaters, matriculated at the same rate as nondebaters, and enjoyed a higher acceptance rate into graduate school programs. In another study, Rogers (2005) determined that debaters were more successful than nondebaters in completing their graduate studies and achieving higher scores on their LSATs and GREs.

Debate participation improves academic performance because it promotes numerous skills that are essential to realizing a high level of educational proficiency. The educational benefits of debate include teaching research skills, acquiring cross-disciplinary knowledge about the world, learning how to organize and construct arguments, improving writing skills, enhancing listening and note-taking skills, increasing student self-confidence, and improving time-management skills.

a. Research
One of the obvious benefits of policy debate is that it teaches research skills in a manner "unparalleled in the world of academics" (Fritch 1993/1994, 7). No undergraduate college class assignment requires as much research as debate does. Robert Rowland argues that "debate, more than perhaps any other educational activity at the university level, teaches students about both the importance of research and the wealth of material that is available" (1995, 101). The research effort undertaken by debaters over the course of a single year's topic is often greater than the work to obtain a law degree or dissertation (Parcher 1998). Many debaters spend as many as 20 to 30 hours per week doing research (ibid.). A typical debate team gathers enough evidence to write thousands of pages of argument briefs.

This emphasis on research is due to several factors. Because debaters are required to debate both sides of a topic, they must collect evidence to support a myriad of arguments. Debate judges also reward evidence more than oratory. There is an expectation that debaters are required to support every point with evidence (Panetta 1990). Therefore, everyone has a competitive incentive to collect as much evidence as possible. In many cases, the best researchers are the most successful debaters (Cheshire 2002).

Because doing research is so integral to competitive success, debaters have a strong incentive to acquire excellent research skills. Unlike most undergraduates who specialize in doing research in their own area of academic study, debaters require expansive research skills. Even when a debate topic is confined to a particular subject area, for example, reducing U.S. agricultural subsidies, debate arguments will emerge requiring research in the fields of economics, political science, law, international relations, the environment, and philosophy. This means debaters must learn to use all available library databases as well as locate evidence from books, government documents, newspapers, and the Internet.

The process of doing debate research is also making debaters more proficient in using computers and a wide variety of new and emerging technologies. On a regular basis, debaters utilize computerized research databases to conduct research (Freeley and Steinberg 2005). While no studies have been done on this point, observational evidence suggests that debaters are more skilled than nondebaters in using sophisticated searching techniques. Because debaters need to locate evidence that supports very precise claims, they become skilled at conducting Boolean searches where words such as OR, AND, AND NOT, and NEAR are inserted to create relationships among keywords in a search query. Debate also teaches techniques in using scanners. Many debate squads now require students to produce their research in digital form. This requires debaters to scan evidence that cannot be downloaded electronically from books and periodicals.

Debate alumni strongly support the belief that debate participation improves research skills. In surveys that ask former debaters how their participation in debate has benefited them, developing research skills is always mentioned as a valued benefit (Hobbs and Chandler 1991; Matlon and Keele 1984). In the most recent studies, the value of research skills has increased in importance. In a survey of lawyers who debated during the 1990s, Katsulas and Bauschard (2000) found that acquiring research skills was ranked as the second greatest benefit of debate participation. A survey by Doyle Srader (2006) of former debaters who are now college educators (but not debate coaches) cited the acquisition of research skills as the most important educational benefit of debate. In a survey of former NDT and CEDA debaters, David Williams, Brian McGee, and David Worth report that a high percentage of these debaters viewed the acquisition of research skills "to be a valued element of debate participation" (2001, 201).

b. Student Knowledge About the World
The knowledge gained by students competing in debate is wide-ranging and substantial. As soon as the college topic area is announced in mid-May, students begin background reading on the topic. When the actual topic wording is announced in July, the intensity of the research effort accelerates to a vigorous pace, as debaters scramble to find as many research materials as possible before the first tournament in September. From this point forward until the last tournament in early April, arguments are revised and created on a continuous basis.

During the course of one debate season, a debate team will produce thousands of pages of argument briefs. Individually, every debater will be responsible for reading and carefully filing them.

The range of cumulative knowledge accrued from compounding several years of debate, is even more astounding. For example, 2009 graduates who debated in each of the past four years, have learned a great deal about four public policy topics: (1) increasing U.S. economic and diplomatic pressure on China; (2) overruling U.S. Supreme court cases involving federalism, school racial segregation, abortion, and military commissions; (3) promoting U.S. constructive engagement with Iran, Syria, Afghanistan, Lebanon, and the Palestinian Authority; and (4) reducing U.S. agricultural subsidies.

Any student who debated over these four years would have learned an incredible amount about some of the great issues and controversies of the twenty-first century. Should the United States engage or confront China? Can U.S. economic pressure force China to respect human rights and intellectual property rights? Should the Supreme Court allow the federal government to have greater control over state governments? Do U.S. military commission trials for enemy combatants violate international law? Can U.S. diplomacy with Syria promote peace in the Middle East? Will constructive engagement prevent Iran from developing nuclear weapons? Will increasing U.S. troops to Afghanistan promote peace? Do industrial farming practices threaten the environment? Do government subsidies for biofuels reduce U.S. energy dependency and global warming? In fact, over a four-year academic debate career, "students grapple with virtually every contemporary issue of American public policy" (O'Donnell 2008b).

However, debaters learn much more than topic knowledge. They also learn a great deal about political institutions and practice. The policy-systems approach essential to intercollegiate debate teaches students about the intricacies of how the three branches of the U.S. government operate. Debaters also learn about current events because they are forced to imagine the passage of controversial policies derived from the yearlong intercollegiate debate topic in a contemporaneous political climate that involves political costs and trade-offs with other agenda items under consideration. This means that in any given year, the top agenda items being pursued in Washington will be hotly debated in the form of politics disadvantages. For example, if the topic requires the affirmative team to advocate reductions in the U.S. nuclear arsenal, a negative team might argue that doing so at this time would trade off with ongoing health care reform efforts.

To be prepared to argue politics disadvantages, debaters must be knowledgeable about all major legislation pending before the U.S. Congress. Subsequently, in addition to the debate topic, students must learn about the pros and cons of a host of public policy issues such as universal health care, immigration reform, cap-and-trade mandates, ratifying the Law of the Sea Treaty, and free trade bills with Colombia, Panama, and South Korea, to name a few.

Since the emergence of critical arguments during the late 1980s, debaters must also be prepared to argue philosophy. The Supreme Court topic gave rise to debates about critical legal studies, feminist jurisprudence, Michel Foucault, and critical race theory. The China and Middle East topics witnessed debates about threat construction, nuclearism, and cultural relativism. The agricultural subsidies topic led to heated debates over the capitalist system and Heideggerian critiques of technology and science. In sum, intercollegiate debate offers a rich curriculum that fosters learning across multiple fields and disciplines—all at the same time.

c. Argument Construction and Organization
Argumentation is one of the important skills for maintaining a vibrant society. This is because "argumentation occurs everywhere, and we deal with it as readers, listeners, writers and speakers on a daily basis" (Inch, Warnick, and Endres 2006, 8). Every professional endeavor involves constructing arguments. Lawyers make arguments in support of their clients. Businesses make arguments to sell products and services. Legislators make arguments to advocate policy changes. Politicians make arguments for why they should be elected. Academics make arguments when they teach and publish scholarship. Argumentation is the lifeblood of society.

Competitive debate is an ideal laboratory for training students in the study of argumentation. Through it, students acquire fundamental skills in argumentation, beginning with how to analyze complex problems. Students learn how to analyze a proposition by identifying the various issues on multiple sides of controversies. Students learn how to construct valid arguments and are taught that sound reasoning and appropriate evidence must support claims. In addition, students learn techniques of refutation in order to defeat poorly constructed arguments, and they are taught how to expose flaws in evidence or reasoning. Students acquire skills in organizing arguments such as prioritizing the placement of arguments as well as packaging them for consumption by multiple audiences. Finally, students learn how arguments interrelate and potentially conflict.

d. Writing

Debate participation improves writing skills in two ways. First, research shows that students who become more fluent speakers develop improved writing skills (Sperling 1996). By improving the oral communication skills of students, debate indirectly enhances their writing skills. This is borne out by research demonstrating that debaters achieve higher scores on writing exams than nondebaters (Peters 2008). Second, the process of crafting briefing papers and preparing speeches enables debaters to practice their writing skills on a regular basis. Writing debate briefs and cases teaches students how to structure and organize arguments. These skills are beneficial to students who are required to write term papers or to answer essay exam questions. Research shows that debate is beneficial in improving students' writing skills (Matlon and Keele 1984; Rothenberg and Berman 1980) and organizational skills (Hill 1982; Semlak and Shields 1977; Williams, McGee, and Worth 2001). College educators claim that the argumentation and organization skills they learned through debate are useful for making arguments to administrators and colleagues, and also help them with their scholarship and teaching (Srader 2006).

e. Oral Communication, Active Listening, and Note-taking

Debaters consistently rank improved oral communication skills as one of the top benefits of participation in debate (Huston 1985; Lybbert 1985; Matlon and Keele 1984; Oliver 1985; Williams, McGee, and Worth 2001). Debate develops oral communication skills in a number of ways. The first, and perhaps most obvious, is that it develops students' ability to deliver speeches in public, as has been observed by coaches and former debaters (Bernard 1999; Giesecke 1981; Pemberton-Butler 1999; Sowa-Jamrok 1994), and demonstrated empirically (Semlak and Shields 1977). Debate provides extensive public-speaking practice and improves self-confidence (Matlon and Keele 1984; Pemberton-Butler 1999; Sowa-Jamrok 1994), two of the most important factors in reducing public-speaking anxiety and improving performance (Lucas 1998). The sheer number of critiqued speeches a debater presents in a typical debate season is not insignificant. Assuming a moderate travel schedule consisting of ten tournaments per year, with six debates (at minimum) at each tournament and two speeches per debate easily yields a tally of 120 unique speeches in an academic year. Most do many more, to say nothing of practice speeches with coaches and teammates both before and after tournaments.

However, debate training and practice also teaches other, less formal oral communication skills. Debaters are paired together in two-person teams and must rely on each other to compete successfully. The ability to communicate quickly and efficiently and to both give and follow directions, sometimes simultaneously, is often the difference between a win and a loss in a particular debate round. This "cooperative communication," sometimes referred to as an "interactional skill" (Hill and Leeman 1997), between partners is significant skill that translates easily to the world outside of debate.

Equally compelling is the extent to which debate develops listening skills. Studies have long established that active listening skills are important, but that most people are passive listeners, retaining only 25% of what is heard (Nichols and Stevens 1957). Active listening has been cited as an important prerequisite for engaging in productive dialogue and for engaging other skills (Goleman 2000). Improved listening and note-taking ability are frequently cited benefits of participation in debate (Freeley and Steinberg 2009; Goodnight 1993; Wood and Goodnight 2006). Competing successfully in debates requires effective responses, and effective responses are possible only when a student has listened carefully and taken thorough notes on their counterparts' arguments.

In addition to presenting and listening to speeches, intercollegiate debate offers a unique opportunity to refine advanced communication skills through cross-examination—a practice that involves interviewing someone with an opposing viewpoint, and thereby engages both listening and speaking skills. Conducting a productive and respectful cross-examination is difficult to learn but is invaluable to public discourse (Hill and Leeman 1997). Further, cross-examination provides a unique opportunity for critical listening—evaluative listening—the type of listening that results in a judgment, which is particularly useful in preparing and executing a cross-examination (Hill and Leeman 1997). As noted by Lawrence Norton, "Selecting the properly worded question to ask at the right time and arranging a meaningful series of questions is a real challenge to the thought process. Knowing how to select the right answer also is based on listening" (1982, 35)·

Debaters also have the ability to interact with coaches—both their own and, through post-debate feedback, coaches from other schools. This increases oral communication skills in two ways. First, the ability to coordinate with your own coaching staff to formulate arguments is another "interactional skill"—requiring students to work with others in a team-based context to create strategies (Hill and Leeman 1997). Current debate practice is no longer "I write the arguments. You deliver the arguments," as characterized in the major motion picture, *The Great*

Debaters. Instead, top-down argument strategies have largely been replaced by a more cooperative model in which debaters hold a great deal of decision-making power regarding the formulation of the arguments they present while also being assisted and counseled in making these strategic decisions by their coaches.

Second, the interaction that debaters have with their judges after debates creates an additional opportunity to both ask questions and develop their critical listening skills—in this situation, their discriminative listening skills, and the ability to gather information while seeking to understand the judge's feedback (Hill and Leeman 1997). Developing the habit of asking for and constructively receiving criticism while seeking to improve fundamental skills serves debaters well in both classroom and workplace settings long after their debate careers are over.

f. Self-confidence and Time Management
There are also a number of indirect ways that debate participation helps to improve students' academic achievement. There is evidence that debating experience makes students feel more confident in their ability to communicate, both orally and verbally (Freeley and Steinberg 2005; Rogers 2002, 2005). This self-confidence may encourage students to participate more actively in class discussions and improve their performance when they give oral presentations or write term papers. Debate also teaches students useful time-management skills. Debaters learn to multitask and process information faster and more efficiently than nondebaters (Parcher 1998). Better time-management skills allow students to complete their schoolwork in a timely fashion.

4. Ethics of Advocacy
Teaching students ethical advocacy has always been mentioned as an important educational benefit of debate (Capp and Capp 1965; Freeley and Steinberg 2005; Hunt 1994; Ulrich 1984; Ziegelmueller, Kay, and Dause 1990). To enforce ethical conduct by participants, guidelines have been promulgated by governing bodies of debate, including the American Forensic Association, the American Debate Association, the Cross Examination Debate Association, and the National Debate Tournament Committee. Rules prohibiting the misuse and fabrication of evidence, rules establishing the eligibility of debaters, and rules prohibiting sexual harassment by students and judges have been adopted.

Through their participation in debate, students learn the importance of conforming to these standards as well as the benefits of participating in a scholarly community characterized by academic integrity. Coaches teach students how to avoid plagiarism and to cite evidence properly. They are also taught never to cite evidence out of context. Students participating in debate receive constant reinforcement from their coaches, from judges, and from other student competitors, stressing the ethical requirement to obey these communal norms. As a result, the misuse, distortion, and fabrication of evidence are extremely rare in academic debate.

At the same time, concerns that debate advocacy is unethical because it emphasizes competitive success over educational learning have been expressed over the years. Some have feared that the emphasis on winning will produce sophists who are devoid of ethical responsibility (Gow 1967; Haiman 1964; Horn and Underberg 1991). If this were the case, students might be more likely to distort the truth and be encouraged to lie. If true, this would be a damning indictment of the activity of debate. Fortunately, this perspective has been totally discredited by empirical research (Rogers 2002, 2005). In fact, research demonstrates that debaters are less likely than nondebaters to distort the truth and ignore conflicting evidence of contrary viewpoints. Moreover, debaters are less likely to engage in situational ethics, that is, to conveniently shift their ethical position depending on the circumstances (Rogers 2002, 2005).

There is a far stronger case to be made that participation in switch-side debating teaches students to form a sound ethical foundation. For example, Star Muir argues that "firm moral commitments to a value system" are "founded in reflexive assessments of multiple perspectives" (1993, 291). By forcing students to defend both sides of an argument, switch-side debating cultivates a "healthy ethic of tolerance and pluralism" and leads students to appreciate the validity of opposing belief systems, while "instilling responsible and critical skepticism toward dominant systems" (Harrigan 2008, 37). This process of debate and self-reflection over time produces a more ethical belief system because it is grounded in critical thought. Nurturing debate about alternative viewpoints and trying on others' ideas through simulated and situational argument is the essence of a free society and the basis for an ethical society.

5. Community Building
Intercollegiate debate has a long history of outreach to a variety of local, national, and international communities, although efforts to foster alignment with constituencies outside of the competitive arena have gathered momentum in recent years. Public debates represent one mode of outreach and community

building and are an active and visible aspect of many intercollegiate debate programs. Such forums allow students who have honed their knowledge and skills through competition to bring the benefits of a debate education to larger audiences—both on the campus and beyond. The CEDA actively encourages intercollegiate debate programs to build community, with a yearly award for the intercollegiate program that best realizes these objectives. Countless examples emanate from intercollegiate debate programs across the country, and many have been backed by strong administrative support—support that recognizes the centrality of debate to the mission of the university. One of the signature events involving multiple institutions in a public debate competition is the James Madison Commemorative Debate and Citizen Forum. Held annually for the past decade, the event is adjudicated by lay judges and is attended by large audiences from the university and the broader community. With financial backing from the university, this forum is indicative of the power of intercollegiate debate to extend the reach of competition to foster civic engagement and public deliberation in local and regional communities.

On the national scene, intercollegiate debate also has a distinctive footprint. For example, to mark the inauguration of President Barack Obama, the Smithsonian Institution sponsored the "Inaugural Debate Series," which involved debates by college teams on the priorities of the new administration (Caputo 2009). These debates, which attracted large crowds to the Baird Auditorium, were held on the National Mall at the National Museum of Natural History preceding the inaugural ceremonies. Another recent initiative, spearheaded by the U.S. Environmental Protection Agency, expands the panoply of public debate options in even more interesting and impactful ways. Initiated by Ibrahim Goodwin, an environmental scientist in the agency's Office of Water, the effort joins experienced intercollegiate debaters from different institutions in debates central to the science policy concerns of the agency. By bringing the talents of intercollegiate debaters to bear in a variety of contexts and environments—ranging from internal workforce training and rule making to public outreach and community decision making—this initiative underscores the relationship between debate and deliberation (Mitchell, forthcoming).

Internationally, several organizations merge debate with community building. The International Debate Education Association focuses on bringing the methods of debate to societies where democracy is in its infancy, while the National Communication Association's Committee for International Discussion and Debate sponsors long-running debate tours between intercollegiate debate teams in the United States and debating teams from both Britain and Japan. On a different tack, several U.S. State Department international youth programs integrate debate training into curricular design (SEEYLI, Ben Franklin). Research testifying to the impact of such initiatives reveals that students who participate in such programs are better positioned to push for increased democratic accountability in these postcommunist states (Mitchell et al. 2006).

Although not always formally tied to the organs of intercollegiate debate, perhaps the most powerful evidence of the benefits of a debate education emanates from the urban debate movement. Spearheaded by intercollegiate debate programs, this effort has matured over the past two decades to bring colleges, middle and high schools, as well as community organizations and philanthropic organizations together in fruitful collaborations designed to bring the virtues of a debate education to underserved urban communities. With outposts in more than 20 of the nation's largest cities and tens of thousands of graduates, the results have been astonishing. As Will Baker notes, "there is no doubt that urban debate leagues using policy debate produce results and engage students that other resources have failed to reach" (1998, 69–70). Linda Collier's (2004) empirical study of urban debate students establishes a strong link between participation in debate and improvements in reading, self-esteem, decision making, GPA (grade point average), and prospects for attending college. Similarly, Carol Winkler's (2010) empirical assessment of urban debate league programs in Atlanta finds even stronger correlations between debate and a variety of academic, behavioral, and social benefits. These students also experience the empowering potential of debate. As Edward Lee, a graduate of the Atlanta league, explains, debate "allows students to take control of their educational destiny and at once make it a site of resistance" (1998, 96).

Furthermore, the benefits of such outreach and community-building initiatives positively impact intercollegiate debate programs. Carrie Crenshaw describes the benefits that college programs gain from involvement with the urban debate movement. College debaters who work with such programs not only improve their competitive skills, they benefit from the experience of giving back to others (1998, 83–84). In addition, experience with such initiatives helps college students to become "well-rounded adults who can see the value of their debate experience in a larger context" (83). Larry Moss (2001) validates this approach arguing that students who have received debate training are obliged to "utilize those skills on behalf of their communities" in order to realize the full benefits of debate.

Additional examples of debate's natural association with civic engagement are provided in "Alternative Debate Models" (see pp 236–41).

6. Fostering Modes of Inquiry

a. Active Learning

Active learning is a mode of instruction that focuses the responsibility for learning on the learner. Charles Bonwell and James Eison (1991) suggest that learning is maximized when learners work in pairs, discuss materials while role-playing, debate, engage in examinations of case studies, and take part in cooperative learning. L. Dee Fink explains that active learning occurs when learning activities "involve some kind of experience or some kind of dialogue" (1999, para. 3)—dialogue with self, dialogue with others, observing, and doing.

Intercollegiate debate fosters each of these learning activities. Dialogue with self involves thinking reflexively about topics, including what a person ought to think about a topic, and includes self-evaluation of the thinking, writing, and speaking, as well as consideration of the role of the knowledge in his or her own life. In order to decide what arguments to advance in a given debate, debaters must think critically about the topic they will be debating. To evaluate their opponent's arguments (as well as to select their own), debaters need to assess their own thinking on the topic as well as research and prepare briefs and speeches. Finally, debaters consider the ways in which the things they learn have impacted their own lives, particularly when the topics involve social issues. Dialogue with others involves "intense" discussion about the issue at hand. Debaters engage in these intense discussions not only in their individual debates but also with coaches and teammates, with frequent spillover outside of the tournament context into a variety of formal and informal social situations. Observation includes listening to someone else doing something that is related to what they are learning about. Debaters are involved in observation when they are listening to the speeches of their opponents, listening to practice debates, and listening to others debate at tournaments. Lynn Goodnight explains that debaters learn to become active listeners, concentrating on the speaker, mentally reviewing what has been said, trying to anticipate what will come next, and noting the kind of evidence that is being used (1987, 6). Doing simply involves a learning activity where the participant "does something." Debaters are involved in doing the debating, analyzing the material, writing the speeches, presenting the arguments, and making the choices that will win debates (Bellon 2000).

Tournament debating substantially increases the intensity of the active learning experience. The drive to win increases the intensity of the discussion, while the attention to detail and the need to think reflexively about the argument and ideas at hand required to do so are all amplified through the competitive lens.

b. Cooperative Learning

There are five essential elements of cooperative learning: positive interdependence; face-to-face interaction; interpersonal and small-group skills; individual accountability and personal responsibility, and frequent use of group processing (Johnson et al. 1991). Each of these elements is thrust upon participants in intercollegiate debate. It is unavoidable.

In order to experience positive interdependence, students must perceive that they "need each other." Participants in intercollegiate debate are competitively interdependent. Given the tremendous research, argument preparation, and scouting burdens, it would be very difficult, if not impossible, for individuals to succeed in debate without the support of the larger team, let alone their debate partner (Shelton 1995). As Ehninger and Brockriede explain, "In this respect debate may be compared with a group of mountain climbers concerned with their mutual safety" (1978, 15). Positive interdependence is manifest in intercollegiate debate because students share research resources and strategies and perform individually assigned roles that contribute to the collective good. To be successful, debaters and coaches must work together in a variety of group processes to share information, coordinate research assignments, and work as a squad at tournament competitions. Similarly, to be a member of a successful team requires a large degree of individual accountability and personal responsibility.

Face-to-face interaction and group processing is promoted when students explain, discuss, and teach what they know to their peers and perform it before judges and opponents. Debaters who work on particular assignments are likely to share knowledge gleaned through research with the entire squad before tournaments, at regular squad meetings, and with teammates before each and every individual contest debate. At some tournaments, more experienced debaters may serve as coaches for younger debaters. On campus, many of the older debaters judge practice debates and work with younger debaters. College students who are former high school debaters assist high school debate programs through coaching or judging. In addition, many high school debate camps are staffed by college students who are responsible for teaching debate to high school students (Bauschard 1998).

Interpersonal and small-group skills, such as decision-making, trust-building, communication, and conflict-management skills are also critical because students debate in teams of two. At every step of the way—from the beginning of the season until the last debate of the academic year—partners must make joint decisions about which arguments to advance at the beginning of the debate as well as which arguments to rely on in later rebuttals (Goodnight 1987, 3). This requires building trust and effective communication between partners. And, when conflicts arise—as they inevitably do—debaters must work to manage conflicts in order to be successful.

c. Intentional Learning

For Carl Bereiter and Marlene Scardamalia, intentional learning is characterized by "processes that have learning as a goal, rather than an incidental outcome" (1989, 363). Marlene Francis, Timothy Mulder, and Joan Stark sharpen this perspective by focusing on its essential attributes. Intentional learning is "learning with self-directed purpose, intending and choosing to learn and how and what to learn. Intentional learning involves five attributes of learning: questioning, organizing, connecting, reflecting, and adapting" (1995, para. 2). Success in intercollegiate debate depends crucially on maintaining each of these aspects.

To begin with, debaters need to learn not only to question arguments made by their opponents but also to question the strength of their own arguments before they decide to advance them in debates. At the same time, debaters need to organize and synthesize arguments and opinions advanced by myriad sources to coherent and concise positions. They must also organize their own research, the work of their teammates, and scouting information collected by tournament participants. Furthermore, developing arguments and preparing them for presentation in debates requires making connections between arguments and opinions derived from many different literatures, connecting arguments with those advanced by one's partner, developing a full understanding of the relationships between arguments in order to synthesize positions for rebuttal speeches, as well as cultivating an awareness of the contested relationships between arguments—arguments presented in any particular debate as well as those advanced by others throughout the academic year.

In order to improve, debaters must critically reflect not only on which particular arguments have proved more or less successful but also on their own skills and the strengths and weaknesses of their team, as well as the strengths and weaknesses of their opponents. Once strengths and weaknesses are assessed, debaters must adapt to those strengths and weaknesses in individual contests in ways that privilege their own strengths while exploiting their opponents' weaknesses.

7. Student Empowerment

In addition to cultivating educational skills, participation in debate has long been recognized as having positive benefits in shaping the personality of students (Mayer 1936). Because debate requires students to debate both sides of controversies, they become more flexible arguers and more tolerant of opposing viewpoints (Bellon 2000; Muir 1993). There is also evidence that debaters are more socially tolerant and less likely to accept conventional social norms (Rogers 2002, 2005). This is a unique benefit to switch-side debating. Rogers explains: "as debaters become exposed to various resolutions and topics for debate, conduct research on both sides of usually controversial social subjects, organize and write briefs for both sides, and go through the process of arguing those positions, they have the opportunity to develop a wider view of differing social perceptions" (2002, 13–14). Research also shows that debaters are more inclined to become members of intercultural organizations and enroll in cross-cultural classes (Rogers 2005). These tendencies are improved and enhanced when debate programs engage in community outreach. Beth Breger observes that these programs "encourage a dialogue" that not only results in "profound learning" but also "becomes the bridge across the chasms of difference" (1998, 67). This finding is consistent with empirical research that has linked service learning with building citizenship (Morgan and Streb 2001).

Empirical research proves that debate involvement enhances beneficial argumentative skills, while reducing verbal aggression (Colbert 1993, 1994). Debate helps students deal with other types of aggression as well. Reflecting on the Open Society Institute's lengthy experience, Breger reports that "debate teaches students to command attention with words, provides students with an alternate outlet for day-to-day conflicts, and gives them a tool with which they can combat physical aggression" (1998, 66–67). As Melissa Wade explains, "If one knows how to advocate on one's own behalf in a way that will be acknowledged by the listener, one does not have to resort to violence to get the attention of decision-makers" (1998, 63). This contention has been confirmed by empirical research that documents a link between debate participation and a sharp decline in disciplinary referrals (Winkler 2009).

The personal benefits of debate extend well beyond social attitudes and behavioral control. Participants often experience debate as a form of personal empowerment. This includes feelings of personal efficacy, educational engagement, and political agency. Robert Branham explains that debaters evaluate what they are told, and therefore come to see their own knowledge about the world as "earned" instead of passively received from instructors or textbooks (1991, 20). Many authors (e.g., Freeley and Steinberg 2009) have noted that debate experience gives students the confidence they need to interact with peers and authority figures. Debaters see themselves as citizens who can successfully engage complex questions of policy. As Cori Dauber explains, debate teaches students that "they ought not be intimidated by the rhetoric of expertise" surrounding policy issues. "They know that they are capable of making and defending informed choices about complex issues outside of their own area of interest because they do so on a daily basis" (1989, 207). This sense of empowerment is not an abstraction. Debaters gain the skills and the attitude they need to engage important issues in their lives and their communities. Gordon Mitchell (1998, 53) outlines the empowering potential of a variety of debate practices. He describes debate as a "political activity that has the potential to empower students and teachers to change the underlying conditions that cause inequities among schools and communities." Reflecting on their study of Latina involvement in debate, Casey Arbenz and Sylvia Beltran conclude, "debate can be a useful vehicle for providing empowerment and educational opportunities lacking in the public school system" (2001, 14).

CONCLUSION

In addition to its many tangible benefits and time-honored virtues, debate is fun. The pleasure that students take in the development and exercise of their speaking and reasoning abilities is a major motivation for why they participate; debate is exciting, challenging, and enjoyable. Both the competitive and collaborative nature of debate combine to create the conditions for participation in an activity that is as intense and satisfying as any in the academy—including intercollegiate athletics. Along the way, participants form lifelong relationships and gain entry to a networked community that is unparalleled in the history of American higher education.

References
Allen, M.; S. Berkowitz; S. Hunt; and A. Louden. 1999. "A Meta-analysis of the Impact of Forensics and Communication Education on Critical Thinking. *Communication Education* 48: 18–30.
Arbenz, C., and S. Beltran. 2001. "Empowering Latinas Through Debate: An Analysis of Success at SCUDL Tournaments of Latina Debaters." Paper presented at the Western States Communication Association's Panel on Debate Outreach in C'oeur D'Alene, Idaho. http://communi-

cations.fullerton.edu/forensics/documents/Silly%20and%20Jason%2002%20NCA%20Paper.
pdf (accessed June 6, 2009).

Association of American Colleges and Universities. 1985. Integrity in the College Curriculum. Washington, DC.

Baker, W. 1998. "Reflections on the New York Urban Debate League and 'Ideafest II.'" *Contemporary Argumentation and Debate* 19: 69–71.

Barber, B. 2004. *Strong Democracy: Participatory Politics for a New Age.* Berkeley: University of California Press.

Barfield, K.E. 1989. "A Study of the Relationship Between Active Participation in Interscholastic Debating and the Development of Critical Thinking Skills with Implications for School Administrators and Instructional Leaders." Dissertation Abstracts International, 50-09: 2714.

Bauschard, S. 1998. "Coaching to Cooperate: The Role of the Debate Coach as a Facilitator of Cooperative Learning." Paper presented at the National Communication Association Annual Conference, New York, November 20–24.

Bellon, J. 2000. "A Research-based Justification for Debate Across the Curriculum." *Argumentation and Advocacy* 36: 161–75.

Bereiter, C., and M. Scardamalia. 1989. "Intentional Learning as a Goal of Instruction. In *Knowing, Learning, and Instruction: Essays in Honor of Robert Glaser,* ed. L.B. Resnick, 361–92. Hillsdale, NJ: Lawrence Erlbaum.

Bernard, P. 1999. "A Way with Words; Florida Forensics Institute Gives Teens a Verbal Boost." *Sun-Sentinel,* Community News, August 25, p. 1.

Bonwell, C., and J. Eison. 1991. "Active Learning: Creating Excitement in the Classroom." ERIC Document Reproduction Service, #ED336049.

Branham, R.J. 1991. *Debate and Critical Analysis: The Harmony of Conflict.* Hillsdale, NJ: Lawrence Erlbaum.

Breger, B. 1998. "Building Open Societies Through Debate." *Contemporary Argumentation and Debate* 19: 66–68.

Capp, G.R., and T.R. Capp. 1965. *Principles of Argumentation and Debate.* Englewood Cliffs, NJ: Prentice Hall.

Caputo, J. 2009. "College Students to Debate Obama's Priorities at Inaugural Event. Around the Mall: Scenes and Sightings from the Smithsonian Museums and Beyond." http://blogs.smithsonianmag.com/aroundthemall/2009/01/college-students-to-debate-obamas-priorities-at-inaugural-event/ (accessed September 8, 2009).

Chemerinsky, E. 2008. "Inner-city Schools Suffer When 'Debaters' Go Silent." *USA Today,* January 31, p. A11.

Cheshire, D. 2002. "Improving Your Research Skills." *Rostrum* 77. http://www.nflonline.org/uploads/Rostrum/pol1102cheshier.pdf (accessed May 25, 2009).

Colbert, K.R. 1987. "The Effects of CEDA and NDT Debate Training on Critical Thinking Ability." *Journal of the American Forensic Association* 23: 194–201.

———. 1993. "The Effects of Debate Participation on Argumentativeness and Verbal Aggression." *Communication Education* 42: 206–14.

———. 1994. "Replicating the Effects of Debate Participation on Argumentativeness and Verbal Aggression." *Forensic of Phi Kappa Delta* 79: 1–13.

———. 1995. "Enhancing Critical Thinking Ability Through Academic Debate." *Contemporary Argumentation and Debate* 16: 52–72.

Colbert, K.R., and T. Biggers. 1985. "Why Should We Support Debate?" *Journal of the American Forensic Association* 21: 237–40.

Collier, L. 2004. "Argument for Success: A Study of Academic Debate in the Urban High Schools of Chicago, Kansas City, New York, St. Louis and Seattle." Paper presented at the Hawaii International Conference on Social Sciences, Honolulu, HI, June 16–19.

Crenshaw, C. 1998. "Sharing the Gift of Debate: Notes from the Tuscaloosa Debate League." *Contemporary Argumentation and Debate* 19: 80–84.

Cross, G. 1971. "The Effects of Belief Systems and the Amount of Debate Experience on the Acquisition of Critical Thinking." Dissertation Abstracts International, 32-06: 3461.

Dauber, C. 1989. "Debate as Empowerment." *Journal of the American Forensic Association* 25: 205–7.

Ehninger, D., and W. Brockriede. 1978. Decision by Debate. 2d ed. New York: Harper and Row.

Fink, L. Dee. 1999. "Active Learning." http://honolulu.hawaii.edu/intranet/committees/FacDev-Com/guidebk/teachtip/active.htm (accessed June 7, 2009).

Fishkin, J.S. 2009. *When the People Speak: Deliberative Democracy and Public Consultation.* New York: Oxford University Press.

Francis, M.C.; T.C. Mulder; and J.S. Stark. 1995. "Intentional Learning: A Process for Learning to Learn in the Accounting Curriculum." Sarasota, FL: American Accounting Association. http://aaahq.org/aecc/intent/cover.htm (accessed July 28, 2009).

Franke, R.J. 2009. "The Power of the Humanities and a Challenge to Humanists." *Daedalus* 138: 13–23.

Freeley, A.J., and D.L. Steinberg. 2005. *Argumentation and Debate: Critical Thinking for Reasoned Decision Making.* 11th ed. Belmont, CA: Thomson Wadsworth.

———. 2009. *Argumentation and Debate: Critical Thinking for Reasoned Decision Making.* 12th ed. Belmont, CA: Thomson Wadsworth.

Fritch, J. 1993/1994. "What's Right with Forensics: The Perspective of a College Forensic Educator." *Forensic Educator* 8: 6–8.

Giesecke, N. 1981. "Who Spends 15 Hours a Week Studying in the Library?" *Christian Science Monitor*, December 14, p. 17.

Goleman, D. 2000. *Working with Emotional Intelligence.* New York: Bantam.

Goodnight, L. 1987. *Getting Started in Debate.* New York: McGraw-Hill.

———. 1993. *Getting Started in Debate.* 2d ed. New York: Glencoe.

Gow, J.E. 1967. "Tournament Debating: A Time for Change." *Journal of the American Forensics Association* 4: 107–11.

Haiman, F.S. 1964. "A Critical View of the Game of Forensics." *Journal of the American Forensics Association* 1: 62–66.

Harrigan, C. 2008. "Against Dogmatism: A Continued Defense of Switch Side Debate." *Contemporary Argumentation and Debate* 29: 37–66.

Higher Education Research Institute. 2009. "The American College Teacher: National Norms for 2007–2008." HERI Research Brief, March. http://www.heri.ucla.edu/PDFs/pubs/briefs/brief-pr030508-08faculty.pdf (accessed June 2, 2009).

Hill, B. 1982. "Intercollegiate Debate: Why Do Students Bother?" *Southern Speech Communication Journal* 48: 77–88.

Hill, B., and R.W. Leeman. 1997. *The Art and Practice of Argumentation and Debate.* Mountain View, CA: Mayfield.

Hobbs, J.D., and R.C. Chandler. 1991. "The Perceived Benefits of Policy Debate Training in Various Professions." *Speaker and Gavel* 28: 4–6.

Horn, G., and L. Underberg. 1991. "Educational Debate: An Unfulfilled Promise?" Paper presented at the CEDA Assessment Conference, St. Paul, MN, August.

Howell, W. 1943. "The Effects of High School Debating on Critical Thinking." *Speech Monographs* 10: 96–103.

Hunt, S.K. 1994. "The Values of Forensics Participation." In *Intercollegiate Forensics*, ed. T.C. Winebrenner, 1–12. Dubuque, IA: Kendall Hunt.

Hunt, S.K.; D. Garard; and G. Simerly, G. 1997. "Reasoning and Risk: Debaters as an Academically At-risk Population." *Contemporary Argumentation and Debate* 18: 48–56.

Huston, D. 1985. "What Should Be the Goals of High School Debate? An Examination and Pri-
oritization." Paper presented at the National Forensic League Conference on the State of High
School Debate, Kansas City, MO. ERIC Document Reproduction Service, #ED272942.

Inch, E.S.; B. Warnick; and D. Endres. 2006. *Critical Thinking and Communication: The Use of
Reason in Argument.* 5th ed. Boston: Allyn and Bacon.

Isocrates. *Antidosis,* trans. by George Norlin. Cambridge: Cambridge University Press, 1929.

Jackson, T. 1961. "The Effects of Intercollegiate Debating on Critical Thinking." Dissertation
Abstracts, 21-11: 3556.

Johnson, D. et al. 1991. *Cooperation in the Classroom.* Edina, MN: Interaction Book.

Jones, D. 2004. "Debating Skills Come in Handy in Business." *USA Today,* September 30, p. B3.

Jones, K. 1994. "Cerebral Gymnastics 101: Why Do Debaters Debate?" *CEDA Yearbook* 15: 65–75.

Katsulas, J., and S. Bauschard. 2000. "Debate as Preparation for the Legal Profession: A Survey
of Debaters from the 1970s to 1990s." Paper presented at the annual meeting of the Southern
States Communication Association, New Orleans, LA, March 29–April 2.

Kuh, G. 2008. *High-Impact Educational Practices.* Washington, DC: Association of American Colleges and Universities.

Lawhorn, B. 2008. "Extracurricular Activities: The Afterschool Connection." *Occupational Out-
look Quarterly* 52: 16–21.

Lee, E. 1998. "Memoir of a Former Urban Debate League Participant." *Contemporary Argumentation and Debate* 19: 93–96.

Lucas, S.E. 1998. *The Art of Public Speaking.* 6th ed. Boston: McGraw-Hill.

Lybbert, B. 1985. "What Should Be the Goals of High School Debate?" Paper presented at the
National Forensic League Conference on the State of High School Debate, Kansas City, MO.
ERIC Document #ED272941.

Matlon, R.J., and L.M. Keele. 1984. "A Survey of Participants in the National Debate Tournament, 1947–1980." *Journal of the American Forensic Association* 20: 194–205.

Mayer, J.E. 1936. "Personality Development Through Debate." *Quarterly Journal of Speech* 22:
607–11.

McBath, J.H. 1984. "Rationale for Forensics." In *American Forensics in Perspective: Papers from the
Second National Conference on Forensics,* ed. D.W. Parson, 5–11. Annandale, VA: Speech Communication Association.

McKee, K. 2003. "The Relationship Between Debate and Critical Thinking with Advanced
Placement Teacher Perceptions of That Relationship." Dissertation Abstracts International,
64-08, 2766.

Mitchell, G.R. 1998. "Pedagogical Possibilities for Argumentative Agency in Academic Debate."
Argumentation and Advocacy 35: 41–60.

Mitchell, G.R. 2010. "Switch-side Debating Meets Demand-driven Rhetoric of Science." *Rhetoric
& Public Affairs* 13: 95–120.

Mitchell, G.R., Pfister, D., Bradatan, G., Colev, D., Manolova, T., Mitkovski, G., Nestorova, I.,
Ristic, M., & Sheshi, G. 2006. "Navigating Dangerous Deliberative Waters: Shallow Argument
Pools, Group Polarization and Public Debate Pedagogy in Southeast Europe." *Controversia* 4:
69–84.

Morgan, W., and M. Streb. 2001. "Building Citizenship: How Student Voice in Service-learning
Develops Civic Values." *Social Science Quarterly* 82: 154–70.

Moss, L.E. 2001. "Beyond an Expansion of Privilege: New Urban Voices and Community Advocacy." *Rostrum* 75 (March): 16–17. Available at http://www.nflonline.org/Rostrum/MarZeroOne/.

Muir, S.A. 1993. "A Defense of the Ethics of Contemporary Debate." *Philosophy and Rhetoric* 26:
277–95.

Murphy, S.K., and J.A. Samosky. 1993. "Argumentation and Debate: Learning to Think Critically." *Speaker and Gavel* 30: 39–45.

National Education Goals Panel. 1991. *The National Education Goals Panel: Building a Nation of Learners*. Washington, DC: U.S. Government Printing Office.

National Institute of Education Study Group. 1984. *Involvement in Learning: Realizing the Potential of American Higher Education*. Washington, DC: National Institute of Education, U.S. Department of Education.

Nichols, R.G., and L.A. Stevens. 1957. *Are You Listening?* New York: McGraw-Hill.

Norton, L.E. 1982. "Nature and Benefits of Academic Debate." In *Introduction to Debate*, ed. C. Keefe, T. B. Harte, and L. E. Norton, 24–40. New York: Macmillan.

O'Donnell, T.M. 2008a. "The Great Debaters: A Challenge to Higher Education." Inside Higher Education, January 7. http://www.insidehighered.com/views/2008/01/07/odonnell (accessed August 4, 2009).

———. 2008b. "As Professors Left Debate, It Became Gamesmanship: Letters to the Editor." *Chronicle of Higher Education* 55 (October 17): 38.

Oliver, P. 1985. "How Well Are We Meeting the Goals of High School Debate?" Paper presented at the National Forensic League Conference on the State of High School Debate, Kansas City, MO. ERIC Document Reproduction Service, #ED272943.

Omelicheva, M.Y. 2007. "Resolved: Academic Debate Should Be Part of Political Science Curricula." *Journal of Political Science Education* 3: 161–75.

Owen, D. 2004. "Citizenship Identity and Civic Education in the United States." Paper presented at the Conference on Civic Education and Politics in Democracies sponsored by the Center for Civic Education and the Bundeszentrale für Politische Bildung, San Diego, CA, September 26–October 1.

Panetta, E.M. 1990. "A Rationale for Developing a Nationally Competitive Debate Tournament Oriented Program." *Argumentation and Advocacy* 27: 68–77.

Panetta. E.M., and D.A. Herbeck. 1993. "Argument in a Technical Sphere: Incommensurate Rhetorical Visions." In *Argument and the Postmodern Challenge: Proceedings of the Eighth SCA/AFA Conference on Argumentation*, ed. R.E. McKerrow, 25–30. Annandale, VA: Speech Communication Association.

Parcher, J. 1998. "Evaluation Report: Philodemic Debate Society." http://groups.wfu.edu/NDT/Articles/gtreport.html (accessed June 2, 2009).

Pemberton-Butler, L. 1999. "Flexing Forensic Muscles—Auburn High School Debate Teams Compete Nationally Thanks to the Districts Commitment and Inspiration of Longtime Teacher." *Seattle Times*, February 2, p. B1.

Peters, T. 2008. "An Investigation into the Relationship Between Participation in Competitive Forensics and Standardized Test Scores." Master's thesis, Regis University.

Pfau, M.; D.A. Thomas; and W. Ulrich. 1987. *Debate and Argument: A Systems Approach to Advocacy*. Glenview, IL: Scott, Foresman.

Rogers, J.E. 2002. "Longitudinal Outcome Assessment for Forensics: Does Participation in Intercollegiate Competitive Forensics Contribute to Measurable Differences in Positive Student Outcomes?" *Contemporary Argumentation and Debate* 23: 1–27.

———. 2005. "Graduate School, Professional, and Life Choices: An Outcome Assessment Confirmation Study Measuring Positive Student Outcomes Beyond Student Experiences for Participants in Competitive Intercollegiate Forensics." *Contemporary Argumentation and Debate* 26: 13–40.

Ross, S. 2002. "Workplace: College Debaters Get Head Start on Exec Track." Reuters News, June 3.

Rothenberg, I.F., and J.S. Berman. 1980. "College Debate and Effective Writing: An Argument for Debate in the Public Administration Curriculum." *Teaching Political Science* 18: 21–39.

Rowland, R.C. 1995. "The Practical Pedagogical Functions of Academic Debate." *Contemporary Argumentation and Debate* 15: 98–108.

Semlak, W., and D. Shields. 1977. "The Effects of Debate Training on Students Participation in the Bicentennial Youth Debates." *Journal of the American Forensic Association* 13: 193–96.

Shelton, M.W. 1995. "Squad as Community: A Group Communication Perspective on the Debate Workshop." Paper presented at the annual meeting of the Southern States Communication Association, New Orleans, LA, March 29–April 2.

Sowa-Jamrok, C. 1994. "High School Students Can't Say Enough About Debate Experience." *Chicago Tribune*, April 24, p. C9.

Sperling, M. 1996. "Revisiting the Writing-Speaking Connection: Challenges for Research on Writing and Writing Instruction." *Review of Educational Research* 66: 53–86.

Srader, D. 2006. "The Impact of Prior Experience in Intercollegiate Debate upon a Postsecondary Educator's Skill-set." Paper presented at the annual meeting of the National Communication Association, San Antonio, TX, November 16–19. http://northwestchristian.academia.edu/documents/0011/5331/Paper.pdf (accessed May 22, 2009).

Ulrich, W. 1984. "The Ethics of Forensics." In *American Forensics in Perspective: Papers from the Second National Conference on Forensics*, ed. D.W. Parson, 13–22. Annandale, VA: Speech Communication Association.

Wade, M. 1998. "The Case for Urban Debate Leagues." *Contemporary Argumentation and Debate* 19: 60–65.

———. 2006. "The Value of Debate: A Report for Tom Jenkins." http://www.debatecoaches.org/wp-content/ev/08-09/jenkinsmemo.doc (accessed May 28, 2009).

Whalen, S. 1991. "Intercollegiate Debate as a Co-curricular Activity: Effects on Critical Thinking." In *Argument in Controversy: Proceedings of the Seventh SCA-AFA Conference on Argumentation*, ed. D.W. Parson, 391–97. Annandale, VA: Speech Communication Association.

Williams, D. 1951. "The Effects of Training in College Debating on Critical Thinking Activity." Master's thesis, Purdue University.

Williams, D.; B. McGee; and D. Worth. 2001. "University Student Perceptions of the Efficacy of Debate Participation: An Empirical Investigation." Argumentation and Advocacy 37: 198–209.

Winckler, C. 2010. "The Impact of Policy Debate on Inner-city Schools: The Milwaukee Experience." In *The Function of Argument and Social Context*, ed. D. Gouran, 565–571. Annandale, VA: National Communication Association.

Wood, R.V., and L. Goodnight. 2006. *Strategic Debate*. New York: Glencoe.

Ziegelmueller, G.W.; J. Kay: and C.A. Dause. 1990. *Argumentation: Inquiry and Advocacy*. 2d ed. Englewood Cliffs, NJ: Prentice Hall.

Alumni Testimonials

The most compelling evidence for the benefits of a debate education comes from our alumni—those for whom involvement in intercollegiate debate had a profound impact on their lives. We hear these stories all the time and we take special delight in sharing them when we encounter fellow debaters during our journey through life. The testimonials included below were solicited from a handful of distinguished alums whose accessibility and eagerness to respond rapidly met with the publication constraints of this volume. However, their witness here only begins to scratch the surface of a much larger alumni testimonial project. The power of such testimony is worthy of preservation, not merely for the sake of preservation, but because it encourages efforts to solicit, collect, and share the stories of the powerful narrative that is debate.

> High school and college debate was the most important part of my education by far. I learned research, time management, and argumentative skills that put me far ahead in my classes and prepared me well for law school. In fact, I found law school much easier than college plus debate; I had to figure out what to do with all my extra free time, and I was already "thinking like a lawyer," often a major barrier for new law students. Moreover, debate's requirement of teamwork offered fantastic lessons in working with others, dividing responsibilities, and collaborating to achieve team goals. I can't say enough good things about collegiate debate, or the people I met (and still know) as a result.
>
> *Rebecca Tushnet, professor of law, Georgetown (Harvard, 1991–95)*

> Debate taught me how to think and research more than any class or experience I had at Harvard or anywhere else. For some students, including me, the motivation to compete and the preference to work independently drives them to learn. In my experience, six elements made policy debate uniquely valuable:
>
> First, the opportunity to creatively learn about and design research arguments is something not available in most classes, where certain required elements are taught and proven on exams.
>
> Second, debate taught me to think quickly. Policy debate is not a spectator sport, but the speed with which competitors are forced to think and speak in rounds trained my brain to work faster.
>
> Third, strategic judgment is required to evaluate and anticipate which arguments must be won to win a debate and which can be sacrificed. That judgment is essential for prioritizing work and life after debate.

Fourth, debate taught me to organize my thoughts to make them clearer. When, in college, I started to apply principles of debate like organization, introductory statements, and concluding arguments to my writing, my writing improved dramatically.

Fifth, debate teaches you to get into someone else's mind, anticipating which arguments would be persuasive to a judge and which ones wouldn't. It is not enough to feel that you know the right answer yourself, you have to convince another observer of your argument. That ability serves debaters well later in life when they have to convince others to take action (be it philanthropic pursuits, policy initiatives, business ventures, academic commitments, or just raising independent, societally productive children).

Sixth and finally, policy debate teaches you to do something. It is not enough simply to make a philosophical argument but one must understand the root causes of certain economic, legal, or foreign policy problems and what actions can conceivably make the world a better place. That drive led me to the world of foreign policy as a career.

For all these reasons, policy debate has been an indispensible element of my education and is an opportunity for students from across the country to compete on a level playing field. For precisely these reasons, we at CSIS have established an internship for 13 years hiring at least one nationally competitive college debater as an intern to take advantage of these unique research and analytic skills.

You just can't get this kind of training anywhere else.

Alexander T. J. Lennon, editor in chief of the Washington Quarterly *and senior fellow in international security policy at the Center for Strategic and International Studies (CSIS), and an adjunct professor of security studies at Georgetown University (Harvard, 1987–90).*

Debate was the most important part of my high school and college education. The training it provided me in analysis, organization, and speaking have been invaluable and I literally use the skills I learned in debate every day. It also taught me how to manage my time effectively and efficiently. The life lessons it provided were equally invaluable. Other than my parents, my high school and college debate coaches were the two people who had the greatest impact on my life.

Erwin Chemerinsky, dean and Distinguished Professor, University of California, Irvine, School of Law (Northwestern, 1971–75)

My sense of the role debate can play in the collegiate experience comes both from having participated in intercollegiate debate, and now, as a college professor, having observed how debate shapes the college experience. Like all extracurricular college activities from athletics to theater to journalism, debate is not for everyone. And, like all activities, it tends to open some doors while closing others. That being said, debate can provide a number of important benefits. It can improve a student's ability to analyze arguments rigorously, to think quickly, to speak publicly, and to conduct research, especially on current affairs and policy issues. It provides an outlet for individuals to compete in an intellectual forum. Lastly, it brings together like-minded students within and across universities, providing the opportunity to forge enduring friendships.

Dani Reiter, chair, Department of Political Science, Emory University (Northwestern University, 1985–89)

With that amount of immersion, each year tackling a new topic, going through the discipline of analyzing, researching, organizing, preparing for refutation, and constantly refining in light of new arguments and changing information—those skills became instinctive, and have remained so. When I'm confronted with a new issue, challenge, or project, my mind immediately goes to questions of identifying key issues, to research (wouldn't life have been grand with Google?!), to wording and organizing a case, to preparing for objections, and to presentation. I don't wonder about how to approach a new topic, it just comes naturally.

Being coached by George Ziegelmueller and his team of assistants has had another lifelong influence on me—an influence on my own classroom teaching. Although I'm a full-time college administrator, I remain a teacher at heart, and I try to teach a public speaking or speechwriting class each semester. I can't imagine having students do a series of isolated assignments without having the opportunity to really improve along the way. You don't learn to speak by being told what to do after the fact, you learn by being coached while you're speaking. That's how I was coached, and that's how I teach to this day. So, the instinct to analyze, and the value of coaching are the two lifelong impacts of my debate education.

Donald N. Ritzenhein, provost, Macomb Community College, Warren, Michigan (Wayne State University, 1964–68).

I was a debater in high school, a debater in college, and a debate coach and judge after college. I don't know any other extracurricular activity that teaches students more about more.

Debate teaches substantive material. For full years, I debated topics like space exploration, national educational reform (twice), First Amendment case law, hazardous waste responsibility, U.S. arms sales, consumer product safety, and foreign trade policy. I had to learn about all these topics as well as implications flowing from them, ranging from policy issues like government spending and federalism and military strategy to the philosophies and deontological constructs of John Stuart Mill and John Rawls and Thomas Malthus.

Debate also, as you would expect, teaches public-speaking skills. I do not contend that the uninitiated want to listen to a debate per se—the speed of the speeches and the technical jargon used in the "game" of debate will confuse most first timers. But the skills learned—clarity, explanation, confidence, organization— are transferable to many other public-speaking opportunities that audiences will enjoy hearing.

More important, to me, than either of these first two benefits is that debate teaches how to think on one's feet. The number of unexpected twists and turns in any given debate round are multiple, and the debater who best understands and reacts to the unforeseen will win.

But there is something more basic than any of those things: Debate reinforc-es—if it does not teach for the first time—that there are at least two reason-able sides to virtually every topic. One does not spend long in competitive debate and retain the idea that there are many absolutes that face us in daily life. Note: I do not at all mean that there are no moral, religious, and scientific absolutes—there clearly are—but I do mean to say that, quantitatively, the number of absolutes is relatively few compared to the number of subjects with which we deal—personally, professionally, ethically, politically—on a daily basis. The debater who is paying attention to this truism is the best debater, as he/she can debate either side of an issue in a given competition equally well, and is the better person, as he/she can value the arguments made by someone who disagrees without simply writing off the disagree-er as a nut/conservative/ liberal/whatever label is convenient. The judge who understands debate best knows that the debater in competition is not always—and may well rarely be— advocating a personally held position but rather is learning and exercising the skills of seeing both sides of a question that will serve the debater very well in life; the judge rewards those skills even if the position is personally anathema to the judge.

Lyn Robbins, senior general attorney, BNSF Railway Company and adjunct professor of law, Baylor University School of Law (Baylor, 1983–87)

My favorite definition of leadership is that of General and then President Dwight Eisenhower. "Leadership," said Eisenhower, "is the art of getting someone else to do something that you want done because he wants to do it." With a little "pc" in mind, I have a definition I suggest you memorize:

Leadership is the ability to get people to do things you want done because they want to do them.

"because they WANT to do them." That sounds to me like "persuasion." Where does that word come from? From the Latin "per suasio," which translates to "through sweetness."

WHAT? Leadership is about sweetness? Most people who think seriously about sound leadership speak in general about possession of solid character and values combined with interpersonal and management skills. That is undoubtedly correct.

I would argue that possession of debate skills adds a very important dimension to sound leadership. Debate provides the essence of persuasion, which is presentation of your ideas in a way that leads others to agree with them. Others? Who? A debate judge, your colleagues on the floor of Congress, media audiences viewing commercials, your boss who allocates scarce resources including pay raises to which others have legitimate claims, the soldiers you are about to lead into battle, the person to whom you are proposing marriage . . . we could go on. In debate, winning presentations include knowledge of the audience and the use of reason, logic, and evidence in confident and appealing styles designed to persuade. In debate, practice makes perfect—or at least better than any other reasonable alternative.

My experience has been that leaders who consistently approach people in their organizations in persuasive ways develop an atmosphere where people automatically want to do their best almost as a matter of habit, where "follow the leader" counts—as opposed to barking out orders and issuing stern directives.

. . . Do you have that short definition of leadership above memorized?
William J. Taylor Jr. is a senior adviser at the Center for Strategic and International Studies and a former U.S. Army colonel elected to the Infantry Officer Candidate School Hall of Fame. He served in tank and rifle battalions in Germany, Korea, and Vietnam, where he was decorated for heroism. After participating as a student in Episcopal Academy's debating society from 1948 to 1952, Dr. Taylor coached and directed the West Point debate team from 1965 to 1981.

We're happy to offer our modest tribute to this activity, which we enjoyed as participants and support as alumni.

We begin by noting the obvious: debate is ideal preparation for careers centered on public policy. It's fascinating to see folks whom we debated, coached, or judged on policy issues, now making or influencing those policies. To name just a few, Larry Summers, running the economy for President Obama; Austan Goolsbee of the Council of Economic Advisers; and Jim Poterba, president of the National Bureau of Economic Research. Leaders such as presidential candidate John Kerry, presidential adviser Karl Rove, and über political strategist Bob Shrum all cut their teeth on policy debate.

A recent feature article in *Washingtonian* magazine is titled "Why College Debaters Dominate Washington's Political Scene," and that pretty well sums it up.

But these are just a few visible examples. Debaters lead many fields of endeavor, in big business, entrepreneurship, education, law, academia, philanthropy. For debaters, sustained later-life achievement is the rule, not the exception. That speaks volumes about the practical skills debaters develop.

And what are those skills? Everybody's list would be different, but you'd have to include these:

- *Intellectual rigor.* Debate is a proving ground where logical fallacy, pretense, and puffery are quickly detected and ruthlessly rooted out. And though we may quibble about decisions in any particular round, debate is ultimately a very meritocratic activity. Whatever your background, with the right stuff you can excel; and the smallest college program can, on any given day, knock out the most favored competitor—especially if the latter lets up for an instant.
- *Rhetorical skill.* Yes, it's been decades since many coaches were professors of rhetoric. But rhetoric is still central to the activity, in the sense of getting across your point concisely, coherently, and persuasively. A point we've often made in speaking to business groups is that everyone, no matter the title or position, is essentially a salesperson. The power to persuade is what it takes to succeed, whether in personal, social, political, or business relationships. Even for the U.S. president, as Dick Neustadt famously observed, the real strength of the office is the power to persuade. Where else but in debate can you learn how to use that power in a competitive situation where your efforts are instantly rewarded with a win or brought up short with a loss?
- *Creativity.* Debate rewards original thinking and out-of-the-box ideas. And often it demands concept formulation in a matter of seconds. Ex-debaters take this for granted, but it is a rare and valuable skill. If you've had to respond extemporaneously to a surprise affirmative case sprung in a tournament elimination round, before an audience of peers, there isn't much that can daunt you in later life.
- *Collegiality.* Participating in an activity where you can't win on your own— where you have to marshal outrageous hours of effort on the part of others and return that effort in kind—is great preparation for a future where there are few opportunities for "solo" success. Today, most organizational experts will tell you that motivating small, flexible, and purpose-driven teams is the direction of the modern enterprise. And they might be talking about a debate squad.

For all these reasons, we think that debate remains the single best preparation any student can have for whatever the future holds. If anyone doubts this, here's a simple thought exercise: of all the debaters you've met since college, have you ever met one who regretted participating? Who thought he would've learned more by hitting the books harder or finding a more fulfilling outside activity? We haven't.

We conclude with a literary analogy that once captured our imagination: the Great Game as described by the writer Hermann Hesse. This was a mythical activity that could capture, through the elaborately symbolic moves of game pieces, the interplay of ideas. Similarly, debate is an elaborately structured competition deploying ideas as game pieces. Within its rigid framework and time structures, skilled players can craft unique, competitive interactions on an immense number of topics, political or philosophical. No topic or flight of fancy is forbidden, except by the need to prevail against a foe alert for any mistake.

A cerebral game, yes. But debate also partakes of the adrenaline surge of public performance; of harsh, browbeating questions; of desperate improvisation; of sudden, bitter defeat; of thrilling, unlooked-for victory. What a ride!

As our own mentor Larry Tribe commented in his memorial to Jim Unger, one of the finest coaches ever to grace the activity, what we remember is "debate as high art, debate as ritual, debate as relentless analysis, debate as bloodless battle." We salute those who continue to advance this activity, which has done so much for us and for so many others. May the next few years keep the activity undiminished, robust, and vital for the generations to come.

Charles E. Garvin and Greg A. Rosenbaum won the 1974 NDT debating for Harvard. In 1979, they teamed again to coach Harvard's 1979 NDT Champion. After graduating from Harvard Law School (Charlie took a side trip to Oxford as a Rhodes Scholar, while Greg simultaneously earned a master in public policy from Harvard's Kennedy School), both began careers at the Boston Consulting Group. They continued to team as principals in Palisades Associates, Inc., a turnaround merchant banking firm, where they have put debating skills to work while controlling such companies as Expressions Custom Furniture, Richey Electronics, TVC Communications, and Empire Kosher Poultry. Palisades became the corporate sponsor of the NDT in 2006 when the Ford Motor Company Fund did not renew its support. Recently, Palisades Associates agreed to continue its NDT sponsorship through at least the 2015 NDT. Greg was recently appointed to the NDT Board of Trustees.

Section I: Professional Development, Research, and Advancement

Status of Standards for Tenure and Promotion in Debate

Tenure and Promotion Working Group

Chair
Robin Rowland, University of Kansas; and co-author, R. Jarrod Atchison, Trinity University, Texas

Members
Derek Buescher, University of Puget Sound
Ryan Galloway, Samford University
Matt Gerber, Baylor University
Jeff Jarman, Wichita State University
Kelly Young, Wayne State University

Advisory Members
Tom Hollihan, University of Southern California
Kelly McDonald, Arizona State University

Approved by:
American Forensic Association
Board of Trustees of the National Debate Tournament
Cross Examination Debate Association
National Debate Tournament Committee
National Developmental Conference on Debate
Western States Communication Association

SUMMARY

At the core of debate is the director who sometimes has the title of "coach." The director is sometimes described as a competitive strategist, playing much the same role in debate that directors/coaches play in athletics. This view is fundamentally incorrect since the very essence of coaching debate involves two key pedagogical goals common across higher education. The two key pedagogical roles fulfilled by the director/coach are teacher and research-team mentor. The director/coach teaches debaters argumentation theory, audience analysis, and a host of other topics. But he/she also teaches them how to research and construct strong arguments. In this way, the director/coach plays a role similar to the leader of a research team. In addition to the pedagogical roles, the director/coach is a mentor, a strategist, a motivator, a planner, an organizer, and often a friend.

Every successful debater has a story about a director/coach who changed his/her life. A successful director/coach can have impact across generations of debaters. In that way, the director/coach also becomes the institutional memory of the activity. Debaters see the competitive demands of the moment, but the director/

coach can see how competitive practices impact long-term pedagogy. Given the many crucial roles that the director/coach plays in debate, it is essential for the health of the activity that appropriate standards are in place for evaluating the performance of the director/coach and providing the same type of reasonable protection against unfair evaluation that the tenure process provides for other faculty members. Without those standards, directors/coaches may be evaluated based on standards that do not account for the unique demands involved in coaching academic debate. The result may be to move the activity toward a situation in which more and more of the coaching is done by nonacademic instructors whose focus is only on competitive success and who lack either a long-term perspective or a pedagogical focus.

The Tenure and Promotion Standards Working Group was convened in order to participate in the ongoing national conversations on assessment and promotion and to provide guidance to units as to the most appropriate way to appoint and evaluate the performance of professionals in debate and forensics. As we note in detail later in this report, debate directors/coaches currently are evaluated based on a wide variety of different standards and through many different procedures. While there are many models for evaluating the work of coaches, only a few of those models provide the stability that the tenure model provides for faculty members in tenure-track positions. This situation is unfortunate. First, current trends in appointment and evaluation encourage the use of non-academic coaches. A tenure model, in contrast, produces a culture dominated by directors/coaches with a focus on long-term pedagogy. Second, it means that directors/coaches lack the protections of other faculty members. As a consequence, in a difficult economic or ideological climate, it may be much easier to get rid of a debate director/coach than other faculty members, a situation that may create instability in the forensics program itself. Third, there is a danger that the incredible time commitment involved in coaching debate may not be rewarded appropriately because the evaluative standards do not account for the pedagogical, professional, and intellectual work of the director in furthering the pedagogical goals of the activity.

To address these difficulties, the tenure and promotion group believes that there are two appropriate models for evaluating the performance of debate coaches. One approach treats the director/coach as a normal tenure-track faculty member, but broadens what can count for academic research. Under this approach, a season of debate should be evaluated as itself a form of research in the same way that a theater production would be considered creative research for a faculty member in a theater department. A few schools already have had the vision to embrace this model. A second approach treats the role of coaching debate as essentially similar to that of faculty who in addition to teaching have a professional performance dimension to their academic assignment. In this way, coaching responsibilities would be evaluated as a kind of professional performance in the same way that the work of a librarian or an academic scientist is viewed as professional performance.

The working group recognizes that when a university grants tenure to an individual, the institution is making a commitment that can extend for 25 or more years. Some universities may be wary of making such a commitment to a debate director/coach, fearing that the director/coach will not continue to work with debate over the long term and instead focus on teaching, administration, or research. The working group believes that institutions can confront this situation by specifying the responsibilities of the director/coach. For example, some institutions may want to create a title and position description for debate that specifies the duties of the debate director/coach and makes clear that any grant of tenure applies in the context of the particular position description. The director/coach would be able to earn tenure with all the rights and privileges associated with it and could be promoted to professor under this approach. Transfer to an alternative tenure line would require review by appropriate administrators as is common with many university appointments such as with department chairs, directors of graduate studies, and basic course directors. The university might give the director/coach a particular title to make this point clear, in the same way that some universities have a different title for a clinical professor than for other faculty members.

A proposed "Standards for Evaluating the Performance of Faculty Debate Coaches," is included at the end of this document. This document was approved by the attendees at the Developmental Conference on Debate at Wake Forest and also by the Board of Trustees of the National Debate Tournament at the same conference. Since the conference, it has been approved by the National Debate Tournament (NDT) committee, the American Forensic Association, the Cross Examination Debate Association (CEDA), and the Western States Communication Association. Based on the endorsement of debate organizations, the standards should be considered by deans and department chairs in crafting the appointment and evaluation standards for future generations of coaches. The standards also may lead to a shift back toward directors/coaches having the protections of tenure, a development that would provide stability to the coaching ranks and also help maintain a pedagogical focus in the activity.

While our focus has been on debate coaches, we think it quite likely that a very similar situation applies to directors/coaches working with forensics and that the same standards that we are proposing for debate would be appropriate in that context as well.

Debate scholarship embraces a wide array of topics, research methods, and modes of presentation and publication. Although we consider this diversity of scholarly practice a great strength of our field, it brings with it potential difficulties as well. Notable among these is the complexity of assessing records of scholarship that include elements not easily captured by the typical categories used in tenure, promotion, and merit review.

Although this document is meant to provide guidelines to assist institutions in the creation of tenure and promotion-related documents we recognize, of course, that each case of professional assessment is an internal matter of departments, colleges, and universities with their own evaluative standards. Directors/coaches expect to be assessed with the same rigor as their colleagues in other fields. We do not presume this document will supersede procedures at individual institutions. Rather, it offers a perspective on the value of scholarly practices that, though distinctive to debate research, may not be as familiar to scholars and reviewers in other fields. Additionally, the guidelines do not offer an exhaustive account of the many roles fulfilled by the director/coach in debate.[1]

In what follows, we first provide an overview of debate in order to explain the importance of the activity and then review the status of tenure and evaluation standards among directors/coaches in various types of programs across the country. A mass e-mail was used to ask directors/coaches to submit information about the nature of their current appointment (tenure track, term appointment, and so forth) and the standards through which their performance is evaluated. In addition to seeking information about appointment and evaluation standards for current coaches, we reviewed material from previous developmental conferences and the statement of debate coaches labeled the Quail Roost document

---

[1] We are heavily indebted to the NCA Performance Studies Division: Tenure and Promotion Guidelines for Understanding and Evaluating Creative Activity, n.d. for the language of these previous two paragraphs. Additional references include Voice and Speech Trainers Association, Inc., Promotion, Tenure and Hiring Resources, 2002; Association for Theatre in Higher Education, Guidelines for Evaluating the Teacher/Director for Promotion and Tenure, August 1992; Good Practice in Tenure Evaluation: Advice for Tenured Faculty, Department Chairs and Academic Administrators: A Joint Project of the American Council on Education, the American Association of University Professors, and United Educators Insurance Risk Retention Group, 2000.

(named after the place where the conference was held), as well as information about how faculty in theater and academic professionals in positions similar to that of a debate director/coach are evaluated. Following the review of current appointment and evaluation practices, we develop a case for the proposed two tracks for evaluating the performance of debate coaches. We conclude with draft standards.

AN OVERVIEW OF DEBATE

The fundamental goal of academic debate in all its forms is to provide students with the critical analysis and advocacy skills they need to build a strong case for a position related to a public controversy. Debate accomplishes this goal through a process in which students prepare for and then attend tournaments on a stated topic. The students, usually in teams of two, research all aspects of the topic, along with underlying issues relevant to the topic, and then prepare positions in order to support and oppose the topic.

The topic is usually a broad statement of policy (or value implying policy) that potentially can be supported or opposed in many different ways. To be successful therefore, debaters must have strong positions related to all of these different ways of supporting or opposing the topic. While the focus of debaters is often on competitive success, that emphasis on competition pushes them to hone their research, critical-thinking, argument-construction, and presentation skills. The competitive aims of the activity are tied directly to the pedagogical goal of training students to present strong and ethical positions on a public issue. In this way, tournaments are best understood as a kind of advanced laboratory for teaching public argument. Debate provides a laboratory not only for teaching argument but also for testing the value of various proposals on a given topic. It is thus both a place for training future policymakers and a place for testing policy proposals. From the perspective of the debater, competitive success may be the primary goal of participation. From the perspective of the director/coach, however, the desire of debaters for competitive success is a powerful prod pushing them to fulfill the pedagogical functions of the activity.

Over the course of a debate season, a team (or individual debater) might compete in as many as a dozen tournaments, comprised usually of six or eight preliminary rounds, followed by a single elimination tournament of teams seeded based on the preliminary results. The process of tournament debate pushes students to do enormous amounts of research and other preparation for tournament competition. The process also forces students to work continuously to strengthen positions on the topic because opposing teams are researching counterarguments to the positions they have developed. Once again, competition serves a pedagogical function.

It should be evident that while debate is often compared to other competitive activities, especially athletics, it is fundamentally different from those activities. In athletics, the fundamental goal of the competition is the competition itself. In debate, in contrast, the competitive aspects of the activity are a means to a pedagogical end. Debaters are motivated by the competition to do an enormous amount of work researching and preparing arguments, work that they would never do in the same quantity or with the same intensity without the competitive motivation.

Why do universities invest in academic debate? The answer is that the power of tournament debate for training students in public argument and advocacy has been demonstrated for almost 100 years. Many academic programs use simulations of various kinds to train students to confront a given issue. For example, both within and outside universities, crisis simulations are common for preparing professionals for a crisis in public health, foreign policy, and so forth. The simulation serves as an educational laboratory to prepare the students on the topic. Debate is best understood as a more general type of educational laboratory, a laboratory that gives students the basic skills they need in order to develop and defend a persuasive and ethical case related to an important public issue.

A REVIEW OF TENURE AND EVALUATION STANDARDS AND APPOINTMENT STATUS IN CONTEMPORARY DEBATE

We received 29 institutional responses to our query concerning the status of tenure and evaluation standards for debate coaches. Ten of the responses involved institutions with nontenure-track appointments while the remaining 19 responses included at least one tenure-track appointment. Several institutions reported a mixture of tenure-track and nontenure-track appointments. In total, the responses represent a wide variety of institutions with one single common denominator—they employ at least one full-time debate director/coach.

After analyzing the responses, three items for consideration emerged. First, there is little uniformity concerning the categorization of debate-coaching activities. Second, there is a wide continuum between institutions that require debate directors/coaches to achieve the same publication record as their traditional faculty colleagues and institutions that do not have any requirements for scholarship from their debate coaches. Third, there are alternative models for evaluating debate as a creative research activity that may help resolve the institutional pressures for increased scholarly production.

Although total uniformity across institutions is impossible, it is our opinion that these items demonstrate that the status of debate directors/coaches across the academy varies so widely from institution to institution that it is difficult to train, prepare, and evaluate current and future generations of debate coaches. It is not surprising, therefore, that none of the responses included an active debate director/coach with the rank of full professor with tenure, and that our anecdotal evidence suggests that few debate directors/coaches have been promoted to full professor in the modern era.

Item One: How Do Institutions Account for Debate-coaching Activities?

Categorizing debate-coaching activities as scholarship, teaching, and/or service represents a major discrepancy between institutional approaches to evaluating debate coaches. Although there is a persuasive argument that debate-coaching activities intersect all three of these traditional categories, few institutions permit debate directors/coaches to submit their activities within all three categories. Instead, with a few notable exceptions, institutions have generally moved toward treating debate-coaching activities as either teaching or service.

The majority of institutions surveyed consider debate coaching as primarily a teaching-related activity. As such, most institutions offer course reductions to allow their debate directors/coaches more time to focus on their debate obligations. The number of reductions changes from institution to institution, but the use of course reductions is consistent across a broad range of institutions. Beyond course reductions, however, the standards for evaluating debate-coaching activities as teaching vary widely.

One struggle that debate directors/coaches consistently confront is how to articulate teaching *effectiveness* outside of competitive success. One director/coach resents the connection between teaching effectiveness and competitive success because despite how effectively a debate director/coach teaches his/her students, "Student talent is still an extremely important intervening variable." The responses demonstrate that traditional measures of teaching effectiveness such as student evaluations are rare for a director's/coach's debate-related activities. We suspect that few of these traditional student evaluation measures would be appropriate for determining the teaching effectiveness of a debate director/coach As a result, rather than focusing on measures for effectiveness, institutions are increasingly developing descriptions of the connections between debate-coaching activities and the educational benefits associated with participation in intercollegiate debate.

Despite the fact that there is a trend toward considering debate coaching as teaching, there is very little consensus on the level of specificity necessary to establish the connection between coaching and the educational benefits of debate. Some institutions have very specific lists of debate-related activities, such as "Directing undergraduate research projects," while other institutions have general statements, such as "Extracurricular student guidance, such as faculty adviser for the undergraduate student organization." As a result of the vague nature of some descriptions, debate directors/coaches sometimes find themselves explaining the basic connections between their debate-coaching activities and teaching while other directors/coaches have the luxury of focusing on explaining their success within specific categories already recognized by the department.

Although the majority of institutions categorize debate-coaching activities as teaching, there are several institutions that consider these activities as solely service related. A research-one institution's tenure and promotion document categorizes debate coaching activities under the service section with a list of other activities such as, "Advising student groups." The director/coach of this institution described his/her institutional categorization of debate as follows, "Debate vaguely counts under 'service.'" This categorization of debate is not limited to research-one institutions. A small private university explicitly evaluates debate coaching only as service. The tenure and promotion document prioritizes teaching as 50% of the evaluation with research and service split at 25% each. The director/coach of this institution wrote, "I teach the same number of courses as the other faculty, have the same research expectations, the same number of advisees and committees, and other university service and then I do debate on top of that."

We acknowledge that every academic institution has unique goals and approaches to its academic culture. The result of the current categorization scheme, however, is that different universities end up describing the same exact coaching activity as either teaching or service, but not both. For example, some institutions consider judging at intercollegiate debate tournaments a unique area for instruction. According to one institution, "The faculty member is asked to critically engage the ideas and performance of student competitors, then to render a decision and provide an oral as well as written critique of the event to the students involved. These activities are recognized and rewarded as teaching activities." A separate institution, however, evaluates judging as second-level service when the debate director/coach presents an "oral debate critique before an audience." Judging debates is a prime example of an activity that can persuasively be articulated as both teaching and service. However, when institutions only evaluate debate-coaching activities as either service or teaching it forces similarly situated activities to be relegated to one portion of a debate directors/coaches consideration evaluation.

Institutions differ between categorizing debate coaching as teaching and/or service, but one consistent paradigm throughout the responses is that coaching debate is not considered a "traditional" scholarly activity. None of the responses included a standard of evaluation wherein debate-coaching activities are considered the equivalent of publishing peer-reviewed articles or having a book published by an academic press. As we will review in items two and three, the relationship between coaching debate and scholarship is complicated by alternative models of evaluation, but none of the responses support an evaluation of debate activities as traditional scholarship.

Item Two: Expectations for Scholarship
The second item that emerges from the responses is that the expectations for debate directors/coaches to produce scholarship exist on a wide continuum. On one end of the spectrum, debate directors/coaches are expected to achieve the same publication record as their traditional faculty colleagues. Five of the nineteen institutions with tenure-track debate directors/coaches have the same publication expectations for their debate directors/coaches as for their traditional faculty. The responses represent a variety of institutions ranging from a Carnegie research-one university that requires two publications in journals of "high quality" per year to private institutions that require 10 publications in peer-reviewed departmentally approved journals. The tenure and promotion documents for these departments do not distinguish between debate directors/coaches and traditional faculty with regard to research.

Almost all of the debate directors/coaches at this end of the spectrum cited an institutional philosophy that debate directors/coaches should be treated the same as the other faculty with regard to publication expectations. One director/coach wrote, "The publication requirement is the same as [for] anyone else in the department—no special privilege for debate." Another director/coach noted, "despite the fact that 45% of my job is assigned service with the debate program, there is not much weight assigned to debate once you get out of our department . . . we are expected to publish 'or perish' as it has been put." In addition to having the same publication expectations, these institutions do not count scholarship on the practice of debate at the same level as traditional academic research unless it is published in one of the top journals as designated by the department. In short, this end of the spectrum does not recognize debate as a scholarly activity, creative or otherwise.

On the other end of the spectrum, institutions do not require their debate directors/coaches to engage in any scholarship. There were over 25 debate directors/coaches represented at this end of the spectrum and all of them were nontenure-track appointments. The positions ranged from directors with the full privileges of a tenured professor except with periodic reviews to one-year adjunct appointments. The majority of these debate directors/coaches have reduced teaching obligations and are evaluated on their debate-related activities and their classroom-teaching effectiveness. Several of these positions are located outside of an academic department and therefore the debate director/coach is evaluated by a university administrator. Within this end of the spectrum, there is a wide variety of institutions from research-one universities with multiple directors/coaches to small private teaching colleges with one director/coach. The one common characteristic is that none of these institutions require their debate directors/coaches to engage in scholarly activity.

While the overall publication expectations vary from institution to institution, there are fewer and fewer debate directors/coaches today who fall somewhere in the middle. In the middle, debate directors/coaches are expected to publish some traditional academic research, but not as much as their traditional faculty peers. Only three institutions have explicit middle-ground standards for scholarly research. Two of the three institutions had vague language suggesting that the debate director/coach should demonstrate a consistent record of publication, but acknowledged that the unique demands associated with the position require the institution to evaluate a candidate's overall contribution. The most explicit middle-ground standard was set by a research-one institution. At this institution, the research requirements for a traditional faculty member require a candidate to either publish two peer-reviewed articles for each probationary year or publish an academic book and five peer-reviewed articles. This institution, however, has a separate description for the debate director/coach, which requires that person to publish at least five peer-reviewed articles during his/her probationary period. Despite the attempt of these three institutions to carve out a middle ground, the overall responses suggest that unless an institution adopts an alternative model for evaluating debate-coaching activities the trend is decidedly in the direction of more publications and less distinction between debate directors/coaches and traditional faculty or toward hiring nontenure-track debate directors/coaches with no expectations for scholarship. In the latter situation, directors/coaches lack the protection and status afforded by tenure.

Item Three: Alternative Models for Evaluating Debate Coaches

Four of the institutions surveyed utilized alternative models for evaluating the activities of their debate coaches. The four institutions represent a large research-one institution, two midsize state universities, and one small private university. All of the institutions have tenure-track debate coaches. Despite the diversity of institutions, the one characteristic they share is that they evaluate debate-coaching activities as a form of scholarship. One institution's tenure and promotion document is adapted from the Quail Roost Conference report and acknowledges that "Within the Department of Communication, the Director of Forensics is a unique position with unique evaluation requirements." The document goes on to describe how the responsibility to be well versed in the relevant literature on the debate resolution permeates all parts of being an active debate director/coach including directing undergraduate research projects, judging intercollegiate debates, and effectively preparing students for competition. The debate director/coach submits these materials in an annual portfolio that is considered a form of research for their tenure and promotion materials.

Two of the institutions borrow their model directly from the performing arts and theater in particular. The tenure and promotion document from one of these institutions identifies "Direction of forensic activities" under the category "Scholarship and Other Creative Activities." The document outlines the standard as follows, "Creating and managing a nationally competitive forensics program and providing leadership at the national level in competition debate are the primary indices of achievement in this category." In this model, the debate director/coach submits a portfolio describing how his/her activities satisfy this standard, and external reviewers evaluate the candidate's success. The other institution utilizes a "career variable interest agreement" that counts debate as a professional activity that is modeled after the standards used to judge the professional activity of theater professionals. These alternative models suggest that a deeper understanding of debate coaching as a form of scholarship can help resolve the tension between requiring scholarship for tenure and promotion or moving the debate-coaching position to a nontenure-track appointment.

IS A TENURE MODEL APPROPRIATE FOR ACADEMIC DEBATE?

The focus on the competitive nature of academic debate along with analogies often drawn in the media between debate and intercollegiate athletics might lead some to argue that the tenure model is not appropriate for a debate director/coach. While the working group recognizes that the tenure model will not fit all institutions, we also believe that it is the most appropriate model for maximizing the value of debate as a means of training future leaders and producing research on argumentation. A tenure model is appropriate for a debate director/coach for the same reasons that it is appropriate for other faculty members. The tenure model both provides appropriate protections for the director/coach and ensures that the director/coach will be viewed as a valuable faculty colleague within an institution and not as a second-class citizen. The director/coach has a great deal to offer his/her colleagues in terms of depth of knowledge of public policy, and an understanding of effective management of a research team, for that is what a debate squad is. This expertise may be lost to the department and larger institution if the director/coach is not viewed as regular faculty member. Directors/coaches lacking a tenure-track appointment are often denied the opportunity to participate on faculty or graduate-student committees. Not only do such rules unfairly harm the career of the director/coach, but they deny to the institution the many insights about argumentation and public policy that a director/coach can provide.

In addition, the tenure model is needed to protect and nurture academic debate as a subfield in argumentation studies. While academic debate is a highly competitive activity, from a pedagogical perspective it is best viewed as an extremely intense form of leadership coaching in order to train the next generation of leaders in a host of fields related to the public sphere. A tenure model is widely seen as appropriate for faculty teaching and doing research in all areas of the curriculum. Precisely the same point applies to debate. The presence of tenured faculty in any subfield guarantees a focus on pedagogy and research. In debate, tenured faculty members provide both institutional memory and a focus on the larger educational purposes of the activity.

TWO MODELS FOR APPOINTMENT AND EVALUATION OF DEBATE COACHES

The review of appointment status and evaluation standards of debate directors/coaches indicates that there are many different models for appointment and evaluation of debate coaches. However, only a few of those models provide the stability and protection of a tenure-track appointment and account for the unique demands of coaching debate. Debate directors/coaches have responsibilities and demands on their time that are very different from those of other faculty members. An appropriate model for appointment and evaluation of debate directors/coaches needs to take into account those responsibilities and demands.

Coaching debate is a form of teaching, but the time demands are much greater than for traditional classroom teaching. Consider the example of a director/coach with a squad of five teams that travel actively and three more that participate occasionally. In order to prepare these teams for tournament travel, a director/coach would have to spend many hours and several evenings a week working with the teams on arguments and listening to practice debates. A team of this size would need to travel to eight or more tournaments a semester in order to provide each of the active teams with adequate competition. Even if the director/coach of the team had help in some form, he/she would need to go to at least eight tournaments and more likely 10 or more a year. Each tournament requires a four- or five-day commitment, including travel days. The time demands we have described are typical for debate coaches. Many directors/coaches spend even more time than in the typical example we have described. There are similar time demands for forms of debate that are focused on individual, rather than team competition.

Of course, directors/coaches do far more than simply prepare teams for travel and attend tournaments. Directors/coaches also recruit high-quality students to their college or university, engage in a variety of alumni-related and other outreach activities, host public debates, do public relations for the program and university, along with many other activities.

Why do directors/coaches spend so much time working with debaters? Another way of considering this point is to ask why such an incredible time commitment is justified in an academic sense? The short answer to this question is that the debaters of today are the academic, business, legal, and political leaders of tomorrow. As is demonstrated in the reports of other working groups, academic debate has served as an excellent training ground for people who go on to shape society. Debate teaches people the research, critical thinking, and advocacy skills they need to deal with problems in the public sphere and elsewhere. Student newspapers often compare the work of the debate director/coach to the work of a football or basketball director/coach. In terms of the time commitment, this comparison is exactly on target. In terms of the impact of the director/coach, however, the comparison is deeply misleading. A successful basketball director/coach trains the next NBA point guard or power forward. It is no exaggeration to say that a successful debate director/coach might train a senator, Supreme Court justice, or president. Former debaters are widely represented in professions related to public argument including law, academia, business, politics, and government. And the debate director/coach accomplishes the aim of training these future leaders without the support system found in athletics by putting in very long hours working with gifted students. A number of studies of higher education recently have emphasized a coaching model. Academic debate is perhaps the strongest and most successful example of a discipline using that model.

The key point is that appointment and evaluation standards need to take into account the time demands of the director/coach and the importance of the work that the director/coach is doing. Two basic problems are present in the current appointment and evaluation models. First, many directors/coaches are evaluated based on standards that do not account for the unique demands of coaching debate. For example, the time demands on directors/coaches mean that they have far less time to work on traditional academic research than do normal tenure-track faculty members in research appointments. It is unsurprising that debate directors/coaches have not produced as much traditional research as other faculty members, given the time demands we have described. This means that applying traditional research standards to debate directors/coaches is inappropriate in nearly all cases. A similar problem occurs in cases where the program attempts to account for the work demands of coaching debate by providing a course release from teaching or other small benefit. While helpful, the demands of coaching a season of debate cannot be balanced by the provision of a small benefit, such as a course release.

Moreover, the application to debate of traditional standards for research is inappropriate because it does not recognize as legitimate the unique forms of research that are produced by debate. Debate directors/coaches assist their debaters in developing innovative arguments on a given topic. The debaters then test those arguments rigorously in competition against teams in the region or throughout the nation. This testing process is a form of peer review, quite similar to what occurs at journals. The ideas produced in this competitive process *are* a form of research. In the arts, it is widely recognized that projects produced in collaboration by a faculty member and a student are a form of creative activity. Similarly, the arguments produced by the collaboration of directors/coaches and debaters are best understood as creative research. Applying traditional standards of research to debate directors/coaches is fundamentally unfair because it fails to recognize the work of the director/coach along with his/her students in producing creative research.

In order to validate the creative research produced by the collaboration of directors/coaches and debaters, the working group recommends that in conjunction with the American Forensic Association, debate organizations create an online journal focused on best practices in creative public-policy research. In addition to providing an outlet for best practices in debate argumentation, the journal also might publish policy analyses about contemporary policy controversies drawn from debate research. The editorial board of the journal would review samples of creative research submitted on a given topic and then publish online those examples of creative research meeting the standards of the journal. The focus of the online journal would be on best practices in creative research related to the particular debate topic and thus would not compete with the mission of existing journals, such as *Argumentation and Advocacy*. However, the existence of the online journal could validate the importance of the creative research produced in the collaboration of directors/coaches and debaters. The online journal also might be a way for the debate community to participate in the dialogue about public policy in the public sphere.

The second problem is that in attempting to account for the time demands on debate coaches, many institutions have created nontraditional academic appointments for debate coaches. These appointments do account for the demands of the activity, but often lack the protections provided to tenure-track or term-appointment faculty members. This situation threatens the stability of coaching. In a difficult economic time, a debate director/coach may be let go simply because he/she lacks the protection of tenure. Also, debate directors/coaches are much more subject to the vagaries of shifting academic ideologies than are faculty members with tenure-track appointments. Another unfortunate effect of present standards is to encourage institutions to hire nonacademic coaches, usually a recent former debater, to direct a program. This coaching arrangement may produce an activity in which the focus is almost exclusively on competition as opposed to pedagogy. It also means that directors/coaches rarely have a long-term perspective.

It seems clear that the solution to the problems we have identified is to create appointment and evaluation models that both account for the unique demands of coaching debate and provide appropriate academic protections for coaches. Our goal in this report is to provide clear, equitable, reasonable, and attainable standards for annual performance evaluation and promotion. While recognizing that institutions may take many approaches to appointment and evaluation standards for a debate director/coach, the working group believes that two possible models for establishing clear, equitable, reasonable, and attainable standards merit particular attention.

Model One—A Professional-Performance Model

Under the professional-performance model, a debate director/coach would be appointed and evaluated in the same way that professionals with teaching, but not research responsibilities, are appointed and evaluated. In this view, a debate director/coach would be evaluated based on his/her professional accomplishments in coaching debate, along with normal teaching and service responsibilities. The professional accomplishments in debate would be assessed through a professional-responsibility portfolio that might include one or more of the following:

• A summary of team-building and other coaching efforts carried out by the director/coach;
• A summary of team performance at tournaments in the review period;
• A sample of research briefs created during the debate season. This material might be published in the online journal on best practices in debate argumentation;
• A summary of the director/coach's work as a judge in debate and how this judging functioned as a means of carrying on an academic dialogue concerning research relevant to the debate resolution;
• Information about public debates and other events in which the debate squad participated;
• A summary of pedagogical efforts training coaches and future directors of debate;
• A summary of efforts to secure external funding for research, programming, and/or outreach and development programs, for example, Urban Debate Leagues (UDLs);
• A summary of alumni development and other outreach efforts;
• Traditional academic research in argumentation and debate in journals such as Argumentation and Advocacy, Contemporary Argumentation and Debate, and Argumentation or the proceedings from argumentation conferences such as Alta, ISSA (International Society for the Study of Argumentation), and

OSSA (Ontario Society for the study of Argumentation), outlets that have played a key role in the development of argumentation and debate/forensics theory and practice (note that such research is not a required part of the appointment);

• Other appropriate information bearing on the professional performance of the director/coach.

The professional-responsibility model recognizes that the demands of coaching make it difficult or impossible for a debate director/coach to fulfill the research mission of other tenure-track faculty members. Rather, the position should be evaluated in the same way that a clinical professor or other professional with teaching responsibilities is evaluated. For example, the basic course director at a number of universities is evaluated under a model in which professional performance takes the place of research in the evaluation scheme. Similarly, a clinical professor managing something like a clinic or laboratory would be evaluated based on his/her work in the clinic or laboratory as well as teaching, and not based on publications. Some universities may want to give the debate coach a particular title analogous to clinical professor in order to account for the nature of the position.

The professional-responsibility model provides an appropriate way of accounting for the massive time commitment associated with, and the pedagogical importance of, coaching debate. Under this approach, a debate director/coach could be placed in a tenure-track faculty line with all the rights and privileges thereof, but evaluated under the professional-responsibility model. The director/coach could be tenured in this position and post-tenure remain in it continuing to fill the position as director/coach. Alternatively, the professional-responsibility model could be used for renewable term appointments of three or five years. The tenure-track model is preferable because it provides greater stability.

The professional-responsibility model accounts for the substantial commitment that acting as a debate director/coach requires and provides an appropriate means of specifying the appointment assumptions and evaluating the performance of a coach.

Model Two—Debate Performance as a Form of Research in a Tenure-Track Model

While the professional-responsibility model is an appropriate means of evaluating the performance of a debate coach, the working group believes that the debate-performance model is preferable. Under this approach, a season of debate would be viewed as itself a form of research in the same way that directing a theatrical production is viewed as a form of creative performance in theater. This model accounts for the enormous demands of debate and also recognizes that academic debate is itself an enormously research-intensive activity. In the course of a debate season, the arguments produced under the direction of any director/coach reach literally hundreds of debaters, judges, and other coaches. In that way, the ideas are presented and tested in a public setting at least as rigorous as the peer-review process for academic publication. The debate-performance model is the most appropriate model for appointment and evaluation of a debate director/coach at any university with a strong research mission. At such institutions, there is every danger that a faculty member on a nonresearch appointment may be viewed as a second-class citizen. Recognizing that debate performance is itself a form of research provides a means of fairly evaluating the work of a director/coach and minimizing the danger that the director/coach will be viewed as academically inferior to other research faculty. Under this approach, a debate director/coach would be evaluated based on his/her research performance in debate, along with normal teaching and service responsibilities.

The debate-performance model requires a means of assessing the research dimension in a season of debate in a way similar to that used in theater to assess the creative performance value in a theatrical production (examples of such standards are included as an appendix to this document). A similar approach is sometimes used in journalism and other disciplines. Drawing on the experience in theater and other academic disciplines, debate directors/coaches could be evaluated based on one or more of the following:

• A portfolio of research materials including research briefs representing a broad sample of the team's research efforts over the course of the debate season. This material might be published in the online journal on best practices in debate argumentation;
• A summary of the director/coach's work as a judge in debate and how this judging functioned as a means of carrying on an academic dialogue concerning research relevant to the debate resolution;
• A two-page statement explaining the intellectual importance of the research produced over the course of the season;
• A summary of pedagogical efforts training coaches and future directors of debate;
• A summary of efforts to secure external funding for research, program-

ming, and/or outreach and development programs, for example, Urban Debate Leagues (UDLs);

• Peer-review statements on the research performance of the team by debate critics certified for their excellence in argument by the National Debate Tournament, the Cross Examination Debate Association, and other appropriate debate organizations, operating under the general sponsorship of the American Forensic Association, the leading professional organization in argumentation studies. In theater, peer reviewers are certified by leading organizations and their views are consulted on the quality of theatrical productions. A similar process would work well in debate and be much easier to organize because of the tournament-focused nature of the activity. The standards needed to be classified as a peer critic would be validated by debate organizations and the American Forensic Association;

• Traditional academic research, including research focused on pedagogical issues in argumentation and debate in journals such as Argumentation and Advocacy, Contemporary Argumentation and Debate, and Argumentation or proceedings from argumentation conferences such as Alta, ISSA, and OSSA, outlets that have played a key role in the development of argumentation and debate/forensics theory and practice (note that such research is not a required part of the appointment);

• Other appropriate information bearing on the professional performance of the coach.

The debate-performance model provides an appropriate model for appointing and evaluating the academic performance of debate coaches. It recognizes the immense demands placed on directors/coaches and provides a means of evaluating that performance that does not risk labeling the director/coach as a non-research and therefore lesser faculty member. Rather, it recognizes that a season of debate involves just as strong and rigorous a commitment to academic research as does participation in the peer-review publication process. Under this approach, a debate director/coach could be placed in a tenure-track faculty line with all the rights and privileges thereof, but evaluated under the debate-performance model. The director/coach could be tenured in this position and post-tenure remain in it continuing to fill the position as director/coach.

In relation to the debate -performance model, the working group urges relevant debate and forensics organizations to study the most appropriate means of certifying peer reviewers. In addition to conducting reviews of tenure and promotion materials, these reviewers might be used in some cases as part of the annual evaluation or third-year review process. It is important that debate and forensics organizations establish rigorous standards for validating status as a peer reviewer in order to guarantee that reviews produced by the peer reviewers receive the careful consideration that they deserve.

APPOINTMENT EXPECTATIONS

In order to clearly establish appointment expectations, it is important that letters of appointment specify the responsibilities of the director/coach and the criteria under which his/her performance will be evaluated both in terms of the annual-merit process and in terms of promotion and tenure. The letter of appointment should articulate the relationship of the director/coach and the debate/forensics program to the mission of the program, department, college, and university.

PROMOTION TO PROFESSOR

In addition to providing a model for promotion to associate professor with tenure, it is important to provide an appointment model and associated standards for promotion to professor. Provision of a model under which distinguished debate directors/coaches can be promoted to professor is important for two reasons. First, the promotion to professor is a sign of substantial professional accomplishment. Without that alternative, even the most distinguished director/coach may be considered a second-class citizen in the department. Second, because attaining the rank of professor takes both time and considerable professional accomplishment, directors/coaches who attain this rank will have long experience with the activity. These directors/coaches play a crucial role in providing institutional memory within the activity and maintaining a focus on pedagogy.

Each of the models for appointment and evaluation that were described earlier could be used to set standards for promotion to professor. The faculty member would again use the portfolio process, but with the aim of demonstrating that he/she was a major intellectual leader in the activity, as defined by the criteria for evaluating the portfolio under either the professional-performance or the debate-performance models.

MERIT EVALUATION

As we noted in a review of the current status of appointment and evaluation standards in debate, many directors/coaches currently are on nonacademic appointments. This method of appointment lacks the stability of the tenure-track model and deprives both debate as a subfield and also particular academic institutions of the insights that the director/coach can provide on a host of academic issues related to public policy, value argument, argumentation, and means of managing a research group. Therefore, while we believe the tenure model is the most appropriate approach for appointing and evaluating debate coaches, we also believe that regardless of the model it is essential for directors/coaches to be evaluated through the same merit-evaluation process as other faculty members, although by criteria appropriate for the director/coach as outlined in this document, and to have access to the same kinds of rewards as other faculty members

Transfer to Alternative Evaluation Appointments

It is important to recognize that the appointment and evaluation standards apply only to cases where faculty members remain actively involved in debate. Meeting the standards for appointment and promotion under either the professional-performance or the research-performance models would not necessarily qualify the individual to shift his/her appointment to a traditional research-oriented appointment. Since the individual would not have been tenured under a research model, his/her accomplishments would not necessarily qualify him/her for such an appointment. This approach has two advantages. First, it encourages debate directors/coaches to remain in the activity by providing them a path for promotion first to associate professor with tenure and then to professor. This should help keep senior directors/coaches involved in debate. Second, it answers the fear of some that debate directors/coaches will be tenured under a nonresearch model and then retire from debate to the department and become unproductive. This would not be possible because the appointment of the director/coach should specify not only his/her assignment to debate, but also that promotion and tenure were accepted under a nonresearch model. Thus, the faculty member could transfer out of debate into a traditional tenure-track faculty line only with the approval of relevant promotion and tenure decision makers at a given school.

Conclusion

The Tenure and Promotion Standards Working Group believes that current appointment and evaluation standards in many cases do not account for the unique demands of coaching debate and fail to provide the stability of the tenure-track model. Current practices also encourage programs to move to a model in which the director/coach is a nonacademic and the focus of the program is purely on competition. The working group believes that this trend is unfortunate and that alternative standards are needed. In this report we have developed a case for two models for appointment and evaluation. In the final section, we include draft language that we hope will be endorsed by various organizations associated with academic debate.

Appendix: Standards for Appointment and Evaluation of Debate Coaches

Preamble—The pedagogical value of debate for training the next generation of leaders in business, academia, the law, and the public sphere is well known. A debater of today often becomes the successful lawyer, academic, business leader, or even senator, Supreme Court justice, or president of tomorrow. Given the pedagogical value of debate, it is important to have appointment and evaluation standards that account for the unique demands of tournament debate. The time demands of working intensively with a group of gifted students to prepare them for tournament competition against other gifted students are enormous. Appointment and evaluation standards must account for both those demands.

It is in recognition of both the importance of the director/coach and the need for appointment and evaluation standards that account for the nature of debate, that _____ endorses the following standards:

MODEL ONE—A PROFESSIONAL-PERFORMANCE MODEL

Under the professional-performance model, a debate director/coach is appointed and evaluated in the same way that professionals with teaching, but not research responsibilities, are appointed and evaluated. Professional performance replaces research in the appointment and evaluation standards applied to the coach. Professional accomplishments in debate should be assessed through a professional-responsibility portfolio prepared by the director/coach in the normal evaluation cycle for the institution. That portfolio should include one or more of the following:

• A summary of team-building and other coaching efforts carried out by the coach;
• A summary of team performance at tournaments in the review period;
• A sample of research briefs created during the debate season. This material might be published in the online journal on best practices in debate argumentation;
• A summary of the director/coach's work as a judge in debate and how this judging functioned as a means of carrying on an academic dialogue concerning research relevant to the debate resolution;
• Information about public debates and other events in which the debate squad participated;
• A summary of pedagogical efforts training coaches and future directors of debate;

- A summary of efforts to secure external funding for research, programming, and/or outreach and development programs, for example, Urban Debate Leagues (UDLs);
- A summary of alumni development and other outreach efforts;
- Traditional academic research, including research focused on pedagogical issues in argumentation and debate in journals such as Argumentation and Advocacy, Contemporary Argumentation and Debate, and Argumentation or proceedings from argumentation conferences such as Alta, ISSA, and OSSA, outlets that have played a key role in the development of argumentation and debate/forensics theory and practice (note that such research is not a required part of the appointment);
- Other appropriate information bearing on the professional performance of the coach.

Under the professional-responsibility model, the debate director/coach should be evaluated in the same way that a clinical professor or other professional with teaching, but not research, responsibilities is evaluated. For example, the basic course director at a number of universities is evaluated under a model in which professional performance takes the place of research in the evaluation scheme. Similarly, a clinical professor managing a clinic or laboratory would be evaluated based on his/her work in the clinic or laboratory as well as teaching, and not based on publications. Some universities may want to give the debate director/coach a particular title analogous to clinical professor in order to account for the nature of the position.

The professional-responsibility model provides an appropriate way of accounting for the massive time commitment associated with, and pedagogical importance of, coaching debate. Under this approach, a debate director/coach could be placed in a tenure-track faculty line with all the rights and privileges thereof, but evaluated under the professional-responsibility model. The director/coach could be tenured in this position and post-tenure remain in it, continuing to fill the position as director/coach. Alternatively, the professional-responsibility model could be used for renewable term appointments of three or five years. The tenure-track model is preferable because it provides greater stability.

MODEL TWO—DEBATE PERFORMANCE AS A FORM OF RESEARCH IN A TENURE-TRACK MODEL

While the professional-responsibility model is an appropriate means of evaluating the performance of a debate coach, the debate-performance model is a more appropriate model at institutions with a substantial research focus. Under this approach, a season of debate is viewed as itself a form of research in the same way that directing a theatrical production is viewed as a form of creative performance in theater. This model accounts for the enormous demands of debate and also recognizes that academic debate is itself an enormously research-intensive activity. In the course of a debate season, the arguments produced under the direction of any director/coach reach literally hundreds of debaters, judges, and other coaches. In that way, the ideas are presented and tested in a public setting at least as rigorous as the peer-review process for academic publication. Recognizing that debate performance is itself a form of research provides a means of fairly evaluating the work of a director/coach and minimizing the danger that the director/coach will be viewed as academically inferior to other research faculty.

The debate-performance model requires a means of assessing the research dimension in a season of debate in a way similar to that used in theater to assess the creative performance value in a theatrical production. Drawing on the experience in theater, debate directors/coaches should be evaluated based on one or more of the following:

• A portfolio of research materials including research briefs representing a broad sample of the team's research efforts over the course of the debate season. This material might be published in the online journal on best practices in debate argumentation;
• A summary of the director/coach's work as a judge in debate and how this judging functioned as a means of carrying on an academic dialogue concerning research relevant to the debate resolution;
• A two-page statement explaining the intellectual importance of the research produced over the course of the season;
• A summary of pedagogical efforts training coaches and future directors of debate;
• A summary of efforts to secure external funding for research, programming, and/or outreach and development programs, for example, Urban Debate Leagues (UDLs);
• Peer-review statements on the research performance of the team by debate critics certified for their excellence in argument by the National Debate Tournament, the Cross Examination Debate Association, and other appropriate debate organizations, operating under the general sponsorship of the American Forensic Association, the leading professional organization in argumentation studies. In theater, peer reviewers are certified by leading organizations and

their views are consulted on the quality of theatrical productions. A similar process would work well in debate and be much easier to organize because of the tournament-focused nature of the activity. The standards needed to be classified as a peer critic would be validated by debate organizations and the American Forensic Association;

• Traditional academic research, including research focused on pedagogical issues in argumentation and debate in journals such as Argumentation and Advocacy, Contemporary Argumentation and Debate, and Argumentation or the proceedings from argumentation conferences such as Alta, ISSA, and OSSA, outlets that have played a key role in the development of argumentation and debate/forensics theory and practice (note that such research is not a required part of the appointment);

• Other appropriate information bearing on the professional performance of the coach.

The debate-performance model provides an appropriate model for appointing and evaluating the academic performance of debate coaches. It recognizes the immense demands placed on directors/coaches and provides a means of evaluating that performance that does not risk labeling the director/coach as a non-research and therefore lesser faculty member. Rather, it recognizes that a season of debate involves just as strong and rigorous a commitment to academic research as does participation in the peer-review publication process. Under this approach, a debate director/coach could be placed in a tenure-track faculty line, with all the rights and privileges thereof, but evaluated under the debate-performance model. The director/coach could be tenured in this position and post-tenure remain in it, continuing to fill the position as director/coach.

APPOINTMENT EXPECTATIONS

In order to clearly establish appointment expectations, it is important that letters of appointment specify the responsibilities of the director/coach and the criteria under which his/her performance will be evaluated both in terms of the annual merit process and in terms of promotion and tenure. The letter of appointment should articulate the relationship of the director/coach and the debate/forensics program to the mission of the program, department, college, and university.

PROMOTION TO PROFESSOR

Each of the models for appointment and evaluation that were described earlier could be used to set standards for promotion to professor. The faculty member would again use the portfolio process, but with the aim of demonstrating that he/she was a major intellectual leader in the activity, as defined by the criteria for evaluating the portfolio under either the professional-performance or the debate-performance models.

Pathways to Innovation in Debate Scholarship

Research and Scholarship Working Group

Chair
Gordon R. Mitchell, University of Pittsburgh

Members
Peter Bsumek, James Madison University
Christian Lundberg, University of North Carolina-Chapel Hill
Michael Mangus, University of Pittsburgh
Benjamin Voth, Southern Methodist University

Advisory Members
Marie-Odile Hobeika, Wake Forest University
Michael Jensen, National Academies

The Research and Scholarship Working Group of the third National Developmental Conference on Debate (NDCD) was tasked by the conference steering committee to:

> Foster research and scholarship by examining the culture and prevailing norms among debate professionals toward research and scholarship, identify opportunities for innovation in scholarship, examine existing outlets and imagine new possibilities for research and scholarship about debate and/or by debaters.

This charge comes at a time when the scholarly dimension of the debate enterprise is undergoing significant transitional pressures. To understand the character of these pressures, it is helpful to situate the current challenges and opportunities within a broader historical context. One way to frame the prevailing milieu is to compare the 2009 NDCD to the two previous major debate developmental conferences at Sedalia, Colorado (1974), and Evanston, Illinois (1984).[1] As Donn Parson notes, the 1974 Sedalia Conference "clearly created a call to research in forensics," encouraging forensics practitioners to expand their scholarly commitments. This call was reflected in resolutions that aimed at "recognizing the diversity of methods possible in forensic research; increasing the dissemination of forensic scholarship; having professional organizations

---

[1] For a treatment of the 1974 Sedalia Conference, see Parson (1990) The reports produced by the Sedalia Conference are available in McBath (1975). Proceedings from the 1984 Evanston conference are collected in Parson (1984).

sponsor and support forensic research; and focusing on the characteristics of those engaged in forensics" (Parson 1990, 69).

One of the first orders of business for participants attending the 1974 Sedalia Conference was to pin down definitions of key terms that would guide conference deliberations. Accordingly, the group defined forensics as "an educational activity primarily concerned with using an argumentative perspective in examining problems and communicating with people" (McBath 1975, 11). Notably, this definition reflected a "shift in thinking from forensics as activities to forensics as perspective for scholarship" that "profoundly influenced subsequent deliberations" (McBath 1975, 12).

A prominent theme percolating from Sedalia concerned the importance of positioning forensics as a scholarly endeavor, not merely a game or sport. Toward that end, Sedalia conferees called for debate programs to integrate with academic departments, for graduate programs to redouble training of future forensics leaders, and for all members of the forensics community to embrace scholarly research as a part of their professional portfolios (McBath 1975, 12–21).

A few Sedalia conferees underscored these overall recommendations with detailed commentary. For example, David Zarefsky joined with Malcolm Sillars to write an essay on "Future Goals and Roles of Forensics," advancing the thesis, "scholars and teachers in forensics should define their interests primarily in terms of their *substantive scholarly concerns, rather than their roles as administrators of activity programs*" (Sillars and Zarefsky 1975, 83, emphasis added; see also Rieke and Brock, 1975, 129–36). This commitment to scholarship was reinforced by a shift in nomenclature echoed by other Sedalia conferees, with the sport-oriented "coach" terminology giving way to terms like "forensics specialist"—a preferred label for describing debate professionals (see, e.g., Hagood, 1975, 101; Keele and Andersen 1975). As Sillars and Zarefsky put it, the sportified "debate coach" definitions have "permitted the hiring of inexperienced candidates for positions often *defined* as non-tenured, with extensive work loads and a range of responsibilities that precludes the time and energy needed for serious scholarship" (1975, 91–92).

The rationale for defining forensics as a scholarly enterprise becomes apparent when one considers how academic scholarship contributes to the long-term vitality of intercollegiate debate by securing institutional support for the activity, bolstering the intellectual freedom of participants, and engendering mutually informing conversations between debate scholars and interlocutors beyond the debate community. As the Sedalia conferees concluded, "programs without any academic affiliation decrease the likelihood that the forensics specialist will be perceived as a scholar whose work is vital to the educational process, and increase the likelihood that competitive activity programs will be regarded as ends in themselves" (McBath 1975, 14).

It is noteworthy that a mere ten years later, Sedalia's ringing call for scholarly research dropped out of the final documents of the Evanston conference almost entirely, save for a few passing references in material produced by the Tenure and Promotion Working Group (Parson 1990, 69, 71). We might hypothesize two reasons for this omission. First, it is possible that the call for redoubled scholarly research relating to debate advanced by the Sedalia conferees was answered, rendering further dwell-time on the issue superfluous. It is certainly the case that in the years between Sedalia and Evanston, debate-related scholarship flourished in a number of outlets, including the NCA-AFA summer conferences on argumentation (Alta conferences) and the *Journal of the American Forensic Association*. But there is a second, perhaps more troubling explanation that accounts for the Evanston conference's exclusion of scholarly research from its agenda. Perhaps an intensifying trade-off between time spent in pursuit of contest debating and time spent in pursuit of research agendas by debate academics forced a choice resulting in Evanston's narrower developmental focus.

Whatever the rationale for the narrow scope of the second National Developmental Conference on Forensics, it is clear that a now thirty-five-year gap in institutional attention by debate leadership organizations to the direction of and prospects for debate-related scholarship warrants redress. As we will detail more fully in the following section, a number of structural trends at the level of contest debating and in the academy more generally have exerted substantial pressures on the character and volume of debate scholarship. Just as time demands are intensifying on coaches to field competitive teams, requirements for tenure and promotion are simultaneously escalating. This double bind has coincided with increased competition for slots in the quality journals that traditionally served as outlets for debate scholarship, or in some cases outright redefinitions of the missions of journals to limit their value as venues for debate scholarship. Adding another twist to this already vexing knot, the increasing "professionalization" of debate, reflected in the decline of tenured debate coaches, has lessened incentives for the coaches to produce debate-oriented scholarship.

Perhaps the greatest paradox resulting from this constellation of factors is that it is growing hard to produce and define a constituency for debate scholarship at the very moment in our public life when such academic work is vitally needed to bolster the quality of public deliberation. This conundrum heightens the salience of our working group's charge, to "imagine new possibilities" for debate scholarship, and to "innovate" by theorizing novel opportunities for forensics specialists to produce academic research. In what follows, we address this challenge by initially assessing key status quo norms and practices that enable and constrain possibilities for scholarly publishing in the intercollegiate policy-debate community (Part One); next, considering how debate's collaborative mode of knowledge production has potential to leverage academic knowledge production (Part Two); and then, taking stock of how the rapid evolution of online digital publishing and the advent of social Web media implicate efforts by forensics specialists to participate in scholarly conversations beyond the tournament grid (Part Three). These preliminary sections pave the way for our closing segment (Part Four), which lays out the working group's specific recommendations and their accompanying rationales.

PART ONE: STATUS QUO TRENDS IN RESEARCH AND SCHOLARSHIP

The tradition of forensics specialists actively producing scholarly manuscripts for academic publication has eroded as debate tournament competition has become ever more labor intensive. Heightened sportification of the debate activity, general decline of interest in scholarly knowledge production on the part of forensics specialists, and reduction of tenure-stream faculty lines for directors of debate are but a few symptoms of the underlying problem Sedalia diagnosed but did not treat.

Debate sportification presents most forensics specialists with a Hobson's choice—produce academic scholarship or coach a successful team, but try both at your own peril. Travel schedules, research assignments, and three- to four-day tournaments combine to exercise a temporal tyranny over those forensics specialists who struggle to find time for academic pursuits beyond the competitive tournament grid. With so much of the time invested in coaching and traveling coming at the expense of teaching and researching, professional priorities devalue academic research. Should one choose to pursue a research agenda and the attendant promises of professional advancement, the choice risks exile from the place one once called home—the tournament site. Thus two realms of rhetorical production, which once were so fruitful in their collaboration, become estranged. One result is that some of the most talented scholars are cornered out of the competitive debate activity because it does not allow them the time or incentive to work on other interests such as publishing and teaching (Parson 1990, 70). Noting that forensics directors shoulder "a combination of teaching, coaching, travel, and administrative duties that boggles the mind," Zarefsky (1980, 21) warned against the tendency of these duties to crowd out scholarly endeavors.

Matthew Brigham's (2008) informal survey of publishing trends on issues related to competitive forensics from 2000 to 2005 (with a comparison to the communication field's flagship journal in its first six years of publication: 1915–20) sheds light on contemporary manifestations of this phenomenon. From 2000 to 2005, 100 articles and 83 book reviews appeared in *Argumentation and Advocacy*. From this group, only 10.1% (19 of 183) of those published pieces touched on issues relating to competitive forensics, with 15 of the 18 full-length articles on forensics coming in two special issues (the 19th was a book review).

Comparing these data with earlier trends, one finds that in its first six years, the field of communication's flagship journal regularly featured articles on competitive forensics—from 1915 to 1920 there were 260 articles and 97 book reviews. Of the 260 articles, 48 (18.5%) were related to competitive forensics, as were 15 of the 97 (15.5%) book reviews. Therefore, of the 357 total entries in this journal during this time, 17.6% (63) covered competitive forensics. In stark contrast, there were zero articles in the *Quarterly Journal of Speech* relating to competitive forensics from 2000 to 2005.[2]

While the sheer intensity of labor involved in contemporary intercollegiate debate accounts for some of the difficulties facing young participants seeking to launch academic research careers, there are also sociological factors complicating the debate-to-scholar metamorphosis. Intercollegiate debate is a social activity shaped by both competitive and collaborative forces. While competitive pressures provide motivation for debaters to do research in order to defeat opposing teams, ésprit de corps spurs team members to work harder with each other on common projects designed to leverage contest-round preparation.

Before a debater presents a new argument at a tournament, for example, the idea has likely been brainstormed collaboratively by partners and other team members, and has been critiqued and refined following coach feedback during practice sessions. The tournament setting adds additional layers of feedback pro-

---

[2] The previous two paragraphs are adapted from a study by Matthew Brigham (2008).

vided by debate opponents and judge comments. Debaters become accustomed to a variety of resources at their disposal: fellow debaters, case lists, old research from former topics, blogs, and e-mail listserves with hundreds of subscribers.

Indeed, debate competitors are socialized into a rapid-reward economy in which their work efforts receive frequent scrutiny from varied audiences. However, the motivational spur provided by this instant-feedback culture can become a hindrance when debaters transition to the academic community, where peer review timelines are notoriously long. For journal submissions, authors can often expect to wait many months (even years) between rounds of editorial feedback. And most basically, in an academic world where assessment criteria are often vague or even nonexistent, scholars find few counterparts to the tournament trophies and speaker point awards that motivate intercollegiate debaters.

The Sedalia Conference advanced a powerful vision for forensics educators. Noting a growing disconnect between academic departments and forensic programs, Sedalia laid out a series of goals that could help to bridge this divide. Unfortunately, while the adopted resolutions were helpful in imagining a new future for forensics, they were less useful in marking precise routes charting courses to such imagined futures. We have already observed how the 1984 developmental conference in Evanston failed to bridge this gap, and although the Quail Roost draft document on tenure for forensics educators (Dauber et al. 1993) emphasized that directors of forensics should be judged comprehensively in tenure and promotion decisions, it developed few innovations designed to stimulate scholarly knowledge production beyond the tournament grid, at most suggesting that forensic directors be provided with research assistants to help them in their presumably solitary publication activities.

PART TWO: COLLABORATIVE KNOWLEDGE PRODUCTION IN DEBATE
Once a solitary enterprise, academic research is fast evolving into an activity where multiple scholars commonly produce knowledge by working together in pairs or teams. In part, this trend is a natural response to the growing complexity and interdisciplinary nature of research topics, whose multifaceted dimensions often overtax the expertise and capability of solo investigators. But changes in the academy's information infrastructure also play a part in facilitating collective scholarly work. Digital interconnectivity, circulation of sophisticated social networking software, and the advent of flexible communication tools, all make collaborative knowledge production increasingly feasible.

While coauthorship is common practice within academic fields such as medicine, economics, the natural sciences, and even some branches of the social sciences (Aonuma 2001, 7), the tradition of collaborative research is less well established in the humanities, although the winds of change are blowing. Amid commentary calling for new modes of knowledge production in the academy (Jensen 2007) and more teamwork in rhetorical scholarship (Aune 2007), surveys document an uptick of multiple-authored publications in the field of communication (Kramer, Hess, and Reid 2007). The publishing landscape is shifting in ways that favor intellectual communities (such as intercollegiate debate) that are able to cultivate and support cross-disciplinary, collective knowledge-production projects.

Co- and group-authored research provides socialization opportunities and material resources that may enable forensics specialists to get a foothold in the world of academic writing. For undergraduate debaters turned graduate students, it provides a support network much like the teams that supported their competitive and intellectual development. For forensics specialists in non-tenure-stream positions who wish to be taken seriously in academic contexts, collaborative research provides a bridge from a service role to scholar role, consistent with the forensics specialists' historical role in shaping the field of speech communication.

Coauthorship seems particularly well suited for members of the debate community because it enacts a familiar process of internal deliberation and argumentation. Mirroring the creation and refinement of argument briefs for competitive debate, the collaborative brainstorming, revision, and decision making that goes into coauthored scholarship involves reworking arguments for eventual presentation to wider publics. Debate teams have honed both formal and informal procedures for co-coordinating intellectual work. These procedures, driven primarily by the pressures of tournament preparation, constitute a rich storehouse of tacit knowledge. Consider that the following modes of engagement in the Debate Authors Working Group approach each have distinct correlates in the competitive forensics setting.

• *Research-area brainstorming and agenda setting,* including roundtable discussion to project the upcoming year's academic projects and set research priorities (correlates with debate team research-assignment brainstorming).
• *Manuscript workshopping,* featuring constructive criticism of drafts in progress generated from multiple perspectives (correlates with small-group research teams working on focused debate assignments).

- *Revision strategy and execution,* involving group conversation regarding how best to respond to "revise and resubmit" peer review (correlates with debate-team strategy sessions focused on how to adapt argument strategies in light of judge feedback).
- *Delivery practice,* executed in practice sessions for oral presentation of research reports to professional audiences (correlates with debate-team practice rounds).

The occasion to work together on scholarly projects affords debate authors opportunities to identify and develop points of overlap between the competitive forensics skill set and the skill set utilized in the generation of publishable academic work. Again, key research skills mobilized in the Debate Authors Working Group model have correlates in competitive forensics.

- *Multitiered latticework of documentation:* Many scholarly publications require authors to undergird their claims with multiple layers of support in the form of footnotes and citations (correlates with conventions of debate brief writing, with "extension" briefs backing up "frontline" arguments).
- *Ésprit de corps:* Authors depend on stimuli from others to break out of creative ruts and maintain writing momentum (correlates with patterns of social support forged in competitive forensics work groups).
- *Audience adaptation:* Successful authors learn to reach multiple audiences by adapting prose accordingly (correlates with the debater's inclination to adapt arguments for a rotating array of diverse judges and opponents).
- *Division of labor:* Scholarly work groups differentiate tasks and parcel them out based on skill specialization (correlates with a debate team's segmentation of assignments to maximize work efficiency).

The preceding lists illustrate how the Debate Authors Working Group model supports scholarly knowledge production by mobilizing skills developed in competitive forensics. This overlapping skill set correlates with work-flow patterns that enable collaborating forensics specialists to "double dip" research efforts, for example, by workshopping scholarly manuscripts during long van rides to and from tournaments, developing academic research projects during periods of downtime at the tournament site, or even using the judge feedback portion of oral critiques to brainstorm new scholarly projects growing out of arguments raised during contest rounds. But the model also promotes intellectual flexibility by drawing from the naturally eclectic and interdisciplinary knowledge base found in the forensics community. From the start, intercollegiate debaters are forced to think outside of and beyond disciplinary boundaries. By engaging diverse topics, debaters necessarily hone modes of thought and research that are detailed yet holistic, sophisticated yet flexible. However, when they enter graduate school, former debaters often face pressure to immerse themselves in a narrow disciplinary matrix and winnow drastically their research focus. Such pressure can further complicate the competitor-to-researcher transition.

The Debate Authors Working Group model has potential to counterbalance this phenomenon by providing a mechanism for debate scholars to maintain contact with the interdisciplinary network of thinkers cultivated in the competitive forensics community. By activating these networks of potential scholars, former debaters can engage in collaborative research and publication that transcends disciplinary boundaries. An additional benefit of these scholarly networks flows from the widespread sense of intellectual curiosity within the debate community. As Cass Sunstein (2007) notes, any group that does not maintain an atmosphere welcoming of dissent is likely to be overtaken by group polarization and groupthink. Thanks to the interdisciplinary nature of debate training, forensics specialists can transcend some of the "turf wars" that typically characterize each discipline's desire to "one up" all others by pointing to its unique and exclusive claim to knowledge.

More widespread collaborative knowledge production in the forensics community will not guarantee a positive future for a sportified activity currently in flux and increasingly under scrutiny. But the prospect of forensics competitors pooling their talent and energy to share the vital lessons of debate with the wider world at least brings into focus a number of hopeful possibilities. Grant monies could be awarded competitively to young debate scholars wishing to buy out portions of their judging commitments at intercollegiate debate tournaments, freeing the scholars to work collaboratively on publishing projects at the tournament site. Rigorous and theoretically grounded systems for academic knowledge coproduction could enable current and former forensics specialists to increase scholarly productivity, thereby strengthening the pillars of institutional support that enable intercollegiate debate to thrive over the long term. Instantiating norms and habits of coauthorship may also make conditions more favorable for argumentation scholars to pursue the sort of interdisciplinary research that is common in fields such as medicine and public health, where collaborative knowledge production is acknowledged as an essential response to the challenge of analyzing multifaceted phenomena.

Part Three: Debate Scholarship in a Digital Age

As sociologist Langdon Winner observes, "technological artifacts have politics" (1986, 19). In other words, choices about communication technologies carry political implications, since patterns of sociality are embedded within technical tools (Keith 2002; McMillan and Hyde 2000). Fortunately, Winner notes that, "by far the greatest latitude of choice exists the very first time a particular instrument, system, or technique is introduced" (1986, 29). Winner's insight punctuates the salience and timeliness of the 2009 Wake Forest NDCD, which comes at a moment when the intercollegiate policy-debate community faces the daunting challenge of understanding precisely how rapid technological change might transform its norms, practices, and even identity as an intellectual endeavor (Edwards 2006).

One technology particularly worthy of consideration in this context is what can be called a Digital Debate Archive (DDA)—an online database that archives, tracks, organizes, and publishes argumentation presented in tournament contest rounds. The general concept of a debate argument archive is nothing new, as the linear "caselist" record of arguments advanced in contest rounds is now an institution in National Debate Tournament (NDT) and Cross Examination Debate Association (CEDA) circles. However, the possible turn to a more ambitious information architecture presents fresh challenges and novel choices. How might near-term choices regarding information architecture and community norms shape the future trajectory of the archive? Does the NDT/CEDA community have a real mechanism for facilitating collective discussion and reflective decision making on this issue? Who will be the gatekeepers determining what content is included and in what form it is presented in a DDA? What incentives will debaters have to share their ideas beyond the contest-round space?

Contest-round debating and argumentation pedagogy have evolved iteratively, with principles from policy debate informing many argumentation textbooks (e.g., Hollihan and Baaske 2004; Rieke and Sillars 1997; Winkler, Newman, and Birdsell 1993), and concepts from argumentation theory shaping the flow of tournament competition. The advent of a DDA is likely to recalibrate this relationship, with the ensuing alterations carrying potential to yield new forms of knowledge production. For our purposes, a DDA organized in a fashion that facilitates the tracking of arguments through time could prove to be a significant research resource for scholars seeking to study argumentation.

As a historical archive, a DDA could document argument strategies and research approaches to particular debate topics, providing a valuable storehouse of data for future scholars interested in studying the intellectual history of argumentation and debate. This function could also support new avenues of scholarship that would investigate argumentation processes by utilizing academic debate as a social "laboratory" (Hagood 1975). Here, the work of academic debaters could itself become an object of study, with the digital archive providing a unique portal for researchers to access phenomena that take place in tournament contest rounds. For example, one might study how new argument formations struggle to gain recognition as legitimate contributions to policy dialogue, or conversely, how they are excluded. Similarly, the content of argumentation advanced on a particular topic could serve as the basis of scholarship, with inquiry focused on how topical arguments unfold in the contest-round setting, and the resulting generalizations compared with argumentation trends unfolding in wider spheres of public deliberation.

The scholarly and pedagogical uses of a DDA could be facilitated or frustrated depending on the format of the archive. A DDA format that privileges pedagogy and scholarly research, perhaps by emphasizing sorting and classification functions, might yield an archive that is teaching and research friendly, with a possible trade-off in competitive utility for tournament contest-round participants. Pondering these trade-offs, it is also possible to visualize ways that a research- and teaching-friendly DDA might potentially transform the competitive contest-round process itself. For example, a DDA organized to provide a mechanism for public recognition of original and innovative research (i.e., possibly through delicious.com-style bookmarking), could both alter the competitive reward economy and create new opportunities for debaters to amplify their work products to wider audiences. Consider that currently, Evazon (Kerpen n.d.) operates a clearinghouse for commodity exchange of finished debate speaking briefs. One section of the Web site lists the "most popular authors" of such finished briefs, ranking them by statistical measures of the number of briefs sold on the Web site. A DDA with sorting and tracking features could support similar competitive indices, perhaps with statistics recognizing debaters whose original arguments were subsequently picked up and run by other teams in contest rounds, or debaters who fashioned the greatest number of original arguments on a given topic.

If a DDA created knowledge toward extra-competitive ends, such as scholarship and debate community outreach, the social capital of participating in collective knowledge production might exceed the competitive incentive for withholding information goods (van den Hooff et al. 2005). CEDA provides some insight into how such incentives could work. Awards for coach scholars and public debate programs offer opportunities to acquire "social capital" for extra-competitive outcomes within the organization. This outwardly oriented knowledge production could have a positive impact on the relationship between debaters and other individuals, such as department chairs and deans, who provide funding for programs but may not know the intricacies of the activity. By providing these figures with access to the copious argument briefs produced for intercollegiate debate competitions, a DDA could create deeper connections with the academy and introduce a new system for rewarding inventive research.

Roughly speaking, the act of publishing research entails preparing material for public uptake, securing editorial sanction, and then announcing the event to facilitate circulation.[3] For many years, this process was structured largely as an economic transaction between authors and printing press owners, with editors often serving as gatekeepers who would vet and filter material. Readers relied on markers of professionalism (quality of print and ink, circulation, reputation of editors) to judge the relative credibility of publications. In the academy, referees employed similar metrics to assess a given writer's degree of scholarly authority, metrics that were rooted in principles of publication scarcity and exclusivity— that a scholar's caliber was in part demonstrated by the ability to persuade editors to publish his/her work.

Acceleration of Internet communication and the advent of digital online publication destabilized these arrangements fundamentally. Publication, previously a one-to-many transaction, has become a many-to-many enterprise unfolding across a complex latticework of internetworked digital nodes. Now Weblogs, e-books, online journals, and print-on-demand book production and delivery systems make it possible for a whole new population of prospective authors to publish material in what Michael Jensen (2008), National Academies director of strategic Web communications, calls an "era of content democracy and abundance."

In content abundance, the key challenge for readers and referees has less to do with finding scarce information, and more to do with sorting wheat from the proverbial chaff (the ever-burgeoning surplus of digital material available online). In the debate community, this is what drives forensics specialists to

---

[3] Portions of this section are adapted from Goodnight and Mitchell (2008), and Woods et al. (2006).

comb through and process copious data in preparation for contest rounds. In the wider world, the pressing nature of this information-overload predicament has spurred invention of what Jensen (2007) calls "new metrics of scholarly authority"—essentially, new ways of measuring the credibility and gravitas of knowledge producers in a digital world of content abundance.

For Jensen, traditional "authority 1.0" metrics, such as book reviews, peer-reviewed journal publications, and journal "impact factors," are gradually being supplanted in popular culture by "authority 2.0" metrics such as Google page ranks, Blog-post trackbacks, and Diggs. Jensen's point is not that these new metrics of scholarly authority are necessarily superior to the old measurement tools, or that they are especially reliable or appropriate for assessing any given author's credibility (especially in an academic context). His point is that they are developing very fast, and becoming more widespread as markers of intellectual gravitas:

> Scholarly authority, the nuanced, deep, perspective-laden authority we hold dear, is under threat by the easily-computable metrics of popularity, famousness, and binary votes, which are amplified by the nature of abundance-jaded audiences. (Jensen 2008, 25)

While Jensen (2008, 25) sees this current trend from an era of content scarcity to an era of content abundance as a "revolutionary shift," a "cultural U-turn so extreme it's hard to comprehend," he also eschews determinism by stipulating that this "is a transformation we can influence." One key avenue of influence entails invention and refinement of what Jensen terms "authority 3.0" metrics—sophisticated instruments that track and measure knowledge creation and dissemination in ways that blend traditional "authority 1.0" principles such as peer review with newfangled digital tools such as *Reference Finder* (a National Academies Press "fuzzy matching" search tool) and Microsoft's *Photosynth*.

Certainly the new metrics present tools for debaters to measure the credibility of online publications, a task that is becoming ever more salient as digital material increasingly finds its way into debate research and tournament advocacy. But a personal connection hints at something greater—Jensen's brother was a successful high school debater under Randy McCutcheon at East High School in Lincoln, Nebraska, so Jensen knows all about inherency, index cards, and spread delivery. And in the debate community's early efforts at collaborative online knowledge production (such as *Debate Results, Planet*

Debate, Cross-x.com, and caselist wikis), Jensen sees seeds of new metrics of scholarly authority.

Consider what takes place in a debate tournament contest round, one held under today's conditions of digitally networked transparency. Debaters present their research on both sides of a given topic, citing evidence to support their claims. Those claims (and increasingly, the precise citations or exact performative elements supporting them) are often transcribed and then uploaded to a publicly available digital archive (a process streamlined by laptop flowing). The yield is a remarkably intricate and detailed map of a whole set of interwoven policy controversies falling under the rubric of yearlong national policy-debate resolution.

Who cares about this? Of course debaters and forensics specialists preparing for the next tournament take interest, as the map provides a navigational tool that leverages preparation for future contests. With refinement, online caselist wikis could be transformed into publicly accessible databases designed to provide resources to policymakers, journalists, and others for interactive study of national policy controversies such as the 2009–10 topic area on nuclear weaponry. Let us say a reporter for the Global Security Newswire is following the START arms control beat. With a visit to a DDA, she could not only pull up hundreds of the contest rounds where arms control was debated, she could click through to find out how certain teams deployed similar arguments, which citations were getting the most play, which sources were cited most frequently by winning teams, and which citations on arms control were new at the last tournament. Such post-mortem analysis of the debate process could enable nondebaters to hypothesis test by "replaying the chess match"[4] that took place at unintelligible speed during a given contest round (see also Woods et al. 2006).

The marriage of a DDA with Jon Bruschke's ingenious *Debate Results* online resource could pave the way for a host of new statistical measures with great salience for a wide array of audiences. Internally, the debate community could benefit from development of a new set of measures and corresponding rewards associated with research outcomes. Who are the most productive individual researchers in the nation? The most original? Which debater or forensics specialist has the greatest "research impact factor" (a possible metric measuring whose arguments tend to be picked up and replicated most by others in contest-round competition). A system for tracking and publishing answers to these questions

---

[4] Michael Jensen's clever phrasing.

could open up a new symbolic reward economy, with potential to counter the drift toward sportification entailed in a strict tournament-outcome-oriented reward structure. The same system could be used to track frequency and mode of source citations, yielding statistics that could answer such questions as: Which experts on nuclear weapons policy are cited most frequently in contest rounds? Which experts are cited most broadly (on a wide range of subtopics)? When a given expert is cited by one side, who are the experts most likely to be cited by the opposing side? Scholars are increasingly using similar data to document their research impact during professional reviews (see Meho 2007). Since the intercollegiate policy debate is driven by an intellectual community committed to the rigorous standards of evidence analysis and hypothesis testing, a strong case could be made that citation in that community is more meaningful than a Web-site hit indicating that a scholar's work product was viewed by an anonymous person browsing the Internet (this is a good example of the difference between a 3.0 and a 2.0 scholarly metric).

Once an enterprise born from the difficulties of engagement with public audiences, academic debate became estranged from its audience-centered origins during the mid-twentieth century. The rise of tournament competition as an organizing telos augured debate's ascetic turn, characterized by heightened specialization, intensified insularity, and fetishization of technique. Rewards for participation in debate rose, but so did entry barriers. Participation rates shrunk, and the activity took on the patina of an exotic sporting event, even attracting a cable sports television network to cover several NDTs in the new millennium.

In charting a course for the future of forensics, the Sedalia conferees envisioned the debate community rounding into a scholarly enterprise that would grow from its audience-centric roots to tackle research questions on such topics as political campaign debates, conflict resolution, public opinion formation, and processes of persuasion (see McBath 1975, 35–36). Now debate's digital turn opens up opportunities for forensics specialists and debaters to recoup the audience dimension of argumentative practice, without jettisoning the wondrous enterprise of fast-talking, evidence-intensive, dynamically reflexive tournament debating.

Choices regarding a DDA's architecture will shape the incentive structure that influences participation rates, demarcate lines of editorial authority, and affect the commodity status of debate knowledge production. On another level, the basic philosophy underlying a DDA will determine whether the technology preserves intercollegiate debate as a primarily insular space or transforms it into a more public enterprise. Furthermore, depending on which design features are selected, a DDA could either reinforce prevailing norms of competition, or introduce new elements into the picture that change the nature of intercollegiate debate entirely.

The foregoing analysis highlights salient dimensions of the NDCD Research and Scholarship Working Group's deliberations conducted before, during, and after the third developmental conference. Working group members began by placing the steering committee's charge in historical context, analyzing previous developmental conferences' treatments of debate scholarship, and taking stock of the role that academic knowledge production has traditionally played in constituting the debate community's academic roots. Next, the working group assessed status quo trends relating to the challenge of producing forensics scholarship in a milieu characterized by heightened sportification of the debate activity, erosion of tenure-stream director lines, the advent of digital scholarship in an age of "content abundance," and increased popularity of collaborative coauthorship as a mode of knowledge production in the academy writ large. These lines of analysis prepared the ground for formulation of seven specific recommendations, outlined in the following resolutions. Each of the resolutions was presented during the NDCD's closing plenary session and endorsed by the full body conference participants.

RESOLUTIONS PRESENTED BY THE RESEARCH AND SCHOLARSHIP WORKING GROUP AND ENDORSED BY THE NDCD PLENARY SESSION
1. The National Developmental Conference on Debate (NDCD) recommends that forensics organizations improve online digital systems for archiving and distributing debate knowledge production. Toward that end we suggest pursuit of a participatory-design process that maximizes benefits of digital archives for the contest-round participants, production of peer-reviewed scholarship, and public engagement.

RATIONALE: An integrated, specialized, and technically advanced archival system, or Digital Debate Archive (DDA), has potential to vastly change the landscape of intercollegiate debate (Woods et al. 2006). Yet there is presently no clear consensus about what specific features a DDA ought to include, nor how such an archive ought to be utilized. Functional concerns about gatekeeping and incentive structures, technical issues about the security and privacy of information stored in a DDA, as well as the concepts, tools, and software-engineering processes that might be used to build one, have yet to be sorted out. The long-term success of a DDA may hinge on the degree to which these outstanding issues are resolved through design processes that prioritize broad-based participation and bottom-up input.

Community-specific computing projects are often hampered by a tendency to utilize nonspecialized software in order to minimize costs and responsibilities (Merkel et al. 2004, 1–2); however, a DDA would be most functional if purpose-built to fit the idiosyncratic conventions of debate competition. Building a custom-tailored archive could be best accomplished by a process akin to what Merkel et al. (2004) refer to as long-term participatory design, utilizing ethnographic techniques and emphasizing end-user involvement during the software-engineering process in order to produce a sustainable system capable of "supporting groups . . . as they identify ways that technology can be used to address organizational and community level problems, and as they develop plans to take on projects involving technology" (Merkel et al. 2004, 2). Rather than turning over the primary responsibility for software projects to engineers, a sustainable participatory approach "see[s] community groups as owners of the projects, not designers" (p. 7) and encourages adaptation over time to specific user needs.

In the context of a participatory model for software development, the potential for disagreement over the details of a DDA can be seen as an asset rather than a liability. Participatory design focuses on "the empowerment of workers so they can codetermine the development of the information system" (Clement and Van den Besselaar 1995, 29) and thereby produces community-specific artifacts that allow programmers implementing a system to better account for users' needs. Participatory techniques are often employed for community-specific projects "because they are deemed more appropriate to the activities than other available conceptualizations" (Törpel 2005, 178). A participatory process grounded in a debate-like format could uniquely leverage the community's argumentative and collaborative skills to construct a DDA with capabilities that would far surpass prefabricated solutions.

While we wish to leave open the possibilities for development of a DDA, we offer some specific suggestions to initiate a discussion about the technologies and concepts that could facilitate the archives' usefulness as a tool for contest-round preparation as well as scholarship and public engagement. Edgar Codd's seminal work in the field of database design can serve as a springboard for conceptualizing the potential of a DDA; his relational model consists of describing relationships between atomic units of data (see Codd 1970). With data stored in nondecomposable domains and organized by relationships among those domains, the information archived in a database can easily be presented to users in configurations that are independent of its internal representation (i.e., the format used by the computer to store the data). For example, a debater's file on a particular position for use in a contest round can be understood as the relation of a series of blocks; those blocks as the relations of specific arguments; those arguments as the relations of taglines, citations, and quotations; and those citations as the relations of authors, titles, journals, and so on. Each constituent unit can be linked to other relations as well: the authors cited in a particular contest round, the evidence produced by a particular researcher on a team, and so on.

Modern database-driven Web applications frequently employ a Model-View-Controller pattern (see Jazayeri 2007), and a DDA might be well served by this approach. The data model, typically powered by a database, consists of the logical components of the information used by the application (e.g., debater, tournament, round, argument, citation, quotation), as well as their properties (e.g., a tournament's name and location) and the relationships among them (e.g., each quotation has exactly one cite). Data are inputted or modified by controllers and exposed to users through views, which translate machine-stored information into human-readable templates.

Multiple views allow the same data set to be displayed to users with different templatic representations for different contexts. It is this feature that may hold the most potential for making the knowledge produced in contest debating useful for academics and the public. The possibilities for computing metrics of authority from this information could facilitate interest in a DDA from scholars outside the debate community. Moreover, while a debater preparing for a tournament might be primarily concerned with a view constructed in the format of a traditional caselist—the set of arguments read by one team in contest debates at a particular tournament—a DDA could also be used to create a dynamically generated annotated bibliography encompassing the vast amount of research conducted by the debate community over the span of a season. An array of alternative views could make the work products of contest rounds more accessible to myriad scholarly audiences, thereby raising the debate community's research profile.

2. The NDCD recommends establishing a publishing outlet that translates knowledge produced in contest debating into double peer-reviewed academic

journal articles. Ideally, the journal will showcase debate's collaborative research model and its ability to impact live public argument with timely interventions.

RATIONALE: Sometimes undergraduate students convert their debate research into term papers, and occasionally more advanced scholars develop dissertations or scholarly articles from topic-area reading they pursued while coaching. Yet for the most part, the voluminous work products flowing from policy-debate competition never reach wider audiences beyond the debate community, and sometimes are never even read in contest rounds. This mothball effect is a shame, not only because the rest of the world might benefit from debate-driven insight but also because young debaters and coaches stand to bolster their scholarly credentials by converting the fruits of their research into peer-reviewed publications. *Timely Interventions: A Translational Journal of Public Policy Debate* is designed to facilitate such conversion by carrying the following types of essays:

1. Policy advocacy essays, where authors pull together their research on a particular policy position (e.g., affirmative case), and write up the case for a general, educated reading audience.

2. Controversy review essays, where authors isolate a particular point of salient disagreement featured in contest-round competition, clarify for a general, educated reading audience why the controversy warrants extended study, and explain how the arguments from contest round debating deepens understanding of the controversy under review.

3. Source review essays, where authors isolate a particular expert whose published work is receiving significant attention in intercollegiate policy-debate competition, detail ways that the source is informing the policy argument, and reflect on how the debate experience yields resources for better understanding the expert's role in the policy debate for general, educated audiences.

4. Forum exchanges, where top experts in the field utilize a debating format to elucidate salient aspects of pressing public policy issues.

As with scholarly, peer-reviewed publications, prospective authors would submit draft manuscripts falling into one of the above categories to an editor in chief, who would then solicit peer review from members of the editorial board (see Appendix 1). As referees with debate experience, peer reviewers would be asked to apply evaluative criteria associated with quality debate argument (e.g., claims stated clearly and convincingly, arguments backed up by support, evidence thoroughly cited), as well as criteria associated with the challenge of translating "debate speak" into accessible prose understandable for a general, educated readership. This latter set of criteria is especially important, given the vision that *Timely Interventions* cultivates a wide readership among policymakers, journalists, citizens, and others interested in learning about that year's given topic area through a debate prism. As an online publication, *Timely Interventions* would publish individual manuscripts serially, upon successful completion of peer review and copyediting. With this procedure, the journal enables articles carried under its banner to be peer reviewed not once, but twice. Prior to going through a round of traditional review by anonymous referees drawn from the ranks of the editorial board and topic-area experts, article content will likely already have been honed and tested during debate contest-round competition. As the NDCD Tenure and Promotion Working Group notes, "this testing process is [itself] a form of peer review, quite similar to that which occurs at journals." The resulting two-tiered system of "double peer review" is designed to ensure that journal content meets prevailing academic standards for rigorously validated scholarship.

3. The NDCD recommends that the American Forensics Association Research Committee exercise professional leadership by including in its annual reports updated lists that identify opportunities for innovation in forensics scholarship intersecting with issues of public concern.

RATIONALE: The tradition of forensics specialists actively producing scholarly manuscripts for academic publication has eroded as debate tournament competition has become ever more labor intensive. Yet the intensity of competition alone cannot account for the dearth in scholarship related to debate. Another important factor is the intellectual history of forensics and argumentation studies in the speech communication tradition. Over the past 50 years the role of debate in the discipline has changed from a leading one to that of a bit player. As David Zarefsky notes in his history of argumentation in the speech communication tradition "debate does not get enough respect" (1994, 6). There are several reasons for the intellectual marginalization of debate, perhaps none more significant than the eclipse of debate by argumentation studies. Zarefsky's (1994) history of argumentation studies illustrates the significant role played by scholarship related to debate in the emergence of argumentation studies. Early works such as Douglas Ehninger and Wayne Brockriede's *Decision by Debate*

(1963) "offered a broader perspective of the debate activity" by lifting debate from the context of intercollegiate competition and applying scholarship related to debate to broader social contexts such as argumentation and decision-making (Zarefsky 1994, 4). According to Zarefsky (1994, 6), this development shifted forensics specialists' scholarly agenda from the species (debate) to the genius (argumentation), producing a rich vein of scholarship and providing forensics specialists with a newfound relevance in the field of speech communication and beyond.

One advantage to the shift from debate to argumentation studies for the forensics specialist was that it afforded scholars an expansive scope of research topics. Once argumentation became a way of looking—a critical perspective—anything from a speech to a piece of music became fair game for scholarship (Brockriede 1975). However, this also meant that the scholarly pursuits of the forensics specialist were taken further and further afield from the specialists' "other job"—coaching debate. Today, there are three pressing reasons to refocus scholarship on debate, and in doing so, revive the tradition of the forensics specialist as academic researcher. First, the prevailing need to bolster the quality of public deliberation points to the value of scholarship designed toward that end. Second, much of the intellectual work currently being done by scholars in a variety of fields including communication studies, public administration, political science, sociology, and psychology, and by professional practitioners who promote and facilitate opportunities for public dialogue and deliberation, tend to either downplay or denigrate debate as a general concept (see, e.g., Flick 1998; Schirch and Campt 2007; Tannen 1998). Third, general understanding of the debate process tends to suffer in a climate where many citizens use dueling monologues such as presidential debates, or *Crossfire*-style television programs as benchmark referents informing their notions of what debate entails.

Forensics specialists are in a unique position to address these problems and jump start an innovative scholarly tradition, which can revive debate as a public deliberative practice and elevate debate in scholarly circles. No community of scholars is more aware of the collaborative and cooperative aspects of debate, more able to catalogue the advantages and disadvantages of advocacy-based deliberative processes, or more capable of organizing, designing, and hosting public debates. In addition, our community of scholars is uniquely positioned to analyze, assess, and critique the strengths and weaknesses of debate formats and designs. Furthermore, by raising the profile of debate as a topic worthy of scholarship we also provide young scholars, who too often feel torn between coaching forensics and pursuing a scholarly career in academia, with an opportunity to do both. As the survey conducted by the Civic Engagement Working Group at this very conference demonstrates, most debate programs are already organizing and hosting public debate events. Scholarship that analyzes and reflects on these events is relatively low-hanging fruit for most forensics specialists and is, at this moment in time, ripe for the picking. Processes of collaboration, public deliberation, and dialogue are the wave of the future—national and local governments, organizations and corporations, and communities are all looking for ways to promote public engagement and facilitate better deliberative processes. As William Keith stated succinctly in his keynote address to our gathering, "Yet while the deliberation train is leaving the station, intercollegiate debate is not on it." That train (a renewed emphasis on deliberation and public engagement) will be ill suited to serve the public good if it leaves the station without a healthy understanding of and commitment to debate.

An annually updated list of suggested topics for scholarly research related to debate and issues of public concern should: (1) help reinvigorate the tradition of debate scholarship; (2) encourage students of debate to make their vast knowledge of debate and deliberation available to wider audiences; and (3) provide forensics specialists, especially young scholars, who wish to position their research firmly within the communication studies tradition, with resources and guidance.

4. The NDCD encourages research and scholarship on topics relating to contest debate-round practice such as argument trends, frameworks, tournament governance, coaching pedagogy, and other related topics. We also encourage debate scholars to extend these research findings to matters of wider public concern. We encourage *Contemporary Argumentation and Debate* to review and publish such scholarship on a quarterly basis.

RATIONALE: Broadening the footprint of debate-related scholarship requires the pursuit of two kinds of scholarly work. The first type of scholarship (perhaps best reflected in resolution no. 2) aims to translate the immense amount of research, thought, and strategizing that takes place over the course of a debate season into useful scholarly work. In advocating this goal, we do not intend to argue for a wholesale shift to translational research on the part of forensics educators. Rather, we also think it incumbent on the debate community to redouble production of scholarship on debate-round theory and practice. Toward that end, it is important not only to utilize *Contemporary Argumentation and Debate* as an outlet for scholarship relating to contest-round trends, but to reach other outlets as well. In making the case for the public benefits of debate as a mode of knowledge production, we might increase the attractiveness of contest debate-round-related scholarship for a broader audience. Alternately, in making the case that debate practices themselves are worthy objects of scholarly inquiry, we also might help to make the case that contest debating is an important and rigorous mode of scholarly production.

5. The NDCD encourages the formation of a mentoring group as a resource for emerging scholars. This group will be composed primarily of former debate coaches comfortable with providing advice and possible review of scholarship. The purpose of this group is to encourage young scholars to produce quality debate research and to provide positive relationships for continuation of the debate scholarship tradition.

RATIONALE: The debate community produces a substantial number of strong academics and scholars. The acute demands of debate coaching often lead coaches to graduate or informally retire into academic circles. These individuals may not be able to provide the intense coaching and research support common to active coaches but they are often interested in supporting debate through mentoring relationships. Through an active solicitation process it is recommended that a list of willing former coaches be added to accessible and relevant Web sites maintained by organizations such as the American Forensics Association.

Such mentor coaches could provide direction in collaborative scholarship projects coauthored with junior coaches and give direct feedback on manuscripts coaches are preparing on their own—particularly those that are relevant to debate theory and practice. Additionally, mentors could suggest research agendas for emerging debate coaches. Finally, mentor coaches might be a resource in the formal processes of tenure and promotion, serving as external reviewers and advisers in tenure case construction.

Mentoring is a traditional and reliable means for improving retention with communities such as the debate-coaching community. In broader academic settings, mentoring has shown a positive relationship to research activity among emerging scholars (Paglis, Green, and Bauer 2006). Such mentoring will likely improve the quality of research and provide a measure of accountability that encourages emerging coaches to prioritize their research work alongside their coaching responsibilities. Moreover, the experience of mentors can help new coaches make sense of the unique demands of coaching that conventional senior academics may have little practical advice to provide. How does one balance coaching and research? How can I delegate my role as a director of forensics to allow time for research? These are the kinds of questions that a mentor can help a young debate coach address.

6. The NDCD should recommend that the American Forensics Association adopt guidelines for collaborative coauthored scholarship.

RATIONALE: In response to concerns regarding abuses such as authorship inflation and downplaying the contributions of junior scholars and graduate students, there have been considerable efforts to address coauthorship as part of ethical research conduct (Drenth 1998; Kwok 2005). Professional associations, institutions, and research journals have developed sophisticated guidelines and practices to determine issues such as who may qualify as a coauthor, how coauthors should be listed in a given article, and what forms of academic recognition are due to each scholar participating in a collaborative project (see, e.g., American Psychological Association 2001; Biagioli et al. 1999).

Inspired in part by these examples, but noting that there is little discussion of collaborative research protocol within the communication field in general and the intercollegiate debate community in particular, the Schenley Park DAWG (Debate Authors Working Group) formed a committee to craft its own coauthorship guidelines. These guidelines (see Appendix 2) provide a framework for intellectual collaboration that enables satisfying and rewarding production of high-caliber academic work. They lay out the stages of knowledge production for each project, calling for the substantial involvement of all contributing authors in the key creative dimensions of conceptual invention, research, and writing/revising (cf. Flanagin, Fontanarosa, and DeAngelis 2002; Jones; 2000, 13).

The guidelines seek to preemptively address potential controversies regarding who qualifies as an author and the order in which authors should be acknowledged in published material. This is an important objective given research showing that disputes stemming from coauthorship arrangements can negatively affect research team morale (Wilcox 1998). Roland Wolseley defines a coauthor as "the writer of approximately half a book's text, sharing equally on space, earnings, and expenses, and participating fully in decision-making" (1980, 20). However, real-world collaboration cannot always be so clearly divided (Day and

Eodice 2001, 137; see also Fox and Faver 1984). The draft guidelines attend to this issue by clearly enumerating the responsibilities of the lead author, senior author, and other coauthors.

Since a key challenge involves convincing institutional audiences of the value of collaborative work products, the guidelines are also accompanied by a work-sheet (see Appendix 3) designed to make transparent each coauthor's contributions to any given project. Such transparency has potential to reduce the phenomenon of "honorary authorship," or "ghostwriting," a problem in the medical field where the proportion of authors whose published contributions do not meet authorship criteria is significant, even reaching 21.5% in one jour-nal (Bates et al. 2004, 87–88; Laine and Mulrow 2005). Future efforts to make contributions to collaborative work products more transparent might involve publication of detailed contributor lists, which already appear in some journals (Yank and Rennie 1999). And as the concept of collaborative knowledge pro-duction evolves in the forensics setting, methods to incorporate and acknowl-edge practical contributions to the research effort could develop in tandem. For example, Wake Forest University undergraduate debaters Alex Lamballe and Kurt Zemlicka recently taught at a debate workshop dedicated to improv-ing high school students' research and speaking skills. Part of the curriculum involved teachers working with students to contribute directly to the 2007 U.S. presidential-debate process. Following the workshop, Lamballe and Zemlicka folded discussion of their teaching experiences into a larger collaborative re-search project. By contributing statistical analysis, background research, and commentary, Lamballe and Zemlicka were able to join the project as coauthors of an academic manuscript. Lamballe and Zemlicka's example could be repli-cated in other contexts, such as undergraduate debaters satisfying coauthorship requirements by contributing contest-round research to collaborative research projects. Such a trend would mirror developments in research fields where prac-tical contributions (e.g., providing patients or research material, carrying out a pilot study, collecting the data) already figure significantly in coauthors' self-disclosure of contributions to articles (Hoen, Walvoort, and Overbeke 1998, 218; cf. Bates et al. 2004).

7. The NDCD endorses the establishment of a U.S. Congressional Speech and Debate caucus and encourages that caucus to foster debate research and scholarship, including the publication of a topic-area packet, and support of a participatory-design process, oriented toward refinement and development of an open source digital debate archive.

RATIONALE: The NDCD Alumni Networking Working Group's initiative to create a "Speech and Debate" Caucus in the U.S. Congress presents numerous professional development opportunities for forensics specialists. In the area of scholarship, the caucus could leverage efforts to heighten the research profile of the academic debate community by reviving the congressional practice of publishing research packets on each year's intercollegiate policy-debate topic and providing resources to support participatory design of an online digital debate archive.

References

American Psychological Association. 2001. "Ethical Standards for the Reporting and Publishing of Scientific Information." In *Publication Manual of the American Psychological Association.* 5th ed. Washington, DC.

Aonuma, S. 2001. "What Is a Coauthor? Scholarly Publishing and Problems of Collaborative Research." *Journal of Kanda University of International Studies* 13: 1–16.

Aune, J. 2007. "Graduate Education and the Organization of 'Research.'" Blogora Web post, February 7. http://rsa.cwrl.utexas.edu/?q=node/1368/ (accessed June 22, 2009).

Bates, T.; A. Anic; M. Marusic; and A. Marusic. 2004. "Authorship Criteria and Disclosure of Contributions: A Comparison of 3 General Medical Journals with Different Author Contribution Forms." *Journal of the American Medical Association* 292: 86–88.

Biagioli, M.; J. Crane; P. Derish; M. Gruber; D. Rennie; and R. Horton. 1999. "Council of Science Editor's Taskforce on Authorship." http://www.councilscienceeditors.org/services/atf_whitepaper.cfm (accessed June 22, 2009.)

Brigham, M. 2008. "Nostalgia or Hope: On the Relationship Between Competitive Debate and Speech Communication Departments—Past, Present, and Future." Paper presented at the 2008 National Communication Association Convention, San Diego, CA, November 21–24.

Brockriede, W. 1975. "Where Is Argument?" *Journal of the American Forensic Association* 11: 179–82.

Clement, A., and P. Van den Besselaar. 1995. "A Retrospective Look at PD Projects." *Communications of the ACM* 36 (June): 29–37.

Codd, E. 1970. "A Relational Model of Data for Large Shared Data Banks." *Communications of the ACM* 17 (June): 377–87.

Dauber, C. et al. 1993. "Report of the Working Committee from the Quail Roost Conference on Assessment of Professional Activities of Directors of Debate Draft Document." www.americanforensics.org/ProfDev/quail_roost.pdf (accessed June 22, 2009).

Day, K., and M. Eodice. 2001. *(First Person)²: A Study of Co-authoring in the Academy.* Logan: Utah State University Press.

Drenth, J.P.H. 1998. "Multiple Authorship: The Contribution of Senior Authors." *Journal of the American Medical Association* 280: 219–21.

Edwards, R. 2006. "Why Computers Won't Destroy CX Debate." *Rostrum* 81, 4: 21–26.

Ehninger, D., and W. Brockriede. 1963. *Decision by Debate.* New York: Dodd, Mead.

Flanagin, A.; P.B. Fontanarosa; and C.D. DeAngelis. 2002. "Authorship for Research Groups." *Journal of the American Medical Association* 288: 3166–68.

Flick, D. 1998. *From Debate to Dialogue: Using the Understanding Process to Transform Our Conversations.* Boulder, CO: Orchid.

Fox, M.F., and C.A. Faver. 1984. "Independence and Cooperation in Research: The Motivations and Costs of Collaboration." *Journal of Higher Education* 55: 347–59.

Goodnight, G.T., and G.R. Mitchell. 2008. "Forensics as Scholarship: Testing Zarefsky's Bold Hypothesis in a Digital Age." *Argumentation & Advocacy* 45: 80–97.

Hagood, A.D. 1975. "Theory and Practice in Forensics." In *Forensics as Communication: The Argumentative Perspective*, ed. J.H. McBath, 101–10. Skokie, IL: National Textbook.

Hoen, W.P.; H.C. Walvoort; and J.P.M. Overbeke. 1998. "What Are the Factors Determining Authorship and the Order of Authors' Names?" *Journal of the American Medical Association*, 280: 217–18.

Hollihan, T.A., and K.T. Baaske. 2004. *Arguments and Arguing: The Products and Process of Human Decision Making*. 2d ed. Long Grove, IL: Waveland Press.

Jazayeri, M. 2007. "Some Trends in Web Application Development." In *International Conference on Software Engineering: Future of Software Engineering*, ed. L.C. Briand and A.L. Wolf, 199–213. Washington, DC: IEEE Computer Society.

Jensen, M. 2007. "The New Metrics of Scholarly Authority." *Chronicle of Higher Education*, June 15. http://chronicle.com/weekly/v53/i41/41b00601.htm (accessed June 22, 2009).

———. 2008. "Scholarly Authority in the Age of Abundance: Retaining Relevance Within the New Landscape." Keynote address at the JSTOR Annual Participating Publisher's Conference. May 13. http://www.nap.edu/staff/mjensen/jstor.htm (accessed June 22, 2009).

Jones, A.H. 2000. "Changing Traditions of Authorship." In *Ethical Issues in Biomedical Publication*, ed. A.H. Jones and F. McLellan, 3–29. Baltimore, MD: Johns Hopkins University Press.

Keele, L.K., and K.D. Andersen. 1975. "Professional Preparation, Status, and Rewards." In *Forensics as Communication: The Argumentative Perspective*, ed. J.H. McBath, 144–55. Skokie, IL: National Textbook.

Keith, W. 2002. "Democratic Revival and the Promise of Cyberspace: Lessons from the Forum Movement." *Rhetoric & Public Affairs* 5: 311–26.

Kerpen, P. n.d. "Evazon." http://www.cross-x.com/evazon/ (accessed June 22, 2009).

Kramer, M.W.; J.A. Hess; and J.D. Reid. 2007. "Trends in Communication Scholarship: An Analysis of Four Representative NCA and ICA Journals over the Last 70 Years." *Review of Communication* 73: 229–40.

Kwok, L.S. 2005. "The White Bull Effect: Abusive Co-authorship and Publication Parasitism." *Journal of Medical Ethics* 31. http://avabiz.com/coauthorship.nsf/presentation/ (accessed June 22, 2009).

Laine, C., and C.D. Mulrow. 2005. "Exorcising Ghosts and Unwelcome Guests." *Annals of Internal Medicine* 143: 611–12.

McBath, J., ed. 1975. *Forensics as Communication: The Argumentative Perspective*. Skokie, IL: National Textbook.

McMillan, J .J., and M.J. Hyde. 2000. "Technological Innovation and Change: A Case Study in the Formation of Organizational Conscience." *Quarterly Journal of Speech* 86: 1–29.

Meho, L.I. 2007. "The Rise and Rise of Citation Analysis." *Physics World*, January: 32–36.

Merkel, C.; L. Xiao; U. Farooq; C. Ganoe; R. Lee; J. Carroll; and M. Rosson. 2004. "Participatory Design in Community Computing Contexts: Tales from the Field." In *Artful Integration: Interweaving Media, Materials and Practices*, ed. A. Clement, F. de Cindio, A.M. Oostveen, D. Schuler and P. van den Besselaar, 1–10. New York: Association for Computing Machinery.

Paglis, L.L.; S.G. Green; and T.N. Bauer. 2006. "Does Adviser Mentoring Add Value? A Longitudinal Study of Mentoring and Doctoral Student Outcomes." *Research in Higher Education* 47: 451–76.

Parson, D.W., ed. 1984. *American Forensics in Perspective: Papers from the Second National Conference on Forensics*. Annandale, VA: Speech Communication Association.

———. 1990. "On Publishing and Perishing: Some Approaches in Forensic Research." *National Forensic Journal* 8: 69–72.

Rieke, R., and B. Brock. 1975. "Research and Scholarship in Forensics." In *Forensics as Communication: The Argumentative Perspective*, ed. J.H. McBath, 129–41. Skokie, IL: National Textbook.

Rieke, R.D., and M.O. Sillars. 1997. *Argumentation and Critical Decision Making*. New York: Longman.

Schirch, L., and D. Campt. 2007. *The Little Book of Dialogue for Difficult Subjects: A Practical, Hands-on Guide*. Intercourse, PA: Good Books.

Sillars, M.O., and D. Zarefsky. 1975. "Future Goals and Roles of Forensics." In *Forensics as Communication: The Argumentative Perspective*, ed. J.H. McBath, 83–93. Skokie, IL: National Textbook.

Sunstein, C. 2007. *Republic.com 2.0*. Princeton: Princeton University Press.

Tannen, D. 1998. *The Argument Culture: Stopping America's War of Words*. New York: Ballantine Books.

Törpel, B. 2005. "Participatory Design: A Multi-voiced Effort." In *Proceedings of the Fourth Decennial Conference on Critical Computing: Between Sense and Sensibility*, ed. O.W. Bertelsen, N.O. Bouvin, P.G. Krogh, and M. Kyng, 177–81. New York: Association for Computing Machinery.

van den Hooff, B.; M. Weyers; D. Peters; and J. de Lange. 2005. "Technological Facilitation of Knowledge Sharing in Communities of Practice." Paper presented at the annual meeting of the International Communication Association, New York, May 26–30.

Wilcox, L.J. 1998. "Authorship: The Coin of the Realm, the Source of Complaints." *Journal of the American Medical Association* 280: 216–17.

Winkler, C.; W. Newnam; and D. Birdsell. 1993. *Lines of Argument for Policy Debate*. Madison, WI: Brown and Benchmark.

Winner, L. 1986. *The Whale and the Reactor: A Search for Limits in an Age of High Technology*. Chicago: University of Chicago Press.

Wolseley, R.E. 1980. "Should I Collaborate?" *Journalism Educator* 34: 19–56.

Woods, C.; M. Brigham; T. Konishi; B. Heavner; J. Rief; B. Saindon; and G.R. Mitchell. 2006. "Deliberating Debate's Digital Futures." *Contemporary Argumentation and Debate* 27: 81–105.

Yank, V., and D. Rennie. 1999. "Disclosure of Researcher Contributions: A Study of Original Research Articles in The Lancet." *Annals of Internal Medicine* 130: 661–70.

Zarefsky, D. 1980. "Argumentation and Forensics." In *Proceedings of the Summer Conference on Argumentation*, ed. J. Rhodes and S. Newell, 20–25. Annandale, VA: Speech Communication Association.

———. 1994. "Argumentation in the Tradition of Speech Communication Studies." Keynote Presentation at the Third International Conference on Argumentation, University of Amsterdam, the Netherlands, June 24.

Appendix 1: Preliminary Prospectus for A New Online Journal Carrying Forensics Scholarship

TIMELY INTERVENTIONS: A TRANSLATIONAL JOURNAL OF PUBLIC POLICY DEBATE

A publishing outlet that translates knowledge produced by the academic policy debate community, showcasing debate's collaborative research model and its ability to impact live public argument with timely interventions.

Editor-in-Chief: Gordon R. Mitchell
Forum Editor: Christian Lundberg
Advisory Board Chair: Robert P. Newman
Founding Members of the Editorial Board

Erwin Chemerinsky, founding dean, University of California-Irvine School of Law (Northwestern University debate alum)

David Coale, partner, K&L Gates (Harvard University debate alum)

Cori E. Dauber, associate professor of rhetorical studies, University of North Carolina-Chapel Hill (Northwestern University debate alum)

Ellen Dorsey, executive director, Wallace Global Fund (University of Pittsburgh debate alum)

Lindsay C. Harrison, associate, Jenner & Block LLP (University of Southern California debate alum)

Michael Horowitz, assistant professor of political science, University of Pennsylvania (Emory University debate alum)

Lee Huebner, director, George Washington University School of Media and Public Affairs Northwestern University debate alum)

Paul Kerr, analyst in nonproliferation, Congressional Research Service (University of Vermont debate alum)

Jeff Kueter, president, George Marshall Institute (University of Iowa debate alum)

J. Scott Maberry, partner, Fulbright & Jaworski LLP (Northwestern University debate alum)

Jeffrey G. Lewis, director, Nuclear Strategy and Nonproliferation Initiative, New America Foundation (Augustana College debate alum)

Allan J. Lichtman, professor of history, American University (Brandeis University debate alum)

Heather Ann Logue, professor of philosophy, University of Leeds (University of Pittsburgh debate alum)

Briana Mezuk, Robert Wood Johnson Health & Society Scholar, University of Michigan Center for Epidemiology & Population Health (University of Pittsburgh debate alum)

Catherine H. Palczewski, professor of communication and director of debate, University of Northern Iowa (Northwestern University debate alum)

Rodger Payne, professor of political science and director, Grawemeyer Award for Ideas Improving World Order (University of Kansas debate alum)

Daniel J. Povinelli, professor of biology, University of Louisiana-Lafayette, Project Director National Chimpanzee Observatories Initiative (University of Massachusetts debate alum)

John C. Roberts, dean emeritus and professor, DePaul University College of Law (Northwestern University debate alum)

Lyn Robbins, senior general attorney, Burlington Northern and Santa Fe Railway (Baylor University debate alum)

Greg Rosenbaum, president and founder, Palisades Associates (Harvard University debate alum)

Paul J. Skiermont, partner, Bartlit Beck Herman Palenchar & Scott LLP (University of Kentucky debate alum)

Cyril V. Smith, partner, Zuckerman Spaeder LLP (Dartmouth College alum)

Benjamin K. Sovacool, assistant professor of public policy, National University of Singapore (John Carroll University debate alum)

Philip Wander, presidential professor of communication, Loyola Marymount University (Southern Illinois University debate alum)

Lesley Wexler, assistant professor, Florida State University College of Law (University of Michigan debate alum)

Danielle Wiese, assistant professor of communication Studies, Grand Valley State University (University of Michigan debate alum)

Appendix 2: Draft Guidelines for Coauthorship of Work Products

Authorship is a significant aspect of academic research, one that deserves careful and rigorous treatment, given its ethical and professional implications. It is important that participants in collaborative debate research projects have a clear, common understanding of the standards for authorship at the outset of each project. As intellectual collaboration is the lifeblood of intercollegiate academic debate, it is appropriate that sound and workable guidelines be developed for translating collective intellectual labor into professional argumentation scholarship.

I. Coauthorship guidelines for collaborative debate research.[5]

The practice of coauthorship should involve the substantial involvement of all contributing authors. Substantial involvement is defined by the following criteria, which must be met by each individual who will be listed as an author in the final work. To qualify as a coauthor, collaborators must contribute at least one substantial dimension of work in each of the following four creative categories.

A. *Inventional Process:* The initial phase of project design sets the foundation for subsequent collaboration. Thus, coauthors should help conceive the project, map the goals and methods for completion of the project, and/or contribute substantial intellectual labor throughout evolution of the project as its trajectory shifts in light of new understandings and research findings.

B. *Writing and Revising:* Substantial written contributions to the collaborative work effort justify the use of the term "author" in the first place; however, "authorship" can be understood in a broader sense to include both the initial contribution of substantial writing and the contribution of substantial written revisions later on in the process. Both of these activities imply a deep investment in the construction of the work at hand. Thus, a coauthor may be understood as an individual who drafts substantial original material or makes written contributions by proposing substantial revisions throughout the creative process.

---

[5] These guidelines are adapted from a document generated in 2006 by the Schenley Park Debate Authors Working Group (DAWG). Exemplars for the DAWG guidelines were drawn from guidelines established by the NHMRC/AVCC (National Health and Medical Research Council/Australian Vice Chancellors' Committee) Statement and Guidelines on Research Practice (1997), http://www.nhmrc.gov.au/funding/policy/researchprac.htm#6. Guidelines developed in other areas of study were also consulted, including those produced by the *Journal of the American Medical Association*.

C. *Research:* Given the importance of research both in terms of the production of scholarly works and the development of arguments for the intercollegiate academic debate contest round, research should play an important role in the collaborative process of coauthorship. For this reason, substantial contributions in this area include setting the initial research agenda through a cooperative process of identifying where the working group should seek out relevant information and what kinds of information are most important to the completion of the project, working through primary and secondary source material in order to identify the most important elements to include in the final project, and finally synthesizing the research that has been completed so as to craft a final coherent product.

D. *Final Approval:* As with any collaborative work effort, it is important that all individuals involved, should they wish to be identified as authors, give their consent to the final project. This avoids confusion, controversy, and delegitimation of the work effort after it has gone on to the publishing phase.

II. Order of Authors[6]
To ensure that all participants have a common understanding of research responsibilities, and to avoid confusion, it is important to establish the order of authors, including a lead author and a senior author (if appropriate).

A. The lead author (listed first) will be responsible for:
• Contributing key written material;
• Corresponding with journal editors and conveying necessary information to other members involved in the project;
• Synthesizing material contributed by coauthors, for example, by knitting together sections, generating thesis statements and implications or conclusions;
• Confirming that the content contributed to the project meets the ethical and quality standards of the group;
• Making final decisions about the order of authors and those included in the acknowledgments.

B. The senior author (listed last) will be responsible for:
• Mentoring the first author in the above tasks;

---

[6] Suggestions on the order of authors are adapted from the British Sociological Association, "Authorship Guidelines for Academic Papers," 2001, http://www.britsoc.co.uk/Library/authorship_01.pdf.

• Providing senior leadership and guidance to the entire group of coauthors throughout the process, from development of the concept to final submission of the manuscript.

C. Those who have made significant contributions (as defined above) are entitled to be included as coauthors. Where there is a clear difference in the size of these contributions, this will be reflected in the order of these authors.

D. All others who fulfill the criteria for coauthorship with equal contributions will be included in alphabetical order of their last names.

E. If all authors feel that they have contributed equally, this can be indicated in a footnote or by directing readers to these guidelines.

Appendix 3: Draft Coauthorship Worksheet

This worksheet breaks down a single scholar's contributions to a collaborative work product. Categories and concept derived from the *Schenley Park Debate Authors Working Group Guidelines for Co-Authorship of Work Products 2.0.*

To qualify as a coauthor for a scholarly article, contributors must demonstrate "substantial involvement" in each of the following areas listed below: invention; research; writing and revising.

Name of coauthor:

Title of article:

- Invention

Check at least one box [ ] Involvement in setting the research agenda [ ] Retrieval of primary or secondary source material [ ] Synthesis of research for presentation in article	*Qualitative description of contribution in this area*

- Research

Check at least one box [ ] Involvement in initial project conception [ ] Assistance in mapping goals and methods for project [ ] Intellectual contribution to drive project evolution	*Qualitative description of contribution in this area*

- Writing and Revising

Check at least one box [ ] Contribution of substantial written text [ ] Contribution of suggested revisions [ ] Execution of substantial revisions	*Qualitative description of contribution in this area*

Development and Advancement in the Coaching Profession: A Report on Professional Debate Coaching Positions and Benchmarks for the Profession

Development and Advancement in the Coaching Profession Working Group

Chair
David Hingstman, University of Iowa; co-author, Taylor Hahn, Clarion University

Members
David Cram Helwich, University of Minnesota
Scott Harris, University of Kansas
Brian Lain, University of North Texas
Jake Thompson, University of Nevada, Las Vegas

Research Assistant
Sean Lowry, James Madison University

SUMMARY

A sound and sustainable intercollegiate-debate program will balance its pedagogical mission and its pursuit of competitive success to suit goals of each institutional sponsor. Debate ought to be pedagogy driven but also is sustained by competition, a key element of an intercollegiate-debate program. Combined, the advantages to a program are numerous. Notably, debate competition attracts and retains able students. The presence or absence of a competitive debate program affects enrollment decisions, and high-school-debate programs are encouraged to visit campuses for university-sponsored debate tournaments and high school summer institutes. Excellence in debate requires many hours of library and Internet research, discussion of potential argumentative approaches to the topic, practice in organizing and presenting arguments under pressure of time limits, and critical review of previous performances. Motivating and proving themselves through competition, intercollegiate debaters are often the most articulate, resourceful, and thorough participants in undergraduate and graduate courses.

Intercollegiate competition gives students the opportunity to be evaluated by a diverse national group of argument critics who are familiar with the subject matter and well-trained in the special requirements of competitive argumentation. Debate tournaments are "seminars in argument practice" for future professional and academic settings, populated with enthusiastic students and instructors. Active involvement in a debate team reflects the academic commitments of the university among a group of other distinguished institutions, providing a unique opportunity for debaters to hone what they are learning, to meet with existing and future contributors, and to network with students and future colleagues at professional and graduate schools. Colleges and universities benefit from the favorable publicity for academic programs and fundraising opportunities that debate competition generates.

This volume elsewhere makes the case for strong faculty involvement in directing and supervising intercollegiate-debate programs. Yet the tasks faced by professionals—financial, travel, on-campus tournament and summer program administration, recruitment and retention of team members, preparation of students for competition, and intercollegiate tournament transportation, judging, and coaching—are both complex and time-consuming. Contemporary competitive debate requires the assistance of a staff of professionals, whether those professionals are also graduate teaching assistants, university staff employees, or volunteers. The Working Group on Development and Advancement in the Coaching Profession ("DACP Working Group") was convened to examine the variety of professional debate coaching positions represented at institutions across the country and to discuss best practices for using the services of coaching professionals and creating opportunities for advancement.

VARIETIES OF PROFESSIONAL COACHING POSITIONS

Using data available from the Bruschke debateresults.com Web site for 112 colleges and universities participating in the Cross Examination Debate Association and/or the National Debate Tournament during the academic year 2008–9, the DACP Working Group developed a typology of coaching positions. The first category, with 51 positions, is made up of tenure-track faculty who are directors or codirectors of the debate or forensics program. This category includes both faculty members who are eligible for full tenure and those who qualify for administrative tenure. *Fully tenured faculty* receive tenure for their overall contributions to research, service, and teaching in their departments. They are eligible to advise graduate students and teach graduate seminars, and serve on departmental and university-wide committees. Should such faculty decide at some point after tenure to give up directing the debate or forensics program, they have the option of doing so if thereafter they meet applicable departmental standards for regular faculty performance. *Administratively tenured faculty* receive tenure primarily on the basis of their record as directors of the debate or forensics program. They are expected to continue active involvement in the debate or forensics program for the length of their academic careers, and service on graduate student committees or other departmental bodies, as well as voting rights, may be optional. Both fully tenured and administratively tenured faculty have classroom teaching obligations and standard university benefits packages as part of their employment contracts. Salary levels generally match the pay scale for assistant, associate, and full professors, although salaries are negotiable depending upon experience. Since many colleges and universities pay on a nine-month basis, directing summer debate institutes on campus may involve significant additional compensation.

The second category, with 22 positions, includes *nontenured faculty directors* of debate or forensics on term contracts where a PhD or equivalent is part of the job requirements. These contracts typically range from one to three years in length, and are renewable indefinitely based upon satisfactory performance. The job title may include the words "instructor" or "adjunct professor," and salary levels are commensurate with those negotiated with other nontenured faculty with valuable professional or administrative experience. The expectations and benefits packages are usually comparable to those of university employees who are classified as "professional staff," although there are usually undergraduate or graduate teaching requirements attached to these positions. These directors are more likely to have obligations to organize and supervise summer debate institutes as part of their regular contract duties. But ordinarily they are exempt from general departmental service and graduate committee work.

The third category, with 17 positions, we have called *lecturers*, even though there may be substantial overlap with the category of nontenured faculty directors of debate or forensics in job expectations and compensation. The differences lie in the required educational achievement (usually MA, JD, or equivalent) and in teaching duties, which are limited to undergraduate courses. Compensation rates and benefits packages are generally somewhat less generous than those for term faculty appointments, and these coaches are less likely to be full directors of debate or forensics and/or directors of summer debate institutes. The employment contracts are also less likely to be renewable, as there are high turnover rates for such positions. Persons in these positions often return to graduate school to earn higher-level degrees or to law or business schools after the completion of their appointments. This type of position is sometimes used to fill a temporary vacancy in a category-one or -two director's job when leaves of absence, illness, or late-year resignations occur. These positions may also be occupied by part-time or visiting lecturers.

The fourth category, with 14 positions, includes those who hold *part-time or full-time staff positions*. To our knowledge, these people are not affiliated with particular academic departments. Usually they are supervised and funded through student activities or dean of student offices, although endowments created through alumni foundation contributions may be used to pay program expenses and fund salary lines. The staff member may be protected by some form of administrative tenure, ordinarily after a three-year period of exemplary job performance, if the position is renewable. But the duties of the position will not be transferable to office employment other than directing or supervising the debate program until approved by the university administration. At several institutions, the staff director also supervises the summer debate institute and receives compensation for that work through the regular salary line. Some programs create one- or two-year staff positions for debaters who have just graduated and want to help their younger colleagues for a short time before they move on to graduate or professional schools.

The final category, with seven programs identified, involves *student management* of the program, with no faculty or staff responsible for the actual day-to-day operations of the program, although they may advise or coach on an ad hoc basis. There may be alumni or other volunteers who help with coaching and travel for minimal compensation and without employee benefits. As in the case of the staff positions, the student organizers generally report on their activities and expenditures to a dean of students, a director of student activities, or student government officers.

With respect to departmental affiliations, almost all of the faculty or professional staff positions are associated with departments of communication studies, although a few are sponsored by departments of political science or public policy, or through centers for undergraduate excellence established by provost or college president initiatives. In addition to student activities or student government funding, staff positions may be supported by offices of summer programs or continuing education.

THE RATIONALE FOR DIVERSITY AND TEAMWORK IN DEBATE COACHING AS A PROFESSION

The unique values and challenges associated with intercollegiate policy debate as a cocurricular and extracurricular activity for students stem from the fact that it encourages educational achievement incentivized by intense intellectual and verbal competition. Few opportunities exist in the undergraduate experience that combine preparation in researching and writing public policy arguments, training in oral advocacy, and rigorous practice in making strategic choices under pressure of limited time. Add to that mix the inducement of peer recognition for advancing to the group of 16 or 32 teams in an elimination-round system producing champions at each tournament. Students who favor academic over athletic interests are enthralled by debate's promise. It is not surprising to faculty members that debaters read more, articulate more clearly, and contribute more to class discussions than other students. While the typical undergraduate may spend winter or spring break on the beach, debaters are in libraries or classrooms preparing for the next set of regional or national tournaments.

Supporting this unique activity administratively over a number of years requires a staff with a wide range of skills and experiences. Illustrating these skills are the categorically different ways that staff members interact with students. Some debate educators recognize debaters primarily as students who represent their colleges and universities when they travel to intercollegiate tournaments. Those travels need to be funded, arranged, and accounted for, and so departmental and collegiate administration and student government relations, airline and hotel bookings, and financial reconciliation practices must be developed. At the same time, new students need to be recruited and national visibility achieved through high school and college outreach and on-campus tournament and summer workshop programs. Others work with debaters primarily as students of argumentation, oral persuasion, and public policy, and need to understand and teach how to utilize Internet and library databases and book collections, how to use computer technology and word processing to transform literature into advocacy materials, and how best to arrange practice sessions in basic oral advocacy skills both at home and between tournament rounds. Still others see debaters and graduate student assistants as participants in an activity that is an extension of the academic curriculum. They emphasize mentoring those students so that what they learn from intercollegiate competition will relate to what happens in the college classroom. Care is taken to see that course work is completed before or after students travel, that students pursue curricular interests that work synergistically with the topics of public policy debate, that their preparation for postgraduate educational experiences is carried through, and that other college students have an opportunity to observe and learn from models of policy advocacy through public and on-campus debates.

Popular television programs about competitive practices in law, business, and medicine, such as *Law and Order*, *The Office*, or *Gray's Anatomy*, reflect a contemporary understanding of the complexity where substantial individual and collective benefits are developed and supervised through a team-staffing approach. Yet the popular conception of many debate programs is that they can be conducted by a single charismatic faculty or staff member who shepherds a group of energetic young people into a national championship team. This (mis) conception is reproduced in the imagination of Hollywood through movies like *The Great Debaters*. While there may have been a grain of truth in this portrayal of a slice of academic life in the United States of the 1940s, the reality of competition as a primary driver of the debate activity itself guarantees that it is no longer a faithful representation. Both the professions and academic debate have become more complicated and demanding for participants because of the genius mobilized by the response to competitive pressures. The required expertise has multiplied as the demands now extend beyond argument form and speaking competence to a wide range of coach demands discussed later in this essay.

However strongly we might wish for a return to some Golden Age of academic debate, we cannot undo years of observation, thought, and information gathering layered in the literature of disciplines relevant to public policy, a complexity that advances with each season. Additionally the heuristic debaters use, the requirement to document each argumentative stance, advance authoritative arguments. We do not discount the breadth and sophistication of the information sources that each of us consult on a daily basis to make decisions in our own lives. Would we expect any less of young policy advocates?

Division of labor and specialization of functions are the hallmarks of modern organizations, and academic cocurricular programs need to follow the model. This explains both the growth and diversity of coaching positions, with tight university budgets accelerating the existing trends. Graduate student assistants in programs with academic departmental affiliations, for example, are expected to master the different categorical skill sets at various points in their involvement as coaches, so they may work very closely with students on research, argument production, and advocacy practices in one year and become supervisors, accountants, and event planners in the next year. Recent alumni, interested volunteers, and graduate students outside of regular departmental affiliations might be engaged episodically to help the team effort in defined or unspecified ways, and their involvement increases the supervisory burden on exiting faculty. Some programs have emphasized increasing numbers of program participants to justify stronger support from student services, and each additional intercollegiate competitive team broadens and magnifies the demands on faculty and staff.

In the remaining sections of our report the working group considers how those who organize debate programs, successful both educationally *and* competitively, are responding both to the challenges facing all cocurricular college and university programs and to the demands peculiar to intercollegiate debate.

FOUNDATIONS FOR PROFESSIONALIZED COACHING IN NEW DEBATE PROGRAMS

Schools that do not currently have a competitive-debate program have the potential to create a dynamic and academically inspired form of competitive scholarly advocacy while simultaneously establishing a powerful recruitment mechanism for prospective students. Unfortunately, it is uncommon for a university to unilaterally establish a well-funded and well-coached debate program. In most cases the creation (or revival) of a debate program begins with the collective desire and dedication of a group of students. For students who want to establish a competitive debate program at their university, a number of strategies can be used to compel official university support.

Groups interested in engaging in competitive National Debate Tournament (NDT)-Cross Examination Debate Association (CEDA)-style policy debate are entering an exciting time in the debate community where digital resources are making research and networking increasingly accessible. Those developing programs should be encouraged to choose their own topics and resolutions, but they should also make use of the massive resources available by focusing on the official NDT-CEDA resolution. New initiatives in the field of *open-source debate* make evidence sharing, such as the Open Caselist, a powerful tool for new programs to engage and compete against established teams. It is no coincidence that the winners of the NDT tend to be the schools with the largest coaching staffs, but the increased distribution and free sharing of evidence and resources have made smaller debate programs increasingly capable of competing against larger institutions. We are now seeing the beginnings of increased resource sharing, with multiple initiatives focusing on regional evidence sharing for groups of developing debate programs. This is one example of dramatic changes occurring in the community that are capable of opening the doors for new participation in debate. Regardless of outside influence, such as an organized campaign by preexisting debate organizations to increase resource distribution, students are independently capable of establishing the foundations for a larger competitive program. The following suggestions are a nonlinear set of options available to students who wish to establish a structured and coached debate program, and eventually developing the capability to maintain multiple professional teaching positions, such as those discussed earlier in this chapter.

For the sake of university recognition, a group of students interested in forming a debate team should focus on initial recruitment and faculty sponsorship. Initial team recruitment can begin by contacting other student organizations, such as political groups, interested in policy discussion in order to establish a base of student interest. All options should be considered, but groups such as the College Democrats or College Republicans are logical places to start. Developing programs should also focus on distributing information in debate-oriented courses. Some examples of suitable courses for information sharing are conflict, debate, argumentation, persuasion, and public-speaking seminars. There is no benchmark number of students who should be active participants in a developing debate team, but organizers should be mindful of any potential minimum membership required by their student government. Failing to meet this minimum requirement could potentially foreclose on the potential recognition of the new debate squad as an official student group that is eligible for school funding.

In addition to interested students, many universities require that officially recognized organizations have a faculty sponsor in order to obtain funding. It is highly desirable that a faculty sponsor be interested in coaching, preferably with a background knowledge of the activity. If no available faculty member has a knowledge of competitive NDT-CEDA debate, a developing debate team should work with any interested member of the university faculty who is willing to contribute to the developing program. Students and interested faculty members will find a plethora of information available on the Internet concerning the duties and obligations associated with coaching a debate program. If students and faculty sponsors are incapable of devoting themselves to competitive policy debate, developing programs should consider the alternative of engaging in campus-based public debates with the intention of eventually transitioning to other forms of competitive debate. Either way, funding and school recognition are critical to the development of any debate program.

Upon establishing a base of student interest and faculty support for the developing program, an interested group should work to obtain a steady source of funding. In the early days of a program, most teams need to work through the normal budgetary process of student organizations, most often requiring the approval of student government bodies. A number of issues arise from student-based funding, as can be seen in student-government appropriations processes. First, these kinds of funding sources tend to be unreliable in the long term, due to the quick turnaround of student government representatives. Second, students who are unfamiliar with the budgetary needs of a competitive-debate program are often unwilling to allocate the appropriate funds to a program, sometimes not realizing that debate requires extensive travel and evidentiary purchases. Finally, student-based appropriations threaten to divorce a debate program from academic avenues of support, implying that the program is a club rather than an academically focused competition. The fragile nature of student-based funding sources makes the establishment of a long-term source of support essential to the continued survival of a developing debate program.

In order to ensure long-term stability, developing debate programs should strive to establish a fixed source of funding from a steady support system. Ideally, a program should be established within a department (most commonly a department of communication) in order to gain a popular support basis while simultaneously gaining recognition as a purely academic organization. Other sources of funding and support can be found through provosts, deans, and department chairs. If the university formerly had a debate program, alumni should also be contacted and asked to support a revival of the activity, either through donation or by contact with the appropriate university administration, directly or sending a letter of support. Support should be procured through a strategic presentation focusing on the well-documented benefits of a competitive-debate program (see Colbert and Biggers 1985; Hill 2002; O'Donnell, "A Rationale for Intercollegiate Debate," pp. 27–56).

A successful and secure debate program requires the establishment of dedicated coaching positions and funding by the university. The amount of coaching available to a debate team is largely contingent on the amount of funding that a university is willing to dedicate to the program, but a number of strategies can ensure continued financial support. The vast majority of qualified (and experienced) coaches are equally capable of teaching at a college level. Universities should try to hire coaches who have the potential to assist the debate team department sponsor with its teaching commitments. A joint coach/teacher position will allow developing programs to establish their place in the department and be identified as a part of the academic program. In addition, coaches who have the potential to teach classes have opportunities to find prospective debaters in their classes.

From a purely financial perspective, university officials should recognize that forgoing professional staff coaches is *not* a wise cost-saving measure. The nature of competitive debate requires each competing team to provide a qualified judge to enter the judging pool. Generally, coaches fill this roll, but if a student-run team wants to compete, they have to hire a judge from a third party. The cost of judging on a round-to-round basis varies with a floor of $30 per judged round and a ceiling as high as $100 per round at national tournaments. The unpredictable market of available third-party judges makes the hiring of these judges costly and inefficient. Hired coaches allow debate teams to circumvent this process and ultimately provide more resources for the money expended. Another disadvantage of hiring third-party judges is that they offer no coaching to the student-run organization. It might be slightly more costly to hire a university-employed coach, but this small cost increase vastly adds to the resources available to students participating at tournaments.

Universities also have much to gain by procuring professional coaches. Scheduled travel and accommodation requirements make student supervision essential to a responsible university-sponsored debate program. Transporting students to a debate competition often requires transportation in passenger vans, which undergraduate students are usually excluded from driving because of insurance problems. For universities that do not have a fleet of vehicles, a debate program has to rent vans for tournament travel, which can be problematic since most rental agencies require customers to be older than the average college student. Furthermore, it is preferred that students be supervised given the distance and time involved in many competitive tournaments. This regular travel and resource management requires a responsible individual to be accountable for budgetary issues, such as registration fees and hotel costs. While many debaters are completely capable of handling the responsibilities of debate team administration, this is an unreasonable burden to place on active competitors. Football players would never be expected to handle hotel reservations, transportation requirements, and equipment procurement. The same logic should apply to debaters, who are heavily disadvantaged when they do not have easy access to coaching and administrative support.

Developing programs and coaches should be aware of the travel and research time that must be dedicated to competitive debate, which can be a deterrent to faculty members who lack experience in the activity. Fortunately, qualified coaches are generally aware of the obligations that come with a career as a professional debate coach. If a program has trouble maintaining the work required to sustain a competitive team, universities with masters programs in related disciplines should consider the creation of debate assistantships. These positions are often established by a sponsoring department and are a useful way of ensuring a consistent stream of new and energetic coaching resources.

The NDT-CEDA community can facilitate the creation of new debate programs through a number of initiatives. Initially, the community should undertake greater efforts to promote debate actively to universities that are not affiliated with a competitive debate community. Debate alumni working at universities without active debate programs provide an easily accessible means of promoting debate to new audiences. NDT-CEDA should also consider establishing district representatives who serve as official contacts to new programs trying to join the debate community. By providing easily accessible forms of contact with community representatives, NDT-CEDA can help students and new coaches through the process of increasing their funding and coaching support staff.

HOW PROFESSIONAL COACHES TAILOR DEBATE PROGRAM ACTIVITIES TO COLLEGIATE EXPECTATIONS AND RESOURCES

Most young coaching professionals learn quickly that they serve many more constituencies, and not only the students who show up to prepare for the first tournament. Academic departments want faculty or instructor coaches and graduate student assistants to play an active role in the intellectual life and service obligations of the department. The debate program must contribute to the department's sense of academic mission and its desire for university and national recognition. University administrators expect the program's activities to be well publicized, and its participants to respect university rules of conduct as well as to attain grades, and other indicators of academic achievement well beyond those of average student performance. Interested alumni take pride in the accumulated records of team victories in national tournaments and of post-graduate accomplishments among individual debaters as a continuation or amplification of what the debate program meant to them as undergraduates. Competing intercollegiate program directors encourage coaches to hold competitions and travel and demand in subtle ways that their staff become active members of the professional debate community. High school program directors want advice, coaching help, and workshop or regional tournament sponsorship in exchange for assistance in recruiting new participants.

Best Practices Approach to Directing a Program

Balancing the numerous and sometimes conflicting demands of these constituencies on a debate program requires careful planning and (re)negotiation from the earliest years of a coaching professional's career. While this report cannot hope to enumerate every element of a management strategy within the limits of its textual space, it will sketch the outlines of a "best practices" approach to supervising and directing an intercollegiate-debate program in light of the multiple-constituency problem. The discussion is organized around two aspects of program development: generating strong institutional support and deploying that support wisely.

Generating Institutional Support

To craft an appeal for more resources that can reach across the range of collegiate constituencies, the coaching professional must first frame the discussion of the justification in terms of what those resources can do. That frame should articulate what this working group terms "meta-level program goals," or the purposes that will guide the day-to-day decisions of coaching professionals and staff members and can be referenced in program review and evaluation. The special value of the meta-level goals statement is that it both informs and warns the constituents that the program is enabled as well as restrained by diverse expectations. One frequently stated goal is curricular: to explain how and why the debate team's ability to meet educational objectives of the particular college or university can be enhanced or undermined by institutional decisions about funding levels. Setting forth the role of argumentation and debate training for a program tied to a department of communication is usually a straightforward exercise. Making the case for a specialized debate program to be a subsidiary project of a humanities or social science college may call for more detailed research and thought, including meeting with prominent academicians both within and outside the institution.

Another goal is competitive: to describe the opportunities for intercollegiate debate that are available to the students and the logistical challenges posed by a yearlong process of institutional participation in debate circuits. To the extent possible beforehand, coaching professionals should be frank about the financial and staffing requirements necessary to achieve different levels of national visibility and tournament success. For this goal, coaching professionals often solicit specific information from other directors whose programs they seek to emulate or from directors employed by schools that university administrators consider "peer institutions of higher learning."

A third common goal relates to public outreach and visibility. How will the program develop and cultivate contacts with important stakeholders within and outside the college or university? What adjunct activities will be conducted in connection with the competitive intercollegiate debate squad for publicity purposes? For example, sponsoring a summer debate institute for high school or college students can be useful in recruiting, employing staff and students, generating academic credit hours, and developing ties with colleagues across the nation. Yet such summer programs may not achieve these goals as well as simply having staff and students seek positions in workshops sponsored by other universities, for example, if the facilities, schedule, or cost structure of the school make it impossible for the programs to compete with those institutions for a limited market of potential enrollees. Furthermore, time spent planning and organizing a summer program trades off with coaching and administrative efforts.

Finally, coaching professionals must carve out a place for themselves and their career plans in the goals statement. What opportunities will the program create for professional development among the members of the coaching staff? How will coaches obtain the administrative and other skills they need to run a small nonprofit enterprise competently and to network effectively with its various constituencies, and what forms of advice and supervision should the institution implement to ensure fairness and accountability? Some meta-level goals statements call for a university-level board of overseers composed of faculty and administrators who have a special interest in the program and who can be called upon to defend it when potentially adverse circumstances arise. If the institution employs faculty or staff with previous debate or forensics program experience, those individuals should be among the first called upon to serve on such boards. These structural specifications within program goals statements work to the benefit of both coaching professionals and the institutions that employ them. Most postsecondary schools no longer assume that a teaching contract is a commitment to a lifetime of service, especially if opportunities for tenure and promotion are not part of the agreement. It is only fair to both coaches and schools that professional skill-building be inscribed into the basic structure and operation of the debate program.

Deploying Resources

Once the goals statement has been formalized to the satisfaction of the coaching professionals, then attention needs to be given to the second aspect of the program, the wise use of resources. Preparation of budget-planning documents is one essential step if the program is to have any hope of sustainability. If possible, program directors should collaborate with university administrators and foundations to draft a clear Memorandum of Understanding about funding sources and financial accountability for the debate program. Many institutions are willing to provide travel and equipment resources, in addition to staff salaries and office space, for program start-up, but that funding is often couched in terms of "seed money" that may not be renewable without strong evidence of program success and service expansion. The criteria for funding renewal and increases should be set forth clearly in the memorandum. Also, acceptable forms of external or alumni support and strategies for seeking it should be detailed in the document. College and university foundations are often willing to open fundraising campaigns for promising programs of undergraduate excellence, but they are sensitive to the risk that special appeals may reduce alumni or external funding for the general operating budget or scholarship accounts. Nevertheless, close relations with these foundations at schools with a tradition of support for debate enable coaching professionals to locate addresses, debate records, yearbooks, and other sources of information for reunions and other alumni contacts. Finally, program directors should familiarize themselves with the institution's rules for financial authorization and reconciliation. Policies about cash advances for team travel, documentation requirements for tournament expenses, limitations on institutional liability for accidents and other problems, and proper procedures for trip approval and credit reconciliation should be thoroughly reviewed with the help of university administrators.

Another important issue of resource management that can be the subject of advance planning is the question of institutional location and networking. When institutions are looking for places to cut their operating budgets, they look first to isolated or small programs that seem to lack constituencies that might complain loudly and persistently about defunding or deep cuts. Hence it is in the interest of the debate program to increase the strength and diversity of linkages to academic and administrative centers within the institution. For academic units, these ties can be strengthened by emphasizing subject-matter connections between policy debate and institutional research and scholarship at the undergraduate and graduate levels. Some schools, for example, have departments or centers that research foreign policy or identity issues that appear regularly and in some depth within the annual policy debate topic. In addition to solidifying agency relationships that will protect the program in times of trouble, such networking creates opportunities for undergraduate and graduate students to document in a more permanent way the extensive research and argument construction efforts of each competitive season.

In our enthusiasm to recommend networking, the working group does not want to conclude without a caveat. Whatever initiatives are undertaken, coaching professionals must be careful to structure them in a way that avoids excessive demands on their time. Conceptualizing the debate team as a bridge between different epistemic communities in colleges and universities is an excellent framework for making argumentation and debate central to intellectual life. Opportunities to bring in students who may not be traveling to intercollegiate competitions regularly or at all, but who could benefit from on-campus and other public-debating experiences, should be pursued wherever possible for the sake of the program as a whole. But in most instances, the coaching professional's work will be evaluated primarily according to the basic outlines of program review: numbers of students served, competitive distinction of the program, and outcomes such as graduation rates and professional school admissions.

SPECIAL PROFESSIONALIZATION ISSUES FOR INTERNS AND GRADUATE ASSISTANTS

The future of debating activities in American colleges and universities depends on the willingness of undergraduate participants to give back to the activity they love. While some will make that contribution in the form of generous financial support for debate programs and volunteer judging and coaching work, many others will be called to replace directors of forensics and assistant coaches when they retire or move to other jobs. This final section of the working group report will discuss how future coaches and faculty members can make a smoother transition from participant to forensics professional.

A. Post-undergraduate Interns

In hard economic times, more college graduates are putting off graduate and professional school for internships and other temporary employment. Intercollegiate-debate programs sometimes create opportunities for their recent graduates to work with their squad in argument preparation, practice sessions, and tournament coaching and judging. What should these assistant coaches keep in mind so that the experience reinforces the desire to enter the coaching profession when the internship ends?

Probably the most important thing to remember is that a career, like Rome, is not built in a day. Some think that their contribution to the short-term success of the debaters will be the sole measure of their value in professional life, even though much of what needs to be learned lies outside of tournament competition. Moreover, some believe that they can improve on the merits of their own undergraduate performance by living vicariously through the triumphs of those who follow. But giving in to these temptations actually can make it less, not more likely that an internship will lead to full-time coaching. First of all, it is easy to assume that working too hard on research will have no bad consequences. The role of researcher trades off with the role of judge if the research compromises fulfilling the commitment of judging. Judges who fall asleep during morning rounds do not merit a reputation for competency. A full year of overwork also risks burnout. Second, excessive ego involvement in the success of particular teams is a recipe for professional disaster. Interns who were patient when they were competitors while interacting with judges and other students as competitors, often turn into surly inquisitors when they cannot extricate their egos e from the results of particular rounds.

Interns can shape their coaching experiences in positive ways to reap the professional benefits of an early start. Initially, the intern can keep his/her options open by exploring productive intersections between policy debate research and potential professional or academic concerns. Rather than spreading themselves too thin by concentrating on case-specific arguments, interns might see an opportunity to investigate some issues in depth from a disciplinary or practical perspective. In addition to developing a specialization for later study, interns may better educate debaters by improving instruction on how arguments can be developed and defended strategically. Should the proposal to establish an online debate research database be implemented, interns would have a channel for beginning a publication track record.

Another path to professional recognition opens from viewing the internship experience as a chance to discover what good coaches do by closely observing their mentors in action. Interns sometimes forget that their new position will and should change their relationship with former coaches as well as with their former colleagues. Interns should pursue every opportunity to participate in coaches' meetings and to ask practical questions about the programmatic reasons behind the judgments that coaches reach both during and between tournaments. Silence maintained out of misguided deference to authority figures could slow or even reverse professional development. At the same time, interns must recognize that their former colleagues who are still debating are no longer the same kind of friends they were in previous years. The legal restrictions on consensual and nonconsensual personal relationships that most colleges and universities impose on all faculty and staff, are ignored by interns at their peril because administrators consider all coaches to hold a supervisory position.

B. Graduate Student Assistants

Most graduate students who coach intercollegiate debate are planning careers in the discipline of communication studies, although future literary, political science, and legal scholars and practitioners, among others, also participate in the activity. Debate coaching is an excellent addition to the graduate educational experience because it sharpens dialectical understanding that is essential to critical scholarship and it develops skills in teaching advocacy practices. It can also help both scholars and practitioners prepare for administrative roles in academic and professional organizations. Nevertheless, as our earlier discussion suggested, coaching work alone does not qualify people for a wide range of positions that include responsibility for directing forensics programs. This section will suggest ways that graduate students can better coordinate their academic and coaching experiences to achieve maximum benefit and increase their options for continuing involvement in the debate-coaching profession.

For graduate students who have or share primary responsibility for directing a program, our previous discussion about recruiting and training staff, publicizing the squad's existence, and expanding its activities seems most relevant. If the program is not sponsored by the student's academic department, it would be wise for the graduate student to determine and then explain carefully to advisers in advance the likely extent of the student's investment of time and energy in debate coaching, which are usually much greater than the demands of ordinary instructional positions Also, the graduate student should demand and reach a clear (preferably written) understanding with the program's sponsoring units about compensation and initial funding commitments.

Communication studies departments have been and continue to be the primary institutional home of debate programs, and there are many opportunities to earn master's and doctoral degrees while coaching intercollegiate and campus debate. Teaching assistantships typically provide a stipend that covers tuition for a full schedule of courses in exchange for coaching duties and two to four class assignments per year. Graduate students typically register for three seminars (nine credit hours) per semester, and are expected to write a major paper at the end of each seminar. To remain eligible for teaching and coaching assistantships, graduate students must maintain what institutions define as "normal academic progress" toward their degrees. Maintaining a proper balance among their responsibilities of teaching class, keeping up with seminar readings and assignments, and coaching and traveling with debaters is a major challenge for many young graduate students. There was a time when faculty members at research-one universities were all too willing to give doctoral students a grade of incomplete when they were unable to finish their seminar papers before the end of the semester. The consequence of this "gift," however, was that some students piled up a large number of incompletes that then had to be cleared from their transcripts, at the expense of summer and inter-semester break periods, before those students could take their comprehensive examinations and prepare their dissertation prospectuses. At most of these universities, strongly discourage graduate students from asking for incompletes. Instead, these students are encouraged to compromise their final essays, and to use future vacation periods to recover from the rigors of the semester and edit their manuscripts for convention presentation and publication submission.

What are graduate students asked to do in assisting with debate programs that makes it essential to devote planning time and psychic energy to working and studying efficiently and effectively? First, graduate students usually work directly with undergraduates on a daily or weekly basis in preparation for and participation in tournament competition. In most instances, the enjoyment that graduate students get from performing these tasks is the reason why they chose to coach debate, so there is little regret about the many hours involved. On campus, graduate students conduct debate squad meetings, listen to practice debates and speeches, help debaters get started on research assignments, edit and critique the written arguments prepared by debaters, and strategize positions against the cases of their more able opponents. On tournament trips, graduate students often drive university vehicles to the competition site, help students register for housing, enter the tournament, find food, provide four or more rounds of debate judging, and work with teams intensively during the 30 to 60 minutes of preparation time before each debate begins. Second, graduate students are often asked to direct or assist in conducting local debate tournaments on campus, which sometimes involve more than 100 high school debate teams, as well as to participate in judging at high school tournaments within their metropolitan area. They are sometimes an integral part of recruiting efforts for new debaters. Third, graduate assistants are expected to meet whatever financial documentation requirements apply to team travel. They sometimes receive university credit cards in their names, which require them to file travel reconciliation data and receipts on a monthly basis or lose charging privileges for tournament travel. Finally, graduate students are occasionally asked to make travel arrangements or perform other administrative chores for the program.

Given this list of potential duties, it is easy to see why graduate student coaching is time-consuming. While a graduate student who is coaching debate typically receives a reduction in teaching load of one course per semester, the responsibilities involved in debate coaching tend to be much greater than those associated with teaching a course. Despite the heaviness of the burden, most graduate students who are not yet ABD assume the extra load stoically, reassuring themselves that they are doing what they love and that there are limited coaching positions available at doctorate-granting universities.

The primary recommendation of this working group is not to discourage graduate students who are potential coach professionals from getting involved in coaching, but rather to urge graduate student assistants to do whatever they can to protect their status as future academicians eligible for quality academic positions that offer the benefits of tenure and promotion. At times, this means that graduate assistants must choose to reduce their commitment to the coaching activities so that enough time will be available for reading and reflection on course materials, for writing and presenting papers at professional conferences and for publication, for improving their classroom teaching skills, and for enjoying some semblance of a social life.

Graduate students are vulnerable to adverse health effects from stress and overwork, and deserve some time and space to relax and heal. Perhaps this means that they will travel to only three tournaments rather than five each semester in fulfillment of their assistantship requirements. It should be the responsibility of debate directors and their faculty colleagues to adjust their expectations of graduate assistants involved in debate coaching so that those students have time to learn and to exercise important nondebate academic skills.

In concert with fair and sensitive treatment is the suggestion that doctoral advisers help graduate student assistants give careful consideration to the kind of academic positions for which they wish to qualify after reaching ABD status. Expectations for tenure-track assistant professors at research-one institutions in the United States have expanded prodigiously in the past 20 years. In addition to completing their dissertations prior to interviews, finalist candidates for academic positions are often expected to have published an essay in a major disciplinary journal by the time of application. Even tenure-track positions in which debate coaching is a primary or major responsibility or at a non–research-one institution where effectiveness in classroom teaching is a more important concern than research, candidates are expected to show on application abundant evidence of their work presented at scholarly conferences and in smaller publications. Once selected for these positions, tenure-track assistant professors are expected to pick up the pace of publication, with dissertations published as books and articles in major disciplinary journals expected prior to the granting of tenure.

Doctoral students who coach debate are thus forced to make tough career choices that determine whether or not they will continue their involvement in debate activity after completing their dissertations. In these decisions, they must carefully consider offsetting risks. On the one hand, that their involvement in debate coaching may slow their publication record, thus diminishing eligibility for academic positions at major universities. On the other hand, giving up debate coaching either in graduate school or after completing their dissertations will remove a major reward of their professional lives. Fortunately, there are still a healthy number of tenure-track academic positions in the United States that take into consideration the competing demands of coaching, teaching and research at the time of the tenure decision. Other essays in this book suggest new ideas about how to combine argument work with students and cutting-edge publication possibilities in the communication and public policy disciplines (see, e.g., Mitchell, "Pathways to Innovation in Debate Scholarship," pp. 93–126). This working group concludes by heartily endorsing these recommendations and encouraging graduate students to investigate ways in which online and specialty journal publications could lead to innovations in interdisciplinary research and practice.

References
Colbert, K., and T. Biggers. 1985. "Why Should We Support Debate?" *Journal of the American Forensic Association* 21 (Spring): 237–40.
Hill, B. 2002. "The Value of Competitive Debate as a Vehicle for Promoting Development of Critical Thinking Ability." In *Perspectives in Controversy: Selected Essays from Contemporary Argumentation and Debate*, ed. K.T. Broda-Bahm, 47–70. New York: IDEA.

Section II: Innovation and Best Practices

Innovation and Debate: Where Do We Go from Here?

Innovations in Debate Working Group

Chair
Karla Leeper, Baylor University

Members
Blake Abbott, University of Georgia
Kelly Congdon, Richmond University
Josh Gonzales, Wake Forest University
Sarah Partlow Lefevre, Idaho State University
Derek Richardson, Atlanta Entrepreneur
Sara Spring, University of Iowa
Scott Varda, Baylor University

Advisory Member
Aaron Hardy, Whitman College

The fact that debating has existed (in one form or another) from the classical era to the twenty-first century is proof of the capacity of debate and those who engage in it to innovate. The ancient Greeks would scarcely recognize a modern debate round where students who have flown in from distant cities take notes on laptop computers and use evidence from sources they have downloaded from the Internet. Despite those differences, our debate ancestors would recognize the ongoing commitment to a competition of ideas present in contemporary debate.

Thomas Edison, perhaps one of the most innovative individuals in history, argued that "discontent is the first necessity of progress" (Edison 1996). A brief review of the literature related to intercollegiate debate makes it clear that we have no shortage of discontent. The National Development Conference on Debate challenged us to think about how the creativity inspired by that discontent might influence debate in the twenty-first century. This essay will discuss how debate might improve its innovative process and how that process will be influenced by factors outside of our activity.

ENHANCING THE PROCESS OF INNOVATION

As we think about innovation in debate, we might be tempted to think only about innovation as a serendipitous process: discovery by accident or necessity. However, innovation can occur intentionally. Treating innovation as a part of our responsibility as educators would require us to regularly and deliberately ask important questions, challenge old assumptions, and take action in the face of change, rather than merely being moved by it.

As a first principle, innovation in debate must become *intentional*. This does not mean that we direct our experimentation to achieve predetermined outcomes. Rather, it means that we are intentional in creating spaces within our activity for innovation to flourish. We participate in an activity that is constructed of rules and norms of our choosing. Making different choices about these can fuel innovation. For example, we might choose to utilize the debate topic as a vehicle to encourage innovation. The topic is a critical variable in the way debate functions, and altering our approach to it can have significant results.

Developing topics with nongovernmental agents, no agent at all, or the debate community as agent can encourage a very different type of discussion than current topics focused on the U.S. federal government as the agent of change. Those debates might assess the efficacy of political action, the morality of individual agency, and the ability of the community to impact the wider world. Another choice might be to select a topic area with resolutions that rotate each semester or month. The rolling focus would alter the way in which students pursue research, argument construction, and the execution of the debate round itself.

The debate community has already used the structure of tournaments to create spaces for innovation. However, tournament directors could choose to go much further than changing time limits, shifting within a narrow range of judging assignments, or canceling one round in favor of public debates. Changes in judging could build bridges with a wider community or provide educational opportunities for students and other interested individuals. Another choice might be to alter the structure of tournaments to require that one or more rounds be judged by a member of the community. If our goal is to provide more students with in-round experiences, we could offer debaters who have been eliminated the opportunity to judge in some capacity on elimination-round day.

Second, the debate community must consistently subject innovation to *evaluation* through a deliberative process. Debate encourages students to think through problems and ideas, to assess them from a multitude of angles, and frequently to imagine a world different from the one in which they live. Coaches and debaters do a good job (generally) of hashing out the implications of argumentative innovations. Unfortunately, we have not always subjected other kinds of innovations that influence debate to the same deliberative process.

Technological advances in research are one good example. The explosion of online research resources such as LexisNexis has dramatically changed debate. The ability to research electronically has equalized the playing field between schools that had large libraries and those that did not. Students now have access to a wider array of experts and material in a more timely fashion than ever before. However, the integration of this technological innovation into our practice has had a profound effect on the ways that students and faculty function at tournaments and on the types of arguments that are made in debate rounds. This essay takes no position on whether those innovations were good or bad. The point is that as a community we have not evaluated how electronic research would change us or how we might change our policies and processes to deal with the influx of these innovations.

Our governing bodies and the coaching community must make decisions about innovations in a deliberative fashion. We must measure every innovation against the core values of our activity: transparency, accessibility, equity, diversity, and the creation of communities of learners. And we must also assess how innovations will impact our community's understanding of ethical and professional obligations.

Third, we must be *reflective* in our innovation. We should engage criticisms of our activity and apply our deliberative model to a process of evaluating current assumptions about debate. We commonly hear coaches and debaters argue that we should use what we learn on any topic to engage our political system. We should be no less committed to engaging our own structures. Setting aside what we believe to be true about debate and its benefits, we must ask whether we really are producing the learners and learning communities necessary for the twenty-first century. Asking this question does not require us to argue that the present state of the activity is unsatisfactory. But we cannot be sure that we are meeting our objectives unless we periodically test whether what we say about ourselves is true.

It may be time to have the debate about debate. Forums such as eDebate have been the site of many discussions about the purpose of debate, whether debate is truly open to all people, and what our public responsibility is. Perhaps it is time to turn our powerful critical lens inward and spend a season talking about who and what we are and want to be. Even if an entire season were not devoted to this subject, it may be worthwhile to devote time at a number of major tournaments to discussions about these questions. The Owen L. Coon Forum held for many years at the Northwestern tournament set aside two hours during the tournament for such discussion.

It may be time to talk about our view of competition. Much of what we do in debate is organized around a particular view of competition. Perhaps it is time to move beyond discussions about what it means to "win" a debate. The criteria for winning incentivize certain practices. What exactly are we choosing to incentivize? What do we want to reward?

Closely tied to our views of competition and winning are our views about the only lasting record of what happens in a tournament debate—the ballot. Many of us grew up with judges who would write a page describing the round and dutifully check the boxes at the top of the ballot to assess our performance in five categories, awarding an appropriate number of individual speaker points to us, our partners, and the other team. The written ballot as a tool to convey the reason for decision has gone the way of the dodo, and speaker points are now given in decimals. Speaker points seem to have become disconnected from meaningful criteria, and, instead, reflect a general sense of whether the debater is competent. It may be time to rethink the feedback judges provide to students. We never hope to lose the in-depth critical review of a student's arguments that a conversation about a specific debate can provide. But perhaps we should ask judges to rethink the ballot and speaker points to reflect a more meaningful set of criteria that address educational priorities that extend beyond any individual debate round.

We also need to examine the judges' role during a debate. We devote very little time and attention to training judges. Arguably judge training should be part of a program of professional development. A focus on professional development could shift our view of the judge as a passive, neutral observer of the debate to the judge as an active participant in the creation of the argumentative moment in a round. As a participant, a judge might have a very different role. That role might include asking questions, evaluating evidence, providing feedback to the teams, or even giving a preliminary assessment of the arguments before the rebuttals. If our goal is education, we might better serve that goal by allowing this expanded role.

The good news is that there is a wealth of material to inform our reflections. Those who have come before us have discussed many ways to improve our processes. We could begin our work by engaging in a process of *retroactive enrich-*

ment and looking at ideas that might have been rejected in another context or under conditions different from those that exist now.

Finally, our innovations must keep our activity relevant to the academy and to our communities. Debate has an opportunity to provide skills and experiences that are important to our society. We can share those benefits with many who choose to participate in debate, but we should also make an effort to provide those benefits to a wider community.

Many debate programs conduct public debates. As valuable as these debates are, there may be ways to enhance their impact. Rather than asking people to come to an auditorium to hear our students discuss an issue of current interest, debaters might more effectively go to an audience and conduct a debate on an issue that is important to them. Debating in front of smaller groups may create an interactive experience that enriches our students and others. Posting and archiving debates online might allow those who cannot attend a public debate to access the event on their own time.

Debaters produce an enormous quantity of research over the course of a year. Much of this work is exhaustive and of a very high quality. After the season, the work typically goes into a file and stays there until another topic requires it. The community should think about ways to make the accumulated work of the season more publicly accessible in traditional publication formats, or electronic venues such as blogs or wikis. In addition to providing a service to those interested in the subject, a publication project such as this could assist students and tenure-track faculty in acquiring publication credit.

DEBATE INNOVATION AND THE TWENTY-FIRST CENTURY ACADEMY
Debate programs depend on the good will and resources of colleges and universities. Innovations will invigorate our activity only if they are consistent with the values and goals of the broader academy. During the past decade, leading national educational policy organizations have undertaken comprehensive studies of the state of higher education (Altbach, Berdahl, and Gumport 2005; Association of Governing Boards of Universities and Colleges 2009; National Leadership Council for Liberal Education & America's Promise 2007). A review of their work provides insight into some external variables that should influence the future direction of intercollegiate debate.

Debate as a High-impact Practice

The various assessments of higher education arrive at fairly uniform conclusions about the work that colleges and universities need to do in the next century. The American educational system has achieved fairly good results during its history, but the burden on it will be great and the consequences of failure will be high. Nothing less than our economy, our civil society, and our future may depend on the ability of educational institutions to meet future needs.

Educators are developing a catalog of what they refer to as "high-impact practices." These practices engage students in undergraduate research, provide opportunities for extensive mentoring experiences, and find ways to connect students' academic experiences to their world outside the classroom. The debate community must pursue innovations that further the argument that debate is an outstanding high-impact practice.

First, *institutions are looking for high-impact practices that enhance students' ability to function in a world with a strong global focus*. There is a general consensus that cultural competency is critical to the educated person in the twenty-first century. As technology has increased our ability to communicate and as the global economy has become more interdependent, the world has become smaller. The crises we face, such as climate change, terrorism, economic inequality, and poverty are global in nature and will require a sophisticated understanding of culture, history, and international affairs to manage them. There is great concern that we are not doing enough to educate our students to be effective participants in this global public square (Reimers 2009).

Debate must continue to make the case that it does a better job than many other academic programs of preparing students to function effectively in a global society. Many of the problems tackled in contemporary debate topics provide opportunities for students to think about problems in a global context, and they encourage students to evaluate the global consequences of American actions.

Additionally, our community has had a history of sponsoring international debates. The experience heretofore has been limited to tours, with international teams visiting our country or an American team visiting a willing international partner. Some other debate organizations such as the International Debate Education Association engage in regular international competitions. It is time for the policy of the Cross Examination Debate Association and the National Debate Tournament community to embrace expanding competition to include international partners. Tournament formats that rely on technology to connect competitors may make this possible. Imagine a future where tournament results include teams from Russia, Japan, or Egypt with the same regularity as they now include teams from California, Texas, and North Carolina.

A second set of high-impact practices encourages students to think in cognitively complex ways. Higher education in the twenty-first century must produce students who can deal with complex problems in an environment fraught with ambiguity. Barriers between disciplines are breaking down, and the truly educated person must be able to integrate knowledge from a variety of disciplines. Just as problems of climate change, terrorism, economic inequality, and poverty are global, they are also complex. We are looking for citizens, scholars, and leaders who can think creatively and bring new approaches to the challenges we face.

Debate is an outstanding vehicle for encouraging students to think in cognitively complex ways and to be creative as well as strategic. Moreover, the ability to think through hypothetical outcomes and to evaluate competing positions creates a level of comfort with ambiguity that will allow our students to exercise leadership in situations in which information is incomplete.

A third goal of high-impact practices is to create students who are literate in a world awash in information. Our students must be technically literate: they must understand the way in which technology produces and disseminates information. Our students must also be information literate: they must be able to assess the quality of the information they consume. And our students must be literate about the conduct of scholarship: they must fully understand the strengths and limitations of the research methods that result in new knowledge.

Debate will be most successful in its innovative efforts if it enhances the literacy of our students in key areas. Debaters were early adopters of the Internet and the research capability that it created. Debate and argumentation pedagogy must continue to emphasize the ability of the form to teach students to critically evaluate information. Moreover, a focus on critical reading of texts and the extensive testing of ideas provides insight into the process of developing complex ideas and thoroughly examining them.

Fourth, strong communication skills are always in demand. The skills of speaking, writing, and participating in groups are even more critical in the information age. There is significant concern that this generation of students is losing its ability to communicate clearly because of its dependence on technology. Innovations in debate must continue to emphasize basic communication skills.

Innovation and the Economics of Intercollegiate Debate

The financial collapse of the early twenty-first century has left Americans skeptical about the effectiveness of many institutions. Companies that have served as the bedrock of the economy, such as General Motors, have gone into bankruptcy. Financial institutions that held the life savings of many have collapsed, leaving nothing but ruined dreams in their wake. And government regulators who were supposed to protect the interests of consumers seem to have been ignorant of or indifferent to the risky practices that were the source of the collapse. The result is one of the highest unemployment rates since the Great Depression, growing numbers of home foreclosures, and massive government deficits as the Obama administration borrows against our future to safeguard our present.

Higher education has not and will not emerge unscathed from this period of skepticism that asks whether institutions are operating in an honest and responsible manner. The steadily increasing cost of a college education has raised eyebrows, engendering calls for state and federal governments to examine the business practices of the higher education industry. Iowa Senator Charles Grassley and New York Attorney General Andrew Cuomo have engaged in rigorous investigations of student lending and international programs, and the expectation is that this is just the beginning of the scrutiny that colleges and universities will face (Fain 2008).

As lawmakers increase scrutiny of higher education, university budgets will face significant pressure (Laidler 2008). The economic downturn has substantially reduced education budgets for public schools. Plummeting endowments have placed private schools in difficult fiscal positions. The decline in the value of the stock market and the evaporation of many investments has reduced the amount of money many families have available to pay for their children's college education. And declining economic fortunes have increased the pressure on governing boards to keep tuition increases to a minimum, even as the demands on the universities' budget for salaries, research infrastructure, facilities, and technology increase (Broad 2008).

Financial conditions in higher education have always had an impact on the practice of intercollegiate debate (Nichols 1936). Debate costs money. There are travel costs, judging fees, the logistics of tournaments, and preparation costs. Tournament debating originally came into being as a way for schools to allow a larger number of students to participate in a greater number of debates for less cost. The continuing economic crisis and the desire to reduce university expenditures will put at risk of being cut programs that are not essential to the core mission of the institution. Universities have even begun to cut costs in sacred cows like athletics, eliminating entire sports and cutting amenities for revenue sports such as football and basketball (Belson 2009). These reports of belt-tightening measures should leave no doubt that intercollegiate debate is entering a time in which it may have to work harder to cut costs and justify its expenditures.

The assumption that debate tournaments should take place on college campuses around the nation may have to be reexamined. During the economic downturn, colleges and universities have followed businesses in reducing conference travel and other travel budgets. Even athletics programs have had their travel budgets tightened (Abrams 2008).

Traveling to other universities to compete may become a phenomenon of the past. Smaller budgets may require the community to find other ways to conduct debates. Advances in technology may make those alternatives more viable than ever before. Corporate America is already exploring such solutions as Web conferencing to connect employees. This essay will discuss the implications of technological advancement on debating later, but economics may play a significant role in accelerating the integration of such technology into the debate format.

Scrutiny of college costs has consequences beyond budget cuts. In order to determine whether consumers are "getting what they pay for" and to evaluate whether state and federal investments in education are paying off, many have called for the evaluation of educational institutions on the basis of outcomes. The Spellings Commission report (2006) is the most notable example of this outcome focus. The philosophy espoused in that report has spread to the agencies that accredit colleges and universities. As a consequence, administrators are interested in whether academic programs can provide data demonstrating that they do in fact teach students the skills they claim to teach.

Debate has not taken advantage of the opportunity to gather data on the skills and abilities of our students on a broad scale. Tournaments could provide us the opportunity to gather data on skill development in public speaking, writing, research, critical thinking, and so on. As we evaluate innovations in tournament management programs and online results management databases, we should think about how we can prioritize gathering data on students' skill levels. These data, encompassing an enormous number of students from a wide variety of institutions, across a number of years, could give us some powerful tools to justify debate and debate-program funding to administrators. We must think about gathering data that go beyond wins, losses, and speaker awards.

Debate Innovation and the Age of Cloud Computing

Educause is a collection of educators who care about the integration of technology in higher education. In 2007 they undertook a careful evaluation of how technological innovations will change the character of the work done by colleges and universities. Their seminal report on the synergy between higher education and technology provides fertile ground for thinking about how debate might innovate in a world defined by technology (Katz 2008).

The characteristics of new technologies make the consequences of their introduction quite different from previous innovations. Phenomenal increases in computing power, miniaturization, and digitization have created revolutionary rather than evolutionary change. We can now process information at a much more rapid rate and we can share that information much more quickly. The result has been advancement at a breathtaking rate.

Technology is now ubiquitous. It is present in nearly every aspect of our lives; and where it is not currently present, we are actively seeking to integrate it. Technology is smaller and more portable than ever before, allowing us to have technology nearly anywhere. Computer networking and wireless connections make it possible to use technology to connect ourselves to others a room or a continent away. Social networking sites and iPhones as well as television and computers, e-mail, and text messages combined to make the swearing in of President Barack Obama the first Web 2.0 inauguration (Jones 2009).

Technological evolution is hard to predict, but is essential for debate to evolve. It is apparent that the twenty-first century will provide innovations that debate must engage in order to remain relevant to students and educators as a means of creating communities of learning. Our community can take advantage of the opportunities technology presents to radically alter debate practices.

We must devote more attention to how we choose technologies and what the consequences of adopting those technologies might be. Choosing some technical directions may foreclose the adoption of others. We must discuss whether we want to embrace the open-source model of technology or engage with commercial entities for purposes of technological development. These questions are difficult to answer and will require that we learn more about the technologies we might embrace.

One of the most important lessons we can learn from prior technological innovation is the value of openness and accessibility. Advancements in tournament management such as the contributions of Jon Bruschke, Rich Edwards, Gary Larson, and Ross Smith are important models for decisions because they embodied the values of transparency and openness. When appropriating technology into our practices, we must make sure that these technologies are appropriate. The double meaning of that term should not be missed. Unless we make the right choices, the technology that we choose must be appropriate or it will appropriate the community.

Technology will allow debate practices to become more effective. Current innovations such as social networking, paperless debate, and virtual debating, as well as near-future possibilities such as online debating or open-source evidence production hold tremendous advantages for the community. In "Deliberating Debate's Digital Futures," Carly Woods et al. (2006) consider the implications of the integration of a single new technology of a "Digital Debate Archive" for the practice of debate. These changes hold promises in efficiency, argumentation, and beyond. However, these resources may also negatively impact the community, eliminating some key skills, fragmenting the community, increasing resource disparities, or reducing spaces for innovation. As we move forward, the community must thinking carefully about these implications.

Technology has already changed our view of the university as a physical place. Many students are enrolled in online courses, and a few for-profit institutions do not even have a physical campus. Technology may similarly disconnect the concept of a debate tournament from a physical space.

Travel impacts debate in many ways. Costs can be considerable, and travel takes students away from school and many coaches away from their families for significant portions of time. The long tournament days can be grueling. The toll on health and professional development can be significant. And the burden of travel may create a barrier to encouraging novice debate. Technology might provide a way to facilitate competition without the physical travel.

As the quality of technology increases, the ability of individuals to use technology to work together is enhanced. Stable Internet connections, high-quality low-cost sound and video equipment, and high-speed data transfers make computer-assisted communication much more feasible and reliable than ever before. The success of unified communication technology will make technology-facilitated gatherings as easy as a phone call.

The growth of participation in virtual worlds by video gamers illustrates the potential for technology to change debate practice. One study reports that the number of hours spent by residents in virtual worlds has doubled, from 10.8 million hours in 2007 to 28.3 million in 2008. One virtual world, Second Life, nearly quadrupled its population during that same time frame to 12.2 million ("A Second Coming" 2008). Virtual collaboration is being explored by a number of corporate entities. For example, the Obama inaugural group had built virtual conference centers in the Second Life platform (Jones 2009). Colleges and universities are not far behind. Harvard has its own Second Life Island, where it actually teaches courses (Crush 2008).

There have been a few attempts to conduct debates using online platforms, although technological limitations have made such attempts difficult. The availability of communication technologies and the economic pressures of the next several years should combine to incentivize the use of these platforms to hold debates. Freeing tournaments from the constraints of location, time, and travel could be the result. We might hold a debate by e-mailing digital video files containing each speech. Judges could watch the video files at their convenience and render a decision via e-mail. Debates could be held in real time via videoconferencing technology. Or we might even hold a tournament in a tournament hotel on an island in Second Life.

Anyone who has ever made a twelve-hour drive home from a tough tournament might readily embrace the idea of holding debates from the comfort of his or her own office. However, there are benefits to the current tournament model. Engaging in face-to-face educational interactions has value. Learning how to travel and seeing other campuses enriches students. And the opportunity to engage with colleagues on a regular basis is professionally meaningful for coaches.

The community must determine what is valuable about the tournament experience and find ways to use technology to balance the personal and economic demands of travel with the benefits of face-to-face interaction. A mixed solution might set up regional tournament sites where teams would travel shorter distances but still engage in national competitions using technological connections with other regional sites.

Conclusion

Each developmental conference has asked its participants to think about where we will find ourselves at the next developmental conference. Interestingly, a review of those earlier essays demonstrates that many of the concerns we have today were shared by those who came before us. The commitment by the debate community to enhance communication and argumentation skills, to be relevant to the academy, to be faithful to the interests of the institutions that sponsor us, and to improve the level of civil discourse in society is strong. Each generation has taken that commitment seriously and has done its best to maintain the health and well-being of intercollegiate debate. Undoubtedly this generation takes its obligation just as seriously. If we are intentional, and use the tools that make us special among academic programs, we will give the participants in the next developmental conference much to write about.

References

Abrams, J. 2008. "College Teams Are Feeling the Squeeze from Fuel Costs." *New York Times*, October 3, p. 3.

Altbach, P.G.; R.O. Berdahl; and P.J. Gumport. 2005. *American Higher Education in the Twenty-first Century: Social, Political, and Economic Challenges*. Baltimore, MD: Johns Hopkins University Press.

Association of Governing Boards of Universities and Colleges. 2009. *Strategic Imperatives: New Priorities for Higher Education*. Washington, DC: AGB Press.

Belson, K. 2009. "Universities Cutting Teams as They Trim Their Budgets." *New York Times*, May 4, p. D1.

Broad, M.C. 2008. "We're Controlling Spending: College Presidents Are Making Hard Choices to Keep Tuition Affordable." *USA Today*, December 1, p. 11A.

Crush, P. 2008. "Virtual Worlds-Virtually Speaking." *Human Resources*, December 1, p. 38.

Edison, T. 1996. *Thomas Alva Edison Quotes*. http://www.thomasedison.com/quotes.html (accessed July 8, 2009).

Fain, P. 2008. "Why Colleges Can't Shake the Feds." *Chronicle of Higher Education* 54, no. 43 (July 4): 1.

Jones, K. C. 2009. "Obama's Is First Web 2.0 Inauguration." TECHWEB, January 20. http://www.informationweek.com/news/government/showArticle.jhtml?articleID=212901451/ (accessed June 6, 2010).

Katz, R. 2008. *The Tower and the Cloud: Higher Education in the Age of Cloud Computing*. Washington, DC: EDUCAUSE.

Laidler, J. 2008. "Colleges Tighten Budgets." *Boston Globe*, November 30, p. 1.

National Leadership Council for Liberal Education & America's Promise. 2007. *College Learning for the New Global Century*. American Association of Colleges and Universities. http://www.aacu.org/advocacy/leap/documents/GlobalCentury_final.pdf (accessed May 24, 2009).

Nichols, E. 1936. "A Historical Sketch of Intercollegiate Debating: II." *Quarterly Journal of Speech* 22: 591–602.

Reimers, F. 2009. "Global Competency Is Imperative for Global Success." *Chronicle of Higher Education* 55 (January 30): 1.

"A Second Coming for Virtual Worlds." 2008. *PR Week*, March 28, p. 24.

Spellings Commission. 2006. *A Test of Leadership: Charting the Future of U.S. Higher Education.* Washington, DC: U.S. Department of Education.

Woods, C.B.; M. Brigham; B. Heavner; T. Konishi; R. Rief; B. Saindon; and G.R. Mitchell. 2006. "Deliberating Debate's Digital Futures." *Contemporary Argumentation & Debate* 27: 81–105.

Best Tournament Practices: Recommendations and Data

Best Practices Working Group

Chair
Rich Edwards, Baylor University; co-author, Jon Bruschke, California State University–Fullerton

Members
Brent Brossmann, John Carroll University
Adrienne Brovero, University of Mary Washington
Shruti Chaganti, James Madison University
Mike Davis, James Madison University
John Fritch, University of Northern Iowa
Mike Hall, Liberty University
Gary Larson, Wheaton College
Will Repko, Michigan State University
Ross Smith, Wake Forest University

Executive Summary

The committee was charged with reviewing a host of possible tournament practices; the initial agenda was a three-page single-spaced document with a list of more possible topics than any committee could dispense within two days. The group chose to focus on those issues that seemed most salient and least governed by any other body. In the end, a surprisingly large number of issues did get discussed and converted into concrete recommendations. Those recommendations immediately follow two initial caveats.

First, the initial recommendation recognizes that this committee was not able to cover all pertinent topics and that some ongoing forum is necessary to give full consideration to the evolving issues of tournament administration. These recommendations should therefore not be interpreted as the only issues tournament directors should consider or plan for. The committee came to the conclusion that ongoing consideration of tournament procedures is a very useful exercise, and that a continually updated document containing the recommendations of best practices would be a very useful product.

Second, the committee sought to balance the need to identify core values with the tournament directors' need for concrete recommendations. Where concrete recommendations are given, they were offered with the recommendation that a "best practices" recommendation was not binding, and that the demands or goals of particular tournaments or divisions might make other choices better ones.

The seven final recommendations of the committee are:

1. Recommendation: a council of tournament directors should be convened to review tournament practice and publish a "best tournament practices" document.

2. Recommendation: as a best practice, tournament competition administrative procedures should be transparent and communicated in advance of the tournament.

3. Recommendation: as a best practice the debate community should consider replacing the 30-point scale with a suitable standardized alternative such as the 100-point scale (70–100) adopted by Wake Forest in 2007 and 2008.[1]

4. Recommendation: as a best practice, our community should strengthen its support for novice debate competition.

5. Recommendation: as a best practice, our community should mindfully structure tournaments to incentivize values beyond competitive success.

6. Recommendation: as a best practice, tournament information should be centralized and tournaments should utilize the most current tabulation and Web-based platforms.

7. Recommendation: as a best practice, judge placement protocols should use ordinal rankings and seek to have all judges hear their full commitments.

The full resolutions and an extended discussion of them, drawn from notes of the meeting, follow. All resolutions were reviewed and edited by the full committee and, except where otherwise noted, received consensus support. All text that precedes the phrase "final report commentary" was language included in resolutions presented by the Best Practices Working Group and adopted without objection at the Plenary Session of the Developmental Conference. Following the discussion of recommendations is a short report on other items of discussion that did not result in recommendations and an appended list of original agenda questions.

1. Recommendation: A Council of Tournament Directors Should Be Convened to Review Tournament Practice and Publish A "Best Tournament Practices" Document.

Rationale:

• Several issues of tournament procedure, such as calendaring, scheduling,

---

[1] The dates were added during the write-up of the final report and were not reported at the conference.

team composition (including mavericks and hybrids), judging obligations, round pairing (including preset procedures, the evening of brackets, the order of tiebreakers), speaker point scales, judge conflict norms, and others, require ongoing review, research, revision, and innovation.

- There is no other appropriate forum for the presentation and debate of these issues.
- Tournament directors are in the best position to review and implement tournament procedures.
- New tournament directors would benefit greatly from a published list of issues, possible solutions, and best practices.
- The Best Practices Working Group should produce a draft of recommendations as a starting place for the Best Practices document.

Logistical notes: All tournament directors should be invited to participate at a meeting; some virtual connection component should be included so that people not physically present can participate. The Council should be convened at least once annually. Ongoing virtual discussion and document production is appropriate. This year's meeting will occur between the California swing tournaments. The agenda will be to develop a comprehensive list of tournament procedures and recommended practices.

Final Report Commentary

Although the Committee was able to make several specific recommendations, such as the use of a 100-point scale and ordinal judge ratings, a much larger list of issues remains uncodified. These issues will be repeatedly faced by tournament directors without a document offering community guidance on how to handle them. There was support for a draft of the Best Practices document to be created prior to the inaugural meeting of the Council of Tournament Directors, and the presumption was that the Council of Tournament Directors would meet at least yearly to review the extant document for possible revisions and to consider issues not in the document that may have become prominent.

There was a feeling that [the] Council of Tournament Directors should start by codifying the resolutions of the Best Practices Working Group into their initial document.

Undoubtedly, important initial work of the Council of Tournament Directors will be to establish governance procedures, membership requirements, and the like. It is important to note that the Best Practices Working Group felt that tournament directors—and not other actors—were the people who should compose the Council and make recommendations about Best Practices. Although charges of undemocratic governance are all too common in the policy debate community, the Council of Tournament Directors would be a definitive step forward in making the issues, consequences, and community feelings transparent. Absent such a group and such a document, tournament directors must make decisions without any codified procedure and without any community input. The Best Practices Working Group recommends that the Council of Tournament Directors strive to make their decision making inclusive.

Finally, it is worth emphasizing that this group should consider tournament calendar issues. A concern was that no other body seeks to discuss and seek community input on the tournament calendar. A particular issue that gave rise to the Council of Tournament Directors recommendation was a concern that, although novice divisions average 17.4 teams,[2] many divisions have only single-digit entries and that although novice divisions are generally offered, they do not always have large entries. Part of the concern may be that the tournament calendar is not well coordinated in a way that maximizes novice division entry size. This issue in particular, and those like it, are the issues that the Best Practices Working Group charges the Council of Tournament Directors with addressing.

Other issues of discussion in the Best Practices Working Group that the Council of Tournament Directors might address included: The appropriate number of rounds for novice division and the value of workshops in lieu of debates, judge placement in novice division, limited evidence divisions, as well as the issues presented in subsequent resolutions.

2. Recommendation: As a Best Practice, Tournament Competition Administrative Procedures Should Be Transparent and Communicated in Advance of the Tournament.

The problem: During tournaments debaters constantly ask coaches: "When does the next round start? Which round is high-high? Why did I hit the top seed? Where do we go for food? When do the pairings come out? Where do I leave my tubs? How was this round paired?" It's easy to blame the debaters for not keeping track of the tournament book, but sometimes there is a simple lack of

---

[2] Data provided by Brent Brossmann taken from debateresults.com; full data are presented below in Recommendation 4.

transparency. Sometimes the tournament book is overwhelming, making the information less accessible.

It is the conclusion of the Best Practices Working Group that there is a need for more transparency, in the form of easily accessible, relatively standardized information. As a bonus, we think this can serve as a template or checklist for both old and new tournament directors of decisions to be made and items to be communicated to tournament participants.

Implementation: There should be a checklist of decisions that need to be made in planning for a tournament. Much of this can be implemented using a template structure that will be available on Debate RESULTS http://www.debateresults. com. (However, it will not make those procedural decisions for you.)

Final Report Commentary
Particular issues included: The type of judge placement system in use, including the use of judge placement in novice and JV divisions; the release time of pairings, which may be intentionally withheld to facilitate a full lunch or rest break; expectations about the length of disclosure time; how rounds are paired (which, if any rounds, are high-high, etc.); how brackets are evened (how decisions are made about which team will get pulled up, etc.); whether hybrid or maverick debaters are allowed, and if they are, how their results will be tabulated (whether they can clear, whether they are eligible for speaker awards, whether they can win, etc.).

There was a strong feeling that the information should be in a central place, perhaps in a distinctive and independently linked portion the invitation. A particular recommendation was that the debateRESULTS.com http://www.debateresults.com Web site would generate a checklist of particular issues to be decided for tournament directors to complete, perhaps with a link to Best Practices recommendations, and that the information would be presented in a more accessible way for tournament participants. Presently, issues like the number of divisions offered and the round a tournament is expected to clear appear on a quick fact sheet and independently of the invitation. A "tournament rules" page might serve a similar function.

Finally, there was a feeling that some sort of feed might be created to communicate changes and tournament announcements, and that one item of transparency was to identify how tournament information would be distributed.

3. Recommendation: As a Best Practice the Debate Community Should Consider Replacing the 30-point Scale with a Suitable Standardized Alternative such as the 100-point Scale (70–100) Adopted by Wake Forest for 2007 and 2008.

Point Inflation and Compression: It has been a well-known phenomenon that points assigned by judges have been both inflating and compressing in recent years. It is now typical that the standard deviation (the range determined by 2/3s of judge point awarded) is less than 1. At the 2009 National Debate Tournament (NDT) with 3,276 scores, the average was 28.08 and the standard deviation was .54 with over 1/3 of the scores being 28. At the point that the standard deviation approaches the smallest discrimination a judge can make (1/2 point), speaker points lose most of their ability to reliably discriminate performance with the small remaining variability in the points assigned by judges having an amplified and idiosyncratic impact on the outcome, particularly for speaker awards.

Final Report Commentary

Gary Larson provided data concerning the point distribution.

The two central concerns on which there was consensus were: (1) the ballot should be adjusted to allow judges to provide greater discrimination, and (2) a new system should be standardized so that judges could become familiar with it, facilitating cross-tournament consistency.

There were dissenting voices that noted some tension between the two goals. The 100-point scale was possible only because there was not ubiquitous use of the 30-point scale, and other candidates to obtain the goal of greater differentiation do exist, such as the University of Southern California quarter-point scale.

Although the 100-point scale did receive the endorsement of the Best Practices Working Group, and although the Best Practices Working Group did recognize the value in a standard system, there should be some room for tournament directors to continue to experiment and innovate new scales that might provide valid means of differentiating debater performance.

Further, there was some difference of opinion about the data presented. Although the Wake Forest data do show a smooth curve, given the Central Limit Theorem (which states that all large samples tend to take the shape of a normal curve) such results would be expected even given random chance. Scales with 1-standard deviation units might be problematic for some applications, but simply treating the data as categorical rather than continuous is a possible solution. There are many well-established means of analyzing categorical data.

4. Recommendation: As a Best Practice, Our Community Should Strengthen Its Support for Novice Debate Competition.

We should continue to support novice debate. Best practices may include:
- Making a commitment to foster novice debate wherever feasible;
- Developing ways to lower the bar for entry into competitive debate;
- Expanding novice workshops as part of the tournament experience;
- Maintaining the integrity of novice divisions even when entries are very low;
- Rotating judge selection processes through divisions to ensure judge quality;
- Increasing the consistency of speaker point assignments in the novice division by providing guidance to the judging pool.

Tournament directors are providing opportunities for novice debate. In the 2008–9 season, 49 of 76 tournaments (64%) had teams enter a novice division. Sizes ranged from 2 to 49 teams, with a mean size of 17.4 entries and a median of 13. Fifteen of the tournaments had single-digit novice entries, suggesting a need for a stronger commitment to novice debate.

A best practice for developing novice debate is to determine ways to lower the entry bar. Contemporary novice debate practice is to include all options open to varsity debate. This can be overwhelming to people new to the activity. Practices such as using limited evidence pools and employing nondebate graduate students as judges should provide easier transitions into competitive debate.

Another best practice is to encourage novice workshops during tournaments. Reducing the number of competitive rounds by one to provide novices opportunities to discuss new concepts and network with themselves and coaches should enhance education and community.

An effort to maintain the integrity of the novice division is also important. Traditional constraints such as not meeting a team multiple times in preliminary rounds are not as important in novice debate if the alternative is to compete against debaters in higher divisions.

It is also a best practice to rotate the order by which judges are assigned within different divisions. Prioritizing varsity and junior varsity debates in every round would result in novice debaters being judged consistently by critics who are not easily placed.

It is a best practice to create a consistent understanding of how speaker points should be assigned in the novice division relative to the junior varsity and varsity divisions. Tournaments should provide guidance to judges as to whether novice speaker points should be assigned relative to other novice debaters or relative to debaters in the varsity division.

Final Report Commentary
It is worth noting that the recommendation made by the Best Practices Working Group is that "it is also a best practice to rotate the order by which judges are assigned within different divisions." This is not the same as endorsing the use of a mutual preference system in the novice division either identical to or different from a mutual judge placement system in the open division. Indeed, the suggestion that judge pools might also include graduate students without debate training highlights this fact.

As will be discussed in relation to Recommendation 7, there is a need to provide novice competitors with educational judging, but there is also a need to develop judges. A system that excludes certain judges from all divisions is contrary to the goal of developing new judges, who may go on to become coaches or program directors.

5. Recommendation: As a Best Practice, Our Community Should Mindfully Structure Tournaments to Incentivize Values Beyond Competitive Success.
Whereas:
1) Almost all of the community's, and any given program's, discretionary resources are spent on tournaments,
2) Competition is a powerful incentive,
3) The practices and values tournaments currently reward may be relatively narrow, and
4) Our conception of tournament, as limited in time and space may be narrow,

We believe tournaments should use incentives and be structured so as to:
1) Be humane. Adequate time for meals, socializing, and sleep should be guaranteed by a workable schedule.

2) Be safe. Tournaments should account for the need for safe travel to and from the tournament.
3) Create a workable and enforceable schedule that accounts for (in addition to, socializing, and sleep) time spent in tabulation, pre-round preparation, judge decision making, and post-round critiques for both preliminary and elimination rounds. Limits on the length of the overall day should be established; in most instances, this should not exceed twelve hours.
4) Create, in more instances than currently exist, opportunities for service, debate community building, training, public debate, and public research that take advantage of opportunities unique to the gathering of a large number of debaters and coaches in a single location.
5) Consider means of limiting demands on coaches so as to be consistent with the above.

Final Report Commentary
Although less specific than other recommendations, this recommendation was strongly endorsed and motivated by the desire to more thoughtfully consider how our goals as educators match the ways that we reward practice. It recognizes that tournament competition is the overriding motivation that drives almost all of our current practice, and as such the most successful reforms are those that align tournament reward structures with pedagogical goals.

In particular, the Best Practices Working Group felt that tournament schedules should be altered, usually in ways that limited the number of preliminary rounds, such that all tournament participants could get more rest. There was a strong endorsement of enforcing schedule times, and the Best Practices Working Group felt that tournament directors should maintain schedule times even when tournament participants were stretching those times to prepare for any given round.

Two specific practices that were discussed were (1) requiring as a condition of entry that participants demonstrated that they had participated in a public debate during the semester that the tournament is held in, and (2) requiring that an academic paper based on debate-related research be submitted at registration. Those academic papers could be ranked and recognition given for them, or the paper ranking could be included as a tiebreaker. Although the paper ranking task would be large, it is not greater than the conference paper rating tasks of many National Communication Association divisions.

Above all, the Best Practices Working Group feels that far too often tournament practice becomes an end in itself and not a powerful tool that professional educators can use to shape practice in a productive, healthy, and pedagogically enriching way. Greater attention should be given to aligning tournament competitive practice with overall forensic values.

6. Recommendation: As a Best Practice, Tournament Information Should Be Centralized and Tournaments Should Utilize the Most Current Tabulation and Web-based Platforms.

Rationale:
• There are many advantages to a standardized repository for tournament information, including:
   o Facilitation of research due to a standardized format;
   o A single location for important tournament information, including invitations, schedules, and updates, making it easier for tournament participants to find the information they need;
   o Improved sharing of tournament-relevant data with necessary parties, including judge preference information, judge conflict information, tournament updates, etc.;
• Tabulation software that is compatible with Web-based data formats is much more efficient than tabulation software with noncoordinated data formats;
• Those who program the centralized data repositories should share format information to other software developers.

Logistical notes: The current state-of-the-art Web platform is debateresults.com, and the current state-of-the-art tabulation system is the Computer Assisted Tabulation (CAT) program. Programs that are compatible with the CAT and debateresults.com conform to this recommendation.

Final Report Commentary
A number of the Best Practices Working Group's other recommendations require that certain decisions be codified into tournament tabulation software, or that tournament directors have, for example, the ability to communicate on a central portal. This necessitates that tournament directors use the most up-to-date software and tournament participants enter those tournaments through central data portals.

In addition, college policy debate has largely relied on the volunteer work of a relatively small number of programmers to conduct its business in an electronic age. Given this reality, there really is no ready labor force capable of compiling data from disparate formats into a single, comparable data set for the very many times that such data collection would serve the community.

7. Recommendation: As a Best Practice, Judge Placement Protocols Should Use Ordinal Rankings and Seek to Have All Judges Hear Their Full Commitments.

Rationale:

• Ordinal rankings accomplish all of the goals of category-based systems and provide additional flexibility.

• It is disadvantageous to the long-term viability of the judging pool to either overuse highly preferred judges (because it contributes to burnout) or to underuse less preferred judges (because it stunts their professional development).

• For large tournaments, empirical evidence suggests that it is possible to place judges to their full commitment and still provide judging for all teams that, with limited exception, will fall in the top 50th percentile. It is reasonable to expect that a handful of debates (less than 5%) may have judges that are rated by some teams as low as the 67th percentile.[3]

• There is not agreement on whether mutuality or preference should be maximized within the ordinal ranking systems. Some feel that team ratings about judging should be honored to the maximum extent possible and they favor schemes that maximize preference. Others feel that high mutuality and lower preference would reduce judge compression (a team being judged repeatedly by a smaller pool of judges) and argument overspecialization. Tournament directors should pursue their own systems in this regard.

Exceptions: The value to placing all judges to their full commitment notwithstanding,

• It is expected that some judges may judge slightly fewer than their full commitment.

• All tournaments should begin with sufficient rounds of judging in excess of what is necessary to finish the tournament.

• This recommendation should not discourage tournament directors who wish to do so to retain additional judges to improve the quality of the pool, reduce the overall judging load on entered judges, or both.

• These recommendations may not pertain to some tournaments with unique goals (such as round-robins or national championship tournaments).

---

[3] These conclusions are based on data Gary Larson presented concerning the 2008 CEDA national tournament.

Final Report Commentary

Mike Hall and Brent Brossmann presented research evidence that some judge "compression" has occurred; that is, teams are being judged repeatedly by a smaller pool of critics than they have been historically.

Brent Brossmann reported that, when decisions as opposed to rounds debated are considered, for the top two teams at the NDT and Cross Examination Debate Association (CEDA), an average of 10¼ judges rendered 33% of their decisions, and 25¼ judges rendered 56% of their decisions. Each of those teams had different slates of judges with some overlap.

Mike Hall presented historical data from a sampling of large tournaments held in 1967, 1968, and 1969. In 1967 there were 66 total ballots rendered for different teams at common tournaments for a possibility of 66 unique judges. Out of those 66 ballots, there were only 4 judges that any team had more than once and no judge that any team had more than twice. In 1968, there were 58 ballots, 5 judges had judged any team more than once, and only one instance of a judge hearing a single team 3 times. In 1969, 49 ballots were considered and there were 8 judges that heard one team twice and no judge who had heard any individual team more than 3 times. The overall pattern of repeat judging was about 16%. As a caveat, Hall opined that judge compression would be higher if regional tournaments were included in the data set.

A related issue concerns the number of debates that teams participate in. Anecdotal recollections of the committee members cited teams that had competed in as many as 162 rounds in earlier historical eras, mostly the 1970s but also including the early 1980s and late 1960s. Researcher Shruti Chaganti discovered that 2008–9 First Round bid applicants all had competed in between 72 and 112 rounds. If indeed teams in the past had more rounds overall and more rounds at regional tournaments, and contemporary teams have fewer rounds and more rounds at national tournaments, it could well be that there is more judge compression in the contemporary era than there has been in the past.

Others were of the opinion that, regardless of the state of historical research, judge compression is obviously a very real phenomenon at contemporary debate tournaments. A strong consensus emerged that judge compression was not healthy for the overall community. Some feared a "balkanization" where teams of different styles never met before a neutral critic to compare and contrast their differing issues and emphases. Others feared judge overuse—that small numbers of highly preferred judges are increasingly being called on to judge beyond their commitment in order to maximize the preferences of the teams. A final concern was that the need to place highly preferred judges in debates between teams of vastly contrasting styles had the effect of privileging that very small number of debates. As an empirical matter, it was demonstrable that in some instances placing judges in those debates first had the effect of lowering the overall judge ratings for all other debates.

An important consideration to note is that there was widespread consensus that, however team preference was to be maximized, current practice frequently results in a number of judges not fulfilling their full commitment. This is undesirable because it increases the demands on the rest of the judging pool and fails to develop new judges who may not be strongly preferred.

Discussion made it clear that some judges were receiving systematically low preferences because they engaged in undesirable educational practices, while others were being excluded simply because they were unfamiliar to the participants. No resolution on the issue was reached, although this does seem like fertile ground for the Council of Tournament Directors to consider, and in particular some means of distinguishing between new judges who are simply untested with experienced judges who are widely unpreferred is beneficial.

OTHER ISSUES OF DISCUSSION THAT DID NOT RESULT IN RECOMMENDATIONS

There was some discussion of the value of large tournaments. Some expressed the opinion that the debate community as a whole tends to give undue emphasis to tournament size. On the other hand, the power of large tournaments to compel practice that might not otherwise occur (such as requiring evidence of public debate participation as a condition of tournament entry) was also evident.

There was extensive discussion of the relationship and value of national versus regional competition and the fact that teams now compete in fewer rounds than they did historically; there were references to teams that competed in 162 rounds during a season, or attended 17 or more tournaments. Generally, action on this item was referred to the Council of Tournament Directors.

There was much discussion and a strong consensus that more emphasis should be given to the construction of the tournament schedule. In particular, tournament directors should identify pairing release times, round start times, decision times, food break times, and student break times that are realistically reflected in the schedule. That is, the times should give participants a reasonable amount of time to prepare for the rounds after the pairings come out, judges should have an adequate amount of time to reach and communicate a decision, and food breaks should be recognized as a set-aside period of time, not simply as round preparation time. Implementation of this was referred to the debateresults.com Web site, which took charge of creating a "schedule generator" function.

Some discussion concerned the use of a central debate evidence database, with deadlines that enforced limitations on the addition of new evidence. The overall idea was to have a central, Web-based place where teams would upload all of the evidence they intended to read at a tournament, and evidence not posted there was inadmissible. A number of logistical issues were discussed. The overall goal of making tournament preparation more manageable and less all-consuming seemed to enjoy support. There was a concern that during-tournament research demands were contributing to a large degree of burnout and unhealthy practice; an evidence deadline might address this issue. The logistical viability of such a system remains open.

The student academic verification rules were discussed. There seemed to be consensus that some after-NDT academic verification was likely to be required by the NDT Committee.

Appendix: Original Agenda

The following is the informal range of topics the Best Practices Working Group considered as a possible agenda. It is presented here so that future bodies, such as the Council of Tournament Directors, have a documented list of possible issues that they might consider.

PROPOSED AGENDA:
Tournament Scheduling and Entry Considerations

• Available divisions: Is a shortage of novice or JV divisions a problem? If so, what can be done to encourage these divisions and to encourage entries in them?

• District tournaments: What, if any, problems do we presently have with numbers of regional/district-level tournaments? What could be done to encourage greater participation in such tournaments?

• Qualification systems: Should the NDT reconsider the first or second round at-large qualification system?

• Tournament Atmosphere/Structure (Big Picture): How can we best make a debate tournament a livable experience? How many prelim rounds/tournament days are optimal for the invitational tournament? Eight? Seven? Six?

• Tournament Communication: How should tournaments communicate to participants procedures, etc.

• Academic accountability: Are changes necessary in competitive practices relating to academic eligibility? Are changes necessary in applicable rules controlling the number of semesters of tournament eligibility?

• Allowing hybrid/maverick debaters: Do invitational tournaments allow this practice? Is there a reason to make a recommendation to invitational tournaments concerning this practice?

• Judging obligations: Are changes in judging obligation systems necessary to improve the availability/quality of judging at tournaments?

• What is the state of Web-based tournament entry systems? Are changes necessary? What does the future hold?

Tab Room Procedures

• What is the future for tournament tabulation software? PlusTab 2, Tab Room on the PC are being developed.

• What is the future of ballot retrieval. Are there superior ways to distribute ballots and retrieve results? Given the digital transition, what is the future?

• How should rounds be paired? Preliminary rounds could be random or seeded and if seeded a predictable method would be needed.

• What power-matching systems should be used? High-high versus high-low?

- How should brackets be constituted? Should a pull be the weakest opposition records and where should pullups be placed in the new bracket, by pulling up middle to middle and/or bringing leftovers down?
- What are the best judge assignment systems? Should assignment be made by ordinal judge rankings as with the National Debate Tournament?
- Should mutual preference be used? If so how many categories should be used and what should be the size of categories? Or should a system of director's evaluation of judge quality be utilized, as happened in the past and common in high school practice). Should random assignment be considered? Should method vary by round?
- Is speaker point inflation a problem? If so, what is the solution? For example, consideration of a higher point ballot. Other alternatives for ranking for speaker awards could consider opposition wins, combined numbers (e.g., opposition win & high/low speaker points), deviation from judge mean points, ranks.

Tournament Rules & Procedures
- Post-round comments: What feedback system(s) would best provide sound forensic education? Does our community have a problem with civility? Would recommendations in this area be useful? Do we need a community norm concerning the amount of time allocated to post-round discussion?
- What should be the rule for online access during a round of competition? Is there a way to allow online access without facilitating delivery of briefs from out-of-round researchers/coaches? Is this even desirable? Are community norms a strong enough corrective against abusive practices?
- What should be the rule/norm for judge conflict? Are there issues that should be discussed here, or are present norms working sufficiently well? Should competitors be allowed to register a Web-based conflict with a judge, or should such a report always come from the judge? For judges who might be unsure of the community norm, should the norm be made specific?

Debate Program Management
- The digital transition: What are the problems (transporting tubs, environmental implications of paper use, copying costs, in-round management of briefs)? What are the available solutions?
- Recruitment: Is there a need to discuss recruiting practices?
- Evidence collection: Does our community need a standard for source credibility/qualification/conflict of interest or is this properly an in-round subject for argument?

Section III: Community and Organization Building

Consolidating Debate Governance: Working Group Recommendations

Governance Working Group

Chair
Gordon Stables, University of Southern California

Members
Andrew Barnes, Georgia State University
Dan Cronn-Mills, Minnesota State University, Mankato
Terri Easley, Johnson County Community College (KS)
Vik Keenan, Baruch Debate, City University of New York
Eric Morris, Missouri State University
ML Sandoz, Vanderbilt University

INTRODUCTION

The governance working group was asked to explore the status of intercollegiate policy debate associations and recommend improvements in organizational structure. Our working group solicited input from a range of debate organizations and included participation from leadership of several organizations and perspectives drawn from the conference participants. This document presents our conclusions.

Our report offers a summary on the state of organizational governance, looking across the policy debate landscape, and suggests longer-term recommendations concerning systemic change. The report also contains a series of action items that could help the community to function better in the near term. More important, we hope the report can spur community deliberation regarding fundamental changes in how debate administers the activity.

STATUS OF ORGANIZATIONAL GOVERNANCE—HOW DO WE GOVERN?

The challenge of governing intercollegiate debate is frustrated by the decentralized, fragmented, and often overlapping nature of the activity, with authority divided among several organizations. Each policy-debate program decides which policy-debate organizations to join, typically on an annual basis. The mix-and-match system finds most programs joining some or all of the following organizations: the American Forensics Association (AFA), National Debate Tournament (NDT), Cross Examination Debate Association (CEDA), American Debate Association (ADA), and Phi Ro Pi. Moreover, these memberships collectively are not inclusive of all schools that participate in policy debate and fail to integrate with many other organizations that deal with nonpolicy debate.

Each organization has its own emphasis and expertise, self-defining as fulfilling a unique purpose. The memberships define their function with emphases ranging from broad novice participation to selection of a national champion. Yet collectively the memberships combine to form the larger policy-debate community with shared interests.

The structure is characterized by organizational traits that differentially motivate rules and regulations, resulting in disparate statutes across overlapping functions and jurisdiction. Basic student eligibility standards, for example, are generally set by the American Forensics Association, but many of the other organizations also contain clauses that allow them to directly follow or adjust those AFA standards. This ensures that even when one organization acts it often has a direct influence on the activities of the others. For example, when the AFA changed its eligibility rules for intercollegiate competitions, moving from academic time-blocks to academic years, organizations that relied on these rules were largely unaware of the decision to change and then had to scramble to adjust their rules and practices. Technological developments are also making linkages more apparent. For example, as the recording and publication of debate videos are becoming more common, organizations often look to each other to determine fair use standards without logic for who decides.

When organizations attempt to synchronize, coordination is often ad hoc. Each organization was designed to perform certain basic functions for its members (provide regional representation, collect dues, often host a national tournament, determine the rules and standards for its specific competitions, etc.) and each of these functions is repeated in various committees and officer corps across organizations. As organizations mature, other responsibilities are added (antidiscrimination officers, press committees, Web-site management, etc.), exacerbating fragmentation and overlap. The result is a patchwork in which committees and officers that are often motivated to cooperate are nonetheless charged with specific responsibilities and "turf" that compete.

This system might be viewed as benign, an inefficient system without material harm. Yet there are costs. While the number of policy-debate programs is arguably stable, there is also a declining number of full-time forensics professionals who are asked to shoulder these responsibilities. The term "forensics professional" intentionally identifies the historical concept of tenure-track personnel who were expected to engage professional responsibilities as part of their tenure. Certainly nontenure coaches provide such services, often filling the gaps with nonfaculty coaches. Over time, absent institutional commitment from professional directors, we increasingly rely on the goodwill and benevolence of very busy coaches who are not rewarded for such service. There is also a distortion in the nature of volunteer service where the greater numbers of coaches gravitate to jobs directly involving competition-related activities, leaving professional development issues in search of leadership.

Generally, debate organizations are situated to perform their core functions of managing competition, yet they are poorly organized to anticipate and prepare for overarching issues. For example, the media environment requires that debate organizations play a significant role in managing the *brand* of policy debate with outside organizations. Yet it is also apparent that when too many organizations "represent" policy debate with larger audiences, the voice lacks reach, authority, or coherence. For these reasons, we believe that the policy-debate community should consider greater organizational coordination.

STATUS OF ORGANIZATIONAL GOVERNANCE—SIGNS OF INTEREST IN GREATER COORDINATION

Several indicators suggest that there is interest in greater coordination, admittedly in an uneven manner. The 1996 "merger" of the NDT and CEDA is one important sign that the community recognized the problems of dividing governance. Ending a split that had lasted over a quarter century, the two organizations agreed to a common annual topic. The merger produced substantial changes in the debate community, from altering regional travel patterns to influencing the ongoing dynamic of which programs defined themselves as interested in policy debate.

On closer inspection, the CEDA/NDT merger represented the first step toward bringing together institutions that shared community values about the nature of academic debate. It brought schools together that might be regionally proximate, but did not typically compete against one another. The adoption of a joint topic might be considered the *1.0 version of an organizational merger*. The accommodation, however, did not make any effort to streamline how the organizations functioned. Each organization continued to mark its own regional boundaries and elect its distinct national and regional officers. Functionally, each debate program was represented by two separate officials but there was little rationale for the duplication. Even though the member schools were almost an inclusive overlap, they continued to elect two regional representatives, with similar (but not identical) boundaries. In the Southwest, this created issues where schools did not have a single region for local competition. This caused practical problems such as the inability to coordinate local travel planning, and it undermined any effective sense of local governance. While some regions informally took steps to coordinate their efforts, the organizations continued to use two different maps to represent the same programs until 2009. In the spring of 2009 the first efforts to coordinate the regions took place in the Southeast and across the West. Currently the organizations still elect two officers for each region, but these efforts at coordination are the first steps toward a single model of regional governance. The idea that each school would have one regional representative assigned to look after its national interests underlies the concept of a 2.0 merger or a truly integrated national organization.

Jointly hosting national tournaments is another area where greater coordination is needed, and there are small signs of progress. Every spring the NDT, CEDA, ADA, and PRP each host a national championship. Several regions host championships for novice and junior varsity students. Even before considering regional end-of-the-season tournaments or national qualifiers, at least seven tournaments that claim to recognize some form of national champion take place from the end of February until mid-April. At present there is no mechanism to coordinate the scheduling or hosting of these events. Because most of these tournaments rotate hosts, when and where a tournament is hosted can have a tremendous influence on the turnout and composition of the event. This dilemma is even more pronounced because several of the tournaments require so many classrooms that they often can be held only during the host school's spring break.

In 2000 (the fourth year following the CEDA-NDT merger), both national tournaments were hosted in Kansas City. Different institutions hosted each tournament (University of Missouri Kansas City hosted the NDT and Jefferson County Community College hosted CEDA Nationals), but schools could attend both events consecutively in the same city. This has not been repeated, and now the two tournaments are often scheduled on consecutive weekends in very distinct locations. In 2009, for example, many schools made the 1,500 mile trip from Pocatello, Idaho, to Austin, Texas, in one and a half days to compete at both CEDA and the NDT. This is the result of a difficult process of coordinating hosting bids and organizational needs. Again, there are limited signs of progress. In 2010, The University of California at Berkeley will play host to both tournaments, using the same campus and hotel facilities, over an eight-day period. There are certainly advantages and problems of a joint tournament, but the current process has not generally been able to coordinate these tournaments, to say nothing of how the tournaments influence all of the other national and yearend tournaments.

Another important moment in the recognition of a greater need for organizational coordination took place in 2008. A very public controversy involving the internet posting of a video showing an ugly post-round confrontation between coaches and judges at the 2008 CEDA Nationals tournament forced the entire policy-debate community to consider its shared linkages. The incident created a media frenzy that exposed policy debate to a great deal of scrutiny from local media, educational press, and university administrations. Because the incident took place at CEDA Nationals, CEDA was thrust into the role of responding to media and institutional inquires. Understandably the AFA, NDT, PRP, and ADA were concerned about CEDA being the lead organization discussing the matter with the national media and the administrations of member institutions. Simply drawing distinctions between that event and an organization or tournament are nuances that fail to resonate in the larger academic and media conversation. Even within CEDA there was tension about who and how the organization should release public statements.

A year after these events it is apparent that despite pedagogical differences we all share a common brand of policy debate. The passage of a CEDA code of professional conduct, now being modeled by the AFA and by other non–policy-debate organizations, can be seen as recognition that every coach, student, and program is interconnected, aware that our problems cannot be limited to just one tournament, program, or organization.

The final sign of recognition of a need for greater institutional coordination is the conference that has produced this report. The conference grew out of the ideas of the chair of the National Debate Tournament and the leadership of the Cross Examination Debate Association, but it could not have produced so much energy and effort, to say nothing of its large turnout, without a collective sense that debate professionals wanted this event. It was significant not just because it had been so long since the last professional development conference, but also because debate professionals gathered not to talk about the upcoming topic or to have a competition. This larger gathering of professionals, many paying their own way because of limited organizational funding, took place because debate professionals saw the need to move beyond the traditional ways that we gather at tournaments.

STATUS OF ORGANIZATIONAL GOVERNANCE—INTERACTING WITH LARGER COMMUNITIES

The 2008 CEDA Nationals controversy is thus not the only example of how the debate community has trouble communicating with the larger world. Increasingly, there are occasions when outside communities reach out to the policy-debate community and when the policy-debate community wants to speak in larger settings. This section addresses the nature of this challenge in our current model of governance.

Historically, debate professionals have resisted efforts to speak in collective voices, preferring instead to have their own distinct communication strategies, with individual programs favoring autonomy. We are comfortable with selecting champions and relating to individual administrative, community, and alumni support. How one program chooses to explain the rationale for its efforts may differ from its neighbor's, and debate coaches have long respected these differences.

Yet, this decentralized model can create problems when outside actors approach what they perceive to be the single entity of policy debate. If an individual is interested only in a specific tournament, directing that inquiry is easy, but how does one answer a query about the larger community? These are not hypothetical questions. In the past few years, debate coaches and organizations have been approached by media, documentary filmmakers, college sports television networks, network studio writers, organizations hoping to expand debate in historically black colleges and universities, and multimedia companies seeking to expand online debating. Some segments of the debate community may be wary of outside overtures, especially from for-profit organizations, but it would be folly to believe that our well-respected community of colleges and universities should be institutionally incapable of even considering such arrangements.

Currently, we are not legally or organizationally constituted to easily address simple requests such as providing consent forms for filming. We do not retain regular counsel to review contracts. Our organizations are incorporated in states across the union and have varying levels of insurance needed to oversee so many students and professionals each season. We are not yet comfortable answering questions about how our obligations to our home institutions intersect with our collective actions. We also take for granted that just about any member can compete against any other member at a given tournament, but this may not be assured in a world of exclusive contracts. Perhaps more fundamentally, most of our governing documents are almost exclusively focused on managing our competitions.

We are not positioned to consider even basic questions such as: who speaks for us? Simply put, we do not have a procedure for the collective to enter into relationships with other organizations. Many will remember the several-year relationship that the NDT developed with College Sports Television (CSTV). In that case, even when faced with an organization interested in promoting college debate through their network it was difficult for debate to respond. Even after it was decided that the NDT was interested in a partnership, questions persisted about who possessed the legal authority to sign contracts representing the organization and its membership. Even in this best case situation, where an outside media organization is self-motivated to publicize our national tournament, negotiating such an arrangement is very difficult.

The problems involved in the CSTV negotiations illustrate a larger issue. As our information age makes it simpler to distribute information, we see a growing interest in activities that teach critical-thinking skills. Outside actors are unlikely to sympathize with claims that we are institutionally incapable of making collective judgments and signing contracts. It is very likely that if our institutions fail to provide the channels for our member schools to negotiate greater visibility and access to emerging communication technologies, they will negotiate such deals on their own and without collective deliberation.

The responsibility to proactively engage larger communities does not require debate programs and institutions to abandon the many unique characteristics that make competition debating distinct. If an organization is primarily concerned with maximizing opportunities for students who do not have forensics experience in high school, this mission certainly can be reconciled with that of another organization that is primarily interested in determining a national varsity champion. We must find ways to acknowledge our differences, even as we recognize the benefits of enhanced coordination.

WHAT'S NEXT? MOVING TOWARD GREATER COORDINATION

That the college policy-debate community is interested in taking the needed steps toward greater organizational coordination is far from guaranteed. Each of the above-mentioned steps has been marked by controversy, and they are only the beginning of substantive change. As much as we endorse the short-term action items contained in this report, they alone cannot resolve our governance problem. If the community were truly willing to move toward coordination, we would need to accept significant institutional reform of each organization and a redistribution of certain core responsibilities.

At a fundamental level, the community would need to accept the essential principle that "we" are willing to recognize these common linkages in the legitimacy of a single primary organization. This effort will likely involve the delicate balance of a federal model of organization, where each of the current organizations clearly defines itself by its core mission and then agrees to function as part of the larger structure. Each organization should retain its core identity or its unique rationale, a process that could be enhanced by removing redundant legislative tasks. If an organization is interested in promoting debate among students without prior competition experience, it need not also be tasked with regulating each and every debate competition. As the central part of this organizational restructuring, we need to move core functions, such as eligibility, tournament scheduling, questions of educational climate and conduct, publicity, and legal incorporation into some central organization.

The committee was heartened by the response of the conference to the recommendation for increased coordination. Far from dismissing the importance of increased coordination, the assembly encouraged even greater centralization, going as far as strongly recommending the creation of a full-time executive director and staff for this new organization. Ross Smith of Wake Forest University noted the success that other debate organizations, including the National Forensics League and the National Association of Urban Debate Leagues, have employed with this model of a full-time executive complementing the work of the coaching community.

Our working group strongly supports the role that a full-time executive director and staff can play in this new structure. When this suggestion was raised within the individual organizations over the past few years, the question generally turned to the feasibility of generating the funding for salary, benefits, and office needs. This important suggestion would necessitate changes in our basic financial model. At present, most of the debate organizations generate revenue to provide for some annual expenses (such as summer business meetings and annual awards), but the overwhelming economic model is built upon using annual dues to defer the costs of the national tournaments. At present none of the organizations pays full-time staff and when one considers the difference between even the combined budgets of all of the national tournaments and what would be needed for a full-time director, intercollegiate policy-debate organizations will need to pursue a different business model. Rich Edwards of Baylor University noted that the National Forensics League has a much larger base of members, events, and competitors; this broader base allows them to support full-time leadership.

The question of national leadership would require the community determine who would hire this staff, another reason to determine the location of central governance. At present none of the organizations are well-suited to this task. As we surveyed past and present leadership from across each of the organizations, we noted the remarkable extent to which individual experience with a specific organization led officers to conclude that some *other* organization was better suited to this task. Theoretically the challenge is simply to gain consent of the members to make the appropriate legislative changes. In reality, there are two sets of barriers that closely resemble what used to be understood as inherency: structural and attitudinal barriers. Without the tool of fiat, the college community will need to decide how best to overcome these challenges.

To build a unified structure, the college community must be willing to empower the leadership of the AFA, NDT, CEDA, ADA, and other related organizations to begin building these common foundations. The unified structure will also require the identification of individuals who are willing to serve as transitional leadership, especially until a sustainable revenue stream develops.

Each organization has some of the necessary institutional components and all must be willing to cede some of their responsibilities. All of the organizations, for example, build upon sections of the AFA code that include questions of competitor eligibility. Every institution is incorporated and has officers devoted to organizing their records and collecting dues. Most of the organizations have some form of tournament sanctioning procedure, even if many have evolved into perfunctory exercises. Both CEDA and the NDT contain legislative assemblies that provide for local representation. These are tasks that relate to each specific organization, but they also identify areas where a common system would serve the larger community. At the very least, this could work as a federalized system in which the central organization provides clear standards for matters such as competitor eligibility.

To make the needed changes these organizations would revise their governing documents in accordance with a larger organizational blueprint. This would eliminate duplicate positions and committees, and it may necessitate a new no-menclature to describe the interorganizational relationships. It may be instruc-tive to consider each organization as a caucus entity functioning within the larger structure, ensuring that specific interests and preferences are preserved for like-minded members, but allowing uniformity where it makes sense. ADA-sanctioned tournaments would therefore still be able to generate and operate within specific rules to govern their competitions, even as much of the rule making would flow from the unified national system of regional representatives.

It is also not obvious which organization should become the new organizational hub. The NDT would need a major overhaul of its infrastructure, which would force it to be responsible for a great many aspects of debate in which it currently has no involvement. CEDA would need to change cultures, from an organiza-tion that has been historically defined in opposition to other models to a base-line structure. The AFA would need to establish ties to communities of coaches that no longer have historical ties with the organization. The AFA and PRP would need to be dramatically restructured to represent all of intercollegiate debate. Alternatively, the community could choose to create a new organiza-tion. This enjoys some cognitive simplicity, but it very clearly runs the risk of magnifying all of the current coordination problems.

Conclusion: Empower the Organizational Leadership to Start Working

It is far less important what name the central organization uses than that the membership endows it with the legitimacy to truly represent intercollegiate policy debate. The final action step recommended by this committee is to em-power the leadership of each of the policy-debate organizations to function as a working group to begin examining and drafting the specific steps that necessary to represent policy debate in a single entity. These steps should be developed in active coordination with the membership and provide the ability to identify a specific, near-term timeline for the introduction of specific legal and legislative changes.

If each of the organizations played an active role in developing new guidelines, with a process that involves the membership, change could be possible. The scale of the task is daunting, but the importance of this effort requires such ac-tion. Without a coordinated voice, the community will continue to fragment and become a weakened presence when engaging outside entities. While there is surprising consensus regarding the advantages of consolidating governance, without the license to exercise leadership, changes will remain hostage to full schedules and inertia.

Finally, only a unified membership has the possibility to reach out to the larger forensics community. There are substantial pedagogical differences among the programs that define themselves as "policy-debate" programs, but we continue to compete against one another. There are many other institutions that also support forensics but have specific pedagogical goals. In a world with a unified structure there is the possibility of allowing these kinds of disagreements to function naturally and indeed to provide a healthy means of discourse. Imagine how differently high school speech and debate organizations such as the National Forensics League would have evolved if member schools were told that their interest in new forms of debate, such as Lincoln-Douglas or Public Forum, would require them to leave the "policy-debate" community. This is the history of the past few decades of intercollegiate policy debate and it has not made us stronger, just more divided.

It is an exciting thought to imagine a future world of intercollegiate debate where disagreeing about how our students should engage each other does not require leaving one community or one organization. Such changes are possible with greater organizational coordination.

ACTION ITEM: ASSESSMENT IN FORENSICS

The educational foundation of forensics is well-established. Numerous scholars have expounded on the cocurricular nature of the activity (e.g., K. Bartanen 1998; Church 1975; Millsap 1998; Stenger 1999). And as Dreher (2008, 26) notes, "forensics is at its core an educational activity."

Yet both in debate and individual events, forensics is taking little heed of contemporary educational practices. In particular, it is not utilizing contemporary educational assessment practices on a regional or national level. Educational assessment should be second nature to directors of forensics. As Pellegrino, Chudowsky, and Glaser (2001, 2) contend, "assessment is always a process of reasoning from evidence." Reasoning from evidence is a core principle and practice underlying policy debate and individual events.

The request for forensics to engage in assessment practice is not new. More than three decades ago, Mills (1979, 1) argued:

If the area of forensics is to regain its former academic and co-curricular prominence, directors of forensics need to adjust to changing philosophies and needs. They must clarify the aims and goals of forensics programs, *establish the significance of co-curricular offerings in forensics,* and demonstrate that forensics deserves a place of prominence in speech communication departments. (emphasis added)

K. Bartanen (2006) reiterated the need for forensics to engage in programmatic assessment. The need is clear, yet the forensic community has largely failed to engage in rigorous assessment of its practices and standards.

Educational assessment serves a number of specific functions, including the validation of how well students are learning. It justifies the effectiveness of educational practices, establishes high academic standards, and measures the progress of students, programs, and organizations in meeting high academic standards (Pellegrino, Chudowsky, and Glaser 2001).

Zelna and Cousins (n.d.) identify seven reasons to engage in assessment. Assessment serves to:
1. Reinforce or emphasize the mission of your unit
2. Modify, shape, and improve programs and/or performance (formative level)
3. Critique a program's quality or value compared to the program's previously defined principles (summative level)
4. Inform decision making
5. Evaluate programs
6. Assist in the request for additional funds from the university and external community
7. Assist in meeting accreditation requirements, models of best practices, and national benchmarks

All seven reasons should resonate with members of the forensic community (especially no. 6 on requesting additional funds).

Forensics is not at the forefront of contemporary education; it has fallen behind on the very practice at which it excels—reasoning from evidence.

Proposals
The governance working group addressed the issue of the forensics community's engaging in educational assessment. One of the most important forward-looking

steps that the debate community can take is to enhance the sophistication of its assessment techniques. The working group believes that both intercollegiate policy debate and individual events defend themselves primarily through anecdotal evidence. Forensics must participate in the same practices as the rest of the educational community and establish national assessment profiles. The governance working group offers three specific proposals:

Proposal 1
Forensic organizations must participate in the development of national assessment profiles for intercollegiate policy debate and intercollegiate individual events. Rationale: The profiles need to be on a national level rather than owned/controlled by any one forensic organization. Individual forensic organizations may add to the profiles to address components that are unique for the particulars of their debate and/or individual event programs, but the basic foundation should remain stable across all organizations.

Proposal 2
State, regional, and national forensic organizations should contribute funding to support scholar(s) who undertake the task of developing the assessment profiles. Rationale: The creation of the documents will be time intensive, demand particular knowledge sets, and require testing before national distribution/implementation. Such a task is beyond the scope of a volunteer and deserves the time and attention of a funded scholar.

Proposal 3
The forensics community should create an online database for collecting and sharing information gathered from individual programs that use the national profiles. Rationale: A national database enables scholars to coordinate efforts based on the national profiles. The data may be used for local programs, as well as by state, regional, and national associations.

On both the formative and summative level, forensics needs to step to the forefront and engage in systematic educational assessment of student learning outcomes.

In 1990, Kay posed a question that the forensic community has yet to answer: if they are of value to the departments asked to support debate (Kay 1990). Assessment profiles will provide forensics with the evidence to answer the question.

Action Item: Coordinate Community College Nationals and CEDA Nationals

For decades, Phi Rho Pi has been the tournament designated to crown a community college national debate champion. Despite continued support for the tournament division, schools that primarily compete in policy debate have been declining for the past five years. In the past few Phi Rho Phi tournaments, there have been only three schools in the policy-debate division.

Phi Rho Pi is a weeklong tournament that hosts various forms of debate events as well as individual events. The entire event is held at a hotel and a school that exclusively competes in policy debate must commit to an entire week since preliminary debates are scheduled over several days to leave room for other events.

In light of the economic downturn, many schools cannot afford to attend the tournament. The cost of travel to the location, tournament fees, hotel rooms, and meals for eight to nine days amounts to a huge chunk of a program's budget.

Recently, community college directors have sparked efforts to coordinate a championship tournament that would facilitate more participation. Offering a shorter and more cost-efficient championship policy-debate tournament is not meant to deter programs from Phi Rho Pi. Programs that include a variety of formats attend Phi Rho Pi because it is designed for a program that does multiple forensics events.

The governance working group thus offers two proposals:

Proposal 1
The Cross Examination Debate Association National tournament should host a community college breakout at the 2010 CEDA Nationals held at Berkeley. Many community college programs are on the West Coast and more community college programs have attended CEDA Nationals than Phi Rho Pi in the past five years. Adding a day to a tournament most community college programs already attend provides more opportunities at a much lower cost. After the breakout, feedback will be solicited about long-term possibilities for a community college national championship.

Proposal 2
The Cross Examination Debate Association should create a vice president of community college affairs. This officer would serve on the executive council as

a consistent voice for community college programs. Additionally, this position would coordinate future possibilities for a community college championship tournament.

ACTION ITEM: POSITIVE VIDEO CONTENT

While occasional audio and video recording of debates is a long-standing practice, recent events have reopened questions about the value of the practice. Through the 2004-6 CSTV coverage of the NDT, there were several disputes over the availability of particular contestants for video coverage. The most notable event was the 2008 posting on YouTube of a post-round argument between two coaches that brought negative publicity to the forensic community. Reaction to that argument, and the publicly posted debate that preceded it, led to the cancellation of a program and challenges for other programs.

Since 2008, many tournament invitations have included policies on videotaping. The most common policy is to allow video recording by all participants for educational use, including private sharing, but to impose barriers on public posting. While such policies have certainly reduced the number of rounds publicly available, it has preserved a reasonable Web presence of debates. While the 2008 incident vividly demonstrated the ability of one person with a video camera to impact the entire community, the process of determining what is acceptable practice varies by the situation.

Although videos can have a negative impact, such technologies have many potentially positive benefits as well. Videotapes of the better debates could accelerate the learning curve for younger debaters, provide a positive image for external communities, help to include those in the community who cannot afford to attend every tournament (or remain through finals!), and provide a richer sense of community (Morris 2006).

Furthermore, the benefits of video are not limited to formal debates. Many tournament moments, and in particular awards assemblies, provide a positive window into the community. Anyone who has dealt with individuals unfamiliar with debate knows that certain questions recur (Why do they speak so fast? Why do they work so hard?). Having a public, video-based FAQ might provide a useful resource of effective communication with these people.

Public display of video is a balancing act. Students have legitimate concerns about public use and misuse of their images. Preserving a forum where students can make arguments that they might not want tied to their future careers is important. Those who invest time and energy in video recording have reasons for doing so, and those reasons also are an important part of the dialogue. All of these concerns will be balanced inevitably, so balancing them in an open and deliberative process is more likely to lead to agreement about how the community should handle such questions. Clarification of such norms might help the community if there is a future incident comparable to the 2008 one.

The governance working group thus offers two proposals:

Proposal 1
The policy-debate community should authorize and endorse, either through current organizations or newly emerging structures, the creation and distribution of positive video content about policy debate. This content might include answers to commonly asked questions, particular presentations at assemblies, educational presentations from particular camps and coaches, synopses celebrating particular tournaments, and so on. Such video need not be filmed exclusively by community members—it may be possible to encourage amateur filmmakers to get involved through the creation of contests that offer either recognition or small monetary prizes.

Proposal 2
The policy-debate community should develop a more unified community position about private efforts to videotape and distribute debate contest rounds. Such a discussion could include consideration of the following: a process for widespread intracommunity private sharing of video content; clarification of whether tournament competitors have a right either to avoid being recorded or request that recordings not be made available to others; a process for selecting the high-quality debates for public publication; a centralized process of managing permissions for public use of recorded video, including opt-in or opt-out processes for particular students or programs, and so forth.

References
Bartanen, K.M. 1998. "The Place of the Forensics Program in the Liberal Arts College of the Twenty-first Century: An Essay in Honor of Larry E. Norton." *Forensic* 84: 1–16.
Bartanen, M. 2006. "Rigorous Program Assessment in Intercollegiate Forensics: Its Time Has Come." *Forensic* 91: 33–45.
Church, R. 1975. "The Educational Value of Oral Communication Courses and Intercollegiate Forensics: An Opinion Survey of College Prelegal Advisors and Law School Deans." *Argumentation and Advocacy* 12: 49–50.
Dreher, M. 2008. "The Peoria Recommendations: Suggestions on Promotion, Tenure and Evalu-

ation for Directors of Forensics." In *Published Proceedings of the National Developmental Conference on Individual Events*, ed. D. Cronn-Mills, 24–31. Mankato: Minnesota State University.

Kay, J. 1990. "Research and Scholarship in Forensics as Viewed by an Administrator and Former Coach." *National Forensic Journal* 8: 61–68.

Mills, N.H. 1979. "The Role of Forensics in Speech Communication: Reassessment Toward the Future." East Lansing, MI: National Center for Research on Teacher Learning. ERIC Document #ED169596.

Millsap, S. 1998. "The Benefits of Forensics Across the Curriculum: An Opportunity to Expand the Visibility of College Forensics." *Forensic* 84: 17–26.

Morris, E. 2006. "Argue into the Camera, Please: An Exploration of the Prospects and Drawbacks of Comprehensive Digital Recording in Policy Debate." *Contemporary Argumentation and Debate* 27: 148–56.

Pellegrino, P.W.; N. Chudowsky; and R. Glaser, eds. 2001. *Knowing What Students Know: The Science and Design of Educational Assessment*. Washington, DC: National Academies Press.

Stenger, K. 1999. "Forensics as Preparation for Participation in the Academic World." *Forensic* 84: 13–23.

Zelna, C., and P. Cousins. n.d. "Assessing Student Learning Outcomes in Student Conduct." http://www.ncsu.edu/assessment/presentations/student_affairs/stu_con_assessing_outcomes.pdf (accessed June 16, 2009).

Constructing Alumni Networks

Charting Post-Debate Networks Working Group

Chair
Scott Segal, Bracewell & Giuliani LLP, Washington, DC

Report Writer
Michael Hester, University of West Georgia

Members
Dave Arnett, University of California, Berkeley
Sarah Holbrook, University of West Georgia
Geoff Lundeen, University of West Georgia
Andrea Reed, Wake Forest University
Christopher Sedelmyer, Vanderbilt University
John Stubbs, Romulus Global Issues Management, Washington, DC
Elizabeth Wiley, George Washington University

Remote
Brad Hall, Office of Al Gore
Sue Peterson, California State University, Chico
Josh Zive, Bracewell & GiulianiLLP, Washington, DC

Directors of debate programs have never had a problem explaining the value of
the activity. Whenever questioned on the subject, coaches are quick to tick off
the advantages of debate participation: critical thinking and argument formulation, research skills, audience analysis, extemporaneous speaking, organization,
constructive and comprehensive skepticism, and real-time analytical skills.
Rarely missed in such exchanges is the opportunity to drop the names of influential individuals who personally cite the crucial role debate played in their
own lives: nearly every U.S. president and Supreme Court justice, corporate
giants like Lee Iacocca, civil rights leaders such as Malcolm X, even pop-culture
figures such as Harry Connick Jr. "Debate alumni" have served as evidence of
the claim that debate produces an informed, productive citizenry with obvious
benefits for all of society.

Yet, while debate educators have had no problem identifying these debate
alumni as essential contributors to a thriving diverse, liberal democracy, we
have ignored the substantial (human, organizational, financial, and other) resource this pool of talented individuals can be for the forensics community of
their origin. Certainly some schools have wisely maintained contacts with their
alumni (Emory, Northwestern, and Wake Forest stand out as three examples),
with excellent results for program stability and strength. More schools need to
strengthen the bonds with their own debate alumni. But the one area with the

greatest potential (and that until now, has received the least attention) is the intercollegiate relationship with former debate participants. As a *community*, we have not taken advantage of the ties we have with thousands of successful and influential leaders.

Before detailing these advantages, a bit of definitional detail is necessary. What does it mean to be a "debate alum" and what criteria constitute the category? Participation is a broad term that encompasses all manner of action—from the student who sacrificed sweat, tears, and time to win national championships to the kid who never sniffed an elimination round, and may never have had the chance to travel. Is a degree of success necessary? Of course not—the ranks of debate coaching have always been filled with exceptional coaches who were never that successful as debaters. What about the debate "groupie"—the one who showed up at meetings or helped out with tournament-hosting duties but never competed? For the purpose of our analysis, these "topicality" debates are unnecessary and perhaps even detrimental. Self-identification should be privileged, the intrapersonal judgment the standard. Do they consider themselves alumni of our activity? Do good feelings of their time in the activity remain? Can they identify particular skills established or honed from their experiences with debate? If building up alumni networks is our goal, turning away those who self-identify as debaters is a losing strategy.

Our essay is divided into four parts. Part I identifies which groups have special responsibilities to establish and maintain institutional relationships with alumni. Part II explores the advantages these relationships can have for schools and the larger debate community. Part III details one specific project—a Congressional Speech and Debate Caucus (CSDC)—with the potential to transform intercollegiate policy debate's alumni relations into political power. Finally, Part IV briefly provides helpful tips for programs that want to improve their own alumni relations.

PART I: AGENT SPECIFICATION
National Organizations

Whose responsibility is it to maintain alumni relations? We begin at the top—the activity itself, as constituted in national organizations. Currently, policy debate is akin to professional boxing in the 1980s, with multiple "ruling bodies" governing across fluid jurisdictions. There are three organizations: National Debate Tournament (NDT) operating under the rules of the American Forensic Association; the Cross Examination Debate Association (CEDA), which spun off from the NDT community in the 1970s only to be part of the "topic merger" in the 1990s; and the American Debate Association (ADA). Very few, if any, schools competing in intercollegiate policy debate are dues-paying members of only one of these, and many are members of all three organizations. There are other organizations operating at the collegiate level, including the National Educational Debate Association, which emphasizes "debate as a practical educational activity . . . rewarding advocacy skills that would characterize other public forums,"[1] and Phi Rho Pi, which facilitates debate for junior colleges.[2] While recognizing the broad range of forensic activities occurring across the country, our focus is on the intersectional activities of ADA, CEDA, and NDT debate.[3]

Each of these organizations—ADA, CEDA, NDT—has as one of its primary objectives to assist with program growth and maintenance. Clearly the development of strong alumni networks is a direct means by which national organizations can achieve this goal. More important in terms of the function of national debate organizations, awareness is needed that prior experience in the activity makes people *not only alumni of a particular program but of the intercollegiate policy-debate community* as well. Cross-institutional ties already exist informally—the spontaneous conversations occurring when two people meeting in business or other settings discover they each share policy debate in common. Formally facilitating these conversations and establishing networks of debate alumni should be a focus of national debate organizations.

Debate Programs/Coaches
The most successful debate programs have, not coincidentally, been the ones to make the strongest efforts to develop alumni relations. Debate coaches need to be the first contact for debate alumni. Even when coaches are new to the program or were not the coach at the time particular alumni participated, they still share the knowledge of debate itself, giving them the ability to "speak the same language" as the alumni. This common frame of reference gives the coach or director an excellent starting point for establishing communication with alumni. As the leader of the current program, the coach also speaks from a position of

---

[1] See http://www.neda.us.

[2] See http://www.phirhopi.org.

[3] This is not a move of exclusion, but intended merely to focus discussion on these three bodies in order to make the point as to how *these* organizations can be most productive as conduits for public policy debate in the United States. A comprehensive listing of debate organizations would rightly contain the extensive activities at the secondary school level, including the National Forensics League and the National Debate Coaches Association.

authority, representing the debate program alumni to which the alumni feel a connection. Finally, even more so than national organizations, coaches have a strong incentive to maintain alumni relations for purposes of program stability.

University Administrators

Administrators have a stake in claiming debate success for the larger university reputation. This already occurs when school presidents and academic provosts cite accomplishments of the debate team as evidence of the school's academic excellence. The historical reputation of debate as an extracurricular activity emphasizing scholarly traits such as research and critical thinking gives it a unique status compared to other intercollegiate competitions.

Achievements worth promoting do not end at graduation. The successes of debate alumni are fertile ground for administrators seeking to enhance perceptions of their university and looking for models from which to draw inspiration for current student bodies.

University Development

Directors of debate and alumni and advancement departments can perceive each other as rivals, competing for funding from the same alumni sources. Rather than competitors fighting over the same slice of pie, they can act as team with the common goal of strengthening ties with alumni. The responsibility for establishing, improving, and maintaining alumni relations is the very mission of University Development. Combined with the particular knowledge of debate programs, the experience and skills of University Development staff are perfectly suited to the task of growing alumni networks. The key is for these university departments to understand the importance of expanding these networks beyond the walls of individual institutions.

PART II: ADVANTAGES

Like all alumni groups, former debaters can provide resources for programs. Traditionally, alumni are asked to donate monetary resources to the university, whether for scholarships, facility upgrades, or undesignated funds. For many debate alumni establishing successful careers, this normal means of alumni support is a logical conclusion.

But debate alumni have so much more to offer. Career placement is one area where debate alumni can be very helpful. Internships, graduate assistantships, and opening positions hold tremendous potential as an avenue for alumni assistance. Law firms are always seeking intelligent, hardworking young people with experience in argument research; and debaters, like any students, are interested in finding employment. This mutually beneficial relationship is not limited to the field of law. Over the past decade, public policy think tanks in Washington, DC, have provided internship opportunities to graduating debaters, with the Center for Strategic and International Studies being the first to reach out to the debate community (initiated by Harvard alumnus and NDT champion Alex Lennon). Other institutions, such as the Pardee RAND Graduate School of Policy Studies in Santa Monica, California, have followed suit.

Recruitment of capable students into the world of debate is another opportunity for debate alumni to grow the activity. Whether they are children of former debaters or alumni's friends with children interested in debate, alumni can serve as an extension of the university and the policy-debate community, reaching out to draw in future debaters.

Finally, debate alumni can often be resources themselves, in the form of external marketing. Involvement in charitable activities in the local community or simply being a "celebrity" face of debate, alumni can enhance fundraising projects with their support. When coaches and university administrators cite the list of famous people who debated, they are using alumni in this capacity.

In addition to employing debate alumni to garner resources, debate programs can draw upon alumni as sources for recovering institutional memory. "War stories" are not just entertaining ways to pass the time during dinner; oral history is a means of solidifying the bonds between generations of debaters. This sharing creates depth, expanding the scope of programs beyond merely contemporary actors. Of course, alumni can serve in an informal capacity when judging debates at local tournaments or providing advice to young coaches.

Alumni can also step in and serve in a formal management capacity. The experience of the Georgetown University (GU) Debate Program in the early 1990s is a perfect example. Alumni from Emory and Northwestern who were working in Washington, DC, stepped in as "emergency coaches," keeping the Georgetown program afloat and enlisting the help of distinguished GU alumni such as Justice Antonin Scalia to advocate for greater institutional support of the debate program. Their efforts paid off with the hiring of a new director and an NDT championship in 1992. This story resonates perfectly with the notion of former debaters being alumni of the activity, as well as of the schools from which they matriculated. The main players in the Georgetown story did not debate at Georgetown; they just happened to be in a position to step in and save a legendary program. This is the kind of transinstitutional support intercollegiate debate can tap into with proper attention to alumni relations.

While alumni have a lot to contribute to intercollegiate debate, they also receive benefits *from* their reconnection with the activity. The placement opportunities discussed above serve both parties. The students gain employment or at least experience in a potential career field, while the alumni's organization gains from the efforts of the debaters. Human resources promote policy debate, as nondebaters observe firsthand the unique talents debaters offer.

Intangibly, these relationships are invaluable as *relationships* as well. The friends in every town on the tournament schedule, the "nostalgia networking" between alumni able to maintain contact through the debate community, the bonds shared by people who devoted (and for some, continue to devote) their lives to intercollegiate debate—it is no exaggeration to claim that the impacts of such relationships are "decision-rule level impacts," in the nontechnical "it's often why we coach." And the "add-on" advantage of such relationships can be very tangible: retention through mentorship. Being able to draw upon the wisdom of alumni would be an amazing asset for the policy-debate community in addressing recruitment and retention concerns—both of programs and coaches. Their experiences in college debate and the transition from debate to the "real world" (academic or business professional) would be a wellspring for young people trying to follow their successful paths. Lucy Keele, longtime Cal State Fullerton director, has often spoken of the "long gray line" in referencing the NDT organization's makeup of debate alumni. That line is profitably envisioned not as one linear strand but rather as a complex series of interlocking strands traversing back and forth between the communities of academic professionals, current debate programs, and the political and business worlds where former debaters now make their home—a web formed by our shared experience with debate.

PART III: CONGRESSIONAL SPEECH AND DEBATE CAUCUS

As a general proposition, a Congressional Caucus is Congressional membership organization that is bipartisan, bicameral, and dedicated to the advancement of a common interest. The concept of "speech or debate" is actually of constitutional significance to Congress because Members may not be prosecuted for what they say in legislative proceedings—a protection of free speech that predates the First Amendment (Art. I, sec. 6, cl. 1 of the U.S. Constitution).

An elementary listing of general rules for Caucuses (or Congressional Member Organizations) can be found at the House Committee on House Administration Web site at http://cha.house.gov/member_orgs.aspx.

There were several goals suggested for a CSDC. First, we wanted to locate members of Congress who have had significant experience with academic debate and test just how important that experience was to their subsequent careers. Second, we wished to establish lines of communication between the academic debating community and policymakers. These lines could lead to specific activities or transmission of information that may be of use as some of America's brightest students delve deeply into any year's topic. And third, we hoped the CSDC could be an effective mechanism to foster real debate in Congress—operationally defined as reasoned exchanges on public policy that foster bipartisanship. This last point is the most ambitious, but is perhaps the best reason for Congress to establish a caucus when examined from the point of view of the institution.

Anyone who has followed recent debates in Congress can see the need for fostering exchange of ideas across party lines. Climate change, health care, immigration reform, and financial reform are but a few of the issues currently falling victim to a lack of constructive dialogue. On the outside, a few institutions are trying to bridge the gap. One of the best-known groups trying to forge agreement is the Bipartisan Policy Center (see www.bipartisanpolicy.org), which is run by Jason Grumet—a talented fellow, a friend, and, yes, a former debater.

Jason was one of the first people in Washington with whom Scott Segal spoke about the CSDC concept. After some thinking on his own, Jason has graciously offered to assist us by allowing the center to be a platform for putting the caucus together. Given its avowedly bipartisan nature, we cannot think of a better place to germinate ideas, host meetings, and provide some needed organizational support. And frankly this is a great way for our project to get a running start.

PART IV: POST-ROUND ADVICE
The potential for developing broad and deep alumni relations within programs and across the discipline of intercollegiate policy debate is huge. The advantages of such institutionalized ties are varied and significant. But as has often been the case in policy debate, the plan is the key. How do we get from here to there?

When teaching our students how to become better debaters, we are likely to mention two common methods: model the actions of those already succeeding and practice. These same methods apply equally well to the individual institution seeking to improve its own alumni relations.

There are several successful models from which to choose an intended course. The University of California at Berkeley rebuilt a policy-debate program almost from scratch by tapping into an alumni base excited to reconstitute a Bears squad that is, after less than a decade, one of the top five programs in the nation. The debate programs at the University of Kansas, Northwestern University, and Wake Forest University have maintained national preeminence by maintaining strong alumni relations. And Emory University combined alumni relations, corporate sponsorship, and the philanthropic goals of urban debate outreach to create a network unparalleled in its power and performance as a leader in debate and community service. While they have each been extremely successful, these programs also have differing histories and approaches to offer other institutions looking for a template to employ.

Two additional tips can be helpful. First, modern communication tools make the creation and maintenance of alumni networks easier than ever. The Internet is the ultimate tool for networking, with Facebook the principal example. Every university has a Web presence. Using the institution's information technology infrastructure allows debate programs to build off of a sturdy foundation. Creating an alumni information link on the debate home page, including biography sections, and providing alumni with e-mail lists are just a few ideas. The value of using online resources to build and strengthen alumni networks is not limited to individual institutions. National debate organizations already have their own Web presences and can employ the same methods listed above. The Cross Examination Debate Association has used information technologies to successfully expand participation in the topic-formulation process, with CEDA blogs providing real-time updates from the topic committee meetings. Online social networks such as Facebook are already being used by individuals and some debate programs at individual universities; the full potential of such channels has yet to be realized. The key will be coordination between the various organizations, both to reduce inefficient redundancies and to ensure that alumni do not fall through the cracks between the ADA, CEDA, and the NDT.

Second, it is important to give agency to alumni. Rather than be viewed either as one-way recipients for information about the latest accomplishments of the squad or ATMs from which to withdraw another donation, alumni need to be recognized for the variety of roles they can play. Judging or coaching at local tournaments, acting as liaisons between the academic and the political or business arenas, guest speakers for campus events, mentors for young debaters and coaches, and advocates on behalf of debate in conversations with university administrators are just a few of the ways alumni can be positive forces for contemporary debate. Providing alumni with a formal means of communicating and for acting as a singular agent can help maximize this potential. The creation of debate alumni councils directed by alumni as advisory boards to the debate team offers just such a mechanism. At the national level, development of a college debate alumni association with delegates from each college debate program (past and present) might invigorate the process of building cross-institutional alumni networks that could bolster the intercollegiate policy-debate community in the aforementioned ways.

CONCLUSION

Anyone who has ever debated in college has a story to tell about their own experiences with alumni and the thrill it gave them to learn about "the good old days." And those who exhausted their eligibility and whose current debate ego runs only on the fumes of past wins know the vicarious pleasure to be gained from communicating with today's debaters. As a community, we have never lacked appreciation for a good war story. What we *have* lacked is a better sense of organization and (ironically) planning. The need for having better alumni relations and the benefits to be accrued from institutionalizing those ties is not a difficult case to make in front of a debate audience. Attention now must turn to the daily work of establishing and nurturing those connections in ways that benefit the debaters of yesterday, today, and tomorrow. The age of the World Wide Web has given us tools previous generations did not have. With a little work up front, the intercollegiate policy-debate community can make an investment in alumni relations that pays dividends for generations to come. "Standing on the shoulders of giants" is a phrase used to describe the credit given to the leaders of previous eras by current leaders. But before we can stand on them, we must first reach out with a welcoming hand on those shoulders, and reintroduce ourselves.

Appendix: Notable Former Debaters from Various Fields

Lamar Alexander: governor of Tennessee and Republican presidential candidate

Jackson Browne: singer and song writer

Jimmy Carter: president of the United States

Hillary Rodham Clinton: first lady of the United States

William Jefferson Clinton: president of the United States

Harry Connick Jr.: singer and song writer

Admiral Crowe: four-star admiral, chairman of the Joint Chiefs, ambassador to Great Britain

Alan Dershowitz: noted attorney and Harvard law professor

Mark Fabiani: Special Counsel to the White House

Thomas Foley: Speaker of the United States House of Representatives

Bob Graham: governor of Florida and U.S. senator

John Graham: director, Institute for Policy Studies at Harvard

Phil Gramm: U.S. senator and Republican presidential candidate

Arianna Huffington: TV commentator and web page host

Lee Iacocca: CEO, Chrysler

Lady Bird Johnson: first lady of the United States

Lyndon Johnson: president of the United States

Barbara Jordan: U.S. representative

John F. Kennedy: president of the United States

Richard Lugar: U.S. senator and Republican presidential candidate

Michael Mazarr: analyst at the Center for Strategic and International Studies, editor of the *Washington Quarterly*

George McGovern: U.S. senator and Democratic presidential candidate

Zell Miller: governor of Georgia

Richard Morris: political adviser to President Clinton

Edmund Muskie: U.S. senator and presidential candidate

Richard Nixon: president of the United States

Michael Punke: director, Center for Competitive Trade

Ann Richards: governor of Texas

Susan Rook: news anchor for CNN

Franklin Roosevelt: president of the United States

Theodore Roosevelt: president of the United States

Robert Rubin: Secretary of the Treasury

Antonin Scalia: justice of the U.S. Supreme Court

Nadine Stroessen: president, American Civil Liberties Union

Laurence Tribe: preeminent constitutional law scholar

James Q. Wilson: preeminent political scientist and government scholar

Woodrow Wilson: president of the United States

Albert Wynn: U.S. representative

Section IV: Agenda for Policy Debates in the 21st Century

Controversies in Debate Pedagogy: Working Paper

Controversies in Debate Pedagogy Working Group

Chair
Edward M. Panetta, University of Georgia; co-author, William Mosley-Jensen, University of Georgia

Members
Dan Fitzmier, Northwestern University
Sherry Hall, Harvard University
Kevin Kuswa, University of Richmond
Ed Lee, Emory University
David Steinberg, University of Miami (FL)
Fred Sternhagen, Concordia College (MN)
John Turner, Dartmouth College

The debate coaches who convened the first developmental conference at Sedalia in 1974 provided a clear definition of educational benefits associated with teaching debate. They agreed that debate and forensics were educational activities "primarily concerned with using an argumentative perspective in examining problems and communicating with people" (McBath 1975, 11). Thirty-five years later, this educational perspective remains relevant, even if the practice of debate that it engenders may differ radically. Debating and coaching debate still have at their core the competitive examination of public controversies through a communicative exchange.

The second developmental conference echoes the first in its rationale for coaching intercollegiate contest debate: its participants support the activity because it provides the finest education for students interested in thinking critically about common social problems and in communicating those thoughts to others. George Ziegelmueller and Donn Parson defined these goals to "include the acquisition of skills in the evaluation and testing of arguments through rigorous analysis, and in the construction of arguments through synthesis" (1984, 37). They go on to discuss the need for professional coaching positions to support debate, explaining that debate coaches fulfill multiple roles, including student adviser, classroom teacher, and program administrator. Debate is a rigorous activity with rewards that reflect the work and dedication of its participants and their coaches. Debate coaches fulfill a role similar to that of lab leaders in the scientific community. While it may be possible to produce research without the advice and direction of a leader, having a professional lead the research team improves performance and it is often associated with a more enjoyable learning environment.

The underlying reasons educators teach debate have not changed much over the course of the past thirty-five years. We aspire to teach students to think critically about the world around them and to effectively advocate public concerns in a variety of situations. There are, however, new and timely challenges in our collective effort to fulfill our basic mission. Communication has evolved tremendously since the last conference at Northwestern University in 1984 and even more since the first intercollegiate contest debate in the United States took place in 1892. As a communication activity, debate has not been immune to the sweeping changes in the speed, scope, and access to information that have resulted from technological advances and globalization. As we reflect on these changes, coaches need to think carefully not only about how we use technology to retrieve information but also about the effect that technology has on debate and on our students. Technology and information systems are not the only issues confronting debate, however, for the most important elements driving the activity of debate are about pedagogy in general, elements that have been with us since the early debates took place among the Mayans, the Greeks, the Buddhists, and others.

Mirroring a charge levied against the Sophists, many contemporary critics of competitive policy debate believe that our specialized discourse has undermined the teaching of debate as a method of training in public speaking. The rate at which debaters speak is not the only concern raised; there are disagreements about the relationship that debate should have with political activism, what level of responsibility debate educators have to correct historic economic, racial, and gender divides, and debate as a competitive versus a cooperative enterprise. These disagreements require us to ask: What are the educational goals that we hope to share with students when we teach debate? If those goals and the practice of debate differ, what is to be done, if anything? These questions drove our group's dialogue and shaped this document. We do not hope to provide a blueprint for resolving conflicting pedagogical approaches, but rather to provide a framework to facilitate discussion of these issues.

The remainder of this essay will be divided into three sections. The first section isolates the pedagogical goals of debate educators in teaching debate. We connect traditional goals with their contemporary counterparts in the twenty-first century. The second section discusses the growing instances in which argumentative practices may bring some of the goals into conflict. In the third and final section of the paper, we offer suggestions for improving the practice of debate that might alleviate some of the tension between competing modes of debate pedagogy. An essential step in improving the practice of debate is to make a commitment to a set of standards for program self-evaluation.

I. PEDAGOGICAL GOALS OF DEBATE EDUCATORS

The first intercollegiate contest debate in the United States was between Harvard and Yale in 1892 (Ringwalt 1897). By the turn of the twentieth century many colleges and universities were participating in the competitions. As debate become more popular and widespread, its practitioners began to recognize the need for a forum where they could discuss their teaching methods with other professionals in the field, and so the *Quarterly Journal of Public Speaking* was founded in 1915. Shortly after the journal was established, a scholarly debate took place about the goals and practices of intercollegiate contest debating, which centered on many of the same issues we confront today. For example, there were concerns that debating had become insulated from the public and that this distance was damaging to the educational goals of the activity (Atchison and Panetta 2009). For some, the shortsighted emphasis on competition obscured pedagogical goals as well, as instructors were producing much of the material that was used in debates, removing the student from the crucial practice of research (Lane 1915). The *Quarterly Journal of Public Speaking*, the predecessor to the *Quarterly Journal of Speech*, provides a rich source of material regarding this early dispute about debate.

One of the major players expressing his concern that debating was becoming merely a game was William H. Davis, professor of English at Bowdoin College. Davis (1916) agreed that debate can function solely as a game, but that this conception deters the activity from reaching its full potential. For Davis, debate offered a way for individuals to more effectively participate in a democratic society and critically evaluate the world around them. He argued that it was only possible to realize these benefits if debaters and coaches could acknowledge that there is some larger truth and that the research and debate rounds pave the way for our understanding of that truth. If coaches and debaters treat debate merely as a search for a win over their opponents, then they will have lost the recognition that the primary importance of debating is not to emerge victorious, but rather, that one receives a valuable education in preparing for and practicing debate.

In "Game or Counterfeit Presentment?" J.M. O'Neill, professor of rhetoric at the University of Wisconsin, disagreed. He argued that teaching and coaching debate as a game does not limit its value in promoting the democratic character of its participants, but rather paves the way for creating informed citizens. For O'Neill, debate teaches individuals how to locate and articulate positions on both sides of a question without privileging one side. In this way "Facility in the three R's of debating—research, reasoning, and rhetoric—is the proper object of instruction and practice in debate" (O'Neill 1916, 194). Both Davis and O'Neill recognized the extrinsic benefits of participation in debate, although they disagreed on whether the practice of debate as a game allows a realization of larger hopes for the activity. Other authors in the early twentieth century recognized the educational benefits of debate, but did not necessarily take sides on whether or not debate should be viewed as a game. In his *Science and Art of Debate*, Edwin Shurter argues that, "Perhaps no study equals debate in the acquirement of the power of logical thinking combined with clear expression" (1908, 11). Many of these early authors were united by their passionate defense of the capacity of debate to promote reflective thinking on the part of its participants.

Today there remains an agreement that a fundamental goal of the debate educator is to facilitate access to rigorous educational opportunities. Other activities such as athletics, academic competitions, and cocurricular experiences may approximate different pieces of the pedagogy of debate, but the synthesis of intensities emanating from competitive debate may be unique in the academic world. There is a variety of educational opportunities available to our students, and forensic educators have multiple goals related to these positive outcomes. We have loosely grouped the educational benefits that coaches emphasize into three areas: research, participation in contest rounds, and the group interaction that comes from integration into a community. Through this division, we hope to highlight the role that competition plays in intensifying the learning experience and the ways that debate provides a means to absorb and generate meaningful clash in a wide array of contexts. These benefits include exposure to innovations in information processing as well as building such skills as the ability to process large amounts of information quickly and efficiently.[1] In addition and perhaps more important, we connect the benefits of competitive debate to university mission statements that promise to increase students' creative thinking abilities and to broaden their understanding of a global community.

---

[1] One example of new information processing would involve a "paperless" debate system (Hardy 2009), even though the students using such a system are encouraged to flow "on paper" instead of their computers. Computer flowing has become increasingly common as a means of processing arguments in the round, although the students using this technique often go back and forth between paper and screen.

Intercollegiate policy debate demands that participants invest substantial amounts of time in understanding the annual resolution. A policy debater typically begins topic research in July and carries on an active research program into early April of the following year. While there are several forms of intercollegiate debate, most lack the research rigor associated with policy debate. Some forms of student-driven debate, for example, are not structured to support the kind of rigorous research and season-long clash characteristic of policy debate. There is little academic comparison between a yearlong investigation of a policy proposition that hinges on dozens of hours of adjudicated debate at a single tournament and a series of extemporaneous oppositional speeches that often do not require an investment of time to generate cited research. In *Argumentation and Debate*, Austin J. Freeley and David L. Steinberg identify the primary benefit of debate as the promotion of critical thinking, a position supported by many others in the field (e.g., Patterson and Zarefsky 1983). Freeley and Steinberg (2005, 2) define critical thinking as, "The ability to analyze, criticize, and advocate ideas; to reason inductively and deductively; and to reach factual or judgmental conclusions based on sound inferences drawn from unambiguous statements of knowledge of belief." Alfred Snider and Max Schnurer (2006) connect the need to think critically with the increasing volumes of information at our fingertips. They argue that now, more than ever, debate provides a valuable skill in sorting useful research from the vast amount of information that is available. The crucial skill that coaches teach students is how to differentiate between information that is available and research that is credible and useful. Evidence—its credibility and the role it plays in a public controversy—is being tested in the Internet age in a way that we could not have previously imagined (Miller 2002). The interrogation of evidence quality has been a core of the practice of coaching debate for nearly a half-century and it is a skill we continue to share with our students today (Newman and Newman 1969).

Many participants and coaches have noted the benefits that come from teaching students to be good researchers. Freeley and Steinberg (2005) isolate several benefits of teaching students to conduct research, including the development of proficiency in inquiry, the acquisition of a detailed knowledge of contemporary issues, proficiency in writing, and proficiency with computer technology. Teaching students to do research includes providing an advanced understanding of how to use online databases, such as LexisNexis, as well as providing an intimate understanding of the print resources available at a given institution's library. And, as the scholarship on argumentation has evolved to include a number of forms of evidence such as narrative testimony and visual rhetoric, coaches now regularly work with students on debate arguments that include such representations (Blair 2004).

While many benefits can be linked to teaching students systematic research habits, other benefits are accrued by teaching students to effectively use the research in contest rounds. Invention, arrangement, delivery, style, and memory in relationship to the deployment and advocacy of research and evidence in debate can help expand a student's preparation for leadership, training in argumentation, training in critical listening, and reflexive judgment about important social issues (Freeley and Steinberg 2005). One of the widely recognized benefits of participation in contest rounds is the thinking process that is encouraged by the rapid progression of argument and the synchronicity of specific clash in relationship to abstract clash and the meaning of the debate resolution, the ballot, and the process.

Another outgrowth of encouraging critical thinking is that it prepares individuals to effectively participate in a democratic society. Snider and Schnurer (2006), Patterson and Zarefsky (1983), Rogers (2005), and Davis (1916) argue for a connection between teaching debaters to engage in critical thinking and their participation in democracy. Rogers studied the effect that debate training had on a student's participation in basic democratic processes such as voting and found that "Debate students were much more likely to consistently vote in political elections" (Rogers 2005, 16). He also discovered that, "The positive correlation between debate and political volunteerism was strong. Over three-quarters of the debate students were directly involved in political campaigns, party work, and/or student organizations" (ibid.), corroborating with empirical research what many debate coaches have sensed intuitively.

Not surprisingly, many universities make it a goal to prepare their students to adequately participate in American democracy. In its mission statement, the University of Iowa (2005) promises to help undergraduates prepare for life beyond college by "Communicating to them the value of community involvement and participation in democratic governance." The University of Georgia (2007) hopes to shape its students into an "enlightened and educated citizenry," while part of Towson University's (2006) mission statement reads like an endorsement of the democratizing effects of debate: "The liberal arts core, combined with a commitment to students' co-curricular experience, also serves to develop intellectual and social skills that will guide students as contributing members of the workforce and of a democratic society." The ability of debate to produce informed citizens fulfills a mission of colleges and universities, as does the next pedagogical goal of teaching debate, providing individuals with communication skills that can be used in both small and large group settings.

Colleges and universities increasingly emphasize the benefits of smaller class sizes and more contact with teachers for an improved undergraduate learning experience. Participation in intercollegiate policy debate provides an academic setting in which students have significant contact with each other, students from other schools, their coaches, and coaches from across the country. Debate coaches are also able to foster the leadership skills of their students through collaboration on some of the crucial aspects of the team. These skills are highly prized by businesses (Jones 2004; Ross 2002) in that individuals who are capable of thinking critically and working with others are able to successfully tackle challenging assignments. Prominent universities also recognize the value of collaborative interaction and involvement. Among them, Macalester College (n.d.) explains that "Students . . . should be able to apply their understanding of theories to address problems in the larger community." Dartmouth College (2009) connects the need for debate and community, stating as one of their core values the support of "vigorous and open debate of ideas within a community marked by mutual respect." Our students learn to manage a challenging community environment at a relatively young age.

The advantages related to shaping students into productive members of a larger community are not limited to interactions with their own team. Traveling to tournaments provides competitors with access to trained professional educators from across the country, giving them the opportunity to learn not only from their own coaches but also from opposing coaches. As part of the larger community of scholars, professional debate educators, in adjudicating and critiquing the debating of students from around the country, are intellectually responsible to their peers and the debaters of other institutions in an immediate and direct setting. This responsibility is reflected in the goal of teaching all debaters to recognize that they are part of a global, multicultural community. Needless to say, J.M. O'Neill's (1916) call to facilitate the skill of rhetoric is especially important when addressing disparate communities. An underlying rhetorical skill that debate encourages in its students is the ability to adapt to audiences. The application of techniques to address particular problems requires the capacity to assess an audience and to ethically adapt to that group. Dating back to the early days of intercollegiate debate, the first question most students ask after learning the name of the opposition for a debate is who will judge it? For many in debate, this becomes a reflexive exercise that travels with former debaters into their chosen professions. Sensitivity to audience in our increasingly diverse world is an essential life skill.

A number of universities have instituted leadership programs in the past twenty years. As Freeley and Steinberg indicated, the intercollegiate debate program has served as a native site of leadership training for decades. There is a variety of compilations of famous debaters who succeeded in all walks of life that can serve to inspire the current generation of competitors. That wide-ranging list includes: Justice Samuel Alito, musician Jackson Browne, physician Henry Heimlich, Congresswoman Barbara Jordan, broadcaster Jane Pauley, law professor Nadine Strosser, and economist Lawrence Summers. In addition to the leadership function, the debate program is ideally suited to teaching students the methods needed to manage small group communication environments. These skills are needed throughout life and in every interaction, let alone the need to manage a wide range of professional fields in the twenty-first century. We look to small groups to generate the innovations needed to improve the quality of life for humans in all fields of endeavors and a debate program is a site where students work in small groups over the course of several years to puzzle through issues generated by the debate process. The effective coach provides both leadership training and group communication skills to members of the squad. Overall, the pedagogical benefits of debate are significant, both as a result of, and pointing to, an animating level of controversy that continues to drive an interrogation of the benefits, the structure, the purpose, and the unique synthesis and rigor of competitive debate.

II. CONTROVERSY, CONTEMPORARY DEBATE, AND PEDAGOGY

In this section, we highlight a challenge to debate pedagogy: the emergence of argument strategies that do not demand a predetermined point of stasis for a debate to take place. By calling into question this long-standing assumption, advocates of in-round stasis construction maintain that the range of issues and strategies used in a debate is more expansive and educationally enriching for all participants. Alternately, traditionalists would assert that debate loses its defining characteristic, a shared agreement, and becomes simply an argument rather than a rigorous and balanced academic debate.

There are at least three types of debate in which traditionalists would claim that incommensurable approaches are exposed. First, some teams assert they are not required to debate the national policy topic. In such cases, a team posits a claim that some concerns trump the obligation to address the proposition. Second, some teams contest the value of debate as a mode of communication. Debate is treated as a device that allows entrenched authorities to sustain power. Finally, some believe that the space used for contest debates could and should be transformed into a location for political activism, or even replaced by discussion where wins and losses take a backseat to a different meeting of the minds.

Currently, the community is working through what some believe are irreconcilable visions of debate. One vision finds its roots in the contract and National Debate Tournament (NDT) eras of policy debate described by William Keith in his keynote essay to this convention. The traditional approach has evolved throughout the years to the point that the resolution is the agreed-upon point of stasis. In the contract era of debate, elaborate multipage agreements predetermined the points of clash. With the innovation of tournaments where multiple schools could participate, the contract went from an explicit agreement to an implicit one. As the period that Keith describes as the NDT era emerged in the 1950s and 1960s, both the stock issues and the resolution proscribed a well-defined implicit point of stasis for the debates. As policy analysis took root in debate in the 1970s, the stock issues lost their influence, and we were left with the resolution serving as the point of stasis. And, as many readers recall, there was a dispute over the role that the resolution itself should serve in a debate in the 1970s when we worked through the counterwarrants and operational definition of the resolution debates. While that was a dispute about what elements of discussion should be foregrounded, the controversy was no less heated than the issues we look at today when we discuss what the point of clash should be in a debate.

When we step back from the debates themselves and attempt to provide an explanation of some controversial contest debates, we observe a conflict over the role that stasis plays in debate. The traditional perspective operates under the assumption that the annual policy resolution is the point of stasis, and argumentation proceeds from that point. For many who affirm the need for a predetermined point of stasis, there are several important pedagogical benefits. They begin with the assumption that by locating the point of stasis in the resolution, there is a commitment to competitive balance. The point of clash is not something that is crafted by a team to suit its own competitive advantage. Both sides start with a transparent set of issues and their work revolves around exploiting niches in resolution-based argumentation.

Advocates of this approach contend that when the point of stasis is determined in the contest debate, this rewards those who adopt new ground, and the resulting debate may have no link to the substance of the annual proposition. The repetitive set of tactical arguments independent of the resolution, it is argued, undermines the competitive balance constituted by resolution-based debate. And, there are many who would claim that lacking a cooperative moment before a debate leaves one without an actual debate. Scholars in the field of political theory have noted that to think that some element of consensus ends debate is a common misconception. Consensus does not represent a certain agreement. Rather, embedded in a shared agreement are the conditions of debate. By affirming a shared claim, we can thus argue and debate (Shively 2000).

A second pedagogical benefit of the resolution's serving as the point of stasis for a debate is that students learn, in detail, about controversial public policy issues. If one looks back on the list of policy resolutions dating to 1947, the breadth of issues covered by each generation of debaters is truly remarkable. To vacate the role that the resolution plays in policy debate would deny many students, who would like to regularly address the annual resolution in their debates, the educational benefits associated with the interrogation of the political case in controversy. For coaches and students interested in debating a particular set of issues, the topic-selection process affords the entire community the chance to focus on a set of issues for the year.

Traditional policy debate advocates believe a third pedagogical benefit of resolution-based debate is that judges are able to make decisions that are the result of interpreting arguments from within a shared worldview. A team's arguments are discussed in a post-debate critique from within a shared paradigmatic worldview. In arguments between students who do not share a paradigmatic worldview, judges are often left to work through the conflict without a clearly defined and collectively shared roadmap. Some of those debates can be decided, in part, by the worldview the judge brings into the debate, although such decision making is frustrating for both competitors and judges alike.

For adherents to the traditional mode of debate, when one retreats from grounding stasis in the annual proposition, there are two predicted intellectual justifications that surface. First, there is the claim that the existence of a resolution (without substantive content) and time limits is enough of a point of departure to allow for a debate. For traditionalists, this move seems to reduce the existing stasis to the point that it has no real meaning. How does the resolution mold the argument choices of students when one team refuses to acknowledge the argumentative foundation embedded in the sentence? What educational benefit is associated with the articulation of a two-hour and forty-five minute limit for a debate and decision where there is not an agreed point of departure for the initiation of the debate? Second, advocates of moving away from a resolution-based point of stasis contend that valuable arguments do take place. Yes, but that argumentation does not meet some of the core assumptions of a debate for someone who believes that treatment of a stated proposition is a defining element of debate. Participants in a debate need to have some type of loosely shared agreement to focus the clash of arguments in a round of debate. Adherence to this approach does not necessarily call for the rejection of innovative approaches, including the use of individual narratives as a form of support or the metaphorical endorsement of the proposition. This perspective on contest debate does, however, require participants to make an effort to relate a rhetorical strategy to the national topic.

When we step back from the debates themselves and attempt to provide an explanation of the practice, we observe an important pedagogical struggle over the role that stasis plays in debate. The traditional perspective operates under the assumption that the annual policy resolution is a point of stasis, and argumentation proceeds from that point. The critical perspective views a debate as a site where competitors negotiate the stasis. While there are coaches who hold the traditional view, others are committed to the benefits associated with negotiating the point of stasis in the contest debate. And, there is a well-defined rationale for that approach. The alternate path takes root in the critical turn in the university community at large and in the debate community itself beginning in the early 1990s. The critical perspective calls for debaters and judges to interrogate many assumptions often taken as a given in a particular debate round. We will outline a rationale for this perspective that will provide a pedagogical defense of it.

Just as there are benefits to accepting points of stasis prior to a debate, one potentially enriching element in intercollegiate debate involves the possibility of argumentation that simultaneously challenges the loci of agreement for debate and enhances deliberative discussion. In other words, the possibility of debating about the very practices of debates—how to evaluate arguments, the role of the resolution, the meaning of advocacy—is one of debate's essential characteristics. The "debate about debate," or the process of defending and setting competing parameters, can occur in many ways. At times, those decisions occur implicitly or prior to the contest round itself, as when two teams agree that narrating personal experience is the most meaningful way to defend or reject the resolution. In other instances, agreement may be partially constituted through acceptance of speech times and the existence of a common topic, but the role of the judge and the value of particular forms of evidence are debated in the round. This built-in space for reflection gives the debate community access to a set of skills such as critical thinking and the application of creativity, both of which are significant for a deliberative process that matters to everyone and maintains flexibility. Being able to fully defend a perspective, including the framing of that perspective, relies on a nascent public space open to a critique of itself and its own expectations. The public space of debate, conceived more as a public intersection than as a predetermined vision of what a public should be, is certainly built on mutual agreement and common notions of how debates take place, but it is equally built on the capability of debating the validity of its own construction.

This self-reflexive check on debate distinguishes it from other communicative activities, such as conversation. Mari Boor Tonn (2005), professor of rhetoric and communication studies at the University of Richmond, contends that simply conversing over an issue can lend itself to groupthink—who can dominate the conversation?—whereas debate takes principles such as an agreed-upon topic and a competitive platform as starting points for the creation of argument options. Because one of those options includes debating about debate, the significance of the choice of what to say and how to say it is rarely lost on students or coaches. Not only do words and ideas matter, but so does their framing and their arrangement. The idea that a debate could feature an argument questioning the existence of that very form of debate in the first place sounds tautological or even vacuous, but it actually demonstrates the extent to which debaters, coaches, and judges (the debate community) commit themselves to full engagement with a topic. Not only are debates about debate possible in the activity, they occur regularly and are a prominent component in the development of advocacy skills, small-group negotiation, and expressing confidence in an academic setting. Allowing the point of stasis itself to be open to discussion, arguing about what we should debate in the first place, enhances the radically democratic potential inherent in the activity. Our realities are full of norms proclaiming to uphold or improve a given notion of society, a certain stasis to add comfort to our perspective. Norms are contingent upon the context in which they are accepted, gesturing to debate as a crucial means for teaching skepticism and questioning, both of which are able to develop in even more intense and valuable ways through the practice of debating debate. Some may see this defense as an extension of post-structuralism into debate, but it is instead perhaps the inevitable outgrowth of the goal of teaching debaters to critically evaluate the world around them. It then becomes far more intrinsic and far-reaching than simply a contemporary sensibility because the crafting of a space for debate that includes putting itself on the table may be what defines debate.

The effects of allowing debaters themselves to negotiate the point of stasis have been discussed in a variety of contexts. In 2004, *Contemporary Argumentation and Debate* published a series of articles in a forum discussion about the influence of the division between policy and nonpolicy teams in NDT/CEDA debate. These authors discuss the effect that challenging the traditional point of stasis can have on debate practice. In "Debate's Culture of Narcissism," Roger Solt (2004) describes the effects of this division and notes that the clash has produced some challenges to the traditional conceptions of debate pedagogy, but has also presented us with some opportunities.

Some of the challenges include the connection of personal experience to argument, as this may encourage emotional displays and public shouting matches (Parcher 2004; Solt 2004). Jeff Parcher (2004) is concerned with the public character of the disputes and the way that using personal experience as evidence within debates means that arguments against these teams inevitably become personal. When discussing incidents such as these, coaches would be advised to remember that the judges are not the only audience to the debate.

As we move forward, intercollegiate debate faces moments that may fundamentally alter both our practice and pedagogy. For example, policy debate faces a changing informational landscape that brings both increased opportunity and increased scrutiny. Our pedagogical practices stand to benefit from the possibility of remote video debates, growing access to resources, and improved ability to communicate with a larger audience. However, that access comes at the price of exposing internal debates for consumption by parties with little familiarity and no vested interest in the institutions of intercollegiate debate. William Keith cites the danger in designing deliberative forums that participants may be skeptical of participating in an institution that is "just talk" without influence (Keith 2002). For some, deliberation is an impediment to timely action. Contemporary debate faces the opposite dilemma—visibility of unconventional styles raises the question—why aren't you just talking? Yet, the pedagogy of speech communication is rooted in an impulse to democratize communication (Keith 2008). In the strong sense, democratization means the expansion of not only who communicates but also how we communicate (Kohn 2000). Debate educators and participants would be wise to remember that any broadening of how we communicate occurs against the backdrop of whom we are addressing. The overlapping publics that form the audiences for debate (fellow debaters, university supporters, and a larger more anonymous mass public) both empower and constrain our pedagogical choices. The problems of "narrowcasting" and group polarization may arise if we fail to take into account the latent larger public audience on which intercollegiate debate depends for institutional support (Keith 2002). Each argumentative choice may generate new intellectual avenues for our colleagues or raise the ire of an audience. As a result, we should consider both innovation and preservation as pedagogical responsibilities.

The need to balance innovation and preservation was particularly apparent at the 2004 National Debate Tournament where several debates and interviews were filmed by College Sports Television (CSTV). Administrators, alumni, and high-school debaters are a constant set of secondary audiences who are interested in the character of argument in intercollegiate debate. That by itself is not a reason for coaches to discontinue teaching critical argumentation, but it would behoove the community to reflect on Parcher's (2004) and Solt's (2004) concerns that continued division within the debate community harms the pedagogical experience for everyone.

While some in our profession lament the loss of the self-contained policy-debate environment of the 1970s and 1980s, many changes in the practice of debate have enriched the quality of debate. In fact, many of the more interesting debates that take place today are the result of questioning the excesses of modeling the role of public-policy analysis in the 1980s. In any truly democratic system, there will be individuals who dissent against the majority of the community. In some sense, the criticism of debate from within is inevitable given that it provides such a protected space for discussion. If one of the benefits that we hope to promote is the democratic engagement of informed citizens, then the toleration of dissent within the debate community is essential to the toleration of dissent in the public sphere.

The risk of incoherence or a breakdown in respect between debate-community members is balanced by the benefit of the consistent scrutiny that critics have applied to the traditional norms and procedures of debate. Many challenges to the traditional liberal public sphere and its emphasis on formal norms of equality, access, and toleration focus on the absence of substantive equality or participation by groups excluded on the basis of race, gender, class, and sexuality. The university is an important site for debates over affirmative action, diversity, and representation. Intercollegiate debate provides an opportunity to confront issues of identity politics, distributive justice, and collective responsibility where persuasive, rather than executive, means are required. The strongest challenges to traditional paradigms and rhetorical styles within debate have generally arisen from students and coaches who lack the significant resources enjoyed by some (Bruschke 2004). Given the backlash against "political correctness" imposed from above, cultivating an intercollegiate community that consistently positions students to grapple with these issues could provide an important alternative model.

Those who are committed to the traditional conception of intercollegiate policy debate should, in fact, celebrate the opportunity to test argumentation against a diverse range of objections. While this may create some discomfort for participants at the moment a debate is decided, the experience is an invaluable one for the student when measured over a longer period of time. In a diverse world, our students will come face-to-face with a variety of approaches to cases of controversy over their lifetimes. Evolving critical methodologies and argumentative styles that push existing limits create content that follows academic innovations and deepens awareness of scholarship and research programs that might not be familiar academic offerings at the student's own university. All academic institutions (particularly communication departments) run the risk of solidifying a particular paradigm or approach too strongly. Conducting research that is presented and evaluated outside of the classroom environment creates genuine interdisciplinary encounters.

Our mass-mediated information age has transformed competitive debate from a private dialogue into an extended public conversation that can encourage the participation of nondebating students, university administrators, alumni, and other community members. While this phenomenon attests to the power of competitive debate to galvanize and facilitate public-policy deliberation, the ease of recording debate performance and the potential for the global distribution of those conversations should force coaches and students to reflect on the speech.

Intercollegiate debate provides a safe space for students and teachers to interrogate the controversial issues of our time. It encourages and supports students who are taking risks in their advocacy and working to improve as researchers, speakers, and leaders. As competitive debate expands to more fully include in its membership people with varied and distinct worldviews, the norms of debate practice will continue to be challenged. This should be celebrated and cultivated because competitive intercollegiate debate is one of the few educational venues that provides students with the opportunity to challenge social and political norms. As always, this development should be celebrated with the cautionary note that our speech must continue to account for the impact it has on secondary and tertiary audiences.

Debates occur in a globalized public space where recordings of these events can be made readily available for observation and commentary by anyone with Internet access. Student dialogue is not always a protected temporality of speech, but Internet availability also allows intercollegiate debate to serve as a galvanizing force for the participation of other stakeholders in our conversations about controversial issues. The democratization of information technology exponentially expands the ability of each of us to influence not only our immediate but also our global communities. As educators, we must teach our students that their speech in this environment is indeed public. This is not to say that all of those risks should be avoided but that they should be acknowledged and understood. One responsibility of debate educators is to preserve a respectful space that encourages others to add their voice to the conversation and does not jeopardize the opportunity of other debaters.

While some may lament the current status of intercollegiate policy debate, we believe that the skills associated with debate are put to good use by alumni. Those trained in debate can make public arguments in support of their position. They are also aware of the profound impact that a distinct audience can play on the outcome of an argument. Whether speaking at a local school-board meeting or addressing the Supreme Court of the United States, debate alumni use the skills acquired through rigorous training to improve the world in which they live.

Other criticisms of debate from within include perspectives on its gender and racial disparities, a criticism that hits at the heart of many universities' emphasis on diversity. The difference between discussions of these issues in a typical academic setting as compared to their discussion within a debate is that in a debate they cannot simply be externalized as outside of the matter at hand, but rather must be confronted at that time and place. In this way debate is self-reflexive about its commitment to diversity and provides a useful forum for challenges to a traditional and privileged mainstream.

III. Reconciling Contemporary Practice and Traditional Pedagogical Goals

While we strongly endorse the benefits associated with debate, there is a need to acknowledge some of the problems the community faces. There are debates in which there is very little genuine argument. When teams start from incommensurable worldviews, the benefits of debate are limited. And, for more than a half century there has been a criticism that intercollegiate debate is an exercise in speed-reading that has forgotten the value of teaching students about persuading a public audience. This is a recurrent concern expressed both by alumni and by people with a passing interest in the activity. For example, a recent feature story written by a sympathetic author on the debate program at the University of Georgia highlighted a point–counterpoint between noted alumni on the virtues of speed in debate. Former governor Roy Barnes lamented the introduction of speed debate in the 1960s while former Christian Coalition leader Ralph Reed acknowledged the advantages of his capacity to speak quickly (Johnston 2008).

In this section, we frame a series of suggested points of contemplation by hitchhiking on the three Rs of debate—rhetoric, research, and reasoning— proposed by J.M. O'Neill in 1916. Audience is a core concept tied to any definition of rhetoric. We affirm the need to respect everyone participating in the community. From there we look at the continuing evolution of research in debate. Our immediate concern is the erosion of tests of evidence credibility in debate, which reflects the age of Internet evidence. Finally, we take a self-reflective look at the reasoning skills we share with students. Our suggestion is that programs engage in self-assessment of not only the reasoning skills we share with students but also a wide-ranging set of issues that impact the operation of a debate program.

One of the core values of intercollegiate debate is that it encourages participants to develop an ability to understand, appreciate, and respect different perspectives on substantive controversies as well as different approaches to the competitive activity. A key aspect to competitive success is to be aware of what one is answering, thus debaters must necessarily identify and evaluate the arguments that the other side is making. This need to appreciate different perspectives applies to three aspects of the debate process: the issues, the other team, and the audience. Criticisms of debate practice that focus on the delivery of the participants argue that debate is disconnected from an analysis of audience, but ignore the ways that debate promotes an externally oriented perspective of the world.

The debate process facilitates the ability to understand different perspectives on issues in many ways. The fact that the debater switches sides and debates both sides of a question develops an appreciation of the fact that there are some valid arguments in support of most issues. In addition to the impact that advocating a variety of positions has on understanding different perspectives on issues, researching one's response to an opponent's claims also furthers this goal. The intensive research that a debater conducts in preparing for competition usually begins with reading the sources in support of the opposition. A thorough understanding of what the other side is contending and what warrants are employed to defend those claims is a critical aspect of crafting a successful response. The desire to win an argument in a competitive format provides a unique incentive to seek out the rationale for perspectives on issues that may differ from the preconceived ideas that the debater brings to the enterprise.

Debate also fosters greater respect for one's opponents, contributing to another advantage of the debate process—the ability to disagree with someone in a civil manner. If one can understand and appreciate difference, one is more inclined to rely on the tools of debate and argumentation—reasoning, research, and rhetoric—to answer the disputed claim.

Our students must learn how to understand, appreciate, and respect alternate perspectives on issues that are controversial. While many in our profession are able and willing to defend the contemporary debate experience (with or without rapid-fire delivery styles) to be a rigorous academic exchange, it would be wise for coaches to show how debaters can adapt to a debate that is an open public exchange of ideas. While the actual contest debate may be a highly technical discursive exchange, debaters should be encouraged to find communicative outlets to improve speaking skills and to hone audience-adaptation techniques.

While the twenty-first century has complicated our understanding of audience, it has also called into question what we define as appropriate debate research and the methods used to share and store that material. We are interested in the evolving formatting of what is presented as evidence in debate. While our group is not uniformly in support of a system of open-source debate it is an issue we briefly address here. Making evidence more usable for novices is something that coaches need to further consider. Regardless of the outcome of the open-source matter, coaches need to reflect on ways to make research more usable for our novices. One possibility is that of using evidence packets for novice divisions. This would be designed to lower the entry-level barriers to participation in policy debate, which, even at the novice level, can be steep. The use of packets could lower the dropout rates of novice debaters in at least two ways: first, packets would increase the predictability of arguments in the novice division, making the likelihood of clash higher, and second, packets would decrease the research burdens on novice debaters.

Another concern of the working group is the need to reflect on the production of evidence and the transition to an alternative evidence type that is different from the traditional "card." Utilizing the citation standards of, for example, an academic essay, has been suggested as a way that debaters could paraphrase evidence rather than relying on a direct quotation (Solt 2004). The benefits of this might include a more easily accessible presentation style that is more closely related to speaking in public rather than for an elite audience, and it also would comprise excellent preparation for academic work. The current debate practice of using a short quotation often focuses the debate on what is said or how much is said, rather than on who said it. While there are some debates about qualifications, these are not as widespread as one might think, given that all evidence is presented essentially as a testimonial. Using a more stringent method of qualification and the presentation of papers, akin to that at an academic conference, might increase the role that coaches have in teaching students about the quality of information that they find. Viewing the production of evidence more as a production of academic material would encourage students to internalize the information that they research and provide an argument with that information.

Another issue the coaching community may confront in the next few years is a move to open-source debate. This system is conceptualized as a system that expands current case-listing efforts to include the full piece of evidence that is used in the debate. There are weaker and stronger versions of open-source debate. The weakest versions could include something like a post-tournament, once-a-semester submission of evidence that has been read to that point. The strongest versions of the system would be a submission of any new pieces of evidence that have been read after every debate at every tournament, a system that would also take considerably more work to process and police. One variant of open-source debate that may be attractive to individuals wanting to honor the work of the most competitive debaters while correcting increasingly lax academic standards would be to construct a system where individuals would provide the full-text version of articles from which they have pulled quotations. While this would make the retrieval of their evidence relatively easy when combined with a traditional citation, it could alleviate some concerns over free-riders who did little to no work, and would also allow individuals to more easily access the context of the source that is being quoted. An open-source system might allow coaches at smaller programs to shift some of their valuable time away from researching or leading research efforts and more toward the rewarding work of strategy discussions with the debaters. Coaches may be able to increase their focus on teaching students how arguments are constructed as well as briefing them on the basics of an argument, as there would be a pool of readily available resources from which they could draw. Additionally, an open-source system might encourage more coaches to focus on the public-speaking component of debate.

Some in our group have reservations about both the operation of an open-source system and its effect on the coaching profession. Some believe that open-source debate might reduce the incentive for debaters to do their own work. Others are concerned that the uploading of information might not be done in a timely and transparent fashion. Finally, there is a lingering concern that while technology is always sold as an improvement of the work environment, we often find ourselves increasingly tethered to technology and our need to produce yet more research for debates with each new wave of innovation.

It is also important to acknowledge that among the growing requisites to participation in intercollegiate debate, participation in high-school debate is now among them (Brushcke 2004). Further expanding the scope of participants beyond individuals with a high-school-debate background would broaden the educational reach of debate as well as provide increased opportunities for traditionally disadvantaged populations to participate. Strong novice programs require the active involvement of an engaged coach, as fellow students rarely have the time to coach novices as well as maintain their academic and competitive duties.

O'Neill's claim of debate's capacity to teach reasoning skills is something that coaches have trumpeted for generations. We work in an era in which academic programs with a portfolio of rigorous systematic evaluations will receive support from university administrations, granting agencies, and our own alumni. Our evaluation process should assess not only the reasoning skills we attempt to impart, but the entire range of pedagogical objectives addressed in this essay. In addition to evaluating our pedagogical goals, a review program should evaluate our progress in successfully implementing changes in debate praxis. There are a few questions that should be addressed in any assessment program. For example, does debate as we practice it genuinely achieve the stated goals outlined in this essay? And, are our choices in teaching, coaching, and directing debate guided by information and/or tradition? Debate coaches are true believers in our art, and have experience and intuition to support what we do. Some positive research (although limited) provides support for the educational values of debate, but, obviously, that practice is not without its critics or skeptics.

Since the days of Protagoras, educators, students, and interested observers have valued the educational benefits of participating in debate. Those engaged in contemporary competitive, evidence-based policy debate are deeply convinced of its merits. Our experience provides strong anecdotal evidence that we do achieve the myriad of learning objectives identified earlier in this essay. Nevertheless, there has been limited systematic investigation that tests our practices in achieving those educational aims. And while the limited research provided does tend to provide support for debate practice in achieving enhanced cognitive skills and values (Chandler and Hobbs 1991; Colbert 2002), positive results are not unquestioned (Greenstreet 1992). Quite simply, more study is needed.

For reasons of accountability, and to improve our ability to select the best available practices for achieving our objectives, ongoing review and introspective study are recommended. While such study may support the activity of debate as it is practiced, conducting research on the educational outcomes of debate participation should not presuppose positive results. Just as we will learn from positive support for our intuitive belief in debate, the discovery of harmful consequences of debate practice or lack of support for debate practice may guide our ability as debate educators to improve the experience for our students.

Opportunities for the publication and dissemination of new findings through our conferences abound. And, participation in such research and scholarship should promote the professional development and institutional support for many debate programs. Further, participation in systematic research about the success of debate provides opportunities for partnerships across the academy, not only among the community of debate scholars but also with professionals in educational leadership and research, sociology, psychology, political science, and other disciplines.

Many coaches collect the statements of debate students and alumni, letters of support from constituencies that we serve, and employers and graduate and professional school teachers of our students and alumni. Such stories and testimonies provide materials for public relations and program promotion. However, if systematically collected, coded, and organized, the same subjects could provide material appropriate for genuine evaluation of our success in designing practices to achieve goals. Research should not be limited to one approach: qualitative and quantitative methods are warranted, and data may be gathered from longitudinal investigation, interviews, survey data, focus groups, testing, and generally, all available resources. The input of students who do not continue in debate should be sought, as well as the rationales of institutional administrators and faculty who elect to discontinue programs.

Beyond simply engaging in research about the large-scale practice of debate, we also have to be aware of the goals that our programs hope to achieve. The role of debate educator presents a variety of responsibilities. These roles include coaching individual debaters and debate teams but should not be limited to that role. Educators working within debate programs minimally face the responsibility for program maintenance. Hopefully, they will be able to strengthen the debate program's ability to foster learning opportunities for participating students. Controversy about practice is certainly not new to academic debate, appearing almost simultaneously with its emergence. Our goal is not to suggest ways to eliminate controversial practices. We not only doubt our ability to accomplish such a goal, we do not believe that it is desirable to eliminate controversy. Academic debate's grounding within dialectic and free speech means that vigorous testing of ideas is a desirable outcome—not a problem to be eliminated. Of course, controversy needs to be managed in ways that are balanced against the other goals of debate and the concerns of external constituencies.

We would suggest that debate professionals pursue systematized methods for program evaluation that would both help to approach areas of controversy positively and, more generally, provide information for program decision makers. Without attempting a comprehensive review of program-evaluation scholarship, we would suggest these principles as guides for program evaluation.
• *Program evaluation should be contextual.* Different programs pursue a variety of appropriate goals, serve diverse stakeholder groups, and deal with different limitations and constraints. Effective program evaluation should respond to those contextual differences.
• *Program evaluation should include considerations for program development and growth and not be limited to concerns for program continuation.* While there is an appropriate role for summative decisions about program continuation, it is a mistake to see summative concerns as the sole issue for evaluation. Rather

we would hope to strengthen the arguments we make about debate programs and, consequently, improve decision making regarding practices within those programs.

• *Debate educators should carefully consider what evidence is used to corroborate program outcomes.* We are uncomfortable with the types of data widely used to support conclusions concerning the benefits of academic debate. This caution should not be read only as a call for more quantitative data. While such data can be useful, program-evaluation specialists support the gathering and use of diverse types of evidence. The evidence might well be gathered through ethnographic narratives, interviews, or other qualitative methods.

• *Program evaluation should not be conceptualized only as goal identification and measurement of goal attainment.* Again, we do not mean to advocate a particular model; rather, we seek to widen the scope of options that might be considered. For example, debate programs might consider Robert Stake's responsive-evaluation model, constructivist evaluation, or Ernest House's deliberative-democratic evaluation. Returning to the theme of controversies in debate, we would emphasize that our intention is to provide tools that would help debate coaches and debate programs make reasoned decisions about controversial practices and, more broadly, the outcomes achieved by debate programs. Toward that end, we have attempted to identify a common set of pedagogical goals that debate educators pursue, to track contemporary practices that conflict with those goals, and to provide some suggestions as to how to harmonize the practice of debate with the goals that we have set out.

Like our predecessors who met at Sedalia, Colorado, and Northwestern University, we remain committed to teaching students how to use an argumentative perspective to address cases in controversy. While, at times, we struggle to have the practice of intercollegiate policy debate reflect all of these pedagogical objectives, there are thousands of policy debates that take place annually in which students exhibit an understanding and respect for the audience, in which the use of compelling and innovative research focuses the discussion, and in which students use reasoning skills to clarify complex policy issues. By maintaining a commitment to an argumentative approach, we can and should be able to continue to navigate the inevitable professional disagreements that often define our chosen profession.

References

Atchison, R., and Panetta, E. 2009. "Intercollegiate Debate and Speech Communication: Historical Development and Issues for the Future." In *Handbook of Rhetoric*, ed. A. Lansford and J. Aune, 317–34. Thousand Oaks, CA: Sage.

Blair, J.A. 2004. "The Rhetoric of Visual Arguments." In *Defining Visual Rhetorics*, ed. C. Hill and M. Helmers, 41–63. Mahwah, NJ: Lawrence Erlbaum.

Bruschke, J. 2004. "Debate Factions and Affirmative Actions." *Contemporary Argumentation and Debate* 25: 78–87.

Chandler, R.C., and J.D. Hobbs. 1991. "The Benefits of Intercollegiate Policy Debate Training to Various Professions." "In *Argument in Controversy: Proceedings of the Seventh SCA/AFA Conference on Argumentation*, ed. Donn Parson, 388–90. Annandale, VA: Special Communication Association.

Colbert, Kent R. 2002. "Enhancing Critical Thinking Ability Through Academic Debate." In *Perspectives in Controversy, Selected Essays from Contemporary Argumentation and Debate*, ed. K. Broda-Bahm, 71–100. New York: IDEA.

Dartmouth College. 2009. "Dartmouth's Mission Statement." http://www.dartmouth.edu/~presoff/mission/ (accessed May 29, 2009).

Davis, W. 1916. "Is Debating Primarily a Game?" *Quarterly Journal of Public Speaking* 2, no. 2: 171–79.

Freeley, A.J., and D.L. Steinberg. 2005. *Argumentation and Debate*. Belmont, CA: Thomson Wadsworth.

Greenstreet, R. 1992. "Academic Debate and Critical Thinking: A Look at the Evidence." Paper presented at the Twelfth International Conference on Critical Thinking and Educational Reform, Rhonert Park, CA, August 9–12.

Hardy, A. 2009. "Paperless Debate: A How-to Manual." http://www.whitman.edu/rhetoric/tech/paperless-complete-manual.pdf (accessed May 26, 2010).

Johnston, L. 2008. "Fighting Words." *Georgia Magazine*. http://uga.edu/gm/ee/index.php?/single/2008/06/30/ (accessed June 3, 2009).

Jones, D. 2004. "Debating Skills Come in Handy in Business." *USA Today*, September 30, p. 3B.

Keith, W. 2002. "Democratic Revival and the Promise of Cyberspace: Lessons from the Forum Movement." *Rhetoric & Public Affairs* 5, no. 2: 311–26.

———. 2008. "On the Origins of Speech as a Discipline: James A. Winans and Public Speaking as Practical Democracy." *Rhetoric Society Quarterly* 38, no. 3: 239–58.

Kohn, M. 2000. "Language, Power, and Persuasion: Toward a Critique of Deliberative Democracy." *Constellations* 7, no. 3: 408–29.

Lane, F. 1915. "Faculty Help in Intercollegiate Contests." *Quarterly Journal of Public Speaking*, 1, no. 1: 9.

Macalester College. n.d."Statement of Purpose and Belief." http://www.macalester.edu/about/purpose.html (accessed May 29, 2009).

McBath, J.H. 1975. *Forensics as Communication: The Argumentative Perspective*. Skokie, IL: National Textbook.

Miller, S. 2002. "Conspiracy Theories: Public Argument as Coded Social Critiques. A Rhetorical Analysis of the TWA Flight 800 Conspiracy Theories." *Argumentation and Advocacy* 39: 40–56.

Newman, R.P., and D.R. Newman. 1969. *Evidence*. Boston: Houghton Mifflin.

O'Neill, J.M. 1916. "Game or Counterfeit Presentment?" *Quarterly Journal of Public Speaking* 2, no. 2: 193–97.

Parcher, J. 2004. "Factions in Policy Debate: Some Observations." *Contemporary Argumentation and Debate* 25: 89–94.

Patterson, J.W., and D. Zarefsky. 1983. *Contemporary Debate*. Boston: Houghton Mifflin.

Ringwalt, R. 1897. "Intercollegiate Debating." *Forum* 22: 633.

Rogers, J.E. 2005. "Graduate School, Professional, and Life Choices: An Outcome Assessment Confirmation Study Measuring Positive Student Outcomes Beyond Student Experiences for Participants in Competitive Intercollegiate Forensics." *Contemporary Argumentation and Debate* 26: 13–40.

Ross, S. 2002. "College Debaters Get Head Start on Exec Track." Reuters, June 3.

Shively, R.L. 2000. "Political Theory and the Postmodern Politics of Ambiguity." In *Political Theory and Partisan Politics*, ed. E. Ponts, A. Gundersen, and R.L. Shivley, 173–90. Albany: State University of New York Press.

Shurter, E.D. 1908. *Science and Art of Debate*. New York and Washington, DC: Neale.

Snider, A., and M. Schnurer. 2006. *Many Sides: Debate Across the Curriculum*. New York: International Debate Education Association.

Solt, R. 2004. "Debate's Culture of Narcissism." *Contemporary Argumentation and Debate* 25: 43–65.

Tonn, M.B. 2005. "Taking Conversation, Dialogue, and Therapy Public." *Rhetoric and Public Affairs* 8, no. 3: 405–30.

Towson University. 2006. "Towson University Mission Statement." http://www.towson.edu/main/abouttu/glance/mission.asp (accessed May 26, 2010).

University of Georgia, Board of Regents. 2007. "Mission Statement." http://www.usg.edu/inst/uga/mission.phtml (accessed May 29, 2009).

University of Iowa. 2005. "The Iowa Promise: A Strategic Plan for the University of Iowa 2005–2010." http://www.uiowa.edu/homepage/news/strategic-plans/strat-plan-05-10/goals/undergrad.html (accessed May 29, 2009).

Ziegelmueller, G., and D. Parson. 1984. "Strengthening Educational Goals and Programs." In *American Forensics in Perspective: Papers from the Second National Conference on Forensics*, ed. D. Parson, 37–48. Annandale, VA: Speech Communication Association.

Alternative Debate Models: Working Group Summary

Participation–Alternative Models Working Group

Chair
Allan D. Louden, Wake Forest University

Author
Theodore Albiniak, University of Southern California

Members
Chris Baron, Baltimore Urban Debate League
Nicole Williams Barnes, National Debate Project, Atlanta
Daryl Burch, Towson University
John W. Davis, Debate Solutions, Baltimore
Lawrence Grandpre, Whitman College
Beth Skinner, Towson University
Ron Von Burg, Christopher Newport University
Anjali Vats, Washington Debate Coalition/University of Puget Sound

As these conference proceedings surely demonstrate, the twenty-first century terrain that debate negotiates looks drastically different than it did when the community last convened in 1985. One of our community's biggest innovations since the first and second Debate Development Conferences—and the focus of this working group—has been the introduction and development of what are commonly referred to as "alternative models" of policy debate. Our working group operationalized the term "alternative models" to include all efforts aimed at expanding the scope of policy-debate participation beyond traditional inter-collegiate tournament competition. These include, but are not limited to: (a) efforts to expand participation in the form of urban debate leagues and prison-debate projects; (b) curricular efforts to expand debate's place in the academy; and (c) public debates geared toward an audience other than that for tourna-ment competition.[1] This section summarizes three separate tasks undertaken by this working group. First, we offer some recommendations for considering alter-native debate models as necessary and invaluable contributions to programs and universities as they develop in the twenty-first century. In particular, we suggest that programs consider the role of alternative models as part of the movement to establish a civic-engagement curriculum at the university level. Second, we highlight some key skills cultivated by policy debate that fit within the concept of civic engagement. Finally, we present outlines of articles solicited from indi-

---

[1] See Anjali Vats in this volume for a more extensive list and a historical review of current alternative debate models (pp. 376–98) .

viduals working directly with these models, and offering their advice, feedback, and suggestions for future development.

MAINTAINING RELEVANCE

Policy debaters usually credit participation in the activity as the single most important factor in their academic achievement and successes beyond. Debate is difficult, time consuming, and complex. The vast amount of research, on-the-spot critical-thinking skills, and full-weekend commitment make intercollegiate travel an option only for the select few who can, and choose to, make it a real part of their educational experience. Given its complex structure and the specialization that accompanies it, traditional tournament competition operates largely in isolation from the departments that house them. Unlike other intercollegiate competitive activities, policy debate lacks a strong public-relations component, making our successes difficult to translate to a wider audience. But, as tournament travel costs and budget requests increase, our community faces a very real challenge: what happens to competitive debate programs if departments no longer possess the funds or the institutional will to sustain the traditional, insulated-competitive model? As conference keynote speaker William Keith aptly argued in "A New Golden Age," defending debate relevance amid a wave of budget cuts and criticism of its insulation could be our biggest challenge well into the twenty-first century.

It is important to note that this trend is not unique to policy-debate culture but plagues the university system as a whole. Universities and higher-education systems increasingly play defensive roles vis-à-vis government agencies, media, and community leaders to both demonstrate and justify the utility of nonapplied, non–revenue-generating research (Chatterton 2000). One example of this attempt to move from a reactive to a proactive stance is the major effort by many universities to change their image from that of an elite institution that simply occupies space in a neighborhood to the image of active community members in their surrounding areas. The establishment of university community-relations departments and partnership with local secondary-education institutions at administrative levels could quickly trickle down to a departmental level, where individual programs will need to demonstrate active engagement in the surrounding community (Soto, Lum, and Campbell 2009). Alternative policy-debate models are well situated not only to meet this need but also to play a role as a creative and innovative solution. As many of our contributing experts note, the central feature of alternative models of policy debate is that they bring undergraduate students and faculty together with members of local communities in direct and engaged academic conversation (whether high-schools students, incarcerated populations, online communities, or the public). This active and collaborative dialogue with nontraditional university communities could form the cornerstone of a university's effort to define its worth for a social environment outside of the research and athletic contexts.

The importance of alternative models exceeds the community involvement they generate. In fact, they are also preeminent examples of newer trends within higher education to develop students' civic and advocacy skills. While there is perhaps a typical generational fear of youth apathy, a comprehensive review of current literature (Galston 2001; Kahne and Sporte 2008) demonstrates a real disintegration of democratic awareness and civic interest among all generations in the twenty-first century. Innovative programs that cultivate the motivation, skills, and network connections for a successful democratic citizenry (Verba, Scholzman, and Brady 1995) will play an increasingly important role in constituting an inclusive and active democratic politics. Alternative debate models could reflect and drive the university and community interest in promoting *civic engagement*.

DEFINING CIVIC ENGAGEMENT

Understandings of civic-engagement programs are often contextually determined. Some scholars describe the term expansively as "those activities which individual academics undertake which in some way involve interaction or engagement with the non-academic community and are related to academic expertise" (Bond and Paterson 2005, 338). This experiential model focuses less on offering access to information about politics or the political system and more on crafting opportunities to understand information about the political world in a format where the utility of such knowledge is immediately apparent (Dudley and Gitelson 2003). The expressed goal should not be about increasing involvement in traditional democratic channels (voting, campaign work, etc.) but should instead be about providing avenues for participation that would both inspire a commitment to learning about the political world and fostering experiences where such knowledge is deployed for the purposes of problem solving (Flanagan and Gallay 1995). The hope is that such an effort will encourage participants to become actively engaged in the world in ways that cultivate creativity and investment in the democratic process.

Policy-debate programs nurture the skills necessary for such a critically engaged citizenry. In addition to the content focused on understanding government policy, the critical-thinking, research, and presentation skills crucial to competitive success in intercollegiate policy debate and developed in alternative models are also essential to advocating and adjudicating issues in democratic deliberations. Our working group also chose to identify the following characteristics that solidify the role of alternative debate models in cultivating civic engagement:

Cultivates public speaking and presentation. Individuals often say they fear public speaking more than death. Policy debate necessitates that students overcome this fear by requiring them both to speak to a live audience and to advance well-researched positions subject to adjudication. Unlike other activities that bolster public-speaking and presentation skills, policy debate emphasizes the importance of advocacy and responding, in a timely fashion, to other well-supported arguments. Policy debate requires interlocutors to be confident in both *what* is said and *how* it is said, a precondition to effective civic participation. When coupled with efforts to include underrepresented communities, those skills become crucial toward developing a political voice and offering a space to exercise that civic agency outside of traditional democratic channels.

Increases service learning. Debate encourages specialized policy experts and students to work with community members to cultivate a knowledge of the political world and offers a process of argumentative presentation and resolution that offers immediately apparent benefits either in the form of competitive success or audience appreciation and participation. Most participants usually agree that working with an urban debate league, in a public-debate setting, or with participation of underrepresented communities directly increases the possibility of competitive success through teaching moments.

Establishes a dialogic climate. Policy debate uses the process of deliberation and discussion to resolve contemporary issues of public concern. This unique communicative climate offers the possibility of reflection and interaction that can serve the interests of multiple parties. Taken outside of an intercollegiate tournament setting, this method can inspire a number of institutional linkages and create a complex interaction between students, educators, and the public. This mutually beneficial partnership between academics and served communities can be an important experiential element of conflict resolution in the context of the political world.

Fosters cross-disciplinary scholarship. Alternative debate models utilize research from multiple academic disciplines, experts in alternate fields, and personal and cultural narratives as evidence for truth claims. This harmonious integration of knowledge across the curriculum is invaluable for recognizing linkages between disparate departments within a method that can highlight the utility for interdisciplinary scholarship.

Promotes critical media literacy. Alternative models teach students not only how to use online sources but also how to evaluate the credibility of those sources and to compare competing truth claims. As more and more information becomes digitized and civic-engagement opportunities take place in online communities, participation in alternative debate models teaches students how to interact with information and each other in a new and invaluable way. Whether through information integration (using multiple types of media to craft arguments), evaluation of the credentials of blogs, or the use of new information platforms to host debates, alternative debate models are at the forefront of crafting critical media skills.

Based on this preliminary investigation, alternative debate models not only reflect efforts to enhance civic engagement but also go above and beyond. Bringing academic experts and specialists into dialogue with underrepresented communities for the purpose of cultivating knowledge, experiences, and processes of exploring the political world is obviously beneficial. Coupling these skills with the requirement to synthesize and organize that information and present it to an audience for the purposes of public discussion, community problem solving, or competitive success enhances the capacity to participate in politics by making the knowledge of the political process seem immediately useful rather than abstractly irrelevant. Alternative models also encourage additional efforts to work with communities to provide services that solve local needs and develop new kinds of skills that will enhance democratic participation as it inevitably changes in the twenty-first century.

SUMMARY AND RECOMMENDATIONS

This conference demonstrated the continued strength and commitment of our community to usher in a new era for policy-debate practice. At the same time, it inspired some important reflections necessary to maintain the health of policy debate. As universities continue to face pressure to diversify their missions, one direction may be in the establishment of university partnerships that cultivate relationships with different or nonacademic communities. Policy debate redefined itself years ago by establishing alternative models beyond intercollegiate tournament competition to include participation with underrepresented groups and members of our local communities. These alternative debate models can be a premiere example of civic-engagement programs that bring the academy and the public together in mutually beneficial conversation that enhances civic knowledge and the democratic process.

Despite the potential benefits of alternative debate models, roadblocks still hinder further development. An informal survey of more than 40 coaches and directors administered by this working group demonstrated that, across the board, each program supports some model: hosting public debates, encouraging students to participate in urban debate leagues, working with underrepresented populations, and others. But the same survey also indicates that such commitments require significant trade-offs in resource and time investments to make those efforts permanent. Further difficulties emerge in convincing intercollegiate debaters to add on other commitments that distract from tournament competition and academic achievement. Finally, the survey indicates that generating audience participation may make the idea of alternative debate models attractive but limit their effectiveness in execution.

Each concern is real. However, this working group recommends that programmatic shifts toward alternative debate models should be sustained and accelerated. The invited essays which follow in sections V–VII provide advice for the development of alternative models and their future viability, grounded in models happening around the nation and world.

References

Bond, R., and L. Paterson. 2005. "Coming Down from the Ivory Tower? Academics' Civic and Economic Engagement with the Community." *Oxford Review of Education* 31, no. 3: 331–51.

Chatterton, P. 2000. "The Cultural Role of Universities in the Community: Revisiting the University-Community Debate." *Environment and Planning A* 32, no. 1: 165–81.

Dudley, R.L., and A.R. Gitelson. 2003. "Civic Education, Civic Engagement, and Youth Civic Development." *Political Science and Politics* 36, no. 2: 263–67.

Flanagan, C.A., and L.S. Gallay. 1995. "Reframing the Meaning of 'Political' in Research with Adolescents." In *Perspectives in Political Science: New Directions in Political Socialization Research*, ed. M. Hepburn, 34–41. New York: Oxford University Press.

Galston, W. 2001. "Political Knowledge, Political Engagement, and Civic Education." *Annual Review of Political Science* 4: 217–34.

Kahne, J.E., and S.E. Sporte. 2008. "Developing Citizens: The Impact of Civic Learning Opportunities on Students' Commitment to Civic Participation." *American Educational Research Journal* 45, no. 3: 738–66.

Soto, A.C.; C. Lum; and P.S. Campbell. 2009. "A University-School Music Partnership for Music Education Majors in a Culturally Distinctive Community." *Journal of Research in Music Education* 56, no. 4: 338–56.

Verba, S.; K. Lehman Schlozman; and H.E. Brady. 1995. *Voice and Equality, Civic Voluntarism in American Politics*. Cambridge, MA: Harvard University Press.

Civic Engagement Through Policy Debate: Possibilities for Transformation

Participation–Alternative Models Working Group

Author
Anjali Vats, Washington Debate Coalition, Seattle, and University of Puget Sound

Despite the intense time and competition requirements of modern policy debate, more of the policy-debate community is moving away from an exclusively tournament-focused model of the activity.[1] As demonstrated by the survey conducted by the work group, civic engagement through policy debate is becoming a community norm as opposed to an isolated practice that characterizes particular teams. Perhaps even more significantly, policy-debate-related civic-engagement activities are becoming increasingly diverse and creative endeavors. Urban debate leagues (UDLs) continue to be an integral and invaluable part of the movement to use policy debate as a means of civic engagement. However, instead of stopping at volunteering with local UDLs or organizing public debates, debate teams and former debaters continue to craft innovative organizations and events to respond to the wants and needs of their students and communities.

The trend toward participation and innovation in civic engagement through policy debate certainly suggests that debate programs see value in expanding their horizons beyond tournament competition. One of the primary goals of the work group was to articulate and highlight some of the most interesting and innovative trends in activities that use policy debate as a means of civic engagement and examine the ways in which such activities can enhance the pedagogical benefits of policy debate, generate value added for college and university administrators, and serve as a stepping-stone to a more inclusive, empathetic, and diverse debate community.[2]

---

[1] This work group was not the first to comment on the trend among college debate teams toward moving outside of the boundaries of tournament competition. For example, Joe Bellon (2002) commented on "activist and outreach programs sponsored by college debate programs" in the context of "Debate Across the Curriculum."

[2] The examples cited in this article are by no means exhaustive or intended to diminish efforts that are not discussed in depth. Rather, a few innovative examples of policy debate as a means of civic engagement are discussed as exemplars. Nonetheless, in an effort to provide a more complete picture of the diverse array of ways in which debate can serve as a means of civic engagement, a catalog of organizations and activities that move beyond a tournament model of policy debate has been included in this book. Debate teams are encouraged to use the catalog as a means of informing and improving their civic-engagement activities.

Theodore Albiniak, in his summary of the alternative debate models work group, defines civic engagement as "those activities which individual academics undertake which in some way involve interaction or engagement with the non-academic community and are related to academic expertise (Bond & Peterson 2005, 338). In this article I embrace that definition, examining the ways in which academic debate can be used as a tool to engage with the community at large.

Initially I explore the concept of civic engagement as employed by policy debaters in a historic context, beginning with the establishment of the country's first UDLs. Second, I advocate for a civic engagement model of debate, highlighting previous calls for a community oriented element in the activity. Finally using prison debates as a case study, I demonstrate the value of civic engagement for debates, community members, and colleges and universities.

Policy Debate and Civic Engagement in a Historic Context
The first UDLs took root in the United States in the early to mid-1980s in Atlanta, Detroit, and Philadelphia (NAUDL 2007). Perhaps responding to the call at the Second National Debate Development Conference that "[t]he benefits of forensics should be available to all persons regardless of ethnicity, race, gender, or handicaps" (Ziegelmueller and Parson 1984, 43). The urban debate movement sought, among other goals, to provide inner city youth with opportunities that they otherwise would not have had to learn critical-thinking skills and participate in a competitive, academically oriented extracurricular activity (Breger 1998, 66–68).

In 1997, George Soros's Open Society Institute (OSI) recognized the transformative potential of interscholastic policy debate and began funding UDLs across the country. Beth Breger of the OSI identified debate as a "crucial empowerment tool for youth" and explained that "[d]ebate enables students to present their views effectively . . . respond to the arguments of those who disagree with them . . . [and] command attention with words" (ibid.). Breger also wrote that debate fosters intercommunity communication, which can become "the bridge across the chasms of difference" and "give these students the tools to stimulate social change" (ibid.). Since 1997 when OSI began supporting UDLs, the face of debate has changed dramatically. There are currently UDLs in more than fourteen major cities, including Dallas, Denver, Seattle, St. Louis, Detroit, New York, and Atlanta (NAUDL 2007). As Will Baker discusses in "Toward an Understanding of the Landscape of Debate Expansion in Urban Areas and Opportunities for the Collegiate Community" (pp. 253–61), each of those UDLs has unique programming developed to suit the needs of its students.

Attempts to use policy debate as a means of civic engagement have not stopped at urban debate. Prison debate projects, such as the one sponsored by the University of Georgia, aim to empower incarcerated youth and reduce recidivism (Georgia Debate Union 2008). The Women's Debate Institute, founded by former debaters, strives to close the gender gap in debate and empower women, both in and out of the activity (Women's Debate Institute 2008). Debate across the curriculum programs aim to incorporate debate into multiple disciplines in order to empower students, improve their knowledge base and communication skills, and teach conflict-resolution techniques (Bellon 2000). The Washington Debate Coalition, founded by debate coaches and former debaters, attempts to build statewide partnerships between debate and nondebate organizations and uses debate as a means of encouraging civic participation (Washington Debate Coalition 2009). *The Debaters*, a Canadian radio program, takes debate to the airwaves and attracts an audience through comedy (CBC Radio Canada 2009). Cooperative projects between the federal government and debate programs, such as agency-sponsored public debates, aim to give debaters a voice in policymaking (Debate Solutions 2008). International debate organizations such as the International Debate Education Association encourage debate competitions that cross borders and cultures (IDEA 2006).

TOWARD A CIVIC-ENGAGEMENT MODEL OF DEBATE

Gordon Mitchell argues, in a 1998 article titled "Pedagogical Possibilities for Argumentative Agency in Academic Debate," that while the academic space of debate affords debaters opportunities to learn, taken to its logical limits, the "sterile laboratory" metaphor of policy debate results in a "spectator posture" that is "highlighted during episodes of alienation in which debaters cheer news of human suffering or misfortune" (Mitchell 1998, 3). According to Mitchell, competitive zeal overwhelms empathy, and, instead of becoming citizen advocates, students lose their civic voices and agency (ibid.). The Second National Debate Development Conference reached a similar conclusion, stating that policy debate breeds "those who are highly articulate but morally insensitive" (Sanoff 1984, 69–70). According to the Second National Debate Development Conference, the tendency of policy debate to create apathetic individuals belies the mission of the activity and "[f]orensics works best and maintains its mission only when it addresses the whole person" (Goodnight 1984, 96).

Despite fears that debate will breed intellectually successful yet unfeeling members of society, the survey conducted by the work group demonstrates that virtually all debate teams are participating in some type of civic-engagement project. UDLs, prison debates, women in debate, community partnerships to facilitate debate, debate across the curriculum, government–debater cooperation, radio debates, and international debates fit key criteria for civic engagement such as the encouragement of knowledge acquisition, informed democratic participation, student empowerment, cross-community communication, and equality of education. Policy debaters have begun to tackle significant social-justice issues and embrace means of connecting with groups inside and outside of the debate community. Nonetheless, the surveys reflect that the extent of these civic-engagement projects varies dramatically and is, in some cases, only sporadic.

Accordingly, even though the trend in the policy-debate community is toward participating in civic-engagement activities, the process of educating students who are both highly articulate and morally sensitive can succeed only if such efforts are consistent and sustained. Given the many benefits of participating in civic-engagement projects, policy-debate teams have no shortage of incentives to follow the trend. The work group concluded that civic-engagement activities not only benefit those outside of debate in the community at large but also provide pedagogical benefits for debaters and their audiences; generate value added for colleges and universities, thus justifying well-funded debate programs; and aid in creating a more empathetic and diverse debate community.

The work group noted that debaters and audiences learn skills by participating in nontournament activities in which they might not otherwise engage. For example, public debates force students to communicate with a variety of audiences; organizing UDL tournaments allows students to practice their real world problem-solving abilities; debating in front of diverse groups aids students in understanding and ultimately empathizing with those around them. Involvement with civic-engagement activities also teaches students vital nonprofit and community organizing skills that can aid them in the working world. These benefits and experiential advantages alone make civic engagement a valuable endeavor. In addition, the benefits of debate to the audience cannot be underestimated. Debate empowers audience members to form and articulate opinions and creates a safe space for discussion of controversial issues. In many cases, debate also provides audience members with a powerful and socially acceptable means of making their voices heard.

Further, engaging with the community demonstrates to college and university administrators that policy debate has benefits beyond the classroom and accomplishes social justice goals for society at large. As Theodore Albiniak note in "Alternative Debate Models" (pp. 236–41), colleges and universities are increasingly describing their goals in the context of social justice and community activism as well as education and research; showcasing the benefits of civic engagement through policy debate can demonstrate to institutions of higher education that the activity plays a vital role in their missions. Indeed, the work group noted that colleges and universities that perceive policy debate as integral to their missions and an asset to their public-relations campaigns are more likely to fund and support their debate teams.

Utilizing policy debate as a means of civic engagement also benefits the policy-debate community by fostering important values such as inclusivity, empathy, and diversity. Civic-engagement programs serve as a means to connect debaters to local and global communities and encourage groups that might not ordinarily participate in policy debate to take part in the activity (Breger 1998). Debaters that are exposed to and take the time to understand the experiences of their fellow competitors are more likely to be welcoming instead of adversarial and purely competitive (ibid.). Linking communities and fostering connections between debaters also encourages students from diverse backgrounds who might otherwise quit debate to stay in the activity despite its flaws, again helping to promote positive values in the policy-debate community.

CASE STUDY: PRISON DEBATES

The example of prison debates demonstrates the multiple benefits of civic engagement identified by the work group. First, prison debates have educational benefits for the students and prisoners who participate in them. Students have the opportunity to spearhead and organize efforts to debate in prisons and conduct research on issues of pressing concern to prisoners and society generally. Students also empirically improve their communication skills when they are required to be cognizant of the likely audience response to the arguments they are making (Logue 1989).[3] Prison debates offer benefits for inmates as well. In explaining the benefits of a prison debate program organized with Towson University, Dan Murray, the principal of the Maryland Penitentiary's school stated:

---

[3] Logue also cites the realization of one student that she "couldn't defense police brutality with cattle prods, etc." to an audience of inmates. While such a revelation may seem obvious to many, debaters in the insular environment of the debate tournament may not develop the skill of tailoring their arguments to their audience.

The men have been in maximum lockup for 20–25 years and they still have viewpoints of the world in the 1960's. These debates expose them to current issues . . . the men are in a professional, formal atmosphere. . . . The debates enhance the intellectual approach of the men (Logue 1989, 5).[4]

The debates provided the prisoners with an invaluable forum to voice their opinions and engage in mutually respectful dialogue with students (ibid.).

Prison debates can also demonstrate to college and university administrators that debate brings valuable programming into the community and encourages civic engagement. Indeed, existing prison-debate programs, such as the Malcolm X Prison Debate Project (2009) in New York City, call on students to help inmates recognize their intellectual potential while in prison; address the exclusion of prisoners from the civic process, thus reducing recidivism; and aid former inmates in transitioning to a life outside of prison once they are released. These goals not only move debate outside the insular world of tournament debating but they also directly relate to the missions and goals of many colleges and universities as articulated by Albiniak.

Finally, prison debates provide a unique and well-documented opportunity for students and prisoners to develop a sense of empathy and responsibility to the community. Debaters who participated in the prison-debate program at Towson University reported that they were able to confront their stereotypes about prisoners, develop an understanding of themselves, and appreciate the need to make debate more accessible to the public (Logue 1989). One recurring realization among the debaters was that the prisoners were intelligent individuals with the intellectual ability to understand and participate in the debates (ibid.). This opportunity for mutual respect and understanding can serve as a springboard for students to practice empathy, and, inclusively, in all parts of their lives. Robert James Branham, late professor of rhetoric at Bates College, best explains the transformative potential of prison debates in the context of civil-rights leader Malcolm X:

In an environment of near-total control and regimentation, speech and debate activities are rare and significant acts of self-determination and resistance. In both prison and society at-large, Malcolm X invested great significance in the power of confrontational speech to enact personal and social transformation. (Branham 1995, 118)

---

[4] While the prison debates provided many benefits for the prisoners, it is worth nothing that the one disadvantage articulated by the inmates was that the debaters, largely white, upper-middle-class students, represented a part of society with which the men could not personally relate.

CONCLUSION

While there is no shortage of literature discussing the obstacles to utilizing debate as a means of social transformation (Warner and Bruschke 2001), the work group unanimously expressed the opinion that civic engagement through debate provides the best opportunity for demonstrating the continuing relevance of policy debate to students, administrators, and society at large in the face of increasing pressure to justify the benefits of the activity. Indeed, if debate teams and former debaters continue to craft creative and innovative means of civic engagement, policy debate can adapt in order to meet, and even exceed, the needs of administrators, debaters, and local communities without fundamentally transforming core characteristics of the activity such as encouraging in-depth research, fostering critical-thinking skills, adhering to strict time limits, and training students to become empowered advocates. By embracing methods of civic engagement through policy debate, in the words of Jon Bruschke, director of debate at California State University, Fullerton, and Ede Warner, director of debate at the University of Louisville, "academic debate will become a stronger, more positive force" (ibid., 21).

References

Bellon, J. 2000. "A Research-based Justification for Debate Across the Curriculum." *Argumentation and Advocacy* 36, no. 3: 161–75.

Bond, R., and L. Peters, 2005 "Coming Down from the Ivory Tower? Academics' Civil and Economic Engagement with the Community." *Oxford Review of Education* 31, no. 3: 331–51.

Branham, R.J. 1995. "'I Was Gone on Debating': Malcolm X's Prison Debates and Public Confrontations." *Argumentation and Advocacy* 31, no. 3: 117–37.

Breger, B. 1998. "Building Open Societies Through Debate." *Contemporary Argumentation and Debate* 19: 66–68.

CBC Radio Canada. 2009. "The Debaters." http://www.cbc.ca/thedebaters/ (accessed June 25, 2009).

Debate Solutions. 2008. Public Performances and Exhibition Debates. http://www.debatesolutions.com/program_development/public_performance.php (accessed June 26, 2009).

Georgia Debate Union. 2008. Prison Debate Information. http://debate.uga.edu/prison/ (accessed June 25, 2009).

Goodnight, G.T. 1984. "Scholarship and the Forensics Community." In *American Forensics in Perspective: Papers from the Second National Conference on Forensics*, ed. D. Parson, 95–98. Annandale, VA: Speech Communication Association.

International Debate Education Association (IDEA). 2006. "About IDEA." http://www.idebate.org/about/index.php (accessed June 26, 2009).

Logue, B. 1989. "A Captive Audience: Debating in a Maximum Security Prison." Paper presented at the Seventy-fifth Annual Meeting of the Speech Communication Association, San Francisco, CA, November 18–21.

Malcolm X Prison Debate Project. 2009. "About Us." http://malcolmxdebates.org/about-mxpd/ (accessed June 26, 2009).

Mitchell, G. 1998. "Pedagogical Possibilities for Argumentative Agency in Academic Debate." *Argumentation and Advocacy* 19, no. 2: 41–60.

National Association for Urban Debate Leagues (NAUDL). 2007. "Urban Debate History." http://www.urbandebate.org/debatehistory.shtml (accessed June 24, 2009).

Sanoff, A. 1984. "A Conversation with James Billington: Universities Have Fallen Down on the Job of Teaching Values." *U.S. News and World Report*, October 1, pp. 69–70.

Warner, E., and J. Bruschke. 2001. "Gone on Debating: Competitive Academic Debate as a Tool of Empowerment for Urban America." Paper presented at the meeting of the Western Speech Communication Association, Coeur d'Alene, ID, February.

Washington Debate Coalition. 2009. "About Us." http://www.washingtondebate.org/about.html (accessed June 25, 2009).

Women's Debate Institute. 2008. "About the Women's Debate Institute." http://www.womensdebateinstitute.org/about.html (accessed June 25, 2009).

Ziegelmueller, G., and D. Parson. 1984. "Forensic Directors as Professional Educators." In *American Forensics in Perspective: Papers from the Second National Conference on Forensics*, ed. D. Parson, 37–46. Annandale, VA: Speech Communication Association.

Section V: Beyond Tournaments—Openings for Debate Programs

Toward an Understanding of the Landscape of Debate Expansion in Urban Areas and Opportunities for the College Community

Will Baker, American Forensics Association, vice president for high-school affairs

The belief in a monolithic Urban Debate League (UDL) has been perpetuated on eDebate and in other forums, often by well-meaning individuals seeking to assist a growing movement. This essay is designed to increase understanding of the diversity that has developed within urban-debate communities and their support organizations, making them dramatically different in culture, programs, and even forms of debate.

BACKGROUND OF THE MOVEMENT

The basis of the modern-day urban-debate movement is described as follows by the prime driving force behind its funding, Beth Breger, former program officer for the Open Society Institute, now with the New York City Department of Education. Breger wrote in the *Rostrum* in October 2000:

> In an effort to support the development of democratic societies in Eastern Europe and the Former Soviet Union, the Open Society Institute introduced high school debate as part of a larger movement to help transform the Soviet, monolithic education structure. Debate was introduced to provide a forum for secondary school students to develop sophisticated communication skills, understanding of current social and political events and a tolerance for different ideas, in order to enable them to participate as citizens in what were becoming newly democratic societies.

> In 1997 the Open Society Institute, an international foundation established by George Soros, turned its philosophy to high school youth in America's urban centers. Based on the urban debate league model developed by Melissa Wade at Emory University, since 1997 the OSI has supported the establishment of urban debate leagues.

> [OSI] typically funds grants to university debate programs in order to conduct outreach into the local urban school districts. The funding provide teachers and students from selected high schools with intensive summer training in policy debate, weekend tournament competitions, on-going

mentoring, debate materials and curricular resources, scholarships to national summer debate camps, and a final awards banquet for students, families, and members of the school community. (p. 14)

Breger's work led to an initial set of 14 programs that became known as "urban debate leagues." The Open Society Institute unified several existing efforts under a single banner, expanded efforts in additional cities, and fostered the largest expansion of high-school policy debate in the past three decades. As the media attention grew and the dollars became more significant, urban debate went through the growing pains that many movements do—differences in philosophy related to ego, expenditures, and mission focus; fracturing of structures; and the inevitable challenges of founder's syndrome as some programs failed while others flourished based often on a set of capacities related more to nonprofit management than debate expertise.

The result is a landscape that has several players and therefore several ways for colleges and universities to engage the movement.

THE PLAYERS
Let's focus on some of the organizations that have founded debate programs in urban areas and garnered attention from the media or the college community. Attempting to describe the work of these organizations in a few words is presumptuous. Those interested should have a conversation with the leadership of each group. The table below presents publicly available information on each entity

ORGANIZATION	MISSION	KEY FACTS
Associated Leaders of Urban Debate (ALOUD) www.debateleaders.org	Promotes debate and youth expression as vehicles for urban education reform and civic participation through a network of independent program partners. ALOUD helps young people make healthier choices and transform their lives.	Launched programs in Cleveland, Columbus, Lancaster, Louisville, and Moore County, NC; restarted program in Seattle. Fifty partner programs serve 250,000 young people. Partner organizations include UDLs, speaking unions, colleges, and youth expression programs engaged in hip-hop, conflict mediation, and/or nontraditional communication outlets.

International Debate Education Association www.idebate.org	Promotes its programs and its mission via a wide range of educational and strategic initiatives, from curriculum development and active citizenship training to international student exchanges and an annual, much-celebrated, international youth forum.	Started an urban debate program in Pacific Northwest with Willamette University; has sponsored international programs since 1999. Provides curricular resources and database support to schools globally for teachers and students.
Middle School Public Debate Program www.middleschool-debate.com	Designed to teach public speaking, critical thinking, listening, and debating to students in the middle grades, the Middle School Public Debate Program (MSPDP) works with teachers, administrators, parents, students, and community members to form sustainable debating leagues and classroom oral-literacy initiatives. The MSPDP is intended to foster debate participation in class and in competition.	Founded programs in California, New York, Philadelphia, and Washington, DC. The program is a community-service and educational-enrichment initiative of Claremont McKenna College and the Claremont Colleges Debate Union Also provides resources for teachers and coaches in other communities.
National Association for Urban Debate Leagues www.urbandebate.org	Facilitates participation in organized debate activities for as many urban students as possible.	Founded programs in Dallas, Denver, Houston, Memphis, St. Louis, and Tampa and restarted programs in the Bay Area, Los Angeles, St. Louis, and Detroit (in total 16 sites, aiming to serve 100 new schools each year)
National Debate Project www.national-debateproject.org	Institutionalizes a collaborative infrastructure to facilitate the use of debate and discussion as a catalyst for educational reform.	Founded programs in Milwaukee, Miami, Memphis, and Nashville; includes five member college.

Program Building

Two organizations consider one of the focal points of their mission to be the expansion and promotion of urban debate: the National Association for Urban Debate Leagues (NAUDL) and the Associated Leaders of Urban Debate (ALOUD).

NAUDL focuses on partnering with school systems to establish high school UDLs with an advisory board to provide local governance. ALOUD customizes its programs to the needs of its primary partner in the community (a school district, a university, a for-profit entity, or a volunteer network) and then creates a high school, middle school, or combination program model based on partner input. The Middle School Public Debate Program (MSPDP) is also engaged in program creation but it does not refer to its leagues as "urban debate leagues."

Curricular Debate

Each of the organizations listed above pursues debate across the curriculum as part of its program model. Several have produced texts to help school teachers bring debate into their classrooms, and more are forthcoming, with the International Debate Education Association (IDEA) and MSPDP leading the way.

Name Confusion

There is not nor has there ever been a "National Urban Debate League," although members of the college debate community and the public at large sometimes identify as such the National Association for Urban Debate Leagues (NAUDL) and the National Debate Project (NDP)—which draws its connections from its cofounder Melissa Wade, considered by many the mother of this movement. A variety of organizations attempts to provide services and spread the power of the movement to different venues. Understanding the diversity of the movement is vital for college debate programs interested in becoming involved since relationship-building with many local leagues will look dramatically differently from city to city, and community to community.

Local Program Innovations

The urban debate movement has been responsible for considerable innovation in the debate world, which helps explains some of the movement's diversity. Some urban debate programs may involve 20–40 students and have a national travel schedule, while others may entail hundreds in local tournaments, and still others provide a mix of the two models. Given the resources of college audio-visual departments and the desire for meaningful research projects in many communication and rhetoric departments, partnering with local debate communities in activities such as those listed below may prove a win–win situation for all involved.

Urban debate programs include:

Community Debate—Also called "public debate," it is part of many programs. In Baltimore, the Baltimore Urban Debate League hosts a month of public debates, where students debate in shopping malls, on buses, and at City Hall. The Rhode Island Debate League and IMPACT Coalition have made public debate a hallmark of their activities, with appearances on cable and network television.

Debate as a Human Resources Training Tool—Based on a model first used in Baltimore for a donor special event, ALOUD has refined a debate-team project that can be used to address communication across authority lines, cross-cultural communications, and also to help women and people of color adjust to communication expectations in the business world.

Digital Debate—The Austin Urban Debate League focuses its expansion efforts on connecting students online through Skype and other programs. This has led them to host debates with teams in Asia, Europe, Africa, and Latin America. Digital debate is also being used in New York City to bring debate to special-needs students. The pilot program in District 75 has seen students "light up" and engage for extended periods of time when previously they often had difficulty focusing for more than a few minutes.

Fee-for-Service—The pressure on youth-development programs to show that they develop smart, articulate young people with critical-thinking and public-speaking skills creates a substantial market for staff development and "one-shot" debate events. This market represents a significant funding opportunity for those with debate expertise that has been identified by program partners in Baltimore, Los Angeles, New York, and Seattle. With the market rate for professional development rising weekly, a competitive pricing structure becomes essential. The IMPACT Coalition has become a leader in structuring fee-for-service agreements with for-profit and nonprofit clients that showcase the skills of their members locally and nationally using debate programs.

Hip-Hop Debate Curriculum—The Seattle Debate Foundation has partnered with the Hip Hop Association, the Hip Hop Congress, and local Seattle underground hip-hop artists to develop a curriculum that connects the power of debate and the expressiveness of hip-hop in an engaging program module. The Seattle group has produced a CD and a DVD, and appeared at the Race & Pedagogy Conference in Tacoma, Washington, at the University of Puget Sound.

Prison Debate—While not the first entity to venture into prisons, staff members from the Rhode Island Debate League, IMPACT Coalition, and Baltimore Urban Debate League have created programs that operate in local jails.

Research on Debate in the Classroom—The Baltimore Urban Debate League, DEBATE-KC, and Jersey Urban Debate League have partnered with their respective school districts to help teachers and students utilize debate in the classroom. Each program has an extensive set of instructional documents that can serve as resources, as well as access to some findings (research-based and anecdotal) that point to what debate can do in classroom settings.

METHODS FOR ENGAGEMENT BY INTERCOLLEGIATE PROGRAMS
Benefits
The benefits to college programs from connecting to urban-debate programs are considerable. These benefits include:
- unique access for recruiting purposes to a diverse pool of students
- new funding streams to sustain the debate program
- positive media coverage for the debate team
- innovative research prospects
- greater visibility and leverage within the university structure
- active engagement of both recent and long-term alumni
- once-in-a-lifetime opportunities for students and coaches to build greater cultural competencies, teaching skills, and awareness of people living in the communities that surround the school

Strategies
Let us use ALOUD to illustrate the approaches for, and pitfalls of, connecting your program to the work of urban debate. College debate teams can engage with the ALOUD to (1) sponsor a new debate program in their area; partner on research projects; (2) create "showcase" events to act as focus groups that can test community interest; or (3) form partnerships with ALOUD partner programs or support existing projects online.

Sponsoring a New Program
After an initial e-mail or phone call from a college squad, ALOUD representa-

tives work with the squad to identify university departments and resources that could provide resources to emerging programs (graphic designers to help with brochures, direct assistance with arguments and preparation from the debate team, audio-visual departments to help create instructional videos and podcasts, communication departments to produce scholarship and research of program effectiveness, etc.). ALOUD then asks interested universities to join its network of partners using whatever approval process is required (e.g., securing needed permission from department chairs, deans, coaches, or via team vote). Next, if a college team wishes to initiate a new debate community, ALOUD will develop a comprehensive proposal for a planning grant that includes gathering stakeholders, making opening presentations to people of influence in the community, drafting letters to approach donors, media, and alumni; and explaining how to assemble a team to demonstrate the program as a needed value. Once the planning proposal is approved by all relevant stakeholders (primary partner, university sponsor, school-system partner, major funder), a "who does what" chart outlines the ongoing responsibilities as each side works together to cement the plans and time line for a pilot project.

In ALOUD's experience, the biggest pitfalls for partner programs are overdelegation (putting in charge of the initiative a student or recent graduate who lacks the capacity or experience to navigate a complex school system); lack of familiarity with the school system (the motivations for having debate in the local schools are often tied to the distinctions of power and perspectives among the alternative, charter, and traditional public schools in the district and outside considerations such as compliance with No Child Left Behind requirements, budget constraints, and restructuring pressures); and an inability to explore all potential access points (there may be a point of entry or ally in the school system based in the Special Projects Office, Charter School Office, or GEAR-UP program, as opposed to the departments that handle extracurricular programs or cocurricular instruction. Finding a sympathetic ear with sufficient power to make things happen is essential).

Showcase Events

For some areas, it is impossible to get past people's built-in assumptions of what debate can or cannot do to create a program in the near term. In these cases, ALOUD can organize partnerships between local community interests and the debate team to stage a one-shot event showcasing the debate squad to illustrate the value of debate. Such events can create new allies and an increased interest in establishing a larger debate community.

Becoming an ALOUD partner

An intercollegiate debate team that has no interest in creating a new debate community can become a partner organization and work with existing partners online or in proximate locations. Teams can serve as online chat centers for kids with debate questions, offer additional coaching support, work as evidence benefactors, and offer technical support from Web design to video editing. Individuals and university teams can also hold fundraisers and provide other support that raises the profile of ALOUD's partners through link exchanges, blog postings, and research assistance (e.g., research demonstrating program effectiveness, methodology, or longitudinal studies). These roles can be worth tens of thousands of dollars to the existing program partners. ALOUD maintains a catalog of the needs of emerging debate communities and longtime partners.

UNDERSTANDING THE "TOXIC" COMMUNITY

Before they become involved in UDLs, colleges must understand their prospective audiences. Many presume that debate is debate and kids are kids. This attitude is misguided and can devastate a program before it begins. Both the Southern California Urban Debate League, run by CSU–Fullerton, and the New York Urban Debate League, run by the IMPACT Coalition, require new debate assistants to read extensively about race, privilege, and school-system operations. ALOUD refers to the new initiatives it forms as "debate communities" rather than "leagues" because the purpose of debate is not simply to give kids an exciting extracurricular diversion but to provide a seismic shift that can help to change the culture and reduce the toxicity facing many of our youth. Without a grasp of the audience, we lose the ability to combat the noxious communities where urban debaters often reside. Larry Moss, Urban Debate pioneer with the Atlanta Schools, explains:

> One of the most salient aspects of the social reality of many of our new urban debaters is that they are residents of toxic communities. These communities are not toxic in an ecological or chemical sense. Rather they are toxic in a social and environmental sense. These communities are byproducts of the logic of economic development, which seeks to configure urban space in a manner best suited to tap the profit potential of existing global economic forces regardless of the impact of such a configuration on community residents. More than most communities, the toxic community is an artful teacher. It teaches subliminally but profoundly. The toxic community provides context for one's strivings. It defines the parameters of

collective expectation. The toxic community is a place where basic social institutions such as the family, schools, churches, and government are not expected to work. It transmits a culture within which behavior deemed aberrant by middle class American standards is nothing less than the logical response to one's desperate conditions. The toxic community inflicts emotional damage and leaves internal scars even upon those residents who maintain an outward appearance of normalcy. The initial response of those residing in America's toxic communities is to seek to escape. Indeed, urban demographers point out that in recent years, minorities are leaving inner city communities and taking up residence in the suburbs more rapidly than are whites. But the toxic community remains. And for every toxic community resident who finds a "way out," that escaping resident is replaced by newer immigrants and a rapidly expanding impoverished youth population whose residential choices are limited to such toxic communities.

For many new urban debaters, the opportunities created by their mastery of policy debate represent a ticket out of the toxic community. Already, we have witnessed communities of privilege expanding to allow room for the rapidly ascending stars of urban debate and we are justly proud of this accomplishment. (2001, 16)

This essay provides a quick primer for those who wish to understand the UDL movement or, better yet, become involved. Whatever approach one takes, the ultimate goal is to help kids. If we work together to pool resources and connect the university community more fully to their K–12 brethren, we can advance debate as a discipline and as a unique resource for kids.

References

Breger, B. 2000. "Overview of the Urban Debate Program." *Rostrum* 75: 14, 51.
Moss, L.E. 2001. "Beyond an Expansion of Privilege: New Urban Voices and Community Advocacy." *Rostrum* 75: 16–17.

Rethinking Debate Education: The Impact of Community Programs and Engaged Scholarship on Debate at Emory University

Melissa Maxcy Wade, Emory University

While debate at Emory has a history that dates back to 1837, the modern organization, the Barkley Forum (the Forum), began in 1950, when Emory debate alumnus and then U.S. vice president Alben Barkley lent his name to the debate organization. While there was an active debate team, the Forum also had a mission of service to the secondary debate community through hosting tournaments and workshops. Since 1972, that mission has evolved, often in unexpected ways, to include a multigenerational, socioeconomically diverse community ranging from elementary school children to volunteers in their seventies, and from academics to nonprofit community partners. There is no question that the Urban Debate League, founded in 1985 in Atlanta as a partnership between the Barkley Forum and the Atlanta public schools, has had a profound impact on debate at Emory University: the success of the intercollegiate debate team, the postgraduate choices of alumni, academically supervised service to literally thousands of socioeconomically challenged students in Atlanta alone (engaged scholarship), and strong university assistance through resources to support the work. The Alternative Models Working Group of the June 2009 argument conference at Wake Forest University sought essays on nontraditional models of debate programs, and the Barkley Forum self-identifies in this category.

This essay includes information given to incoming first year students to help them understand the variety of ways to participate in debate at Emory. The following quotation is framed in the Barkley Forum offices and expresses the overarching philosophy of the organization:

> The world of individualistic competition is experienced every
> day; the world of harmonious unanimity is fully realized only in
> sporadic flashes of togetherness, glimpses of what might be if
> only people would cooperate and their purposes reinforce, rather
> than undercut, one another.
>
> —Robert Bellah, *Habits of the Heart*

Bellah captures the essence of objections to competition in Western culture. We often perceive competition to be negative because it privileges the achievement of the individual over the health of the community. Competition is linked with corporate culture's privileging of short-term gain over long-term vision. Deborah Tannen's book, *The Argument Culture* (1998), suggests that individualistic competitive argument has so saturated our society that we struggle to locate community. "Debate" is seen to have trumped "discussion" as a primary vehicle for the exploration of ideas. Implicit in this notion is the idea that one has to "win" by marginalizing other participants, that debate is inherently, and inappropriately, divisive. The Red State/Blue State political and cultural schism is a potent example. The result of this poor image of debate can potentially skew the rich education available through the rigorous discourse of the tournament setting.

At this moment in American history we desperately need the critical-thinking skills generated by competitive academic debate. These skills should be available to all in society, but especially to those who face persistently unequal educational structures. One of the most serious barriers to true reform in education is the resistance of those who have developed powerful interests in retaining the status quo. Our economic interests have become increasingly dependent on advertising for products that are often of low quality and little utility. It has been argued that it takes uncritical consumers to participate in such a system:

> Think of the economic tragedy that would occur if schools taught critical thinking. If they encouraged individuals . . . to think original thoughts. If they taught the philosopher's secret that nothing important can be bought. . . . If they nourished a love of quality. Who would crave the mountains of junk our mass-production economy distributes? . . . Who would fill evenings with televised fantasies in place of living? How could the mass economy survive with the training "schools" provide? We'll never get a handle on school reform until we understand this . . . symbiosis. (Gatto 2001, 41–42)

How, then, do we teach critical thinking? In the world of academic debate it is a foundational tenet that competition motivates intellectual achievement. On a highly functioning debate team, competition motivates individuals to cooperate for the good of the community as well as the individual. The exploration of ideas and research gives rise to both individual and group ownership of learning. Teachers and students work together in ways that encourage partnerships for learning. Paulo Freire (1970) calls this kind of collaboration the path to a liberating education, one that encourages democratic dialogue and critical thinking.

Democratic dialogue is a powerful antidote to traditional education's penchant for the development of authority dependence in students, where they "rehearse their futures as passive citizens and workers by learning that education means listening to teachers tell them what to do and what things mean" (Shor 1993, 29). The dialogic antidote allows teachers and students to collaborate so that students experience the self-discovery inherent in learning, and value the partnership of their teachers in that process. Such collaboration is at the heart of the programs of the Barkley Forum.

OVERVIEW AND MISSION

The Barkley Forum is a successful, nationally ranked intercollegiate debate program, cost-effective substitute for many aspects of an academic communications department, and community service entity that is well known outside of Emory and modeled nationally. The department has strong academic, programming, national, and international community service components, which makes it an attractive recruitment tool for high-quality students for the Office of Admissions.

The Barkley Forum is located in the Division of Campus Life. The mission statement indicates that the division "strengthens and enhances Emory University as a community of learning through our programs, activities, services, and facilities. We create a welcoming and supportive environment with a commitment to model and teach holistic well-being, ethical leadership, community service, and global citizenship."

The mission of the Barkley Forum supports the division mission statement in teaching holistic well-being, ethical leadership, community service, and global citizenship through its community of learning. In addition to achieving national success in intercollegiate tournament debate, the Forum works in the field of education reform, and its mission is to promote debate as a tool for empowering urban youth living in the poorest of Atlanta's communities.

COMPONENTS OF THE BARKLEY FORUM

The Forum is divided into three broad areas: the intercollegiate debate team, engaged-scholar and community programs, and administration. *The intercollegiate debate team* features competition and training opportunities for beginning, experienced, and advanced undergraduates. The *engaged scholar and community program* opportunities include: the Glenn Pelham Foundation (a nonprofit foundation supporting debate and urban debate education initiatives), the

Atlanta Urban Debate League (UDL), the Middle School Debate League of Georgia, the Computer Assisted Debate Program (targeting students from Atlanta Housing Authority communities), the Debate Center at Georgia State University, the Debate Across the Curriculum teacher-training program, the College Bridge Program (advising students on successful college application), various programs in the national UDL network, and emerging international debate work in South Korea, Columbia, Hong Kong, Singapore, and other countries. Participation in these programs takes the form of volunteering, academic internships, grant-funded fellowships, formal academic-assessment and educational-evaluation training, and research for academic publications.

Emory does not have an academic-communications department, but Barkley Forum graduates have been regularly admitted into top doctoral programs in communications. More than 40 alumni hold graduate degrees in communications, and all of them received teaching fellowships based, in part, on their teacher training in the UDL. Seven recent graduates serve in Teach for America as a result of their UDL work. Alumni serve or have served as executive directors of UDLs in Atlanta, Boston, Los Angeles, Memphis, Miami, Milwaukee, Nashville, and Washington, DC. Others assist with UDLs in Chicago, Dallas, Houston, Kansas City, Milwaukee, Nashville, Newark, New York City, Tampa, and Washington, DC. Further, more than 60 -Forum alumni have attended Ivy League graduate and professional schools. Ten recent debate alumni currently attend Harvard Law, and Harvard's doctoral program in international relations, and Yale Law; all 10 participated in advanced UDL/engaged-scholarship work.

RATIONALE FOR COMMUNITY PROGRAMMING
More than 130 Emory graduate, professional, and undergraduate students participate annually in Barkley Forum programs. The Forum enjoys substantial support from Emory University, largely because of the symbiosis between the intercollegiate debate team, community programs, and engaged-scholarship components of the organization. Community programming is *equal* to competitive success in the budget process supporting the Forum. The UDL, international consulting, and related service programs have generated a steady stream of positive national press for Emory. The Forum has brought in over $3 million of grant money for UDL and international programs over the past 12 years. The Board of Trustees has recently approved a funding drive for a $10 million endowed Center for Debate Education. The Forum is a top initiative of the new *Campaign Emory* and has earned a $2 million endowment opportunity, which our alumni are committed to raising. This support flows from all aspects of the Forum op-

erating in concert. Without the debate team the community programming efforts would be significantly impaired through the loss of high-quality instructors. Without the community programs the debate team would have fewer coaches and smaller travel budgets.

Internal evaluation data suggest that many Emory debaters have stayed in college tournament debate (when the workload became daunting) through being reenergized by working with UDL students. It is also significant that Emory students who leave college tournament debate remain active members of the Forum in UDL work. Through the engaged-scholar efforts, Emory debaters and nondebaters receive unique educational opportunities that augment their more traditional classroom learning, and lead to significant postgraduate opportunities.

Barkley Forum community programming success is notable. The UDL program has been replicated in 24 cities and has served 35,000 urban students (Harris 2006), 90% of whom finished high school; and 75% attended college (Morris 2002). Atlanta continues to be a national laboratory for new and related programs through Emory's consortium with Georgia State, Tennessee State, and New York University, identified as the National Debate Project.

Training Programs

Barkley Forum students in intercollegiate debate have the opportunity for an annual August preschool preparation for the September–April competition season at an off-campus debate retreat. These five days introduce students to the Forum, debate coaches, topic research, community building, and community program opportunities. Weekly research meetings, daily opportunities for research, argument theory and performance instruction from coaches, and post-tournament practice, rebuttal re-dos, and strategic research constitute ongoing training.

In early September there is a training program for engaged-scholar and community programs that consists of a half-day group training and a four-hour practicum at a middle school tournament the following day. While most incoming Emory debaters have a history of community service, engaging students in an educational setting that ranges from second to twelfth grades, from affluent urban schools to socioeconomically challenged schools in the same system, particularly at-risk students living in Atlanta Housing Authority communities, and a multiracial, multiethnic population, is a challenging environment. Ongoing training leads to different certification levels, opportunities for advanced academic work in the Division of Educational Studies, and leadership and teaching skill development.

Rounding out participation opportunities are the 60-year-old Barkley Forum for High Schools (BFHS) tournament and the Emory National Debate Institute, held every summer for middle-school and high-school students and teachers on three campuses.

EXPECTATIONS FOR BARKLEY FORUM MEMBERSHIP

The Forum has over 700 alumni, one of the most loyal groups in the university. There is a reason. We genuinely believe that debate is a gift of profound educational value, skill development, and preparation for activist lives that serve the advancement of society in law, education, government, medicine, social justice, nonprofit, business, theology, and other unique employment settings. That gift should be shared with underserved populations so that all siblings in the human family have empowered voices to advocate for themselves. Our work is philosophically anchored in collaboration. The expectations for membership are the result of discussions between staff, student debaters, academic interns, and also reflect the voices of university administrators and faculty.

Students are expected to participate in a minimum of organizational and community service activities to earn the basic privilege of participating on the intercollegiate debate team. Those members not on the debate team also participate in organizational and community service, but the full benefit of that participation is determined by levels of time invested and "certification" levels achieved. Most debaters increase their organizational and community service as their time at Emory advances, and are also eligible for the benefits of more advanced work. Some examples include:

Expectations and Opportunities for Engaged Scholars
• Complete beginning certification protocol in September
• Volunteer for one semester weekly in either the Debate Center, Computer Assisted Debate program, or both
• Complete judging certification for UDL tournaments
• After one semester you are eligible for EDS 472 (seminar in urban education) and 497 (undergraduate directed reading) or EDS 597 (graduate directed reading)
• Completion of EDS 472 generates advanced opportunities; 497 may be taken twice

Advanced Opportunities for Engaged Scholars

- Formal training in administering reading, communication apprehension, and student data-assessment protocols
- Collaborative Institutional Training Initiative (CITI certification). Required for every party who is involved in the assessment process
- Potential for Institutional Review Board (IRB) process for original research and grant administration. Principal researchers must demonstrate compliance with their university IRB process; involves submitting a research plan (with necessary reporting documents) and following through on that research plan without deviation
- Participation in an ongoing multicity study of UDL impact on reading, communication apprehension, discipline, grade-point averages, attendance, and dropout rates conducted by the National Debate Project
- Formal training in field-testing curriculum and educational evaluation methodologies
- Participation in writing for publications in academic communications, education, urban education, psychology, and other disciplines
- Work on compiling curriculum from the various Atlanta and Milwaukee UDL programs, and assisting with the current teacher-training project on Debate Across the Curriculum
- Work with international debate programs in various countries with potential for academic credit, supervised internships, and volunteer work.

CONCLUDING REFLECTIONS

The Barkley Forum's 1950 mission of intercollegiate tournament debate and service to the secondary-school community has certainly evolved in major ways in the past 59 years, but the original notion that debate develops critically important skills that should be shared has remained. The UDL was founded on the notion that education is not equal, despite the rulings of the Supreme Court and the laws of the states. In fact, Jonathan Kozol (1992) is right to argue that we have compulsory unequal schooling in the United States, and that our nation operates in a system of educational apartheid (Kozol 2005). It has been our experience that bringing underserved populations to the world of debate has changed Emory debate. The conversation across the socioeconomic divide is a powerful, mutually nourishing dialogue.

Emory staff and students teach debate differently from the ways in which we were taught, having been guided by the UDL students' seeking changes in instructional method. We constantly revise and renegotiate our relationships with various actors in the university and community settings in service to the amazing children we find attracted to debate. Our program targeting secondary students in Atlanta Housing Authority communities has received national recognition from the U.S. Department of Justice as a successful gang-prevention program. We are working on a separate initiative to disrupt the "school to prison pipeline" through a national criminal justice reform group, *Behind the Cycle*. Academic work on teaching debate in African American vernacular English to support "literocracy" in education is informed by the voices of our housing-authority students. A psychology class at Emory judged our UDL tournaments last semester, and then the UDL kids judged the Emory students in their final academic classroom debates. None of us initially working in UDL programs twenty years ago foresaw the directions in which our work would be taking us.

Emory debaters have benefited in a myriad of ways from moving outside the traditional work of research and intercollegiate tournaments. Engaging those outside the privilege of the university setting yields a rich experiential education that has transformed Emory debaters for decades. Many find a deeper commitment to traditional policy debate with an eye toward changing inequality; others have benefited from more nontraditional ideas sparked by exposure to students from different experiences. Barkley Forum staff and students are constantly impressed with the variety, creativity, and depth of our UDL students.

The UDL continues to develop through a process of trial and error. Emory debate staff and students have made so many mistakes, learning the vital heart of respect through multiple instances of disrespect. Our work is by no means error free or all inclusive. In fact, every mistake is our teacher, and we have come to value our all-too-ordinary capacity for misjudgment as leading us to the next steps. But there is no question that community engagement has transformed our understandings of the power of debate education and the depth of competitive tournaments as laboratories for learning.

References

Freire, P, 1970. *Pedagogy of the Oppressed.* New York: Herder and Herder.

Gatto, J.T. 2001. *A Different Kind of Teacher: Solving the Crisis in American Schooling.* Berkeley, CA: Berkeley Hills Books.

Harris, T. 2006. "Urban Debate Leagues—A Growing Phenomenon." *Urban Educator* 15, no. 3 (March): 6–8.

Kozol, J. 1992. *Savage Inequalities: Children in America's Schools.* New York: HarperPerennial.

———. 2005. *The Shame of the Nation: The Restoration of Apartheid Schooling in America.* New York: Crown.

Morris, H. 2002. "League of Their Own." *U.S. News & World Report* 132, no. 21 (June 17): 50–52.
Shor, I. 1993. "Education Is Politics: Paulo Freire's Critical Pedagogy." In *Paulo Freire, A Critical Encounter*, ed. P. McLaren and P. Leonard, 25–35. London, New York: Routledge.
Tannen, D. 1998. *The Argument Culture: Moving from Debate to Dialogue*. New York: Random House.

Reaching the Dropout Population: Seeking Government Grants

Carol Winkler, Georgia State University

More than 1.2 million students drop out of U.S. high schools annually (Office of the Press Secretary, 2010). Only about 50% of the students enrolled in high school in the 50 largest cities earn a diploma (Swanson 2008). While the dropout rate has historically resulted in lost tax revenues and has drained social services, it now contributes to what many refer to as "the school-to-prison pipeline." Because arrests of dropouts are 3.5 times higher than those for students who complete school (Bourne 2003), many students who fail to finish high school land in prison or the juvenile justice system.

Debate offers an effective remedy for increasing affective, behavioral, and cognitive engagement for at-risk youth in the nation's schools. Studies of participants in debate show that they have higher self-esteem, lower communication apprehension, more verbal assertiveness (which trades off with physical aggression), higher grade-point averages, improved reading skills, heightened critical-thinking abilities, and higher school attendance than their peers. While most of the earlier research targeted high school and college debaters from suburban communities or those from schools that could afford to compete in national competitions, urban debate has emerged as an increasing focus of research.

In 2005, First Lady Laura Bush featured the Computer Assisted Debate (CAD) Program in targeting middle school children from Atlanta's public housing communities as the signature school program for her Helping America's Youth Initiative. More recently, the Department of Justice, through the Bureau of Justice Administration and the Institute for Law and Justice, invited partners in the CAD program to describe the program and its impact at two national conferences on preventing gang violence in public housing communities. As an outgrowth of the expressed interest of various districts in replicating the program at those conferences, CAD representatives now serve as technical consultants to the Department of Justice as part of their Project Safe Neighborhoods (PSN) initiative. Since 2001, more than $1.5 billion has been spent on the PSN program.

Those interested in using debate to help prevent crime should focus on four key strategies:

1. Develop programs that target the children most at risk: poor, minority students who are academically challenged. Focus on middle school-aged students in order to reach them before they join gangs or become completely disengaged from school.

2. Build partnerships with community organizations (such as housing authorities, public school systems, local law enforcement, and other groups that work with at-risk youth, e.g., Boys and Girls Clubs of America). These partnerships are essential in building the collaborative environment needed for your debate project to succeed, and these groups have the necessary resources that can help build long-term sustainability for the projects.

3. Include tracking of disciplinary referrals (suspensions and disciplinary incidents) in any assessment protocols of your programs. Many students will move away from violence and other disciplinary problems in the schools as a result of finding their voice through debate, which in turn, will make the programs attractive for future funding.

4. Contact the U.S. attorney or police chief who serves your area. They can request Computer Assisted Debate Project training through the Institute for Law and Justice that will help build the necessary partnerships. For more information, review the Web site at http://www.engageyouth-ilj.org/school_based_programs_cad.html.

References

Browne, J.A. 2003. "Derailed: The Schoolhouse to Jailhouse Track." May. http://www.advancementproject.org/sites/default/files/publications/Derailerepcor_0.pdf (accessed February 28, 2009).

Office of the White House Press Secretary. "President Obama Announces Steps to Reduce Dropout Rate and Prepare Students for College & Careers." http://ww.whitehouse.gov (accessed March 1, 2010).

Swanson, C. 2008. "Cities in Crisis: A Special Analytic Report on High School Graduation." April 1. http://www.americaspromise.org (accessed January 31, 2009).

The Challenge to Reestablish Intercollegiate Debate at Our Nation's Historically Black Colleges and Universities

John W. Davis II, Debate Solutions, LLC

Where would young James Farmer, or John Hope Franklin Jr., or Barbara Jordan have an opportunity to debate today? Not at Historically Black Colleges and Universities (HBCU) like so many did in the 1930s, 1940s, 1950s, and 1960s, nor at many of the debate powers competing at intercollegiate tournaments each weekend. Recently recalled his debate career, Dr. Franklin told me that he debated for Fisk University between 1931 and 1934, and was in a contest against New York University in 1932, three years before the famous James Farmer debate as told in the film *The Great Debaters*.

The complete history of debating would fill many volumes, but a few salient facts should be mentioned. While the origins of debate are lost in the remote reaches of history, we do know that people were debating in Africa at least 4,000 years ago. For example, Egyptian princes debated agricultural policy at the pharaoh's court (2080 BC). Debate became the quintessential American art and the nation's continuing struggle to create a more perfect union is a history written by the great debates of the day. Almost all leaders of the American Revolution and the early national period were able debaters who had studied argumentation in the colonial colleges or in the community debating "societies," "lyceums," and "bees" that flourished throughout the country, most notably the "Spy Club" at Harvard, which by 1722 was debating contemporary issues.

Secret debating societies flourished among both enslaved and free Africans in America during the nineteenth century. Debating societies were viewed as the training grounds for the leaders and foot soldiers struggling for freedom. Their weapons were words, not guns, and they believed that reasoning, critical-thinking, and public-speaking skills were the ammunition needed for victory.

The evidence demonstrating the educational and leadership value of debate is overwhelming; increased literacy, improved grade-point averages, and improved graduation rates. A long historical record demonstrates that debaters prove to be effective advocates for themselves and their communities. During the mid-1990s alone, a strong majority of members of Congress had competitive debating experience.

Why then have debate programs at HBCUs suffered such a precipitous decline? This trend constitutes a significant missed opportunity—vast talent resources go unnoticed and our national competitiveness is hampered. There have been many efforts in the past to include minorities and encourage HBCUs to participate, but many have not taken up the offer.

Compared to intercollegiate athletics and other costly endeavors, debate is, dollar for dollar, an efficient use of institutional resources. It requires no multi-million-dollar complexes, playing fields, stadiums, or expensive equipment. All that is necessary are classrooms, coaches, office supplies, and support for travel and research. Debate is an inexpensive, educational, and effective way to both promote schools and enhance the quality of the academic experience.

Seventy-five years ago Melvin Tolson built a highly competitive debate team around a talented young James Farmer at Wiley College (an HBCU) to crack the color barrier. At that time in our nation's history, white universities would not debate HBCUs on large national stages. Despite our national progress since that color barrier was cracked, according to the official list of qualifying teams, only Howard University stands among all other 105 HBCUs as having qualified for the nation's first true national debating championships (now the National Debate Tournament [NDT]) in 1952 and 1954.

I have been involved in debate since 1974. For decades as a competitor, lawyer, coach, and historian I have seen the difference it can make in the lives of young African Americans and every other group that takes part. That is why I, along with Timothy O'Donnell (chair of the NDT and director of debate at the University of Mary Washington—one of the top national teams) and my colleague Jeff Porro, launched the Debate Consortium (the Consortium) in September 2008.

The Consortium's mission is to build capacity for cutting-edge pedagogy and undergraduate research in the art and practice of argumentation and debate on crucial issues of American public policy at many of the nation's HBCUs. It includes building bridges between agencies of the federal government and HBCUs as well as forging durable partnerships between Consortium debate programs and existing nationally ranked intercollegiate programs. With strong support from the White House Initiative on Historically Black Colleges and Universities, we use the authority pursuant to Presidential Executive Order 13256 (et seq.), designed to make the organs and resources of the federal government accessible to HBCUs, and to create opportunities for academic institutions to collaborate on specific debate projects surrounding controversial issues central to individual federal agencies.

I am happy to say we have gotten some great response, but a much more systematic and resource-based effort is needed to build team capacity. We simply cannot do it alone.

The movement to rediscover debate has already begun. Urban debate leagues at the middle- and high-school levels are flourishing, and *The Great Debaters* will undoubtedly cause demand for debate to surge in the coming years. However, these leagues cannot shoulder the burden of a nationwide debate renaissance alone. They need colleges and universities to take a leadership role.

Specifically, higher education must do three things. First, HBCUs need to create viable opportunities for high-school graduates, particularly those from Urban Debate Leagues, who seek to continue their debate education after high school. Creating new programs and reinforcing existing programs is essential.

Second, and equally important, we must recruit, train, and produce a new generation of professional debate educators. There are many middle schools and high schools around the country eager to offer debate opportunities to students, but they are unable to find qualified teachers with debate experience because the demand for quality coaches far outstrips the supply. To meet this shortfall, our institutions must generate capacity by fielding debate programs that give students opportunities to learn the coaching craft through rich individual learning experiences. In addition, thoughtful consideration should be given to the ways in which such a commitment spurs curricular innovation at both the undergraduate and graduate levels as well as educational partnerships of local, regional, and state constituencies. Finally, the creation of new opportunities to join the debate teaching fraternity must move in lockstep with efforts to retain, reward, and renew our best debate teachers.

Third, as the nation's longstanding incubators of free expression, innovative thinking, democratic deliberation, and social change, colleges and universities must do more to promote the role of debate as a necessary component of a well-functioning society. Strong debate programs are essential because they showcase best practices. Debate programs are and should be key players in efforts to foster civic engagement and democratic responsibility.

The Great Debaters reminds us that the values of debate are the values of the academy itself. Even critics admit that debate's insufficiencies are due as much as anything to insufficient institutional commitment to a debate education. To be true to our core values, we need to promote the activities that create better students and better citizens. Debate does this. An America where academic debate becomes a prominent fixture on every campus would be a better America. Every college and university has many James Farmers strolling the hallways and quadrangles of its campuses; but we must lay the foundation for achievement. There will be no better opportunity to bring this to fruition than the one that now lies before us. The time for debate is now.

Thus far, ten HBCUs have expressed an interest in starting a debate team in the 2009/10 academic year: Hampton University, Savannah State, Norfolk State, Lincoln, Fayetteville State, Voorhees College, Morgan State, Kentucky State, Huston-Tillotson, and St. Paul's College. Prairie View A&M University and the University of the District of Columbia have expressed interest in starting up programs during the 2010/11 academic year. I hope you will consider sending out a short reminder or nudge to others to help the marketing process (or perhaps stir up some competitive spirit).

And that is why I am calling upon the National Debate Tournament Committee and the Cross Examination Debate Association to collaborate together with HBCUs to achieve significantly greater diversity within the body of university participants within the next five years.

In sum, America gains a broader national benefit when it brings to the table all of the top talent it has to offer in any given endeavor. We need help from America's political, civic and business leaders to end a system that retards our national benefit and underdevelops large segments of our society.

Broadening the Base of Investment in Challenging Economic Times: Communicating the Case for Evidence-Based, Cost-Effective Debate Interventions

Scott Deatherage, executive director, and Eric Tucker, chief academic officer and deputy director, National Association for Urban Debate Leagues

INTRODUCTION

A. Overview

Policymakers and institutional investors face a challenge to identify academic interventions that most cost-effectively and significantly improve outcomes for students in low-performing urban public schools. The National Association for Urban Debate Leagues (NAUDL) seeks to provide high-quality information about how urban debate influences the student outcomes that prospective supporters care most about, by studying the effectiveness of urban debate programs with methodological rigor and peer-reviewed research. The NAUDL increasingly works to share investigator-initiated research that demonstrates that Urban Debate Leagues (UDLs) improve academic achievement by increasing graduation rates, secondary literacy, and college and career readiness.[1]

UDLs, like all debate interventions, require resources to thrive. Transportation, tournament administration, coaching salaries, hired judges, and reams of copies add up. The prolonged economic downturn means school systems, municipalities, and states are bringing a renewed rigor and toughness to education funding decisions, potentially jeopardizing funding for activities such as debate.

For many debate programs, maintaining or growing the capacity to serve students requires obtaining financial support to complement a line item in a school district's budget. Individuals, corporations, and foundations can be solicited as possible sources of funding for debate programs. To thrive and grow, the debate community must also find strong and proactive voices to advocate for financial support from local, state, and federal officials, while applying the creativity and research skills instilled by participation in debate to identify possible untapped sources of government funding.

---

[1] See, for example, http://www.urbandebate.org/urbandebateworks.shtml; and http://www.urbandebate.org/policyandpractice.shtml.

Current economic circumstances put debate programs, like so many social interventions, in an undesirable situation: needing to secure additional sources of external funding while such funding is the scarcest it has been in decades, causing heavy competition for charitable and state resources. Compounding this dilemma, the emerging policy context demands evidence-based, research-backed practice, privileging innovative interventions proven to work and with the capacity to go successfully to scale.

The premise that guides the NAUDL's engagement with potential institutional investors is that cost-effective programs whose positive impacts are supported with strong evidence are most likely to receive financial support. Advocates for debate, this chapter argues, must learn how to frame the benefits of debate in language that will appeal to policymakers and institutional investors who prioritize cost-effectiveness. Debate interventions must also commit to work with academic researchers to examine the educational and social impact of student participation in debate on non–debate-related outcomes, such as graduation rates, secondary literacy, and college preparedness. Credible, peer-reviewed, scientific evidence demonstrating the benefits of debate is an essential component—perhaps the most important one—of securing lasting institutional investments in debate programs across the nation.

The challenge for debate programs is this: advocates for debate and urban debate must consider how they can more effectively communicate with corporate, foundation, individual and government policymakers, decision makers, and investors about why funding for debate should be a priority in a world of scarce resources. This chapter uses the NAUDL's experience making the case for urban debate as a cost-effective intervention to share insights on the broader relevance of evidence-based advocacy for debate.

B. Meeting the Challenge with Aggressive Evidence-based Advocacy: The Approach of the National Association for Urban Debate Leagues

Meeting the challenges presented by the new economic realities and policy context will require well-crafted advocacy across the debate community. The NAUDL has been recalibrating its advocacy efforts to secure financial investments for UDLs with considerable success, even in this tough economic climate. The lessons NAUDL has learned, and its current advocacy strategy, can provide insight for those in the debate community seeking to obtain further support.

Specifically, the NAUDL has developed both the organizational capacity to engage investors and a development strategy to communicate with and obtain support from institutional investors across the nation. In seeking to develop these capacities, the NAUDL has engaged in dialogue with policymakers at all levels of government, as well as the individuals and boards who make decisions about corporate and nonprofit charitable giving. NAUDL has taken advantage of this dialogue to listen to what factors policymakers and donors evaluate in deciding how to allocate resources—criteria with increasing relevance in times when those seeking support must prove their worth amid the clamor of many competing causes for smaller resource pools.

This essay examines how NAUDL pursued its organizational and development strategies to advance its overall mission of facilitating participation in organized debate for as many urban high-school students as possible. The hope is that, in reflecting upon our own experience, we might identify themes and insights relevant to the debate community more broadly.

BUILDING THE ORGANIZATIONAL CAPACITY TO ENGAGE INVESTORS IN CONVERSATIONS CENTERED ON COST-EFFECTIVENESS

The NAUDL has made three principles the bedrock of its efforts to build organizational capacity: leadership, expertise, and strategy. These principles start with a hands-on board, which is highly engaged in the organization's management and strategic development, and provides expert advice regarding the challenges and opportunities that confront the NAUDL. This section will discuss the three principles in depth, explaining how NAUDL has built from the basis of this foundation.

A. Leadership

The NAUDL Governing Board comprises senior executives who are committed to the NAUDL mission. The board is extensively involved in overseeing the NAUDL's strategy, making financial contributions, and securing outside funding. In addition to the Governing Board, the NAUDL has constituted an Honorary Board and a Young Professionals Leadership Board. These three entities bring a range of sustainability-oriented capacities and embody the professionalism and discipline that the NAUDL seeks to bring to each organizational endeavor as well as to communicate to investors. The NAUDL boards are replete with individuals who are successful leaders, across the business, government, civic, and education sectors.

B. Expertise

The NAUDL staff brings a wealth of urban debate experience to the organization. The senior leadership brings over 100 years of combined experience in coordinating debate programs, coordinating academic research, and leading Urban Debate Leagues. More recently, the NAUDL has recruited recent law-school graduates who have been "deferred" from starting with their respective law firms. These "Urban Debate Advocacy Fellows" bring a passion for debate and the academic expertise that comes with obtaining a law degree. In addition, league directors partner with local school systems and business and civic leaders to ensure teachers have the support necessary to succeed as coaches.

Such expertise, in addition to the talent and professionalism of the staff, reassures supporters about the return on their investment, enhancing the Urban Debate Network's claims of cost-effectiveness and significant academic improvement.

C. Strategy

The NAUDL has worked to distill the organizational components and practices that it believes are essential for success into its urban debate programming and infrastructure to provide long-term educational benefits to low-income students and students of color. The NAUDL "best practices approach," which calls for school system ownership supported by a set of strong external partners organized into an Urban Debate Commission/Urban Debate League Advisory Board, is research based and has been refined through field testing.

The NAUDL has also made the strategic decision to collaborate with investigator-initiated research projects that rigorously examine the educational and social impact on urban students of participating in high-quality policy-debate programming. This priority opens up new avenues of research to academics, driving important education research questions. The relationship also makes it possible for the Urban Debate Network to benefit from an emerging body of scientific, peer-reviewed articles reflecting on the influence of urban debate on education metrics such as graduation rates, secondary literacy, and college readiness.

The NAUDL's most substantial accomplishments in recent years resulting from its enhanced capacity have been hosting the first several Chase Urban Debate National Championships, building eight new Urban Debate Leagues, and strengthening UDLs in Boston, Detroit, and Rhode Island. Along with a series of additional conferences, the National Championship weekend brings students, teachers, administrators, and supporters from about 20 cities together to compete, share knowledge, raise awareness, and celebrate on a scale never before seen in urban debate. Additionally, the NAUDL has worked to secure school district support and local funding to bring debate programs to more than 145 high schools that previously did not have access to debate.

DEVELOPING A SUSTAINABLE, LONG-TERM SOURCE OF REVENUE
Building durable, high-quality Urban Debate Leagues is the top programmatic priority of the NAUDL. Indeed, the mission of facilitating participation in organized debate for as many urban high-school students as possible assumes persistent growth and success across time. To realize its mission, the NAUDL requires a long-term revenue base, supplemented by the strategic use of short-term funding to meet specific goals.

This section focuses on what the NAUDL has learned from its dialogue with the different types of investors and how it has adapted its advocacy for urban debate as a transformative educational intervention.

A. Individual Support
Individual donors are critical to the long-term success of the NAUDL and the Urban Debate Network, and should be considered critical to any debate program seeking to establish a long-term source of funding. The NAUDL's individual donor base largely consists of former debaters who have a personal affinity for the activity. In light of this, debate programs should build alumni records and actively stay in contact with their alumni.

The NAUDL has significant unrealized potential for support-driven growth. The NAUDL has found that there are three components to successfully soliciting individual contributions: increasing the number of donors, obtaining larger gifts from annual donors, and improving annual donor participation rates. While obtaining new donors is important, relationships with donors need to be prioritized, cultivated, and maintained.

B. Foundation Support
The NAUDL has worked to create effective, professional proposals to foundations that communicate key ideas and strengths. Active collaboration with entities that have experience in successfully advocating for funding from foundations enabled the NAUDL to improve its in-house development capacity,

putting us in a position to draft effective foundation proposals. These materials have enabled the NAUDL to rely on foundation funds to propel network growth. The NAUDL now solicits significant foundation support on behalf of leagues during their building phases and at critical junctures in their life cycles, all while leveraging broad support for UDLs as local enterprises.

C. Corporate Support

The expansion of the NAUDL's organizational capacity allowed it to engage corporate leaders and corporate foundations, seeking their support. The NAUDL has developed relationships with prominent debate alumni working for potential national corporate sponsors. Over time, the NAUDL has utilized its organizational capacity to develop strategic plans for corporate outreach. At the core of those plans are advocacy documents and professional promotional materials, aimed at attracting new corporate investors.

One prominent argument made in the advocacy materials is that urban debate contributes new, underrepresented, and diverse students to the employment pipeline. This argument is most effective with respect to law firms, which are particularly concerned about the racial, ethnic, and gender composition of the pipeline of legal employees. Modern law firms, in the aggregate, are less diverse than the white-collar workforces of their corporate clients. Corporate clients have taken notice of the lack of diversity within the legal profession and have begun weighing a law firm's diversity more heavily in deciding on legal representation. This pressure from corporate clients has caused law firms to support initiatives and programs that are demonstrating cost-effective ways to improve diversity within the legal profession.

Debate—and urban debate in particular—is poised to make this claim. The analytical, research, and advocacy skills that make for good debaters are also a solid intellectual foundation for good attorneys. UDLs, as a cost-effective means of increasing graduation rates, secondary literacy, and college readiness, increase the number of students of color in the "legal pipeline" by helping significant numbers of such students to successfully complete high school.

D. Special Events

The NAUDL has established that major fundraising events, such as its annual dinner, can effectively develop a synergy between individual, foundation, and corporate donors. Allowing members from all three categories of donors to interact with each other and see the degree of strength and support from donors of all types further reinforces positive perceptions of giving to the NAUDL. Debate programs that involve alumni with institutional supporters can similarly benefit.

E. In-kind Support

Obtaining "in-kind" support has been a crucial goal, since it provides a key means for the NAUDL to improve its organizational and development capacity. Broadly speaking, the NAUDL seeks partners who can provide one or more of the following:

Supportive Entrepreneurial Leadership for Urban Debate. Established and recently graduated professionals in fields such as management consulting, information systems, marketing, and political consulting might take special projects with the NAUDL lasting from a day to a year.

Creating Teams of Social Entrepreneurs. The NAUDL believes that teams and networks of social entrepreneurs working together accelerate and spread social impact. It thus seeks out professionals to collaborate with the NAUDL staff and Governing Board to move particular organizational priorities forward.

Building Organizational Infrastructure. To build a vibrant, national network of catalysts for and sustainers of urban debate requires tools and support systems to deliver robust, sustainable leagues. The NAUDL seeks to partner with organizations to create needed infrastructures and codify proven practices in areas such as performance metrics and measurement, intranet-based data management, strategic planning, expansion initiative planning, configuration strategy, financial and operational systems, marketing and communications, development, access to social financing, corporate-sponsorship models, model-project impact evaluation, and social-networking approaches for UDLs.

Providing Pro Bono Legal Counsel. Attorneys can provide legal advice and assistance to the NAUDL and to local Urban Debate Leagues, prepare submissions to federal and local governments on matters of public interest, and conduct other legal work.

F. Federal Support

Unfortunately, only limited federal government support for urban debate currently exists. However, the NAUDL believes that once the visibility of the Urban Debate Network's approach reaches a tipping point, UDLs will be able to attain federal financial support.

The NAUDL believes its National Urban Debate National Championship competition can serve as an essential networking catalyst to unite key players. The NAUDL's advocacy at these events will focus attention on urban debate as a critical education and youth-development initiative and use sound research to suggest urban debate as a significant, cost-effective strategy to promote the improvement of public education.

Securing federal funding for UDLs would have a ripple effect across the debate community. Stronger UDLs would be able to afford opportunities for more students, both regionally and nationally.

Looking Ahead: Building a Platform for Diversified, Sustainable Funding Premised on the Cost-effectiveness Case

Following from its general drive to secure individual, foundation, and corporate investors, the NAUDL has developed the following specific strategies to obtain and increase institutional support going forward. Debate programs that want to increase external support may wish to model some or all of the following strategies:

• Further developing the campaign for individual donors, including running special events and receptions for prominent former debaters, which over time will yield a broad base of supporters who contribute financially and politically.
• Identifying and engaging grant-making foundations that may invest in demonstration projects that seed UDLs, and field experiments that evaluate UDLs as an exemplary instance of academically rigorous Out-Of-School-Time programming. These projects would produce vibrant local organizations and evidence that may be used to secure future support.
• Identifying and engaging corporations drawn to the national profile of the Urban Debate Network, which may provide sponsorship to expand and strengthen local UDLs that leverage local investment.
• Cultivating partners (such as universities, think tanks, nongovernmental organizations) who supply in-kind resources and opportunities to the Urban Debate Network.
• Engaging urban educational entities, who can be courted nationally in a manner that will produce local political and social capital to help build new UDLs.
• Tailoring advocacy so that local school district line items are influenced by the precedent of cities that have invested in urban debate.
• Building national momentum and advocacy to help secure federal earmarks for UDLs.

CONCLUSION

The current economic downturn has taken its toll. Many school-district budgets are unstable, while others are suffering cuts. Even while debate programs' need for external funding from institutional investors is at its strongest, the amounts being given by charitable donors are the lowest in recent history. More than ever, advocates of debate must present the activity as a cost-effective means of improving the educational outcomes of participating students.

The NAUDL has learned from its dialogue with individual, foundation, and corporate investors, and has improved its organizational and development capacity in light of those conversations. The NAUDL listened to the investor community about the importance of having solid, empirical evidence, justifying the donor's charitable giving. As a result, the NAUDL has forged academic partnerships, which have produced credible, peer-reviewed data proving that participation in urban debate has significant impacts on participants' graduation rates, secondary literacy, and college preparedness. These conversations can be one basis for advocating debate as a cost-effective intervention to improve educational outcomes.

The NAUDL's emphasis on organizational capacity has allowed it to build a staff with the leadership, expertise, and strategic insight to learn from the NAUDL's ongoing dialogue with institutional investors and to tailor its advocacy accordingly. By maintaining good relationships with alumni through effective communication, programs may receive both financial donations and in-kind donations that may then be useful in obtaining foundation or corporate donations (e.g., an alumnus who is now a business consultant agrees to design advocacy materials for a presentation to a foundation).

Even in tough times, debate programs can still grow and provide additional opportunities to their students. The NAUDL's efforts provide one potentially useful approach that existing debate programs can employ to realize their full potential.

Section VI: Pedagogical Innovations

The Allred Initiative and Debate Across the Curriculum: Reinventing the Tradition of Debate at North Carolina

Christian O. Lundberg, University of North Carolina at Chapel Hill

Most of the essays in this volume deal with issues surrounding the everyday operations of an intercollegiate debate team, tournament practice, and the professional advancement of debate educators. The purpose of this contribution is a bit different: the main goal of this essay is to provide one model for how to extend the benefits of debate beyond or even entirely outside the purview of the competitive intercollegiate debate team to the general population of colleges and universities. This essay is aimed at two audiences: debate educators who seek a model for building capacities for debate beyond the specific ambit of their programs, and another audience of readers at colleges and universities without a competitive intercollegiate debate team. For the first audience, I would like to argue that debate teams and coaches take a more active role in extending debate education to student populations outside of the debate team for the sake of building on-campus support for their programs, tangibly demonstrating that the resources university administrations put into debate programs serve more than a very narrow and highly specialized population of students. For those at a college or university without an active debate program, I would like to suggest the Allred model as one way of continuing and extending a commitment to building cultures of debate at our colleges and universities. For readers in both audiences, I have attempted to compile, update, and extend on the state of the art in scholarship defending debate pedagogy and debate across the curriculum initiatives. I also briefly lay out the basic structure of the Allred model, offering it as one way of embodying a commitment to debate as a pedagogical tool that complements the whole of the undergraduate curriculum and as one model for cultivating capacities for democracy in the college classroom.

THE STATE OF DEBATE ACROSS THE CURRICULUM

The debate-across-the-curriculum movement is the primary locus of advocacy for expanding the benefits of debate beyond competitive high school and intercollegiate debate teams. A number of pilot projects have been undertaken in K–12 settings, including, for example, Kansas City's pilot project at the University Academy, and the National Debate Project's Computer Assisted Debate project in the metro Atlanta area. Despite the increasing amount of scholarship justifying the integration of debate practices into college and university curricula, the primary sites of innovation in debate across the curriculum are concentrated in K–12 programs. Though there have been advances in implementing communication-across-the-curriculum measures in higher education, it is unclear that very many of these initiatives actively promote debate as a subset of communication across the curriculum. While a few of these initiatives are organized around an oral-communication component (for instance, Virginia Tech's CommLab program, http://www.commlab.vt.edu), the majority of these programs either integrate oral-communication components into a writing-across-the-curriculum model, or privilege writing as the primary focus of their pedagogical efforts.[1]

There are a number of initiatives associated with debate programs to increase the profile of debate on college campuses, and these initiatives may be one of the primary outlets for the spirit of debate across the curriculum in the absence of the letter of systematic curricular reform. Public-debate initiatives at a number of colleges seek to engage the campus community in debate activities outside the ambit of the classroom (debate programming at the University of Pittsburgh, the University of Mary Washington, and James Madison University come to mind as prominent examples, though there are others).

Perhaps the comparatively slow uptake of debate across the curriculum at colleges and universities is due in part to the large number of "competitors across the curriculum": writing, technology, critical thinking, information literacy, and so on. Competitors for studies across the curriculum are often advocated by departments that traditionally have a powerful voice in curricular decisions, such as English departments. The strength of the competition for themes across the curriculum seems daunting, but it is also possible that even with the powerful case that forensics educators have to make about the benefits of debate, we have not made the argument for debate across the university curriculum as forcefully, persistently, or systematically as we might like to.

Despite the relative scarcity of systematic initiatives promoted by college forensics programs to implement debate-across-the-curriculum projects,

---

[1] Examples include the Campus Writing and Speaking Program at North Carolina State University (http://www2.chass.ncsu.edu/CWSP/index.html), the program in Communication Across the Curriculum at Southern Illinois State University (http://cola.siuc.edu/WritingAcrosstheCurriculum.html), and Communication Across the Curriculum Ideas at Presbyterian College (http://web.presby.edu/writingcenter/faculty/cacPC.html). Thanks to Ron von Burg for providing a list of communication-across-the-curriculum programs.

it is worth noting that debate practices are expanding across college and university curricula. Ruth Kennedy argues that "just as writing assignments have been incorporated across the curriculum, debates have been successfully used in a variety of disciplines including sociology, history, psychology, biotechnology, math, health, dentistry, nursing, marketing, and social work" (2007, 185). The expansion of debate practices provides an opportunity for those tied to the National Debate Tournament (NDT) and the Cross Examination Debate Association (CEDA) communities to play an active role not only in promoting debate but also in helping to shape the debate practices outside of competitive tournament debating. But this is not just a question of influencing the quality and content of debate across the curriculum: the expansion of debate practices on campus without the influence of the debate team poses a question for the role of debate programs as good college and university citizens. The question is whether debate programs are utilizing the immense capacities for public dialogue that they inculcate in their students to assist in campus debate activities, to teach debate skills, and to make a concrete difference in the academic climate at colleges and universities. Influencing on-campus debate activities provides two benefits for competitive intercollegiate debate teams: taking a role in already existing on-campus, in-class debate activities would help to make the case that debate teams are actively involved in the campus intellectual climate, and would also help in translating the benefits of our experiences with debate to the broader college and university public.

The expansion of debate practices has been accompanied by a significant increase in scholarship defending debate's pedagogical benefits. Authors in a stunning number of fields, many of whom have no discernible tie to competitive intercollegiate debate, advocate for in-class debates as an invaluable pedagogical tool. The case for debate has been made recently in the context of: business education (Combs and Bourne 1994; Schroeder and Ebert 1983), dentistry (Scannapieco 1997); economics (Vo and Morris 2006); English and composition (Dickson 2004); health education (Gibson 2004; Temple 1997); history (Musselman 2004); international relations (Omelicheva 2005, 2007); marketing (Berdine 1987; Roy and Macchiette 2005); math (university level; Legrand 2001); medicine and nursing (Garrett, Schoener, and Hood 1996); psychology (Bauer and Wachowiak 1977; Budesheim and Lindquist 2000; Elliot 1993; Gorman, Law, and Lindegren 1981); political science (Omelicheva 2007); public policy (Keller, Whittaker, and Burke 2001; Mitchell 2000); religious studies (Watson 2004); science education (Simmoneaux 2001); social work (Gregory and Holloway 2005); sociology (Crone 1997; Dundes 2001; Huryn 1986); and technology studies (Glantz and Gorman 1997).

Given this expansion of debate practice and scholarship, the time has come to reframe the assumptions that inform calls for debate across the curriculum by the college debate community. Debate's expansion across the curriculum is fueled, in part, by factors external to the competitive intercollegiate debate community's efforts to promote debate, including increasing institutional commitments to deliberative democracy and public engagement. The questions that confront allies of competitive intercollegiate debate within this context are: how to ensure that we have an appropriate voice at the table in promoting and shaping debate practices; how to make the case for best practices; and how we might best connect the broader movements in the academy with the work that we do as competitive-forensics educators.

I would like to suggest that we engage in a minor but important reframing of the call for debate across the curriculum. There are two prominent ways of envisioning such a debate: one that views the role of those promoting debate across the curriculum as an attempt to expand the number of courses with debate components, and one that views debate as an integrative experience that helps students to do the work of weaving together the often-fragmented components of a university curriculum into an integrated education in the liberal arts and sciences. In the first instance, the goal of debate across the curriculum is to maximize the number of places where debate is taking place: that is, to expand debate as a practice. In the second instance, the primary pedagogical goal is to cultivate debate as a core component of education in the liberal arts and sciences, or put differently, to understand debate as a critical capacity that enhances a college or university's already existing educational goals. These two options are certainly not mutually exclusive, and debate advocates should pursue both: but competitive intercollegiate debate programs and forensics educators are perhaps uniquely situated to make the case for the second option. As I envision it, debate, conceived as a portable technology for promoting a rigorous and integrated education in the liberal arts and sciences can make a significant difference in the intellectual health of our colleges and universities. Our goal, then, should be to frame debate programs as clearinghouses for cultivating on-campus debate capacity. This positions debate teams to be significant centers for promoting on-campus dialogue and for promoting debate as a tool that achieves the individual pedagogical and broader civic goals of higher education. The challenge, as any debater knows, is to make sure that debate advocates do the research and strategizing necessary to make the case for debate practices.

The Case for Debate in College Classrooms: Improving Critical Thinking

One of the most repeated claims for the benefits of debate is that debate enhances critical-thinking skills. This claim is significant both because of the intrinsic good of inculcating critical thinking in a student's whole university experience, and because improved critical thinking is often assumed to be one of the most important benefits of higher education. A common reservation about critical-thinking pedagogy is that the movement to improve critical thinking across the curriculum has stalled. Many commentators note that the definition of "critical thinking" has become so broad that "critical thinking" outcomes can be argued for any element of the curriculum. As a result, there is a widespread sense that critical thinking has become somewhat vacuous as an educational outcome (Ten Dam and Volman 2004, 360). Conservative critics have noted that a more global education in argument and "critical" deliberation has been substituted by the indoctrinating effects of mere ideological screed—here critical thinking is assumed to mean indoctrination in leftist critique as opposed to a more ideologically balanced inculcation of thinking and analytical capacities (Zelnick 2008).

These impasses in critical-thinking pedagogy afford the debate-across-the-curriculum movement an opportunity. Debate-across-the-curriculum practices can jump start critical-thinking pedagogy, providing a robust counterargument to the two main objections to the value of emphasizing critical thinking in the classroom. First, defining critical thinking through debate practice provides specific and assessable outcomes for critical-thinking pedagogy. Debate pedagogy articulates the goal of critical-thinking pedagogy as the inculcation of a facility for evaluating argument forms, argument interactions, and the relationship between argumentative claims and the evidence presented to justify them in a given context. Thus, debate pedagogy reinforces and provides specificity regarding outcomes to a curriculum in critical thinking that advances "attention to the development of the epistemological beliefs of students; promoting active learning; a problem-based curriculum; stimulating interaction between students; and learning on the basis of real-life situations" (Ten Dam and Volman 2004, 359). Second, debate practices address the conservative critique of critical thinking by providing a pedagogical practice where all sides of a question are open to contestation in a balanced, rigorous, and systematic way. If the conservative critique holds that universities have become havens for leftist thinking at the expense of the play of the free market of ideas (a critique that has real implications for the health of higher education), debate offers a near-perfect rejoinder that our colleges and universities are not only open to all arguments, but perhaps more significantly, that colleges and universities have built into their curricula a forum that necessitates the critical interrogation of arguments from all sides of our ideological divides.

The evidence that debate promotes critical thought and evaluation of arguments on their own merits is quite compelling. Joe Bellon's landmark article on debate across the curriculum cites a number of quantitative and qualitative studies supporting the claim that debate experience significantly boosts exactly these types of skills (Barfield 1989, cited in Bellon 2000, 166; Brembeck 1949; Colbert 1987). Jeff Parcher's (1998) summation of the same literature concludes that:

> Colbert and Biggers noted that "50 years of research correlates debate training with critical thinking skills" (1985, 212). Keefe, Harte, and Norton reviewed the research and concluded that, "[m]any researchers over the past four decades have come to the same general conclusions. Critical thinking ability is significantly improved by courses in argumentation and debate and by debate experience." (Parcher 1998, 2)

The most authoritative study to date, Mike Allen, Sandra Berkowitz, Steve Hunt, and Allan Louden's (1999) meta-analysis of forensics education, substantiates a strong link between debate practice and improved critical-thinking skills. The meta-analysis of Allen et al. demonstrated that participation in debate produced significant benefits for students' critical-thinking capacities, demonstrating a substantial comparative advantage in cultivating critical-thinking skills when compared to other activities intended for that purpose (Allen et al. 1999, 18). Some have argued that this effect is due in part to self-selection, claiming that motivated and articulate students naturally make their way to debate. Specifically addressing the question of self-selection in measures of critical thinking, the study demonstrates that longitudinal data support the claim that debate participation both increases critical thinking relative to nonparticipation, and, perhaps more significantly, that students' critical-thinking skills increase as their experience with debate increases (p. 20).

The analysis of Allen et al. refutes an earlier analysis by Vincent Follert and Kent Colbert (1983) on the grounds that the latter analysis did not take into account average effects of debate participation. Follert and Colbert's study employed a relatively static "vote-counting" method that specified conditions for a yes/no conclusion about the benefits of forensic participation on critical thinking, and simply counted the number of yeses compared to the number of nos. Of the 47 studies Follert and Colbert evaluated, 28 demonstrated an increase in critical-thinking capacities, and 19 did not. On these grounds, the Follert and Colbert study concluded that there is not a consistent "body of evidence" supporting debate's capacity to increase critical-thinking skills (1983, 2). Allen et al. conclude that when one takes into account a broader body of data in a meta-analysis, weighing studies for sample size and average effects, there is substantial evidence that forensics participation increases critical-thinking skills (1999, 24). They conclude:

> The most important outcome of the present meta-analysis is that regardless of the specific measure used to assess critical thinking, the type of design employed, or the specific type of communication skill training taught, critical thinking improved as a result of training in communication skills. The findings illustrate that participation in public communication skill building exercises consistently improved critical thinking. Participation in forensics demonstrated the largest improvement in critical thinking scores whether considering longitudinal or cross-sectional designs. (Allen et al. 1999, 27)

Sandra Berkowitz's recent reevaluation of this analysis extends this conclusion, arguing that as one specifies the content of critical thinking by articulating its subcomponents, the correlation between debate and critical thinking becomes even more robust. "The results," she argues, "confirm what many of us already know: training in . . . debate . . . has clear and demonstrable effects on critical thinking development" (2006, 57).

There is a strong theoretical and pedagogical rationale for these findings. Alfred Snider and Max Schnurer make the case for debate across the curriculum by arguing that "because debate teaches students to evaluate evidence, to form their own opinions based on research rather than knee-jerk reactions, and to present their views clearly and persuasively, it imparts skills that are useful in virtually any field of study" (Snider and Schnurer 2002, 11). Perhaps more important, in their view, debate instills an *ethos* for education that is both critical and cooperative, as they argue: "students work together in teams to prepare their arguments, debate teaches the virtues of cooperation and, once the debate itself begins, friendly competition" (ibid.).

Kennedy argues that debate participation is one of the few college-level pedagogical practices that forces an integration of the cognitive functions that define critical thinking (Kennedy 2007, 184). In Kennedy's accounting, an all-too-common focus on the transmission of information in the form of curricular content has worked at cross-purposes with cultivating the necessary skills in deliberation, analysis, and evaluation that support critical thinking. Kennedy sees debate as one of the best alternatives to embody a commitment to cultivating critical thinking. Citing critical-thinking theorists, she argues that the real challenge is to move the pedagogical relationship with students from a focus on *what* to think to a focus on *how* to think:

> Because debates require listeners and participants to evaluate competing choices (Freeley and Steinberg 2005), they follow Vygotsky's call for the type of social interaction that develops higher-order psychological functions as well as critical thinking skills by moving up Bloom's Taxonomy. . . . The lower order thinking skills of knowledge, comprehension, and application focus on rote learning or *what* students should think, whereas the higher order thinking skills of analysis, synthesis, and evaluation focus on *how* to think: "The short-term objective of acquiring knowledge should be tempered with the long-term goal of training the mind to think analytically and critically" (Vo and Morris 2006, 16). Instructional strategies such as debate and case studies are better suited to the development of students' higher order thinking skills than traditional instructional strategies such as lecture (Roy and Macchiette 2005). Critical thinking skills used in a debate include defining the problem, assessing the credibility of sources, identifying and challenging assumptions, recognizing inconsistencies, and prioritizing the relevance and salience of various points within the overall argument. (Kennedy 2007, 185)

Debate also holds promise in answering the second criticism of critical thinking in education, namely, that "critical thinking" in the modern university is simply code for left-wing indoctrination. The stakes in this claim are significant for the future of critical thinking in the academy, and more significantly for the health of the academy itself. The idea that college education has become less about developing a commitment to knowledge, inquiry, and analytical skill than a boot camp for ideological indoctrination is a common theme. Often such arguments are marshaled in efforts to cut college and university budgets (including research budgets), calls to eliminate tenure, and efforts to impose content controls: the success of any of these measures would have significant implications for the health of the academy, and, perhaps more important, for free academic inquiry. With a renewed commitment to debate, colleges and universities would be able to say to their critics that they are doing everything possible to create campus climates where students are educated, not indoctrinated, where argument from all sides of our ideological divides are open to full, frank, and respectful discussion.

As one measure of this claim, studies demonstrate that debate is a useful tool in minimizing the appearance of instructor bias. Debate minimizes instructor bias by shifting the locus of the classroom from a monologue aimed at the inculcation of one person's point of view into a discussion where opposing sides engage in debate around critical propositions of policy, theory, or value. The result of this shift is that students become a vehicle for conveying pedagogical contents, and, more important, structural balance in the discussion inheres as a result of debate's dialectical exchange. Additionally, debate creates an openness toward the arguments on all sides of an issue as students have a strategic incentive to listen to the other side of an argument, and defend positions that do not reflect their initial viewpoints. "Schroeder and Ebert (1983) assert that debate . . . [minimizes] instructor bias; . . . when students defend a position they oppose, they must at least temporarily transcend their own bias. By learning about both sides of a controversial topic, students are more open-minded and better able to see another person's viewpoint" (Kennedy 2007, 185).

THE CASE FOR DEBATE IN COLLEGE CLASSROOMS: ACADEMIC PERFORMANCE AND PEDAGOGICAL PRACTICE

The evidence for debate's beneficial effects on critical thinking is robust, but it is still possible to ask whether debate in the classroom improves academic performance. Intuition and anecdotal evidence suggest that the critical-thinking and analytical skill cultivated by debate translates to better academic performance. Minh Luong, a professor in the Ethics, Politics and Economics Program at Yale provides a representative anecdote: "as a college professor, I note that my top students are most often . . . debaters who actively participate in class discussions and articulate persuasive arguments both in class and on written assignments" (Luong 2000, 35). Empirical evidence confirms this intuition: Michael Cronin claims that "Students report . . . their courses are improved due to the incorporation of debate as a teaching/learning activity and feel that debate should be used again in these courses" (Cronin 1990, 12–13).

Jean Goodwin's study of in-class debates confirms Cronin's claim for greater self-efficacy in learning. Specifically, Goodwin found that in-class debates reinforced the goals of existing curricula in three ways. First, students engaged the course content more "deeply" because debate exercises required more careful and detailed reading of the course materials, and forced reflection on these themes "throughout the week" (Goodwin 2003, 162). Debate complemented other course objectives: "The great majority of students (79%), however, focused on how the debates had encouraged or indeed 'forced' them to better learn course content" (ibid.). Second, the group work surrounding debates invited students to integrate a broad spectrum of their peers' opinions on the course matter, most important, by providing a competitive incentive to listen to, understand, and integrate opposing viewpoints (ibid.). Third, debate promoted a "personal connection" to the course material by necessitating that students decide on and articulate an individual opinion on the material (ibid.).

The conclusion that we should make from this evidence is that debate's multiplier effects on the existing curriculum extend beyond better critical thinking: they are also intimately related to the ways that debate promotes pedagogical best practices. In-class debating integrates pedagogical best practices into the classroom by creating a cooperative, multidimensional learning environment. Frank Duffin's (2006) study of debate-across-the-curriculum initiatives in Rhode Island High Schools collected state-level data in 2001–4 and compared the learning outcomes for students involved in the initiative with those of students who were not involved. Duffin's study found that debate fostered "multidimensional and heterogeneous transfer of learning" (p. 148). The result of these practices was "a learning environment that was open, fluid, and democratic, as opposed to closed, rigid, and hierarchical . . . [promoting] learner-centered environments, knowledge-centered environments, assessment-centered environments, and community-centered environments" (ibid.).

Debate's ability to foster pedagogical best practices makes in-class debating a better vehicle for advancing learning than the two primary modes of instruction in the college classroom: the essay and the lecture. Kennedy cites compelling evidence based on student self-assessments that debate is much better than lecturing for student learning in terms of content mastery, critical insight, and, perhaps most important, in eliciting discussion from students who would not otherwise participate (Kennedy 2007, 185). There is a similar benefit of debate when compared to essay writing, providing an argument for a mixed curriculum of debating, lectures, and essay writing as a best pedagogical practice:

In addition, while written essays are used more frequently than debates, Gregory and Holloway (2005) contend that debates extend students' critical thinking and argumentation skills more than essays and that they demand additional performance skills that essays do not. Assessing students in a variety of ways—with both writing and oral assignments—gives more students an opportunity to excel. (Kennedy 2007, 184–85)

THE CASE FOR DEBATE IN COLLEGE CLASSROOMS: APPLICATION AND INTERDISCIPLINARITY

Part of the benefit of debate in this regard is that more than simply fostering student engagement with the curricula by incentivizing mastery of the material and engendering a cooperative learning environment, debate practices also facilitate the application of course material to students' everyday lives (Kennedy 2007, 183; Martens 2005, 4). Debate practice is uniquely effective in fostering application because it demands that a student have a relatively comprehensive grasp of a subject area, but, more important, that they articulate a position relative to the issues in the debate, and evaluate the competing claims that they might make in relation to the strength of the evidence that supports them (Schuster and Meany 2005). Thus, debate practices foster not only engagement with an issue but also an evaluation of a student's position relative to an issue in the light of the best arguments for and against a proposition. Debate offers privileged access not only to content mastery, or even opinion formation, but what is more important is that it bridges the gap between the theoretical knowledge inculcated in the classroom and the specific personal stands that one might take both toward a specific resolution and, more broadly, toward the critical argumentative connections that a given resolution for debate accesses. Debate then has the potential to create a depth of inquiry and evaluation relative to the classroom curriculum that is unparalleled both in terms of knowledge of a subject area, and perhaps more significantly, in terms of a set of owned investments relative to the propositions at hand.

Finally, the curricular benefits of debate extend beyond engagement with materials in a given course toward the concrete application of educational contents that spans disciplinary divides. Strategic incentives in a debate often lead to consideration of materials that are not directly related to the readings and assignments. In-class debates provide a fertile site for students to make conceptual connections across the curriculum. It is not uncommon for the issues in a policy debate, for example, to lead students to research in economics, behavioral sciences, political science, and public policy, as well as to issues deeply rooted in the traditions of ethics, political theory, or philosophy. Thus, in-class debates provide one very tangible way of inviting students to integrate the work that they do in a number of classes. Here debate serves as a powerful tool for countering what is an all-too-common tendency for undergraduates to specialize in increasingly narrow areas by promoting a kind of thinking and strategizing that is interdisciplinary by nature and that invites an exploration of the intersections between a student's various fields of study. Expanding debate might create a powerful double movement that deals with some of the most trenchant critiques of modern educational practices: debate both cultivates analytical, research, and evaluative skills that are portable across all curricula (Snider and Schnurer 2002), and invites problem-centered interdisciplinary thinking while enhancing the benefits of intense study in a specific area. In a climate of increasing emphasis on interdisciplinarity as a hallmark of educational best practices, debate provides a crucial means of realizing a commitment to conversation across disciplines in the classroom.

THE CASE FOR DEBATE IN COLLEGE CLASSROOMS: BENEFITS BEYOND THE UNIVERSITY

So far, I have focused primarily on the benefits of debate for instruction in colleges and universities. The benefits of expanded debate practice, however, extend well beyond the walls of the academy. One of the primary benefits of debate that extends beyond a student's time at school is that debate cultivates robust communication skills, a task that modern colleges and universities have let slip from their pedagogical priorities. Bellon cites evidence of widespread agreement that colleges and universities are failing in the task of inculcating oral communication skills (Bellon 2000, 163). Bellon argues, citing William Semlak and Donald Shields (1977), that debaters are "significantly better at employing the three communication skills (analysis, delivery, and organization) than students who have not had debate experience" (Bellon 2000, 166).

Some argue that there are alternate places where students might learn to speak effectively, such as public-speaking courses. This objection would have merit if the only issue in oral-communication skills were facility in delivering speeches. The unique communicative benefits of debate often get lost in discussions about communicative competencies, in part, because so many educators fail to realize that communicative competency is broader than delivery skills. Debate teaches critical skills in organizing one's thoughts, thinking on one's feet, managing conflict, arguing, analyzing, and responsibly dealing with the claims of one's interlocutor. This broad collection of skills, all of which flow in some way from the combination of increased critical-thinking skills, attention to other points of view, and the practice of delivering one's speech to an audience has substantial benefits in terms of students' capacities for life beyond college.

Most of us believe as a matter of everyday experience that oral-communication skills contribute to success in the university and the world beyond it. The pragmatic benefits of in-class debating for the future career advancement of students have not been studied directly to the best of my knowledge. There is a substantial body of evidence from competitive intercollegiate debate that participation in debate creates a skill set that directly and materially impacts the potential for a student's career advancement. Usually in making this argument, debate advocates list the incredible number of highly successful people who were debaters. (presidents Jimmy Carter, Richard Nixon, Lyndon Baines Johnson, and John F. Kennedy; Supreme Court justices Samuel Alito, Antonin Scalia, and Stephen Breyer; politicians Ted Sorenson, Bob Schrum, and Karl Rove; former U.N. secretary Kofi Annan; captains of industry such as Lee Iacocca; media personalities such as Oprah Winfrey and Tom Brokaw; and legal thinkers such as Lawrence Tribe and Erwin Chemerinsky all usually fall somewhere on the list—though there are a plethora of others.) According to Jeff Parcher, one survey showed that "over 80% of all current members of Congress were on their school's forensics team" (1998, 8).

Of course, it is difficult to say beyond a strong intuition what role debate played in the success of each of these people, and self-selection provides a powerful counterargument to citing a list of successful former debaters as a justification for debate. At the same time, there is good anecdotal and empirical evidence supporting the claim that debate directly contributes to students' future prospects. For example, recent newspaper articles have cited testimonials from chief executive officers (CEOs) who attribute their success in large part to participation in debate (Jones 2004; Ross 2002). Many of the CEOs attributed their success to the research and organization skills learned in debate, and, perhaps more important, the CEOs found training in debate to be uniquely situated to the business world because it taught them to "make decisions under pressure and in a timely manner" (Jones 2004). This anecdotal evidence comports with the nature of the business world as a site requiring difficult decisions under conditions of time pressure and incomplete information. In this context, it is a substantial asset to cultivate the ability to manage deliberative processes by taking arguments on all sides into account while simultaneously articulating a clear and well-reasoned plan. That businesses recognize this fact is evidenced by the increasing emphasis on competitive deliberative decision-making models. For example, Parcher argues that "there is strong empirical evidence, for example, that utilizing devil's advocacy helps improve the understanding of strategic problems. In fact, devil's advocacy has been used successfully by a number of companies for this exact purpose" (Parcher 1998, 2, citing Schwenk 1988). As a result, debate serves as an important training tool for inculcating decision-making skills that produce substantial direct benefits for students who seek the private-sector careers that put a high premium on solid decision making.

The broader effects of debate on future career success are also well documented in the self-assessments of debate alumni. Parcher cites a survey by Jeffery Hobbs and Robert Chandler 'that concluded "that debate alumni overwhelmingly agreed that debate experience had aided them significantly in their professional careers" (1998, 5; see also Williams, McGee, and Worth 2001). Hobbs and Chandler argue that:

> Training in debate provides students with a positive experience which helps them to develop skills which will be needed in their professions. Several respondents, in response to the open-ended questions, reported that debate was the most valuable educational experience they received . . . this survey overwhelmingly supports the idea that participation in policy debate provides significant benefits for those entering the professions of law, management, ministry and teaching. (1991, 6)

It seems that private-sector employers agree with this assessment, at least if hiring practices are any indicator of the qualities and experiences that make employees attractive. Ted Sheckels surveyed Midwest businesses hiring managers, finding that many of them "listed debate first among twenty other activities and academic specializations that an applicant might present on a resume" and also found that "debate was the 'overwhelming' first choice preferred activities by recruiters at major law firms" (Sheckels 1984, 2, quoted in Parcher 1998, 5).

Debate participation also substantially increases leadership and administrative skills. Mel Levine (2005) laments that colleges do not prepare students for life beyond graduation, and offers debate practice as a way of helping to instill crucial leadership skills, including capacities for critical thinking, time management, and organizational skill. Self-assessments of debate alumni provide empirical validation for Levine's claim. Bellon cites a study by Anthony Schroeder and Pamela Schroeder (1995, 19), who surveyed educational administrators, and found that their respondents "overwhelmingly" saw debate participation as the "single most important educational activity they engaged in," and as a significant asset in building their administrative and leadership skills (Bellon 2000, 169). Both Parcher (1998, 7) and Ronald Matlon and Lucy Keele (1984) argue for the strong link between debate participation and leadership skills, citing the significant number of former debate participants who hold important leadership positions in politics, the academy, professional organizations, and the military. Matlon and Keele argue that:

> positions held by former NDT debaters read like a "Who's Who" in leadership. Here is a sample of positions currently or once held by competitive debate alumni: A Cabinet member; Congresspersons; presidents of bar associations, colleges and universities; educational leaders; ambassadors; commanding officers in the military; numerous state and federal government elected and appointed positions; publishers; bankers; corporate board chairpersons; and judicial positions at all levels including law school deans and attorney generals. (Matlon and Keele 1984, 195)

It is clear from this evidence that debate participation provides students a substantial leg up in their future vocational endeavors. And without question, these arguments comprise one important benefit of debate participation. But the benefits of expanding exposure to debate do not simply inhere at the level of individual success beyond the university: one of the strongest warrants for debate practice lies in the broader social effects of debate participation. Debate practices cultivate skills that significantly enhance the prospects for a vital civic and democratic life.

On Debate and Democratic Culture

The social goods generated by debate extend beyond the benefits of making students better critical thinkers or more effective and desirable employees. Expanded debate participation in the classroom cultivates capacities for democratic citizenship. I argue for these benefits by addressing critiques of debate practice holding that debate cultivates an ethos that is harmful to democracy. I highlight three of them: the criticism that debate engenders oppositional binaries that undermine cooperative deliberation (or, that debate is reductive and antagonistic); the criticism that debate contributes to an overly parochial conception of democracy (debate promotes democratic insularity); and the criticism that oral-communication skills are less important for democracy than they used to be (advocating for debate participates in a naive democratic nostalgia).

The first criticism, which is primarily held by critics of debate in the deliberative-democracy movement, argues that because debate practice tends to reduce issues to a simple pro and con, and because debate involves a level of competitive antagonism, debate forecloses the richer democratic possibilities available through more open and cooperative models of deliberation (see, for example, Tumposky 2004). The second critique, primarily associated with former debaters Ronald Greene and Darrin Hicks, argues that the ideology of switch-side debating expresses an aggressive vision of liberal democracy, promoting an insular conception of American democratic exceptionalism. For Greene and Hicks, the problem is not debate itself, but rather the way that debate as cultural technology serves as an alibi for a normative conception of democracy that authorizes intervention in places that do not practice an American version of liberalism: "creat[ing] a field of intervention to transform and change the world one subject (regime) at a time" (Greene and Hicks 2005, 101). The third critique, often forwarded by critics of deliberative democracy, argues that debate privileges an outdated notion of democracy as pegged to the unfettered agency of the reading and speaking citizen, and as a result, promotes an inattention to the institutional and technological forces that define the context of modern life. This is a critique that has become increasingly prevalent recently, but it ultimately has its roots in Walter Lippmann's critique of the idea of "the public" (Lippmann 1925).

In response to the first critique, which ultimately reduces to the claims that debate overdetermines democratic deliberation and that it inculcates an unhealthy antagonism, a number of scholars have extended the old maxim that dissent is critical to democracy in arguing that debate is a critical tool for civic deliberation (Brookfield and Preskill 1999; Levinson 2003). Gill Nichols (2000, 132) argues that a commitment to debate and dissent as a core component of democracy is especially critical in the face of the complexity of modern governance, rapid technological change, and an increasing need to deal with the nexus of science and public policy. The benefits of in-class debate espoused by Stephen Brookfield, Meira Levinson, and Nichols stem from the idea that debate inculcates skills for creative and open-minded discussion of disputes in the context of democratic deliberation: on their collective accounting, debate does not close down discussion by reducing issues to a simple pro/con binary, nor does it promote antagonism at the expense of cooperative discussion. Rather, properly cultivated, debate is a tool for managing democratic conflicts that foregrounds significant points of dispute, and then invites interlocutors to think about them together creatively in the context of successive strategic iterations, moments of evaluation, and reiterations of arguments in the context of a structured public discussion.

Goodwin's study of in-class debate practice confirms these intuitions. Goodwin's study revealed that debate produces an intense personal connection to class materials while simultaneously making students more open to differing viewpoints. Goodwin's conclusion is worth quoting at length here:

> Traditional teaching techniques like textbooks, lectures, and tests with right answers insulate students from the open questions and competing answers that so often drive our own interest in our subjects. Debates do not, and in fact invite students to consider a range of alternative views on a subject, encountering the course content broadly, deeply and personally. Students' comments about the value of disagreement also offer an interesting perspective on the nature of the thinking skills we want to foster. The previous research . . . largely focused on the way debate can help students better master the principles of correct reasoning. Although some students did echo this finding, many more emphasized the importance of debate in helping them to recognize and deal with a diversity of viewpoints. (Goodwin 2003, 158)

The results of this research create significant questions about the conclusion that debate engenders reductive thinking and an antagonism that is unhealthy to democracy. In terms of the criticism that debate is reductive, the implication of Goodwin's study is that debate creates a broader appreciation for multiple perspectives on an issue than the predominant forms of classroom instruction. This conclusion is especially powerful when one considers debate as more than a discrete singular performance, but as a whole process of inventing, discussing, employing, and reformulating arguments in the context of an audience of comparatively objective evaluators. In the process of researching, strategizing, debating, reframing stances, and switching sides on a question, students are provided with both a framework for thinking about a problem and creative solutions to it from a number of angles. Thus, while from a very narrow perspective one might claim debate practices reduce all questions to a "pro" and a "con," the cumulative effects of the pedagogical process of preparing for, performing, and evaluating a debate provide the widest possible exposure to the varied positions that a student might take on an issue. Perhaps more significantly, in-class debate provides a competitive incentive for finding as many innovative and unique approaches to a problem as possible, and for translating them into publically useful positions.

Goodwin's study is even more damaging to the claim that debate promotes an antagonistic ethos that is unhealthy for democratic deliberation. According to Goodwin's study, in-class debating promotes consensus and cooperation more than it promotes antagonism. The cooperative benefits of debate pedagogy are perhaps most compelling when held up against the background of the readily available modes of public democratic discourse that students might employ without debate training. The idea that one can eliminate antagonistic and even competitively driven democratic discourse is, quite frankly, unrealistic. Democratic politics are almost irreducibly related to the articulation of interests and agendas that are at odds with other interests and agendas in the public sphere. If the empirical life of actually existing democratic discourse is any measure, there is no shortage of issues over which American democracy is caught on the rails of seemingly irresolvable disputes. Questions such as the future and content of higher education, moral issues such as same-sex marriage and abortion, and foreign-policy questions often invite not only vigorous, but hotly contested and hostile discourse in the public sphere. The question is not will there be democratic deliberative deadlocks, or even heated debate, but rather how will we most productively manage such deadlocks?

Because they are also citizens, students will inevitably be put in the position of arguing in public about one or more of these questions, and to be sure, we are not dealing with very many of these disputes productively in the public sphere as currently constituted. As one of the few common touchstone experiences that profoundly influences the views and practices of democratic life together or future leaders, corporate movers and shakers, media moguls, teachers, and everyday citizens, colleges and universities should take a more active role in equipping citizens with the tools to productively manage the rough and tumble of democratic life. Universities inculcate practices of citizenship that students carry over into public life, whether such practices are inculcated with care, intentionality, and deliberation or by simple inattention. Thus, those detractors who reject debate as engendering unhealthy democratic antagonism are on shaky argumentative ground on two separate accounts: even if debate practices engender a degree of antagonism, they are certainly better than the prevailing modes of public discourse; and, beyond the speculations of those who are primarily arguing against a caricature of debate, the best empirical studies of actual debate pedagogy indicate that debate inculcates precisely the kind of argumentative capacities that can correct for the antagonistic failings of democratic deliberation.

Debate provides a critical and perhaps unparalleled tool for building democratic capacities because it creates incentives to listen to opposing arguments, and, more important, to think them through on their own terms, if only, at first, for the sake of strategic due diligence. Kennedy's compilation of studies substantiates the claim that debate creates better listening skills, and further, that the empirical effect of increased listening in the context of debate is a significantly increased possibility for opinion change compared to other pedagogical strategies (Kennedy 2007, 184, 185). Kennedy's study is worth quoting at length here because of the strength and breadth of empirical evidence that she marshals:

> opponents believe that participation in a debate merely reinforces a student's existing beliefs rather than promoting an objective analysis of an issue. However, Simonneaux (2001) reports that in all of his studies, the only time the students in his biotechnology classes . . . have changed their opinions has been when they participated in a role play or debate. In Budesheim and Lundquist's (2000) research study of 72 students in three psychology courses at Creighton University, the students who defended a position they already supported almost always maintained their original viewpoint, whereas the students who argued a position inconsistent with their initial opinion were more likely to change their opinion. The response of the audience proved to be unpredictable, as only 52% maintained their original positions. Green and Klug (1990) reported similar results in that the sociology students who defended their initial viewpoint did not change their view, whereas those who were initially neutral or initially opposed the view they defended often changed their view in support of the side they debated. Johnson and Johnson (1985) found that 11 and 12 year old students who studied controversial issues independently were less likely to change their opinions than those who engaged in debate with others. (Kennedy 2007, 186)

This potential for opinion change, especially when compared to other pedagogical methods, makes it difficult to sustain the thesis that debate engenders inflexible antagonism. One explanation for these results is found in Goodwin's study, which validates the idea that debate creates a framework for cooperative group learning around contested issues. Goodwin concludes that her "results point to the value of debate-across-the-curriculum for promoting small group communication and for fostering divergent perspectives on course topics" (Goodwin 2003, 157). In her accounting, practice in structured debate is ultimately the core determinant of whether students learn to see debate as cooperative democratic problem solving, ultimately subsuming debate's antagonistic impulses within a broader sense of openness to opposing viewpoints, or whether students will parrot already culturally available and, frankly, bad models of debate that circulate in mass media.

But the ideological openness and opinion flexibility produced by debate are not simply reducible to listening or to better group-communication processes, though these are significant benefits in and of themselves. One of the primary reasons why debate processes promote managed antagonism and a cooperatively open-minded ethos for democratic education is debate's unique capacity to inculcate argumentatively based role-playing. Ostensibly, one of the significant drivers of the intense antagonistic impasses in contemporary American public deliberation is that often times such impasses are underwritten by a fundamental inattention to the best merits of the other side of a democratic dispute's arguments and motivations. Mitchell (2000) argues that debate provides a pitch-perfect antidote to this problem by inviting students to inhabit the argumentative frame of those with whom they might not agree. The result of this practice is that students are more able to productively interrogate their preexisting opinions in the light of public argument, and simultaneously are called to engage in an evaluative reformation of their stances on the issue at hand.

Cumulatively, the incentives that in-class debate creates for evaluating all sides of an issue, strategic innovation in addressing the resolution, openness to differing points of view, listening, opinion change, and role-playing make debate a democratic technology par excellence. Debate is a deliberative technology that extends democratic discourse by providing capacity for better-informed and more clearly articulated positions on contested issues, while simultaneously (and even perhaps paradoxically) producing a citizen who is more likely to listen to, engage, and even be changed by the opinions of others. The crucial question here is not whether the debate process has drawbacks. Rather, the crucial question is whether or not debate is the best alternative among the available alternatives for democratic discourse. Democratic discourse is, by its nature, contingent, imperfect, and only undertaken under conditions where competing interests are at stake and where there is no unassailable normative claim to decide a dispute. In this light, the paradoxical ability of debate to both clarify and strengthen convictions while cultivating openness to a diversity of opinions and social positions makes it perhaps the best alternative among necessarily imperfect modes of democratic talk.

While these arguments address the first critique of debate, they are also the kinds of claims that underwrite much of the force of Greene and Hicks's critique of debate as a cultural technology. I take Greene and Hicks as exemplars of the idea that debate creates an insular conception of democracy, in part because of their recent reception by the debate community, but more specifically because Greene and Hicks's argument taps into a significant cultural meme regarding debate—that debate creates an arrogance regarding proper analytical and democratic practice that works at cross-purposes to valuing other modes of deliberation. It is worth noting that Greene and Hicks are not arguing against debate per se, but rather against the cultural appropriations of debate, and that despite their critique they have been supportive of debate as a pedagogical practice. The primary point of Greene and Hicks's critique is that debate is a *technology*, that is, a habituated technique for organizing speech. In their reading, debate, as a technology of discourse, regulates not only what can be said in public, but how it will be said, and to what broader cultural and political effects this technique can be yoked. In this reading, debate as a technology is open to any number of cultural appropriations, which reaffirm the desirability of a mode of democratic deliberation in ways that may be both productive and destructive. In this light, it is possible to say that debate has benefits for the individual student participants, but also that the larger cultural implications of debate are that it has too often served as a mode of legitimating an American democratic exceptionalism at the expense of other forms of political speech. One of the implications of marking debate as a cultural technology, and more specifically as a habituated technique for discourse, is that the character of debate is not given in advance, but is open to constant rearticulation—as a technology debate can be articulated to certain undesirable ends, but it is also amenable to being articulated differently. This, in fact, is one of the great virtues of debate compared to other means of dialogue: that it not only invites a constant reinvention but also creates strategic incentives for such reinvention.

Debate shares this commitment to reinvention with democracy: one of the great virtues of democracy, noted in Greek antiquity and reiterated by modern-day theorists from John Dewey to Jacques Derrida, is that democracy is amenable to critique, reformulation, and improvement. Dewey captures this notion in the idea of "creative intelligence," which holds that the very contingent conditions that invite democratic life together in the first place also allow for the creative and deliberative reformulation of democracy in response to its challenges (Dewey and Moore 2007). Derrida (2001) has argued similarly that democracy's best feature is that it is both revisable and perfectible. The implication of democracy's revisability and perfectibility extends both backward into an account of democracy's founding conditions and forward to its ideal future: to a "democracy yet to come" (Derrida 2001). Perfectibility and revisability imply that the democracy we have now is neither perfect, complete, nor guaranteed in advance. At the same time, perfectibility and revisability imply that whatever democracy's failings, the founding condition of democracy also invites the possibility that democracy will exceed its current iterations and be made anew, into something that is better. As democratic technology and technique, debate builds a structural commitment to perfectibility and revisability into democratic discourse, by suggesting that current conditions of democratic life be open to critical analysis and that our common democratic life might be lived differently. Because debate practice highlights both the revisability and perfectibility of democratic life, on balance, the best answer to the drawbacks of debate's current cultural articulations is, to put it bluntly, more debate.

Specifically, by the very practice of holding critical questions up for public contest, debate pedagogy inculcates an ethos that sees democracy as not already here, but as something in the making, so much so that a commitment to debate embodies both the strongest critique of and best hope for perfecting democratic politics—debate practices, by their nature, relentlessly rearticulate democracy. More pointedly for Greene and Hicks's critique, the best way out of a broader sense of democratic insularity lies in turning debate toward the presuppositions of American exceptionalism, a move present in the most simple act of debate: that is, in pointing out that there is something flawed in the status quo or in our conventional approaches to fixing it. Debate practice contains within itself the conditions for exceeding the current articulation of democracy and simultaneously cultivates capacities that provide concrete political hope that we might realize a democracy that is different from the one we have now. The alternative, to give up on debate, leaves not only the insularity of debate's articulation to democracy intact, but more important, leaves the whole edifice of American exceptionalism, which is rooted deeply at many sites beyond debate, fundamentally untroubled.

The final critique of debate pedagogy that I address is that debate practice promotes a naive conception of the speaking citizen that is inappropriate to our current democratic context. This critique of debate, while useful in highlighting the changing conditions of governance that implicate all of us, fails on two accounts. First, even though the citizen speaking in public may not hold the same sway it once did (if it ever did), speech does make a difference in a number of democratic processes: political speech influences how people vote and to whom they contribute money, and it makes a significant difference at a number of sites in the administrative apparatuses of modern government (for instance in public notice and comment practices). More important, even if the romantic vision of the individual citizen's speech changing the course of democratic life is a bit overblown in our context, political speech makes an important difference in noninstitutional practices of political socialization: political speech not only influences who we will vote for but also sets the bar for what we will put up with, profoundly influences our views regarding the legitimacy of public policies, and determines the range of opinions to which we are exposed. Thus, even if debate practices do not directly access the levers of power, they might play a significant role in the production and reformulation of our political culture.

The second major problem with the critique that identifies a naivety in articulating debate and democracy is that it presumes that the primary pedagogical outcome of debate is speech capacities. But the democratic capacities built by debate are not limited to speech—as indicated earlier, debate builds capacity for critical thinking, analysis of public claims, informed decision making, and better public judgment. If the picture of modern political life that underwrites this critique of debate is a pessimistic view of increasingly labyrinthine and bureaucratic administrative politics, rapid scientific and technological change outpacing the capacities of the citizenry to comprehend them, and ever-expanding insular special-interest- and money-driven politics, it is a puzzling solution, at best, to argue that these conditions warrant giving up on debate. If democracy is open to rearticulation, it is open to rearticulation precisely because as the challenges of modern political life proliferate, the citizenry's capacities can change, which is one of the primary reasons that theorists of democracy such as Dewey in *The Public and Its Problems* place such a high premium on education (Dewey 1988, 63, 154). Debate provides an indispensible form of education in the modern articulation of democracy because it builds precisely the skills that allow the citizenry to research and be informed about policy decisions that impact them, to sort through and evaluate the evidence for and relative merits of arguments for and against a policy in an increasingly information-rich environment, and to prioritize their time and political energies toward policies that matter the most to them.

The merits of debate as a tool for building democratic capacity-building take on a special significance in the context of information literacy. John Larkin (2005, 140) argues that one of the primary failings of modern colleges and universities is that they have not changed curriculum to match with the challenges of a new information environment. This is a problem for the course of academic study in our current context, but perhaps more important, argues Larkin, for the future of a citizenry that will need to make evaluative choices against an increasingly complex and multimediated information environment (ibid.). Larkin's study tested the benefits of debate participation on information-literacy skills and concluded that in-class debate participants reported significantly higher self-efficacy ratings of their ability to navigate academic search databases and to effectively search and use other Web resources:

> To analyze the self-report ratings of the instructional and control group students, we first conducted a multivariate analysis of variance on all of the ratings, looking jointly at the effect of instruction/no instruction and debate topic . . . that it did not matter which topic students had been assigned . . . students in the Instructional [debate] group were significantly more confident in their ability to access information and less likely to feel that they needed help to do so. . . . These findings clearly indicate greater self-efficacy for online searching among students who participated in [debate]. . . . These results constitute strong support for the effectiveness of the project on students' self-efficacy for online searching in the academic databases. There was an unintended effect, however: After doing . . . the project, instructional group students also felt more confident than the other students in their ability to get good information from Yahoo and Google. It may be that the library research experience increased self-efficacy for any searching, not just in academic databases. (Larkin 2005, 144)

Larkin's study substantiates Thomas Worthen and Gaylen Pack's (1992, 3) claim that debate in the college classroom plays a critical role in fostering the kind of problem-solving skills demanded by the increasingly rich media and information environment of modernity. Though their essay was written in 1992 on the cusp of the eventual explosion of the Internet as a medium, Worthen and Pack's framing of the issue was prescient: the primary question facing today's student has changed from how to best research a topic to the crucial question of learning how to best evaluate which arguments to cite and rely upon from an easily accessible and veritable cornucopia of materials.

There are, without a doubt, a number of important criticisms of employing debate as a model for democratic deliberation. But cumulatively, the evidence presented here warrants strong support for expanding debate practice in the classroom as a technology for enhancing democratic deliberative capacities. The unique combination of critical-thinking skills, research and information-processing skills, oral-communication skills, and capacities for listening and thoughtful, open engagement with hotly contested issues argues for debate as a crucial component of a rich and vital democratic life. In-class debate practice both aids students in achieving the best goals of college and university education and serves as an unmatched practice for creating thoughtful, engaged, open-minded, and self-critical students who are open to the possibilities of meaningful political engagement and new articulations of democratic life.

Expanding this practice is crucial, if only because the more we produce citizens who can actively and effectively engage the political process, the more likely we are to produce revisions of democratic life that are necessary if democracy is not only to survive, but to thrive and to deal with systemic threats that risk our collective extinction. Democratic societies face a myriad of challenges, including: domestic and international issues of class, gender, and racial justice; wholesale environmental destruction and the potential for rapid climate change; emerging threats to international stability in the form of terrorism, intervention, and new possibilities for great power conflict; and increasing challenges of rapid globalization, including an increasingly volatile global economic structure. More than any specific policy or proposal, an informed and active citizenry that deliberates with greater skill and sensitivity provides one of the best hopes for responsive and effective democratic governance, and by extension, one of the last best hopes for dealing with the existential challenges to democracy in an increasingly complex world. Given the challenge of perfecting our collective political skill, and in drawing on the best of our collective creative intelligence, it is incumbent on us to both make the case for and, more important, to do the concrete work to realize an expanded commitment to debate at colleges and universities.

THE ALLRED INITIATIVE

For reasons beyond the control of any one actor, the competitive intercollegiate debate program at the University of North Carolina, Chapel Hill, ended in 1999. The loss of a program that had produced a robust debate tradition (a tradition that included a top speaker at the NDT and consistent participation in elimination rounds) was significant for reasons beyond the already lamentable loss of a vibrant tradition in the college-debate community. The loss of the debate program also represented, whether recognized or not, a significant change in the identity of the university. A commitment to debate is literally inscribed into one of the most recognizable manifestations of Carolina pride: the ever-present Tar Heel Blue. The school's colors came from a split in what was origi-nally the Carolina Debating Society, the first and most prominent student group at America's first public university. The Debating Society was established in 1795, and a few years later it split into two separate groups: the Dialectic Society and the Philanthropic Society. The Dialectic Society, which was interested in making debate one of the defining features of life at Carolina, took Tar Heel blue as its color, and the Philanthropic Society took white. One might claim that as a historical fact, nothing is more truly Carolina Blue than believing in the public, intellectual, and civic benefits of debate.

The current reincarnation of debate at North Carolina is the direct result of a professorship funded by an alum committed to the original meaning of Carolina Blue. In 2001 Jeff Allred established the "Jeff and Jennifer Allred Initiative in Critical Thinking and Debate." The Allreds' gift was motivated by Jeff and Jen-nifer's desire to reinvigorate a culture of debate at Carolina, and to extend the substantial benefits that Jeff gleaned from participation in debate to the whole Carolina community. My role in this narrative is as a direct benefactor of the Allreds' gift, specifically as a professor charged with the task of implementing the Allred Initiative.

The most immediate impact that the Allred Initiative has on the culture of debate at Carolina is through the Joseph P. McGuire first-year seminar se-ries, which supports an average of two sections a year of the first-year seminar "Think, Speak, Argue." The initiative targeted first-year seminars as a primary site for advancing debate on the assumption that first-year seminar experienc-es set the tone for the rest of a student's college experience, and because the first-year seminar program aims at cultivating norms for students' academic and social conduct while at the university. Thus, the first-year seminar is a debate-intensive experience that aims to cultivate an ethos of debate across the curric-ulum by providing students with experience in thinking through, researching, strategizing, and conducting debates. The goal of providing a class centered on debate early in a student's career is not only to provide students with skills that will benefit them throughout their university education but also to invite them to see all of the learning activities they will undertake at the university through the lens of their debate experience.

The seminar is broken into three distinct phases, with the goal of progressively building the capacities necessary to have formal fully structured debates. In the first section, "Think" the students read texts from scholars in argument and critical thinking, including Stephen Toulmin's *The Uses of Argument* (1958), John Dewey's *How We Think* (1991), and Harry Frankfurt's *On Bullshit* (2005). The main goal of this section is to introduce students to argument as a way of engaging issues, and to provide a framework for what counts as truly critical thinking. Exercises in this section include taking a significant and current public text and diagramming it with the Toulmin model, as well as reading news coverage of current events to spot fallacies. In the second section, "Speak," the students practice basic public-speaking skills, and are introduced to introductory concepts in rhetorical theory, including how to read an audience and how to think about choices for framing arguments, as well as how to listen for and unpack the rhetorical strategies of other speakers. The primary readings in this section include Aristotle's *On Rhetoric* (2006) and Lloyd Bitzer's "The Rhetorical Situation" (1968). The goal of these readings is to give students a sense that arguments do not occur in a vacuum, but rather that arguments occur only in the context of a community of listeners who take up positions both relative to their individual interests and within the coordinates of a persuasive situation.

The third section of the course, "Argue," takes up more than half of the instructional time. In this section, students are paired into teams of four and are expected to research both sides of a collaboratively generated resolution at least two times. The resolutions, which are the focus of debate for the entire semester, have included fairly controversial issues, such as the death penalty, American intervention in Iraq, global warming, affirmative action, and educational reform. I encourage the students to pick controversial resolutions on the basis of easily available materials, and, more important, to teach them that debate practice provides a comparatively safe space in which to explore positions on hotly contested public arguments. The debates become progressively more complex. The first debate includes four constructives and four rebuttals, and the students debate the resolution without a plan. The students receive basic instruction in how to write an affirmative case and how to write disadvantages. In the second debate we include cross-examination time, and invite the affirmative to define their relationship to the resolution by writing a plan. In the third debate the negative is allowed to introduce an alternative proposal to the affirmative's plan. The fourth debate is a no-holds-barred affair, where each side is allowed to employ any argument that they can generate, as long as it is substantiated with good evidence.

Every student who is not participating in a debate on a given day is required to serve as a judge, and is assigned the task of writing a ballot for the debate and providing oral critique to the debate competitors. I grade the ballots quite carefully, paying closer attention to students' rationales for how they vote than to their performances in the debate. I have been consistently surprised by the care and thought that student judges put into their decisions.

The goal of the seminar is ultimately to get undergraduates to carry their debate experience into the broader university community by getting them to take up the mantle of promoting debate practice. The final graded element of the class is a debate community-service project. To fulfill the assignment, individual debate teams may pick one of two options. The first option is that the team teach students not in the class how to debate, and then coach and judge a debate between the students they have recruited. The second option charges an individual debate team with holding a public debate on an issue related to the semester's topic. Teams are required to set up an event, recruit an audience, and to hold a pre-debate poll and post-debate vote and discussion of the audience's stance on the resolution. Ultimately, we would like to take advantage of the debate capacity that these practices build over time by holding an on-campus debate tournament for a small cash prize with teams composed of students who have participated in the seminar debating with students who do not have debate experience. The goal of this initiative to both develop the debate capacities of university students, and to expand the social impact of these capacities by incentivizing students to educate their peers in good debate practice.

Four things have surprised me about the experience of running the seminar. First, I have been surprised by the ability of students who are (in most cases) completely new to debate to pick up the basic skills of competitive policy debate. One of the most rewarding elements of the seminar in this regard is to observe how quickly and intensely the students' commitment to debate grows as their skills grow. As students begin to grasp the process of debate, the amount of time they spend preparing for the debates expands quite significantly. The time investment that the seminar students make is indicative of something that is perhaps more significant: the seminar students have been making the case for debate to their nondebating cohorts. Seminar students are proselytizing for debate, telling their peers about the fun and the benefits that they have derived from their debate experience. Second, I have been pleasantly surprised to see how the strategies generated by the teams eventually become quite intricate and nuanced. On at least two occasions I have copied cites from students to relay to college teams or to use at high-school institutes. The evidence and arguments generated by the death penalty and global warming resolutions in particular reflected a precision and depth of warrant that quite frankly astounded me. Third, I have been pleasantly surprised by the community of argument that seems to emerge in each class. Students take quite seriously their responsibilities in performing well in the debates and in judging. Students in the seminar pay attention to their peer judges' input and modify their strategies accordingly. Finally, I have been impressed with the ways that students in the seminar integrate work from other classes into the seminar debates. I have seen students cite evidence from arguments learned in the economics classroom, the political-science classroom, and studies that they have encountered in various science classes.

Cumulatively, these four pleasant surprises provide one of the best cues to how the debate community might reformulate its call for debate across the curriculum. My experience in the seminar has convinced me that in-class debating can meaningfully inculcate the best ideals of an education in the liberal arts and sciences: a spirit of inquiry, an appreciation for rigorous argument, and a sense of the interconnectedness of the various disciplines pursued under the ambit of a university education. Debate can so effectively cultivate these ideals that it behooves us to make the case for debate as a touchstone experience that provides students an unparalleled lens through which to pursue, and, more important, to integrate and to make publically effective the work that they do in classes across the university. Thus, if there is one strategic lesson to take from the Carolina experience, it is that debate educators and advocates should make a bolder case for debate practice as a core of undergraduate education. Rather than simply promoting debate in as many places as possible, we should be making the case for more courses that frame debate as a critical introduction to life at the university, and as a practice that makes all the goals of our colleges and universities more achievable.

On a practical level, this means that interested debate educators should offer more courses that are available earlier in an undergraduate's career that pursue the traditional goals of the argumentation course in combination with opportunities for concrete debate practice. On a broader level, this means that debate educators need to make the case consistently and vociferously for debate in their departments and at the more general level of the university as an unparalleled academic and democratic practice.

One important precursor to increased advocacy for in-class debate could include more active encouragement of forensics professionals' work in this area by national competitive debate organizations. Simple steps that might make this goal more achievable include better public relations and information management by organizations that support competitive debate under the rubric of a classroom-debate teaching-resources initiative, including the creation of a central site for collecting syllabi that integrate the traditional goals of the argumentation course with concrete debate practice, as well as more visibly highlighting materials that make the case for debate in the classroom. It may also be useful for competitive intercollegiate debate organizations to make materials available that document debate best-pedagogical practices, and that provide contact information for a network of teachers who are also interested in doing the work of making debate education available to the university at large, as well as a central database or at least easily accessible bibliography that documents the work done in an increasing number of fields on debate pedagogy.

In the end, a more coordinated and aggressive campaign by organizations that support debate to make the case for debate as a core of education in the liberal arts and sciences might make a significant difference in promoting best-debate practices in the classroom, and might even provide useful ammunition to debate educators on the ground who would like to make the case for the invaluable benefits of debate participation. Such a campaign would also provide a useful argument for debate programs to expand their resources by demonstrating an impact on college and university communities at large. Many of us whose lives have been so positively impacted by our debate experience feel an obligation to expand debate's benefits beyond the debate team to our colleges and universities, and perhaps to the public sphere at large. It is time for us to do what we do best—to make the case.

References

Allen, M.; S. Berkowitz; S. Hunt; and A. Louden. 1999. "A Meta-analysis of the Impact of Forensics and Communication Education on Critical Thinking." *Communication Education* 48, no. 1: 18–30.

Aristotle. 2006. *On Rhetoric: A Theory of Civic Discourse*, trans. G. Kennedy. Oxford: Oxford University Press.

Barfield, K.D. 1989. "A Study of the Relationship Between Active Participation in Interscholastic Debating and the Development of Critical Thinking Skills with Implications for School Administrators and Instructional Leaders." *Dissertation Abstracts International* 50-09A: 2714.

Bauer, G., and D. Wachowiak. 1977. "The Home Court Advantage: A Debate Format for the Teaching of Personality." *Teaching of Psychology* 4, no. 4: 190–204.

Bellon, J.A. 2000. "A Research-based Justification for Debate Across the Curriculum." *Argumentation and Advocacy* 36, no. 3: 161–75.

Berdine, R. 1987. "Increasing Student Involvement in the Learning Process Through Debate on Controversial Topics." *Journal of Marketing Education* 9, no. 3: 6–8.

Berkowitz, S.J. 2006. "Developing Critical Thinking Through Forensics and Communication Education: Assessing the Impact Through Meta-analysis." In *Classroom Communication and Instructional Processes: Advances Through Meta-Analysis*, ed. B.M. Gayle, R.W. Preiss, N. Burrell, and M. Allen, 43–60. Mahwah, NJ: Lawrence Erlbaum.

Bitzer. L. 1968. "The Rhetorical Situation." *Philosophy and Rhetoric* 1, no. 1: 1–14.

Brembeck, W.L. 1949. "The Effects of a Course in Argumentation on Critical Thinking Ability." *Speech Monographs* 16: 177–89.

Brookfield, S., and S. Preskill. 2005. *Discussion as a Way of Teaching: Tools and Techniques for Democratic Classrooms*. San Francisco, CA: Jossey-Bass.

Budesheim, T., and A. Lundquist. 2000. "Consider the Opposite: Opening Minds Through In-class Debates on Course-related Controversies." *Teaching of Psychology* 26, no. 2: 106–10.

Colbert, K. 1987. "The Effects of CEDA and NDT Debate Training on Critical Thinking Ability." *Journal of the American Forensic Association* 23, no. 2: 194–201.

Colbert, K., and T. Biggers. 1985. "Why Should We Support Debate?" *Journal of the American Forensic Association* 21, no. 3: 237–40.

Combs, H., and S. Bourne. 1994. "The Renaissance of Educational Debate: Results of a Five-year Study of the Use of Debate in Business Education." *Journal on Excellence in College Teaching* 5, no. 1: 57–67.

Crone, J. 1997. "Using Panel Debates to Increase Student Involvement in the Introductory Sociology Class." *Teaching Sociology* 25, no. 3: 214–18

Cronin, M. 1990. "Debating to Learn Across the Curriculum: Implementation and Assessment." Paper presented at the sixtieth annual Southern States Communication Association Convention. Birmingham, AL, April 5.

Derrida, J. 2001. *On Cosmopolitanism and Forgiveness*, trans. M. Dooley and M. Hughes. New York: Routledge.

Dewey, J. 1988. *The Public and Its Problems*. Athens: Ohio University Press.

———. 1991. *How We Think*. Amherst, NY: Prometheus Books.

Dewey, J., and A.W. Moore. 2007. *Creative Intelligence: Essays in the Pragmatic Attitude*. Whitefish, MT: Kessinger.

Dickson , R. 2004. "Developing 'Real-world' Intelligence: Teaching Argumentative Writing Through Debate." *English Journal* 94, no. 1: 34–40.

Duffin, F. 2006. "Debating Toward Dialogue: Using Debate as a Means to Transfer Collaborative Theory into Practice." *Controversia: An International Journal of Debate and Democratic Renewal* 4, nos. 1 and 2: 137–48.

Dundes, L. 2001. "Small Group Debates: Fostering Critical Thinking in Oral Presentations with Maximal Class Involvement." *Teaching Sociology* 29, no. 2: 237–43.

Elliot, L. 1993. "Using Debates to Teach the Psychology of Women." *Teaching of Psychology* 20, no. 1: 35–38.

Follert, V., and K. Colbert. 1983. "An Analysis of the Research Concerning Debate Training and Critical Thinking Improvements." Paper presented at the sixty-eighth annual meeting of the Speech Communication Association, Washington, DC, November. ERIC Document #ED238058.

Frankfurt, H. 2005. *On Bullshit*. Princeton, NJ: Princeton University Press.

Freeley, A.J., and D.L. Steinberg. 2005. *Argumentation and Debate: Critical Thinking for Reasoned Decision Making*. Belmont, CA: Thomson Wadsworth.

Garrett, M.; L. Schoener; and L. Hood. 1996. "Debate as a Teaching Strategy to Improve Verbal Communication and Critical Thinking Skills." *Nurse Educator* 21, no. 4: 37–40.

Gibson, R. 2004. "Using Debating to Teach About Controversial Drug Issues." *American Journal of Health Education* 35, no. 1: 52–53.

Glantz, S., and B. Gorman. 1997. "'He Said, She Said' Debating with Technology." *Technology Connection* 4, no. 7: 14–16.

Goodwin, J. 2003. "Students' Perspectives on Debate Exercises in Content Area Classes." *Communication Education*, 52, no. 2: 157–63.

Gorman, M.; A. Law; and T. Lindegren. 1981. "Making Students Take a Stand: Active Learning in Introductory Psychology." *Teaching of Psychology* 8, no. 3: 164–66.

Green, C., and H. Klug. 1990. "Teaching Critical Thinking and Writing Through Debates: An Experimental Evaluation." *Teaching Sociology*, 18, no. 4: 462–71.

Greene, R., and D. Hicks. 2005. "Lost Convictions: Debating Both Sides and the Ethical Self-fashioning of Liberal Citizens." *Cultural Studies* 19, no. 1: 101–27.

Gregory, M., and M. Holloway. 2005. "The Debate as a Pedagogic Tool in Social Policy for Social Work Students." *Social Work Education* 24, no. 6: 617–37.

Hobbs, J.D., and R.C. Chandler. 1991. "The Perceived Benefits of Policy Debate Training in Various Professions." *Speaker and Gavel* 28: 4–6.

Huryn, J. 1986. "Debating as a Teaching Technique." *Teaching Sociology* 14: 266–69.

Johnson, D., and R. Johnson. 1985. "Classroom Conflict: Controversy Versus Debate in Learning Groups." *American Education Research Journal* 22, no. 2: 237–56.

Jones, D. 2004. "Debating Skills Come in Handy in Business." *USA Today*, September 24, p. 21.

Keller, T.; J. Whittaker; and T. Burke. 2001. "Student Debates in Policy Courses: Promoting Policy Practice Skills and Knowledge Through Active Learning." *Journal of Social Work* 37, no. 2: 343–55.

Kennedy, R. 2007. "In-class Debates: Fertile Ground for Active Learning and the Cultivation of Critical Thinking and Oral Communication Skills." *International Journal of Teaching and Learning in Higher Education* 19, no. 2: 183–90.

Larkin, J.E. 2005. "Developing Information Literacy and Research Skills in Introductory Psychology: A Case Study." *Journal of Academic Librarianship* 31: 140–45.

Legrand, M. 2001. "Scientific Debate in Mathematics Courses." In *The Teaching and Learning of Mathematics at University Level: An ICMI Study*, ed. D. Holton, 127–35. Netherlands: Kluwer Academic.

Levine, M. 2005. "College Graduates Aren't Ready for the Real World." *Chronicle of Higher Education* 51 (February18): 14.

Levinson, M. 2003. "Challenging Deliberation." *Theory and Research in Education* 1: 23–49.

Lippmann, W. 1925. *The Phantom Public Sphere*. New York: Transaction Books.

Luong, M. 2000. "Forensics and College Admissions." *Rostrum* 75 (November): 34–35.

Martens, E.A. 2005. "The Instructional Uses of Argument Across the Curriculum." *Middle School Journal* 38, no. 5: 4–13.

Matlon, R.J., and L.M. Keele. 1984. "A Survey of Participants in the National Debate Tournament, 1947–1980." *Journal of the American Forensic Association* 20: 194–205.

Mitchell, G.R. 2000. "Simulated Argument as a Pedagogical Play on Worlds. *Argumentation and Advocacy* 36, no. 3: 134–50.

Musselman, E. 2004. "Using Structured Debate to Achieve Autonomous Student Discussion." *History Teacher* 37, no. 3: 335–48.

Nichols, G. 2000. "Citizenship: The Case of Science." In *Teaching Values and Citizenship Across the Curriculum*, ed. R. Bailey, 126–36. New York: Routledge.

Omelicheva, M.Y. 2005. "Global Politics on Trial: Using Educational Debate for Teaching Controversies of World Affairs." *International Studies Perspectives* 7: 172–86.

———. 2007. "Resolved: Debate Should Be a Part of Political Science Curricula." *Journal of Political Science Education* 3, no. 2: 161–75.

Parcher, J. 1998. "The Value of Debate: Adapted from the Report of the Philodemic Debate Society, Georgetown University." http://www.debateleaders.org/The%20Value%20of%20Debate. htm (accessed June 2, 1998).

Ross, S. 2002. "Workplace: College Debaters Get Head Start on Exec Track." Reuters, June 3.

Roy, A., and B. Macchiette. 2005. "Debating the Issues: A Tool for Augmenting Critical Thinking Skills of Marketing Students." *Journal of Marketing Education* 27, no. 3: 264–76.

Scannapieco, F. 1997. "Formal Debate: An Active Learning Strategy." *Journal of Dental Education* 61: 995–96.

Schroeder, H., and D. Ebert. 1983. "Debates as a Business and Society Teaching Technique." *Journal of Business Education* 58: 266–69.

Schuster, K., and J. Meany. 2005. *Speak Out! Debate and Public Speaking in the Middle Grades.* New York: International Debate Education Association.

Semlak, W.D., and D. Shields. 1977. "The Effect of Debate Training on Student's Participation in the Bicentennial Youth Debates." *Journal of the American Forensic Association* 13: 194–96.

Sheckels, T.F. 1984. *Debating: Applied Rhetorical Theory.* New York: Longman.

Simonneaux, L. 2001. "Role-play or Debate to Promote Students' Argumentation and Justification on an Issue in Animal Transgenesis." *International Journal of Science Education* 23, no. 9: 903–27.

Snider, A., and M. Schnurer. 2002. *Many Sides: Debate Across the Curriculum.* New York: International Debate Education Association.

Temple, M. 1997. "Using Debate to Develop Health Literacy." *Journal of School Health* 67, no. 3: 116–17.

Ten Dam, G., and M. Volman. 2004. "Critical Thinking as a Citizenship Competence: Teaching Strategies." *Learning and Instruction* 14, no. 4: 359–79.

Toulmin, S. 1958. *The Uses of Argument.* London: Cambridge University Press.

Tumposky, N. 2004. "The Debate Debate." *Clearing House* 78, no. 2: 52–55.

Vo, H., and R. Morris. 2006. "Debate as a Tool in Teaching Economics: Rationale, Technique, and Some Evidence." *Journal of Education for Business* 81, no. 6: 315–20.

Watson, J. 2004. "Educating for Citizenship: The Emerging Relationship Between Religious Education and Citizenship Education." *British Journal of Religious Education* 26: 259–71.

Williams, D.E.; B.R. McGee; and D.S. Worth. 2001. "University Student Perceptions of the Efficacy of Debate Participation: An Empirical Investigation." *Argumentation and Advocacy* 37: 198–209.

Worthen, T.K., and G.N. Pack. 1992. "Classroom Debate as an Experiential Activity Across the Curriculum." Paper presented at the seventy-eighth Annual Meeting of the Speech Communication Association, Chicago, October 30.

Zelnick, S. 2008. 'Critical Thinking' Minus Criticism and Thought." The John William Pope Center for Higher Education Policy. http://www.popecenter.org/issues/article.html?id=2097/ (accessed June 12, 2009).

Co-opetition: A Strategic Approach to Debate Organization Politics and a Proposal for Skills-based Debate Instruction

Will Baker, American Forensics Association, vice president for high-school affairs

Programs and organizational leaders from various forensics groups have spent an inordinate amount of time and energy on proving their superiority to each other, sometimes accompanied by veiled attacks on the value of each other's work. This essay calls for the adoption of a co-opetition model as a strategy for moving forward in interagency relations. Rather than a benign détente, co-opetition recognizes the need for organizations to compete at times and cooperate at other times, both toward their strategic advantage. I have borrowed liberally from the language of Adam Brandenburger and Barry Nalebuff, professors in economics at Harvard and Yale universities, and applied it to a debate-team context to advocate for changes in our thinking and in our pedagogical approaches to on-campus competition.

THE THEORY OF CO-OPETITION

As Nalebuff and Brandenburg explain in their award-winning book *Co-Opetition: A Revolution Mindset That Combines Competition and Cooperation* (1996):

> [T]he common viewpoint is: "Business is war." The language of business certainly makes it sound that way: outsmarting the competition, capturing market share, making a killing, fighting brands, beating up suppliers, locking up customers. Under business-as-war, there are the victors and the vanquished. The ultimate win-lose view of the world comes from author Gore Vidal:

> **It is not enough to succeed. Others must fail.**
> But the way people talk about business today, you wouldn't think so. You have to listen to customers, work with suppliers, create teams, establish strategic partnerships—even with competitors. That doesn't sound like war. Besides, there are few victors when business is conducted as war. The typical result of a price war is surrendered profits all around. Just look at the U.S. airline industry. It lost more money in the price wars of 1990–93 than it had previously made in all the time since Orville and Wilbur Wright.

The antithesis to Gore Vidal's worldview comes from Bernard Baruch, a leading banker, a leading banker and financier for much of this century:

You don't have to blow out the other fellow's light to let your own shine.
Though less famous today than Gore Vidal, Baruch made a whole lot more money. . . .
In fact, most businesses succeed only if others also succeed. The demand for Intel chips increases when Microsoft creates more powerful software. Microsoft software become more valuable when Intel produces faster chips. It's mutual success rather than mutual destruction. It's win-win. The cold war is over and along with it the old assumptions about competition. (p. 3)

This does not mean business is peace. It simply means that business is strategic and a simple us–them, zero-sum approach falls incredibly short of what is needed for success today. We have to identify how others complement what we do as well as how we compete with them for an advantage.

When thinking through business models, people are conscious of their customers, their suppliers and their competitors. They seldom outline their complementors, although that group is a vital element of success. A player is your complementor if customers value your product more when they have the other player's product than when they have your product alone. A player is your competitor if customers value your product less when they have the other player's product than when they have your product alone.

Debate organizations are complementors in the Nalebuff and Brandenburg model. *Many coaches may want to consider this complementor role and therefore leverage the relationship appropriately.*

At most institutions, a university official or principal or donor can say yes we have a debate team or no we do not. They are seldom versed in the style of debate. They know debate is valuable and want to support it for their students and they are excited when we win. Accepting that our battles over format are internal considerations that are viewed as irrelevant by many outside entities opens up different directions for how we approach our engagement and notions of competition.

A Debate Team Value-net Assessment

Value nets outline the key pieces of organizational strategy—customers, suppliers, competitors, complementors. We take Brandenburger and Nalebuff's model and language and apply it to a debate-team context.

The University's Debate Team's Customers

Who are the customers of a debate team? They are students, primarily. To the extent we say that is true, we make students "clients." They are engaging in an activity and should follow the guidance of the coach. Debate teams have other customers. Parents are customers when they decide whether their child can participate or pay for their trips. University departments and student governing bodies are customers when they pay to have the debate team travel or when they allocate resources/space for the team. Another very important customer group is donors/program alumni. They seek fulfillment, prestige, or the opportunity to shape future generations in return for their contributions. All customers are free to take their "business" elsewhere (to activities other than debate).

The Suppliers

A team's suppliers are primarily its staff and administrators. Since universities are in the business of disseminating information, they are also in the market for ideas. Thus, publishers of books, blogs, and journals, and providers of electronic information services (such as LexisNexis and WestLaw) are suppliers as well.

The Competitors

Debate teams have no shortage of competitors: teams compete with one another for students; departments compete for budget money. Meanwhile, college presidents, along with their development officers, compete for the checkbooks of alumni as potential donors. They compete not only with other university teams but also with other types of teams, including sports teams, academic teams, and debate and speech teams that exist at their own university but compete in other forms of the same activity. Technology increases competition among schools. As videoconferencing becomes better and cheaper, digital debates will grow in importance as an option and the justification for travel teams will become harder and harder.

The Complementors

Debate teams, though they compete with one another for students and faculty, are complementors in creating the market for higher education in the first place. High-school students are more willing to invest in debating in college, knowing that there are many schools where they might participate. The list of complementors for a debate program is huge. Elementary, junior high, and high schools complement debate teams. Hotel accommodation is an important complement to debate teams, offering wireless service, copier access, and a business center for research. There are many, many other complementors aw well—24-hour copy shops, coffee shops, pizza and ice cream parlors, and more. These businesses all make a point of locating close to university campuses. Our ability to leverage these resources by creating a positive environment for the "debate industry" dramatically transforms the ability for everyone to succeed. If a hotel chain bidding to host multinational debate competition were guaranteed an extra 3,000 rooms, imagine the leverage each event would have in the negotiations. The same logic extends to copier companies, airlines, and other vendors. The total industry size of debate programs reaches well into the millions when we look at the full range of suppliers. Many overlap across formats. We should analyze these possibilities and consider the formation of a negotiating team that could leverage the areas where we complement to the benefit of all.

On Campus Competition

For most, the above concept of cooperating nationally for improved pricing, especially in this environment, seems reasonable, if logistically daunting. However, the greater challenge is when the concept of co-opetition strikes close to home. How can the emergence of a new debate team be beneficial if you had a monopoly previously? There are two strategies for obtaining benefits:

1. **Framing**—Often people jump to the defense of their format of debate, lambasting interlopers to protect their precious ground. This reaction often occurs without the benefit of the answering the most critical question: *Is the available pie decreasing or increasing?* For example, suppose that the new team results in a funding increase in student activities from the dean's office or your department, or merely greater sympathy to the importance of debate. If that is the case, it changes the entire ballgame.

Market growth is a concept that all university presidents understand. If, rather than defending your program, you identified the newcomer as proof of the success of your program and the growing interest in debate, you could argue that this is a perfect time to consider your university's strategic advantage (created by your team) and the university might consider increasing the travel fund, starting an endowment, seeking grants to bring debate into the surrounding community, or integrating debate into more activities at the school. All of these represent huge win–win opportunities where both the newcomer and the long-standing program can speak about the benefits of debate rather than saying "this form is not valuable," which lessens everyone's perceived value of debate while perhaps creating short-term security.

2. Positioning—When a debater says, "I used to compete in x but now I'd like to try y and participate in your program," directors have a few choices. Some want nothing to do with the student and point him to the x team so the student can continue to do x. Some directors will explain the differences between x and y, and attempt to discourage the student. Still others, if they think the student is hardworking, will advocate for them to give y a shot and support his efforts to do so. The value of the final approach can be seen on a team-by-team level. Rather than resisting efforts by students or other faculty to develop or bring new types of debate programs on campus, program directors should put systems in place to support such efforts and position them to best advantage the new program and their current team in the eyes of the administration. Working together always takes less energy than working in opposition.

A Call for Skills-based Debate Instruction

The final element of the complementor strategy is being able to expand debate to students in the lower grades. Most forms of debate include common elements: refutation, cross-examination, the desire for good extension and rebuttal, evidence, and analysis. Many people begin teaching debate with format as the driving force but the above skill sets could also be the driving force. In most cases, the type of debate only matters much later.

When we start new Associated Leaders of Urban Debate (ALOUD) programs, we resist naming the format so that the maximum number of kids can be engaged. In many of our leagues, we run a policy tournament, a Lincoln–Douglas (LD) tournament and then a public debate where the kids are get excited and understand the core value of debate without it being tied to format. This process would seed debate as a concept in many places so that advocates could emerge without the biases of their predecessors. Just as racial stereotypes are learned, the feelings about format often reflect views based on the instructor's experiences more than on realities.

Teaching Format First

While it varies from case to case, the order of instruction for teaching format first would look like this:

1. Introduction to debate
2. Explanation of this particular format of debate
3. Introduction to the topic
4. Evidence
5. Building arguments for the affirmative and negative
6. Skills-based instruction (note-taking, cross-examination, refutation, etc.)

The strategy can be justified in any number of ways:
- The order is logical.
- Introducing the topic early enables students to apply examples to the skill set they are learning. It enables students to apply the practical to the theoretical.
- They will not be interested in debating if they do not know the topic.
- The topic is a key driving force.
- The format is the basis of what we do. It defines us.

A skills-based model would invert the order, making the format the last item taught and focusing on the skills earlier in the process:

1. Benefits of debate
2. Note-taking
3. Cross-examination
4. Refutation
5. Evidence
6. Topic selection
7. Building arguments
8. Format

In new communities that ALOUD has initiated, we have seen anecdotal evidence that inverting the order has had a stimulating impact on the educational process.

1. Coaches tie the instruction to many, varied examples because the lesson plans are not connected to a particular topic. Released from the shackles of format, they can explain the benefits of debate generally and more easily associate them with public notions of debate (e.g., *The Great Debaters* movie or the presidential debates).

2. Smaller is better. When students are working with a smaller number of in-

dividual pieces of evidence rather than trying to learn an entire 1AC or 1NC at the outset, they can become more familiar with the warrants of each card, compare their evidence better to their opponents, and use cards for illumination not simply for support.

3. Students stay involved longer. We have been able to recruit large numbers of debaters and retain them for longer. Most of the places where ALOUD has started debate communities have lost less than 3% of the debaters originally involved and added a significant number of new debaters throughout the season.

4. Teacher involvement in the selection of format and topic creates a sense of ownership and increased capacity for a structured program that can be integrated into the learning objectives of the school and the larger school district.

For some, the teaching of format first is a badge of honor. They feel that x or y format is more educational and opens the door to more students. The existence of intercollegiate teams of every stripe that are successful and attract numerous students (Emory in policy, Western Kentucky in LD, Claremont in parliamentary, and Vermont in worlds) points to the underlying reality that the educator and program, not the choice of format, are the determining factors of success and program growth.

The point is not that format selection or advocacy is inherently bad. In fact, as students advance and mature and seek out more outlets, they may choose a particular format or inevitably migrate to one format over another based on tournament proximity, director/administration preferences, pedagogical objectives, or other factors. The key element is to avoid passing on stereotypical notions about the strength of one format of debate over another and to create a pathway that will lead to success regardless of the ultimate format choice.

In a larger sense, this method creates fans of debate rather than fans of a format first. This creates a context for support in later life regardless of a particular director's disposition or pedagogical choices. So when a director leaves or a new program begins in the area, or an opportunity for a new summer camp develops, format differences do not become a barrier for engaging students in the power of debate education.

CONCLUSION
We can save money, expand our reach, and change the language of debate and

how it is thought about by working together on common rules and language. Assuming that the presence of more and different debate teams reflects the strength of your program and not a weakness, will open the door to new opportunities for expansion.

Educational Convergences: The Potential Relationships Between Parliamentary and Policy Debate Communities

Derek T. Buescher, University of Puget Sound

The Third National Debate Development Conference (NDDC) in 2009 continued the work of the first two conferences in 1975 and 1985. Similar to those two conferences, the primary attendees and perspectives present were from the policy[1] debate community and, notably, members of the National Debate Tournament ([NDT] and, in 2009, the Cross Examination Debate Association [CEDA]). Considering that the primary form of intercollegiate debate practiced in the United States during the 1970s was that endorsed by the NDT and that the CEDA did not host its first official national tournament until 1985, this focus on policy/NDT style of debate makes sense.[2] Yet, in his overview of the 1975 meeting, conference director George Ziegelmueller astutely described a scene of diverse forensics participation, practice, and instruction. Ziegelmueller even declared the "Nature of the Forensics Conference" as needing to "permit broad based and representative input from within the entire forensics discipline" (1975, 3). As someone whose background was CEDA value debate, who coached CEDA, then NDT, then the National Parliamentary Debate Association (NPDA)-style parliamentary debate, then took over a traditional CEDA program in the Pacific Northwest, and developed a concurrent parliamentary program, I have borne witness to the changing nature of academic debate. It is this changing nature that rests at the heart of this essay. In 2009 the numerical dominance of CEDA/NDT participation is not what it was in the 1970s. A diversity of national debate programs, perspectives, and philosophies suggests the 2009 participants of the NDDC should not only heed Ziegelmueller's (1975) words from more than 30 years prior: "to permit . . . input" from across the

---

[1] I am compelled to point out that parliamentary debate is also "policy" debate, since parliamentary debate tackles questions of policy. Nonetheless, in this essay, when I use the term "policy debate" or "policy debate community," I refer to that format practiced by CEDA/NDT.
[2] Organizationally, CEDA began in the early 1970s, prior to the first development conference. The American Parliamentary Debate Association (APDA) formed in 1981 shortly after the first "Worlds" tournament in Glasgow, Scotland, in January 1981 (see http://www.apdaweb.org/about/history). The National Parliamentary Debate Association (NPDA) formed in the early 1990s, officially changing its name from the Western States Parliamentary Debate Association to the National Parliamentary Debate Association in February 1993 (see, "An Early History of the NPDA," at http://cas.bethel.edu/dept/comm/npda/npdahistory.html). And, NFA-LD did not emerge as a college-level event until the early 1990s.

debate/forensics discipline but also openly recognize and embrace the multiple forms and practices of intercollegiate debate.

In this short essay I address two primary questions. First, what is the history of parliamentary debate? And, second, what is the future of parliamentary debate with particular attention to potential relationships with CEDA/NDT. Before I answer those questions, I will offer a brief overview of the primary distinctions in rules and format between parliamentary and policy debate. More important, I wish to contextualize my answers to the two primary questions with two points that drive my understanding of debate. First, debate is an organic activity. How debate is practiced at any one time depends on its previous interpretations and modes. In addition, as I will demonstrate relative to parliamentary debate shortly, debate continues to change. It is not static, and organizations that have attempted to create rules to maintain a particular type of debate practice have, thus far, been unsuccessful. Every new debate style that has posed itself as an alternative to faster, technical, more evidenced-based debate has become more like the thing from which it turned.

Second, the purpose of debate is education. I believe that because debate programs are housed within educational institutions, their primary purpose is the education of students, not winning, although the two are not mutually exclusive. The conflict, if you will, between members of debate groups, and notably within the NPDA over the past year,[3] calls into question what is meant by education and education to what end. Although I tend to agree with Ron Greene's (2003) more critical approach to education, I do not see myself in the majority on this point. Indeed, much of the debate about debate format mentioned above centers on what is deemed proper education of students. Crudely, this may be viewed as a contest over the definition of skills (speaking to an audience; understanding reason; grasping the basics of research). This is not a debate I will complete in this essay, but I think it necessary for debate organizations and

---

[3] Both formally and informally, members of the NPDA have spoken out regarding the evolution of debate style and practice within NPDA over the past year. Formally, the NPDA Executive Council published a list of structural changes to the national tournament and the sanctioning of member tournaments. This document, known as the *Kirksville Consensus*, also included a preamble that described a desire to return to early (read mid-1990s) practices of parliamentary debate (NPDA, 2008). Informally, a number of NPDA members used the "parli-list-serve" over the waning months of 2008 and again after the 2009 National Tournament to voice concerns over the changing style of NPDA debate. Notable in this latter lamentation was Skip Rutledge of Point Loma Nazarene University (see https://lists.bethel.edu/mailman/private/parli/2009-April/040582.html) and my own response to Skip at https://lists.bethel.edu/mailman/private/parli/2009-April/040586.html).

practitioners to define, assess, and even challenge models of forensics education. Instead, in this essay, I hope to leave those unfamiliar with parliamentary debate with a better understanding of the activity and its potential future directions.

PARLIAMENTARY AND POLICY DEBATE DIFFERENCES

To those unfamiliar with parliamentary debate, but familiar with the format of policy debate as practiced by CEDA/NDT, I offer a brief description by way of distinctions. This description focuses on debate practices of the National Parliamentary Debate Association and the National Parliamentary Tournament of Excellence (NPTE). There are four primary rule differences between parliamentary and policy debate: resolutions, preparation time, quoted material, and speeches.

First, parliamentary debate does not use a single resolution. Instead, each debate begins with the announcement of the resolution for that round. Although generally phrased as questions of policy, resolutions are sometimes phrased as questions of fact or value, a mixture of all three, or even as metaphorical or declarative statements. While some tournaments use topic areas that are announced in the weeks prior to the tournament, many do not, and instead rely on a norm of current events as the ground from which to draw topics. Because parliamentary debate employs a different resolution in each debate, although repetition does occur across tournaments, the approach to research is distinctly different from that found in policy debate. As with policy debate, generically applicable arguments are common, but students are expected to have a strong understanding of a broad range of topics as opposed to a highly technical expertise of a narrower area.

Second, parliamentary debates do not have preparation time during the debate. The absence of preparation time means students need to be quick on their feet. Debaters are expected to arise ready to speak and answer their opposition's arguments at the moment their opponent finishes. Taken together, these two components—the changing resolutions and the expectation of nearly immediate response—define the extemporaneous nature of parliamentary debate. Although the absence of preparation time may lead some to criticize parliamentary debate for not allowing debaters to develop detailed responses, the difference in evidence makes this point less relevant.

Third, parliamentary debate, contrary to popular phrasing, does require evidence to support argumentative claims, but does not allow quoted material to be read in the debate itself unless the debaters have copied it by hand during the preparation time between topic announcement and the start of the debate. This difference is probably the singular significant difference between parliamentary debate and CEDA/NDT. In one respect, the absence of quoted material downplays the reliance on authority so central to policy debate, and from this perspective, the rule potentially forces students to develop the warrants for their arguments rather than the evidence to support the claim they wish to make. Since parliamentary debaters do not need to rely on quoted evidence and are required to be prepared to debate nearly any conceivable topic of note in the news, this is a second primary aspect in the difference in research between parliamentary and policy debate.

Finally, parliamentary debate as practiced by the NPDA has only two rebuttals and no cross-examination period. In lieu of cross-examination, opponents are allowed to ask questions after the first minute and prior to the last minute in each constructive speech. After the four constructive speeches, the debate closes with only two rebuttals. This means the negative block is distinctly different than in policy debate as the last negative speech follows the second negative constructive. The negative rebuttal needs to extend key positions, synthesize the debate, and, in some circles, still offer a "line-by-line" response similar to the second affirmative constructive in CEDA/NDT debate. Similarly, the affirmative rebuttal needs to synthesize the debate and answer the negative rebuttal while, in some circles, also answer all the arguments offered by both the second negative constructive and the negative rebuttal.

Debate Is Organic: History of Parliamentary Debate

In this section I provide a brief overview of the changes in debate practice over the past two decades. Before I venture too far, I need to note that others know these histories better than I do and that I cannot speak for these organizations or for the variety of voices present in these organizations (see, e.g., Trapp 1997). In addition, my attempt at history is largely my history and should be read as such.

In one way, we would be wise to view the origination of CEDA debate as an attempt by forensics educators to focus, or perhaps refocus, debate practices on persuasive speaking in an argumentative context. That CEDA formed from programs previously involved in NDT debate and attempted to create a series of structural rules that impacted the type of performances students could undertake seems to provide the necessary evidence for seeing CEDA as a move away from how debate was practiced in the day. In many ways, the formation of the NPDA is cast within a similar shadow. The early practitioners of parliamentary debate in the Western United States,[4] those who came to form the NPDA, were attempting to create more extemporaneous styles of debate that were slower, less research intensive, and focused on broader audiences. In the words of Robert Trapp (1996), one of the organization's first leaders, "the NPDA is dedicated to the promotion of reasoned and informed public debating" (p. 85) and "in parliamentary debate, argument is aimed at a 'universal audience" (p. 86). Elsewhere, Trapp explained the focus on audience: "Because parliamentary debaters are expected to be clear in the structure of their reasoning and because parliamentary debaters use information from the public forum, the format is one which is accessible to public audiences. Parliamentary debate at its best is an event that ought to be enjoyable and educational for public audiences seeking information, education, and even entertainment" (Trapp 1997, 298).

Trapp's views were not and are not isolated. Many practitioners and teachers of parliamentary debate saw the activity as a return to audience-centered argument within a distinctly public context. Then and now, they wished to train students to be able to rise at any number of public events and argue from an informed position to a broad audience. The attractiveness of this style of debate (extemporaneous and public oriented) drew many forensics educators who not only saw the educational merit of such teaching but also saw a more accessible form of debate to a less-experienced student population. Parliamentary debate provided a format that required less technical knowledge, less time dedicated to research, and slower delivery rates. A student with no high-school experience in debate could learn how to argue in a public setting arguably more easily and more rapidly than a college student new to CEDA/NDT.

Here I wish to make a slight diversion into the Northwest parliamentary community because I think the story is telling and it is what I know best. In the mid- to late 1990s the Northwest maintained several strong CEDA programs that also competed in NDT. The region had a viable regional circuit that maintained open- and junior-level debate tournaments. In the early 2000s, in part as a result of the rise of parliamentary debate in the region and changing programs, several programs ceased to participate in CEDA/NDT. Outside of the format of CEDA/NDT, cost and perception on educational merit were major factors. CEDA/NDT cost programs more in terms of coaching, computer and other technology,

---

[4] The APDA was established as a governing organization to oversee an extemporaneous style of debate "patterned after the style of platform debate first made famous at Oxford University." ("This style of debate gained popularity in the Northeastern United States and many of its participating schools travel to the "Worlds Debating Championships.")

copying, and travel resources. And the problem grew exponentially. In 1996 there were 12 Northwest programs with teams competing in the open division of CEDA. In 2001 there were eight programs; in 2008, three. As some programs moved away from policy debate, tournaments failed to reach critical mass, and regional teams struggling to maintain their policy programs while investing in younger, less-experienced debaters could no longer do so.

Arguably, the trend that virtually eliminated policy debate in the Northwest is now occurring within the ranks of parliamentary debate. Nationally, many programs are opting out of NPDA/NPTE and choosing to compete in British parliamentary, also known as Worlds, format tournaments instead. The number of programs fielding open-level parliamentary debaters at Northwest tournaments is shrinking and, as it does, this means that junior and novice divisions become less sacrosanct. More coaches and programs already disillusioned by the stylistic shifts in open-level parliamentary debates turn to other formats. If the trend continues, so does the potential for history to repeat itself and parliamentary debate to dissolve into British format, evolve into something else entirely, or be absorbed back into CEDA/NDT. This leads me to the second question driving this essay.

PARLIAMENTARY AND CEDA/NDT FORMATS: POTENTIAL RELATIONSHIPS

I begin this section with a word of caution. It is not my intention, nor do I think it wise, for CEDA leadership to pursue a rejoining of ranks between NPDA/NPTE and CEDA/NDT. This idea has made its way into some discussions of traditional CEDA/NDT coaches, but I do not believe similar discussions have circulated within the parliamentary debate communities. It is likely not wise for CEDA/NDT to think of itself in a colonizing light regarding NPDA/NPTE because to do so may only hasten more into the British/Worlds formats. Still, parliamentary debate has undergone significant stylistic as well as practical changes since its early days of the mid-1990s. On balance, the debates have become, for good or ill, more policy oriented, more research driven, more technical, and faster. In many ways, parliamentary debate practiced in the open-level elimination debates of major tournaments mirrors that of CEDA/NDT, even though the debates do not contain quoted material, are still slower, contain less blocked-out arguments, and only have two rebuttals. Certainly, parliamentary debate has not become CEDA/NDT debate, but the formats and practices are more similar than they were ten or even five years ago. Indeed, many in the parliamentary community now borrow heavily in argumentative format, style, and strategy from arguments originating out of the CEDA/NDT community, but a merger between organizations akin to that between CEDA/NDT is nowhere on the foreseeable horizon.

It is possible that some programs will begin to drift back to competing in CEDA/NDT, but those numbers are likely small, would be insufficient to the CEDA organization, and may run the risk of only further damaging already struggling regional debate. This is not to say that bridges may not be built. Given the changing style of parliamentary debate, some students and programs might conceivably travel to and compete in some CEDA/NDT tournaments. The potential for integration raises the final points I wish to discuss; ones intimately related to the potential relationships between CEDA/NDT and NPDA/NPTE: access and recognizing the merits of debate as debate.

Access

Earlier I mentioned two central elements regarding debate, education, and organic qualities, and discussed how many programs chose to leave CEDA/NDT for NPDA/NPTE because the barriers to access seemed fewer to overcome. My own anecdotal experience as a coach certainly suggests the latter to be true: younger students who have less or no experience out of high school, despite the best efforts of well-trained coaches, struggle to survive in policy debate. Of course, notable exceptions exist, but they are exceptions and not the norm. Faster debate, more technical debate, heavier research burdens all run the risk of turning students away from the activity because of the initial hurdles in competition and, not without merit, successful competition.

As I see it, the central element in any relationship between CEDA/NDT and NPDA/NPTE is access. As such, an overt relationship will most likely require concessions by CEDA/NDT regarding the development of novice and even junior debate,[5] the use of evidence, and even the judging pool/use of mutual-preference judging. It is my belief that our duty as forensics educators is to find a way that allows for debate to develop, as it seems always to have done (but perhaps is occurring even faster), and reduce barriers to entry and access into the activity. This is no easy task. The joint development of accessible debate

---

[5] As an aside, I believe one of the more devastating and anti-educational practices in debate organizations is the summation of sweepstakes points. I do not think I overexaggerate when I say that nearly every CEDA meeting contains a discussion about novice and junior eligibility. Without sweepstakes these discussions may very well become moot points, and directors/coaches would approach the placement of their students relative to their best educational outcomes and personal growth rather than on the potential accumulation of sweepstakes points.

and organic debate requires concerted support from national and regional organizations working together; the construction of viable regional circuits that provide cheap debate in recognition of the economies of scale embodied within competition; the protection of novice and junior divisions; and the fostering of judges and coaches who take seriously their goal of educating students about practices of debate at all levels. I think we have a strong core for the latter, and I believe with work we can develop the former three. Working together, the leadership of CEDA/NDT and NPDA/NPTE could lay significant foundations for fostering debate while securing their working relationships with each group. Finally, I turn briefly to the idea of fostering debate as the central relationship between the national organizations.

Celebrating Debate

The strongest relationship that may be built between the parliamentary and CEDA/NDT communities rests on the core of what debate is: a celebration of argumentation as a tool of teaching. Over the past several years I have *suffered* through far too many conversations and discussions about which form of debate is better. My response has become: "all forms of debate have merit and all forms of debate have issues. We would be remiss to think any format is perfect." What CEDA/NDT gives students is a unique educational experience. And, so does NPDA/NPTE, or British style, or any number of formats. Elitist responses on being the best will do little to build the larger communities of academic debate and are much more likely to undermine all communities. Different forms of debate achieve similar ends, if not differently, and to differing extents. Different forms of debate need to be different or they do not really serve a purpose. It makes sense for the leadership of CEDA/NDT and NPDA/NPTE and NFA-LD and Worlds to come together and think collectively about how each fosters a community built on education about argumentation and debate. It makes sense for each to celebrate the other as a means to helping each to try, if not adopt, different styles and approaches. And, it makes sense that these organizations work together to foster debate education to as many students as possible while also seeing the benefit of advanced training for some and more broad-based approaches for others. Ultimately, it is my hope that when we gather and use the phrase "academic debate" it never means one format and always foregrounds the first word of the phrase.

References
American Parliamentary Debate Association (APDA). n.d. "Parliamentary Debate." http://www. apdaweb.org/about/ (accessed August 5, 2009).

Greene, R.W. 2003. "John Dewey's Eloquent Citizen: Communication, Judgment and Postmodern Capitalism." *Argumentation and Advocacy* 39, no. 3: 189–200.

National Parliamentary Debate Association (NPDA). 2008. *Changes to National Tournament Operating Procedures and Rules of Debating and Judging.* https://lists.bethel.edu/mailman/private/parli/attachments/20080906/2cdec132/ChangestoTOP-VersionFinal-0001.doc/ (accessed August 7, 2009).

Trapp, R. 1996. "Parliamentary Debate as Public Debate." *Argumentation and Advocacy* 33, no. 2: 85–87.

———. 1997. "Parliamentary Debate." In *Intercollegiate Forensics: A Project of the Northern California Forensics Association*, ed. T.C. Winebrenner, 291–318. Dubuque, IA: Kendall Hunt.

Ziegelmueller, G. 1975. "National Development Conference on Forensics." In *Forensics as Communication: The Argumentative Perspective*, ed. J.H. McBath, 1–7. Skokie, IL: National Textbook.

Section VII: International Debate Opportunities

New Models for Debating: The USA Learns from the World

Alfred C. Snider, University of Vermont

I started debating in the seventh grade in 1962. I started coaching a high-school team in 1969. I started coaching a university team in 1972. In 1996 I had my first encounter with debating in other countries when I traveled to Serbia. Since then I have conducted debate training in 27 different countries. I began each training experience by teaching the participants about U.S. policy debate and applying it to the various formats I encountered in their area. But, in the process, they were teaching me about what they do and how they do it. When I taught at the first International Debate Academy in 2002 in Slovenia, we used the World Universities Debating Championship (WUDC; Worlds) format. Likewise, when I took a team to the first International Spanish Language Debate Tournament in Chile, I also encountered this format. In 2006 I allowed one of my teams to participate in this format, and they attended the WUDC tournament in Vancouver and the U.S. Universities Nationals in Claremont, California. The next year I allowed other teams on my squad to participate in this format, a choice bolstered by the decision of many policy coaches in the Northeast to add the Worlds format to their tournaments. Consequently, my teams had a lot of experience in this format when they finally went to international tournaments. Many naysayers in our region thought that the addition of a Worlds format to our tournaments would spell the end of policy debating. The reality has been quite different, as the policy divisions are larger and the Worlds divisions are growing. Now my team does both policy and Worlds formats; both sides of the aisle are healthy. Last April we hosted the U.S. Universities Debating Championship and over 120 teams attended; Vermont reached the semifinals and Harvard won the finals.

The Worlds format (also known as British parliamentary) is the fastest growing debate format in America. Many National Parliamentary Debate Association (NPDA) teams are turning to this format; it is increasingly popular with American Parliamentary Debate Association (APDA) teams; and a number of policy teams are trying it (though almost all of them retain policy debate as a separate format). The National Forensic League is considering adding a variant of this format to their competitions. Ten of the thirty-two teams reaching the elimination rounds at WUDC in Cork, Ireland, December 2009–January 2010 were from the United States. As president of the World Debating Council, Neill Harvey-Smith said at U.S. Universities this year, "America is the fastest growing site for WUDC format debate, and unfortunately for the rest of the world, they are getting very good at it."

Below I summarize the key elements of Worlds format and include a link to a more detailed set of rules later in this piece.
• While there may be three or more judges in a room there is only one ballot. After the debate, judges discuss the debate, come to a consensus decision, fill out the one ballot, and then call the debaters back into the room to explain the decision.
• The format calls for four teams of two people, each of whom has a unique name:
• Opening Proposition: Prime Minister; Deputy Prime Minister
  o Closing Proposition: Member Proposition; Proposition Whip
  o Opening Opposition: Leader Opposition; Deputy Leader Opposition
  o Closing Opposition: Member Opposition; Opposition Whip
• Judges rank them 1–4 at the end of the debate.
• Each participant gives one seven-minute speech.
• The topic, or "motion," is announced 15 minutes before the debate. During the preparation period after the announcement, debaters may not talk to coaches or others, nor can they use the Internet. They may consult casebooks, but they can bring into the debating room only notes they write during preparation time.
• The format does not include cross-examination, but members of the opposing side may rise for points of information (POI) during the middle five minutes of each speech, and while the speaker may decline them, he or she is expected to take two during each speech. These are composed of a short (5–15 second) remark or question followed by a short response from the speaker.
• The proposition (Government) case is expected to set up a good debate, not try to run from the issues or avoid them based on technicalities. Opposition teams are encouraged not to dispute unconventional cases, but to debate them out and let the judge penalize the proposition team as appropriate. Policy debate veterans may have difficulty understanding this approach, but it works out quite well, and debates focus on the major issues.
• The first proposition speech lays out their case for the topic. The second through sixth speeches have a balance of refutation-rebuilding and the presentation of a new issue. The last two speeches are expected to summarize the entire debate and may not introduce new arguments.
• Because of the international nature of the debate and the desire to make

it accessible and appealing to all intelligent citizens, Worlds debate uses no specialized jargon.

- Because of the international nature of the debate, the focus of the debate is rarely on one country, and the assumption is that the debate is applicable to all countries where the topic would be relevant.
- Worlds debaters make considerable reference to current events, philosophy, and the social sciences, but the format does not permit quoted evidence, because no outside materials can be brought into the debating chambers.
- The motions tend to come from current events and have a tight focus, such as "This House would support bombing of terrorist bases in Pakistan," or "This House would force-feed anorexics."

Many of the differences between coaching and participating in this format are subtle but are rather obvious once you have been involved for some period of time. In Worlds debate

- The coaches/trainers do not work with the students on the topic once it has been given to them. It is all up to the students. They cannot talk to the other students on their side or their opponents. They may only speak to their partners. Consequently, there is much less feeling of competition among the coaches than there is in policy debating, as the competition is between the students alone. This is why Worlds coaches describe themselves as "trainers."
- Debaters are not involved in a stark "win–loss" situation but can place at some point in-between. This makes the relationships between debaters before and after the round a bit more cordial.
- The relationships between the debaters and judges are also cordial, as a panel of three agreed on the decision and the fine distinctions between the places first through fourth are more understandable than a decision of win or lose.
- Before major competitions judges are briefed, tested, and evaluated based on their scoring of a demonstration debate. This information is used to initially rate the judges for assignment as chair, panelist, or trainee.
- The judges are also competing. After every decision, debaters fill out evaluation forms on the judges and the judges evaluate each other. Higher-rated judges are used in the better debates in the elimination rounds in the tournament, and the highest-rated judges are announced as "breaking" judges. Judges, therefore, are highly motivated to do a good job and satisfy the students and the other judges.
- International debating displays impressive diversity, with many women and minorities participating. Those who believe that policy debating alienates women or minorities will be pleased with the Worlds format. Cultural differences tend to be respected.

- Training of debaters is very different from policy debating. Because debaters do not know what position they will take or what the topic will be, training focuses on basic skills (speaking, argument building, refutation, points of information, etc.) and on constructing proposition and opposition cases for a variety of motions. Last year I worked with my students to brief over 300 motions, a strategy that obviously benefited them in light of the short preparation period between the announcement of the topic and the debate.
- Students still must work very hard. The breadth of knowledge needed to perform well in this format is considerable. Debaters spend hours each day reviewing the news and keeping up on the details of current events. The format may look easy, but it is very difficult to do well.
- This format is very easy for new debaters. They can be in a debate almost immediately and learn by doing from there.
- Inviting a member of your administration or a potential donor or important alumni to see one of these debates is not a problem because they will find the debate understandable and comprehensible. The lack of jargon helps first-time observers to fully understand the content. Likewise, you can easily stage public debates; audiences find them interesting and dynamic.

I think that American policy debate has the best theoretical foundation of any type of debating in the world. The level of sophistication in argument is considerable and impressive. However, it is not the be-all and end-all of debating. The Worlds format has had incredible benefits for my program and my students. Last year I had the largest number of students ever (and 37 years of coaching is a long time) who attended tournaments in both formats. Because we could send students in both formats to the same tournaments in the Northeast, our costs did not increase considerably. Because of the great opportunities for international travel, alumni are more willing to make contributions to fund them. It is both economically and pedagogically feasible to do both.

In the twenty-first century we need to be in a position to take advantage of the explosion in debating in many, many countries as well as the many exciting tournament opportunities that exist. Making a decision to add the Worlds format to your local tournament and to attend similar local tournaments is an important beginning.

Appendix 1: WUDC Speech Guide

Modeled on WUDC rules, with some changes

Speech	Speaker	Length	Content
1	Prime Minister 1st Prop Team	7 minutes	Interpretation of motion Case for the prop (1–2 major points)
2	Leader Opposition 1st Opp Team	7 minutes	Refute prop case Present new reasons to reject the motion
3	Deputy Prime Minister 1st Prop Team	7 minutes	Defend and extend prop case Present new reason for the motion
4	Deputy Leader Opposition 1st Opp Team	7 minutes	Refute new prop reason for the motion Refute original prop case Present new reason to reject the motion
5	Member Proposition 2nd Prop Team	7 minutes	Refute new reason to reject the motion Introduce major new argument for the motion—lead the debate in a new direction without being disloyal
6	Member Opposition 2nd Opp Team	7 minutes	Refute new reason for the motion Introduce major new argument against the motion—lead the debate in a new direction without being disloyal
7	Proposition Whip 2nd Prop Team	7 minutes	No new issues Refute previous speech new arguments Summarize the debate and case for the prop
8	Opposition Whip 2nd Opp Team	7 minutes	No new issues Summarize the debate and the case for the opp

No preparation time between speeches.

Speakers 2–6 should balance refutation with new material.

GENERAL ADVICE

• Make well-developed major arguments in favor of your side of the motion. Focus on better arguments as opposed to more arguments.

• Balance refutation and rebuilding with presenting new materials.

• Offer points of information only to the opposing side.

• Stay active by trying to make points of information.

• Be loyal to the other team on your side; do not contradict them or argue against them, but you are still competing against them.

• Only contest the Government interpretation of the motion as a last resort.

Appendix 2: Judging Guidelines

Keep these things in mind when ranking and scoring the teams. Although all debate formats have much in common, Worlds debate (WUDC-BP) does differ from other forms.

Teams need to fulfill their roles in order to finish first or second:
• 1st Government team—sets up a good debate and does not try to avoid the issues through obtuse interpretations; offers a debatable case and proves and defends their case well; does not avoid debating the big issues by narrowing the debate too much.
• 2nd Government team—leads the debate in a new direction with arguments; summarizes the entire debate in the last speech.
• 1st Opposition team—refutes the 1st Government case and introduces strong arguments against the motion.
• 2nd Opposition team—leads the debate in a new direction with arguments; summarizes the entire debate in the last speech.

Speakers must fulfill their roles:
• New material should be well developed and contain proofs and examples. Fewer well-developed arguments are better than many shallow arguments.
• Debaters are expected to refute new issues introduced in the previous speech.
• Speakers should take at least two points of information and offer numerous POIs during the debate.
• This format is not "line-by-line." Speakers are expected to deal with the important issues in the debate, but not every argument.

Speakers must show excellence in argument development. To do so they must:
• Clearly show the link between the motion and the argument they are presenting.
• Explain the argument fully so that the judge understands it well.
• Prove the argument through the use of examples, statistics, historical analysis, or any other legitimate support mechanism.
• Indicate why this argument is extremely important in deciding the fate of the motion. In other words, show "impact" and "importance."
• Have clear steps in organizing the logical flow of the argument.

Judges should consider presentation and delivery:
• Good delivery and presentation serve to enhance the arguments made, and should be rewarded.

- Good organization helps the debate and should be rewarded.
- Good language use enhances persuasion and should be rewarded.
- Speakers should be persuasive to an audience of intelligent citizens.

Other issues judges should consider:
- The opposition should only question the 1st Government interpretation of the motion in EXTREME circumstances: when they are being abusive and ruining the chance for a good debate. When in doubt, the opposition should debate the interpretation out. Make fun of 1st Government, but debate out the interpretation.
- The two government teams and the two opposition teams should be "loyal" to each other. They should not contradict each other's arguments or actively disprove them. While they are competing, they are on the same side. Judges should penalize disloyalty.
- Politeness is a must. Punish rudeness.
- The offering of points of information should be quietly done and should never disrupt or distract the speaker. The speaker has the floor and should not be disrupted.
- There are no such things as "points of order."
- Government teams may not role-play, time shift, or space shift in their case (they cannot say, "This is the U.S. Supreme Court, we are lawyers, the judges are justices, and the date is 1848").
- Teams may set a motion in the present in a place where it is appropriate, for example, "This House would grant amnesty to illegal immigrants" might be set in the United States or the European Union, where it is an issue.

After the debate:
- The judges ask the debaters to leave the room.
- If there is more than one judge, they come to a joint decision on ranking and points. The designated chair of a panel facilitates the discussion among the judges.
- Judges may have to compromise with other panelists.
- Judges make their consensus decision and map out their explanation. They rank the teams 1–4.
- The chair will then fill in the ballot and hand it in, usually to a runner who collects the ballots and takes them to the tabulation room.
- The judge or judges call the debaters back in and explain the decision. This will involve the disclosure of rankings but not points. The judge or judges will often use 10–15 minutes to explain, compliment, and suggest improvements.

Speaker point range:
- 85–89 = Flawless. The kind of speech you would see in an excellent final round at an international tournament.
- 80–84 = Excellent. The kind of speech that one of the top-five speakers in the tournament would give.
- 76–79 = Above average.
- 75 = Average speech.
- 70–74 = Below average but shows promise.
- 65–69 = Serious deficiencies in argumentation presentation or role fulfillment.
- 60–65 = Seriously wrong in almost all ways, 60 is the lowest score.

Resources
Debate Central: http://debate.uvm.edu/learndebate.html.
SAMBA Worlds Guidelines: http://debate.uvm.edu/dcpdf/sambaworldsguidelines.pdf.
Videos of WUDC debates. Search for "BP" or "WUDC" at http://debatevideoblog.blogspot.com.

Prospering in a World of World Debate

Noel Selegzi, Open Society Institute

Debate has gone global. No better evidence of this exists than the increase in both the number and diversity of universities competing in the World University Debating Championship (WUDC). At the 1981 inaugural WUDC, hosted by the University of Glasgow, 43 teams representing seven countries participated. This year's WUDC, hosted by Turkey's Koç University, involved 400 teams from 60 countries (Harvey-Smith 2010).[1] More teams would have participated but space constraints required Koç to limit registration; all available spots were claimed within minutes of the opening of online registration, and the tournament had a long waiting list. In the past five years, more than 300 universities have sent teams to the WUDC. These numbers will only continue to rise as debate expands into Africa, Asia, and Latin America.

The increasing popularity of the WUDC and other international debate events both reflects the growing popularity of competitive debate and drives it. The opportunity to compete internationally and to join a global network of universities that support debate programs on their campuses has made debate more attractive to students and university administrators worldwide.

In this essay, I respond to the question of how NDT/CEDA (National Debate Tournament/Cross Examination Debate Association) debate programs can prosper in world debate. I believe that the NDT/CEDA community must answer this question itself. Directors of NDT/CEDA debate programs must define for themselves what they think it means to prosper and decide how much they are willing to adapt so that they can take advantage of the opportunities offered by the changing world of academic debate. As a point of departure, I want to describe the reasons why the Open Society Institute (OSI) chose to support debate globally and domestically, and describe how it measures the success of the debate programs it supports.

OSI DEBATE PROGRAMS

OSI does not view debate as an end in itself but, rather, as one means to open societies.[2] Since 1994, OSI has been promoting the expansion of debate inter-

---

[1] For more information on the World University Debate Championship, see http://flynn. debating.net. For commentary, news, and information on global debate activities in many different formats and contexts, see http://globaldebateblog.blogspot.com.

[2] For more on the Open Society Institute, see http://www.soros.org.

nationally through its Network Debate Program and its support of the International Debate Education Association (IDEA); domestically, OSI has established and supported urban debate leagues and the National Association of Urban Debate Leagues (NAUDL).[3]

OSI measures the success of the programs it supports by their inclusiveness and the quality of the educational experience they provide. While OSI-sponsored debaters have achieved competitive success locally and internationally, competitive success has never been OSI's primary concern. OSI gives special attention to the participation of young people living in areas where economic, political, or social injustices have limited their ability to speak in an open and informed manner on the critical issues affecting their lives and communities. OSI assesses programs using two primary criteria: (1) their ability to develop in their participants the skills required to engage fully in the economic, social, and political life of their communities, and (2) each program's success in inspiring both tolerance for the opinions of others and commitment to resolving differences by the force of argument, not the argument of force. In an increasingly globalized world confronted with threats that do not respect traditional geopolitical boundaries, OSI also supports debate that encourages young people to consider public policy from a perspective other than their own. Accordingly, OSI continues to support events that bring together debaters from the many countries in which it operates.

COMPARING STYLES

Early on, OSI concluded that no single Platonic or highest form of debate existed; OSI also realized that pragmatic considerations would have to inform its goals. Thus, the context in which OSI was trying to achieve its goals would, at least in part, determine the debate formats it would support. A debating community can choose whether it wants debates to be inclusive and publicly accessible or it prefers to address a more limited audience. A rigid adherence to a singular view of what constitutes good debate will make it difficult, if not impossible, for a debate program to benefit from increasing globalization. Indeed, that some NDT/CEDA coaches may be unaware of the increasing popularity of global debate may be the result of differing debate styles—the WUDC style that is largely driving the increased popularity of debate differs markedly from NDT/CEDA style.[4]

---

[3] For more on OSI's Network Debate Program, see www.soros.org/intiatives/youth; for IDEA see http://www.idebate.org; and for the National Association of Urban Debate Leagues, see http://www.naudl.org.

[4] For the uninitiated, the Wikipedia entry on debate (http://en.wikipedia.org/wiki/Debate) provides a good overview of the different debate formats, including the two that are the focus of this essay.

Rather than list all of the differences between WUDC-style parliamentary debate and NDT/CEDA-style policy debate,[5] I highlight the five differences that work to make WUDC style more suitable than NDT/CEDA style for global debate.[6] First, the WUDC style is a four-team format in which teams compete for rankings as opposed to wins and losses. Two teams representing the "government" or "proposition" side speak in favor of the topic and two teams speak in "opposition." In this respect, WUDC-style parliamentary debate differs not only from NDT/CEDA-style policy debate but also from other forms of parliamentary debate in which only two teams compete. The four-team format has some obvious practical advantages: more debaters can participate in rounds and fewer rooms and judges are needed. Another advantage of the four-team format, which can be easily overlooked in open societies, is that judges are only asked to rank the teams in the round—they are not required to decide which side won the debate. In contexts where judges are fearful of appearing to contradict government orthodoxy, the difference between being asked to rank teams as opposed to voting for or against a team supporting a controversial proposition is not insignificant.

Second, where the NDT and CEDA debate a single topic for an entire academic year, a hallmark of WUDC style is that a new topic is presented for each individual round of debate and announced only 15 minutes before the debate is scheduled to begin. Where the team that wins the National Debate Tournament will have debated just one topic throughout the entire year, the team that wins the WUDC will have debated 13 different topics over the course of just one tournament and will likely have debated more than 100 topics over the course of the academic year.[7] Thus, where NDT/CEDA-style debate requires

---

[5] Throughout this essay, I have chosen to use the admittedly awkward terms "NDT/CEDA-style policy debate" and "WUDC-style parliamentary debate." I have done so because it would be wrong to promote the identification of either the NDT/CEDA-style policy debate as the one and only form of policy debate or the WUDC style as the only style of parliamentary debate. Similarly, though NDT/CEDA-style debate is practiced primarily in the United States, it is important not to equate NDT/CEDA-style policy debate with debate in the United States. At this point, the NDT and CEDA represent an increasingly smaller minority of both the global and domestic debate communities.

[6] For a guide to WUDC-style parliamentary debate, see Steven Johnson (2009). See also Alexander Deane (n.d.). For NDT/CEDA-style policy debate, see Austin Freeley and David Steinberg (2008) and Alfred Snider (2008). Although focused on secondary-school, not university, policy debate, Gary Alan Fine (2001) provides a valuable introduction to the world of NDT/CEDA-style policy debate.

[7] WUDC style expects teams to treat the topics as "closed," meaning the teams present a case that is tightly and obviously linked to the topic presented for debate. Violation of this norm generally does not become a topic for debate: "topicality" is not a stock issue in WUDC-style parliamentary debate as it is in NDT/CEDA policy debate. However, WUDC judges are

debaters to have an in-depth knowledge of a single topic, WUDC-style debate rewards a broad knowledge of many topics. While debating a single topic all over the world for an entire year would have benefits, the problems inherent in trying to determine what topic would hold the interest of a global debating community for that period are daunting.

Third, in NDT/CEDA-style policy debate, teams are generally expected to warrant the claims they make with "evidence" in the form of quotations from citable sources. Success will often be determined on the basis of the quantity and quality of evidence that a team is able to present. Given that teams are debating a single topic for the entire year, they are expected both to possess and to be able to present specialized and significant knowledge of that topic. In WUDC-style debate the topics change from round to round, thus, debaters are not expected to have anything more than a general knowledge of the topic. Teams that may have a specialized knowledge of a particular topic are expected to present it in a manner that a nonspecialized audience will understand. However, this does not mean that WUDC-style parliamentary debates are not research-based. Weaker WUDC teams might limit their preparation for a tournament to a quick review of the most recent issues of the *Economist*, but the best teams will have spent considerable time researching issues and topics. Lack of knowledge will doom a WUDC team. At the same time, not requiring debaters to have specific knowledge of a single issue ultimately makes WUDC debate more inclusive than the NDT/CEDA format. Teams from places where access to information is limited or restricted will be able to be more competitive in tournaments where they are not expected to come prepared with large amounts of evidence on a single topic.

Fourth, while no rule mandates that NDT/CEDA-style debaters speak quickly, many will commonly engage in speed-reading or "spreading" during the rounds.[8] In contrast, debaters in WUDC tournaments are expected to present their arguments in a manner that allows an ordinary person to follow them; teams are judged not only on what they say but also on how they say it. Judging debaters on how well they speak may, at first glance, seem inappropriate in a global context where English is the predominant language, as it would disadvantage

---

expected to penalize first-proposition teams that offer cases that do not hew closely to the topic. Whether this leaves too much discretion in the hands of the judges is an interesting question.
[8] To get a better sense of spreading, see "Policy debate 101," www.youtube.com/watch?v=h7Py3iExosA; "The National Debate Championship 2006," www.youtube.com/watch?v=zT8t4liEHwU; and "Policy Debate in the News," www.youtube.com/watch?v=86VS6uHdVGo. See also, the documentary Debate Team (Green Lamp Pictures, 2008).

nonnative speakers and allow native speakers to substitute style for substance. However, in practice, insisting that debaters present their arguments in a manner consistent with the way debate might take place in a deliberative public forum, such as a regional or national legislature, benefits nonnative speakers—who would have difficulty comprehending "spreading." At the WUDC, teams cannot speed up to try to leave their opposition behind or rely on jargon-laden or obscure language to avoid engaging their opponents. Required to present their case in a manner that an educated, but not specialized, audience can follow, WUDC debaters are forced to speak clearly and deliberately. While they can sometimes use humor or other rhetorical devices to try to hide a lack of knowledge of the topic, WUDC debaters are not consistently awarded a high rank on speaking ability alone. Regardless of whether teaching young people to speak quickly helps to improve their memory or other cognitive skills, as some NDT/CEDA coaches insist, a debate format that encourages debaters to speak at upward of 300 words a minute will have, at best, only a limited appeal.

Finally, NDT/CEDA judges have much greater latitude in deciding the standards or "paradigms" they employ in adjudicating debates, and teams usually have a say about which individuals will judge their debates. NDT/CEDA tournaments commonly feature a practice called "mutual-preference judging": teams rank the member of a tournament's judging pool based on their desire to have that judge assigned to their debates, software is then used to assign judges to debates based on these rankings. The computer will try to ensure that opposing teams prefer their judges equally. Whether this mutual-preference judging has made NDT/CEDA debate more or less inclusive is contested within the community, but it certainly has made it less important for judges to adopt paradigms consistent with one another. At WUDC-style tournaments, on the other hand, a chief adjudicator will instruct judges on the standards they are to employ, and a judge is expected to follow those standards, not his or her own preferences, when ranking teams. While WUDC debaters do rank their judges, they do so only at the end of a debate, after the judges have provided their analysis and reasoning to the debaters. The chief adjudicator then uses these rankings to assess the overall quality of the judge. Judges who receive consistently lower ranks are assigned to less important debates or placed on judging panels with more-experienced or higher-ranking judges. This practice works to limit the variety of judging paradigms within the WUDC debating community, making it much easier for this style of debate to become a global format.

NDT/CEDA IN THE WORLD OF GLOBAL DEBATE

NDT/CEDA coaches have tried to introduce NDT/CEDA style to an international audience, but, with Japan a notable exception, the format has yet to find much acceptance. Proponents of NDT/CEDA-style debate might argue that nothing in the NDT/CEDA rules precludes teams from speaking at a conversational pace or requires debaters to use jargon or employ nontopical advocacy. Ultimately, however, the NDT/CEDA community must recognize that its style is unlikely ever to expand much beyond the borders of the United States. The globalization of debate, nonetheless, presents NDT/CEDA coaches with a valuable opportunity to expose their teams to a format and style of debate that, while not necessarily better than their own, does offer valuable educational opportunities. To thrive in a world of global debate and to offer their teams the best opportunity to flourish in and benefit from that world, NDT/CEDA coaches should take advantage of the opportunities the WUDC format offers. While only a few NDT/CEDA tournaments take place outside the United States and relatively few international teams travel to the United States to compete in NDT/CEDA tournaments, an increasing number of WUDC-style tournaments are held regularly around the world—I believe NDT/CEDA debaters would benefit from entering this arena.

For those who view NDT/CEDA-style policy debate as the highest form of debate, the globalization of debate may be largely irrelevant, perhaps even threatening. I suspect that some members of the NDT/CEDA community worry that NDT/CEDA programs attending the WUDC are promoting tourism over "real" debate. When I first started working with OSI to promote debate outside the United States in contexts where either no tradition of academic debate existed or where authoritarian and totalitarian governments had suppressed that tradition, some coaches insisted that introducing anything other than NDT/CEDA debate was condescending or patronizing: "Why introduce an inferior form of debate, when you could introduce them to the highest?" I do not believe, though, that these sentiments are predominant within NDT/CEDA community. The NDT/CEDA community is not overly parochial; I suspect that if NDT/CEDA debate had found a global audience, the NDT/CEDA community would have gone global along with it. Admittedly, given the amount of time and effort needed to prepare teams to compete on the NDT/CEDA circuit, questioning what real benefit the globalization of other forms of debate brings is reasonable. However, I do think that the vast majority of NDT/CEDA programs would profit from globalization.

Even if an NDT/CEDA program measures success purely in terms of its won–loss record on the domestic NDT/CEDA circuit, the primary benefit that coaches will likely find in the world of world debate is a broader pool of potential debaters from which to draw. Although NDT/CEDA-style debate is extremely rare outside the United States, many fine secondary-school debate programs around the world focus on English-language debate. Despite the U.S. government's myopic policy that makes obtaining a visa increasingly difficult for students, the United States remains a favored location for study abroad. With many U.S. colleges and universities wishing to increase their number of international students, NDT/CEDA coaches might find the world outside the United States fertile ground for recruiting. I do not believe that the lack of high-school NDT/CEDA-style debate experience will prove to be a handicap for foreign students. With English the lingua franca of global debate, scores of well-qualified foreign students could be valuable additions to NDT/CEDA squads. Of course, the NDT/CEDA coach must make sure that the foreign students are fully aware of the differences between the style they are used to and NDT/CEDA style.

The globalization of debate also provides NDT/CEDA coaches with new opportunities for their students. Some NDT/CEDA coaches view the parliamentary debate formats that dominate the global debate scene as simply inferior to the NDT/CEDA style. However, one characteristic of the WUDC debate format is that, while it is extraordinarily difficult to master, it is relatively easy to introduce. Experienced NDT/CEDA debaters will have little difficulty adapting to WUDC-style debate; in addition, opportunities to debate abroad or to debate locally in international competitions might entice recruits to join NDT/CEDA programs. Some program directors may fear that providing their students opportunities to participate in WUDC-style parliamentary debate will entice debaters to abandon NDT/CEDA for what they perceive to be a less rigorous format. However, the few programs that do compete on both the NDT/CEDA and global debate circuit are flourishing. For those NDT/CEDA programs struggling to attract students, the growth in popularity of the WUDC parliamentary-debate format should be seen as an opportunity, not a threat.

Additionally, the skills that NDT/CEDA debaters will need to develop to compete successfully in WUDC events will not only make them better debaters on the NDT/CEDA circuit but also prove to be valuable assets in the world outside of competitive debate. For instance, WUDC community norms make it impossible for teams to rely on technical debate argumentation or other techniques to avoid addressing the specifics of a topic. These norms force teams to be prepared to debate a wide variety of topics. Consequently, teams must read both broadly and deeply on a wide variety of issues. Similarly, regardless of how much research NDT/CEDA teams have done and how many sources they can cite, teams will always be presented with arguments they are unprepared to refute with cited sources. In these instances, the skill of responding with analytical arguments and appeals only to common knowledge, skills that the WUDC format emphasizes, will benefit the NDT/CEDA debater. Any university debate program should ensure that its alumni have the critical-thinking skills and a breadth of common knowledge so that they do not always need to rely on evidence by authority to make their case. Further, while NDT/CEDA teams can continue to hone their ability to speak as quickly as possible at their own tournaments, the ability to present arguments to an audience either unable or unwilling to follow speakers trying to say as much as they can in the least amount of time is a valuable skill that readily transfers to the world outside the tournament venue. With mutual-preference judging it is conceivable that an NDT/CEDA debate team would never have to debate before judges who would require them to speak at a conversational pace. To succeed in a WUDC-style debate, however, debaters must learn to make their points within fixed time limits without the benefit of speaking at an artificially rapid pace.

Even if NDT/CEDA program directors firmly believe that theirs is the highest form of debate, by adopting a more ecumenical and more inclusive approach to debate, they can take advantage of the enormous opportunities that the globalization of debate can offer their students.

References

Deane, A. n.d. *The Debating Handbook*, www.britishdebate.com/universities/resources/guide_deane.pdf.

Fine, G.A. 2001. *Gifted Tongues: High School Debate and Adolescent Culture*. Princeton, NJ: Princeton University Press.

Freeley, A., and D. Steinberg. 2008. *Argumentation and Debate*. 12th ed. New York: Wadsworth.

Harvey-Smith, N. 2010. "State of the World of Debate: A Sketch of the University Debate Landscape." Report prepared for the Open Society Institute, February.

Johnson, S. 2009. *Winning Debates: A Guide to Debating in the Style of the World Universities Debating Championships*. New York: Idebate Press.

Snider, A. 2008. *Code of the Debater: Introduction to Policy Debating*. New York: Idebate Press.

The Growth of Asian Debate: Implications for America

Jason Jarvis, Georgia State University

There can be little argument that debate is thriving outside of the United States. The World University Debating Championship is now so large that it is almost impossible to hold and features an average of 300–350 teams every year. Regional championships are vibrant and continue to expand with the European Championship, Asian and Australasian Championship all having record levels of attendance. Without a doubt, the fastest growing region in the world for debate is Asia. There is now a regional championship for Northeast Asia, the Northeast Asian Open, and plans are afoot for a South Asian championship as well (on top of region-wide Asian championships in both Asian and British parliamentary formats).

Since 2000, Asian debate has exploded at universities and high schools across the region, and inside cultures and governmental structures that have often been opposed to the development of democratic voices.

The growth of Asian debate is *important to American debaters and debate professionals* for several reasons:

- *Asian debate, a young and largely unstudied region-wide collective of debate communities, represents fertile ground for research about debate.*
The first Asian debate championship took place less than 20 years ago. The region as a whole only began participating in debate in the 1990s. Debate in Asia is young in comparison to debate in other regions of the world and its current form represents only 15 years of development. The first Asian institutions to participate in debate were located almost exclusively in Southeast Asia. In 2004, the first Northeast Asian Open held in Seoul, Korea, marked the beginning of what has so far been snowballing growth in China, Korea, Japan, and Taiwan. Similarly, South Asia hosted the Asian championship for the first time only recently (2008) in Dhaka, Bangladesh (and again in 2009). The development of these communities is startling in its rapidity, but is also fascinating because it has taken place in countries with cultural traditions that discourage public confrontation (Korea, Taiwan, Japan), in countries with underdeveloped democracies (Malaysia, Thailand, Singapore, Bangladesh), and in countries that are staunchly nondemocratic such as China.

Asian debate communities hold promise for examining the nature of how debate communities develop and what practices are best suited for encouraging the growth of debate in cultural or political environments that mitigate against the values and skills taught through education in debate. Furthermore, interesting questions arise about how the development of a debate community among educated elite students will impact the future of a given nation. Will the thousands of Chinese students participating in debate competitions every year learn democratic values? Or, will they learn skills that simply help them to solidify the hold of the ruling Communist Party? As the American debate community is a global leader in debate scholarship and theory, Asia would seem to be a ripe area for academic research related to debate.

- *Non-American debate communities have developed solutions to problems that have plagued American debating for years, which might be useful for envisioning practical changes to American practice or convention.*

For many years, American debate formats have struggled with the lack of diversity in tournament participation. While this issue is not unique to America, it is one that critical members of the debate community have struggled with for quite some time. Asian debaters have created unique solutions that can serve as starting points for a discussion of reforms in American practice.

Korean debate, for example, is entirely female dominated. Tournaments have regularly featured women in speaker awards and elimination rounds, and they routinely make up over half of all entries into competitions. Malaysian debaters have confronted the issue of sexism in debate by hosting a Women's Intervarsity Tournament for several years now. The entire tournament is hosted by women and allows only female participants. This tournament is all the more remarkable because Malaysia (for political and cultural reasons) is not a country known for the advancement of women socially or in the workplace. However, the community has created a safe space for the development and enfranchisement of women in the community through their annual competition. The existence of the competition and the publication of its results highlight the importance of community wide tolerance and equity within tournaments. Similarly, the Australasian Championship has taken the more radical step of integrating affirmative action into its entry procedures. All contingents participating in the competition must have a minimum percentage of women among their members (including judges).

- *Asian debate communities represent a multicultural recruiting bonanza for universities that want to expand within the global community, and the growth of debate offers enhanced job opportunities to debate professionals.*

Asian debaters are already beginning to trickle into the American debate community, with at least one Korean high-school student having joined the Emory debate team in the fall of 2009. This trend is likely to persist as students continue debating upon enrolling in an American university. Moreover, university students who continue their education at the graduate level represent an as yet largely untapped multicultural resource that could enrich the educational environment of debate teams across the United States.

At the same time, the growth of debate represents expanded job options for debate educators at both the secondary school and university levels. University English departments as well as international studies programs conduct the majority (if not all) of their classes in English. Many of these universities go out of their way to recruit qualified faculty members who have a graduate degree from an American university. Increasingly, these schools are looking for qualified candidates with a background in public speaking and debate to support the growing interest in debate.

In sum, the growth of regional debate offers an array of options for interested scholars, students, and educators. American debate has both much to learn from and much to teach to international debaters. If an ongoing dialogue and exchange of human resources can be achieved then both Asia and America stand to benefit from the ideals embodied by the deliberative process of debate.

Appendixes

Appendix I: Debate in Research, Practice, and History: A Selected Annotated Bibliography

Sarah Spring, University of Iowa; Joseph Packer, University of Pittsburgh; and Timothy O'Donnell, University of Mary Washington

This selected annotated bibliography is organized both chronologically and thematically. While the annotations present only a glimpse of the vast scholarship on debate, in its scope and totality, the collection offers insight into the great variety of complex and contested perspectives on debate—as an academic pursuit, a method of inquiry, a basic course in argumentation, and a competitive practice. While many of the selections could fit in multiple sections, the categories identified below emerged during the course of editing this collection. They are designed to offer an overall sense of the major thematic areas that have emerged over the past century and that are very much alive in the proceedings of the Wake Forest conference collected in this volume. Collectively, this bibliography points the way for future research on the activity of competitive debate—an area of inquiry that remains fertile terrain for scholarship.

Textbooks

The textbook is undoubtedly one of the primary resources for examining the history and rhetoric of debate in the United States. Insofar as it represents a more or less final-form statement on the state of the art of debate in the argumentation classroom it is significant historically. At the same time, in its capacity as an introduction to debate for large captive student audiences in classrooms across the country and beyond, it stands as a significant force for shaping public understanding of debate. The list that follows is representative, rather than comprehensive.

McElligott, J.N. 1855. *The American Debater: Being a Plain Exposition of the Principles and Practice of Public Debate*. New York; Chicago: Ivison & Phinney; S.C. Griggs & Co.
  McElligott's classic is a practical guide to effective debating of the period. It seeks to teach "deliberative eloquence" and provides instructional advice on the practice of argument. It includes transcripts of debates as well as templates for sample constitutions for literary societies for institutions seeking to create debate organizations.
Alden, R.M. 1900. *The Art of Debate*. New York: H. Holt.
  Alden outlines the nature of academic debate, particularly in terms of style, structure, and practice at the turn of the century. While dated, it is especially useful as a record of the value of debate in the curriculum of higher education during the period.

O'Neill, J.M.; C. Laycock; and R.L. Scales. 1917. *Argumentation and Debate*. New York: Macmillan.
This textbook provides an early justification for and outline of academic debate. It lays out the basic aspects of debate in terms of style and preparation. It offers interesting insights into early models of debate practice.

Shurter, E.D.B. 1917. *How to Debate*. New York: Harper.
Shurter's textbook outlines a rationale for debate. It is particularly aimed at students in higher education. The book seeks to distinguish itself from other textbooks by emphasizing its focus on an approach to debate that is accessible to a "lay" audience of democratic citizens.

Shaw, W.C. 1922. *The Art of Debate*. Boston and New York: Allyn and Bacon.
Shaw's textbook instructs students in the art of debate and argumentation, emphasizing the structure and style of arguments.

Baird, A.C. 1928. *Public Discussion and Debate*. Boston: Ginn.
Baird's first book presents his perspective on the models of discussion and debate. Throughout, he emphasizes debate as a means of reaching wise decisions. The influence of John Dewey and the value of debate as a method to train citizens in deliberative democracy are evident in this work.

Lahman, C.P. 1930. *Debate Coaching, a Handbook for Teachers and Coaches*. New York: H.W. Wilson.
Lahman's textbook is an instructional manual that outlines practical debate advice and tactics. One section of the book contains a historically valuable survey of contemporary high-school and intercollegiate debating.

Baird, A.C. 1943. *Discussion: Principles and Types*. New York and London: McGraw-Hill.
This later textbook effort from Baird broadens the scope of his earlier work (1928) through its focus on the techniques and values of public discussion. Baird continues to advance the notion that public discussion is valuable to the function of a healthy democracy.

Courtney, L.W., and G.R. Capp. 1949. *Practical Debating*. Philadelphia: Lippincott.
Courtney and Capp's textbook provides instruction on academic debate and argumentation practices. In addition to the focus on the practical, the text includes contemporary examples drawn from public address as well as a number of illustrations.

Baird, A.C. 1950. *Argumentation, Discussion and Debate*. New York: McGraw-Hill.
Baird's postwar textbook continues to draw inspiration from pragmatism and Dewey. The text provides a thorough explanation of debate theory and practice and seeks to inculcate civic education with the methods of debate.

Potter, D. 1954. *Argumentation and Debate: Principles and Practices*. New York: Dryden Press.
This book offers a collection of debate articles edited by Potter and commissioned by DSR-TKA (Delta Sigma Rho-Tau Kappa Alpha). It is designed to offer a broad scope of opinion on debate theory and practice. It offers both practical instruction on debate and historical accounts of debating practices in the United States.

Kruger, A.N. 1960. *Modern Debate: Its Logic and Strategy*. New York: McGraw-Hill.
Kruger's textbook follows previous efforts to explain debate practice and technique. In addition, part five of the book provides a full transcript of a debate from the controversial 1955 intercollegiate debate topic discussed in Greene and Hicks (2005).

Ehninger, D., and W. Brockriede. 1963. *Decision by Debate*. New York: Dodd, Mead.
Ehninger and Brockriede's textbook is considered one of the most influential books about debate. It offers instruction in the practice of debate while considering in historical and philosophical terms the principles of logic and argument. As in Baird (1950), the strain of Chicago pragmatism is evident insofar as the book aims to influence civic and democratic debate in the United States. An appendix includes a transcript of the 1961 final round of the National Debate Tournament.

Windes, R.R., and A. Hastings. 1965. *Argumentation & Advocacy*. New York: Random House.
Windes and Hastings's book is explicitly "not a book on intercollegiate debating," but rather

aims to broaden the teaching of argumentation for a more general population. While clearly using techniques of tournament debating to talk about argument, the authors translate this perspective for an audience that values deliberative democracy.

Brooks, W.D. 1966. *Introduction to Debate.* New York: Exposition Press.

Brooks's short textbook is another tome that aims to use debate to confront modern social and civic challenges. It offers simple explanations of basic debate principles and includes teaching exercises in each chapter.

Kruger, A.N. 1968. *Counterpoint: Debates About Debate.* Metuchen, NJ: Scarecrow Press.

This collection of essays offers insight into the controversies surrounding the practice of academic debate. It covers disputes over debate's relationship to truth, the tournament model, and the use of handbooks.

Wood, R.V. 1972. *Strategic Debate.* Skokie, IL: National Textbook.

Wood's textbook is meant to be used as a practical guide to intercollegiate debate. It offers students strategic advice aimed at provoking critical-thinking practices.

Sanders, G.H. 1982. *Introduction to Contemporary Academic Debate.* Prospect Heights, IL: Waveland Press.

Sanders's text, designed for use in the college classroom, explains debate without extensive use of jargon.

Patterson, J.W., and D. Zarefsky. 1983. *Contemporary Debate.* Boston: Houghton Mifflin.

Patterson and Zarefsky's well-known textbook provides a thorough perspective on academic debate practice. The book is notable for its extensive deployment as a textbook in high-school and university courses.

Ziegelmueller, G., and J. Kay. 1997. *Argumentation: Inquiry and Advocacy.* 3d ed. Boston: Allyn & Bacon.

This book outlines the state of argument theory. It is designed as a textbook for argumentation classes.

Freeley, A. J., and D.L. Steinberg. 2005. *Argumentation and Debate: Critical Thinking for Reasoned Decision Making.* Belmont, CA: Thomson Wadsworth.

This textbook provides instruction on the structure of arguments, types of debate, and other debate skills, and includes a useful bibliography and exercises for in-class debates.

Debate, the Communication Field, and the Academy

A wide-ranging conversation about the relationship between intercollegiate debate and the larger institutional structures in which it resides has persisted for the past century. While not unrelated to the other themes identified in this collection, a palpable voice in the literature calls for debate to reexamine its connections to both the communication discipline and the larger university. For some, it is crucial to the viability of debate. For others, it is because debate has much to offer both the field of communication and the larger university.

Davis, W.H. 1916. "Is Debating Primarily a Game?" *Quarterly Journal of Public Speaking* 2, no. 2: 171–79.

Davis argues against thinking of academic debate as a "game." Instead, he suggests that debate should be considered training for real-life deliberation.

O'Neill, J.M. 1916. "Game or Counterfeit Presentment." *Quarterly Journal of Public Speaking* 2, no. 2: 193–97.

O'Neill argues that one can view debate as a game without trivializing the activity and permitting immoral behaviors associated with sportification.

Thompson, W.N. 1944. "Discussion and Debate: A Re-Examination." *Quarterly Journal of Speech* 30, no. 3: 288–99.

Thompson argues that educators too often focus on the secondary benefits of debate and public speaking. This has meant that programs have cut debate because they believe these secondary benefits can be acquired elsewhere. Thompson believes educators ought to reassert the primary benefits of debate and public speaking.

Schug, C.H. 1952. "A Study of Attitude Toward Debate." *Speech Teacher* 1, no. 4: 242–52.

Schug conducts a study of the attitudes toward debate of college administrators, college officials, and college teachers in related subject areas outside of academic debate.

Crane, W. 1953. "The Function of Debate." *Central States Speech Journal* 5: 16–17.

Crane provides a justification for debate as central to the liberal arts experience. The article argues that debate is critical to providing students the tools to become democratic citizens.

Bradley, B.E. Jr. 1959. "Debate: A Practical Training for Gifted Students." *Speech Teacher* 8, no. 2: 134–38.

Bradley notes the postwar boom in science education and laments the lack of interest in using debate to promote similar and equally worthy goals. He cites the value of debate in creating opportunities for superior students, particular in high school.

Bennett, W.H. 1972. "The Role of Debate in Speech Communication." *Speech Teacher* 21, no. 4: 281–88.

Bennett considers the tenuous relationship between debate and speech communication. He suggests ways in which debate can and should contribute to the discipline.

Pearce, W.B. 1974. "Forensics and Speech-Communication." *Bulletin of the Association of Departments & Administrators in Speech Communication*, no. 7: 26–32.

Pearce conducted a study to assess the attitudes of the speech-communication field toward forensics. His results indicate that many in the field believe that forensics exists independently of the larger discipline of speech communication.

Sproule, J.M. 1974. "Constructing, Implementing, and Evaluating Objectives for Contest Debate." *Journal of the American Forensic Association* 11: 8–15.

Sproule believes that the criticism of debate relies on a mindset that views the objectives of the activity instrumentally. Instead, he suggests that a new standard be established where the rationale for debate is stated and then empirically evaluated.

McBath, J.H. 1975. "Forensics and Speech Communication." *Bulletin of the Association of Departments & Administrators in Speech Communication*, no. 11: 2–5.

McBath summarizes the findings of the National Development Conference of Forensics, which include suggested standards for forensic coaches.

Rowland, R.C., and J.E. Fritch. 1989. "The Relationship Between Debate and Argumentation Theory." In *Spheres of Argument: Proceedings of the Sixth SCA/AFA Conference on Argumentation*, ed. B.E. Gronbeck, 457–63. Annandale, VA: Speech Communication Association.

Rowland and Fritch argue that considerable room exists for debate theory and argumentation theory to develop in conjunction. They suggest that debate can serve as a laboratory for argumentation theory and point to several debate issues that can be examined in terms of current argumentation theory.

Kay, J. 1990. "Research and Scholarship in Forensics as Viewed by an Administrator and Former Coach." *National Forensic Journal* 8: 61–68.

Kay argues that forensic scholarship should elucidate and cultivate the connection between forensic activities and larger questions of the communication field. He identifies the need for change in competitive debate activity if it is to develop as a laboratory for communication studies.

Aden, R. 1991. "Reconsidering the Laboratory Metaphor: Forensics as a Liberal Art." *National Forensics Journal* 9, no. 2: 97–108.

Aden considers the vision in the 1974 development conference that proposed the "laboratory model" for debate. He argues that such a model is counterproductive to the aims of debate as part of the liberal arts tradition. For Aden the laboratory model comes with the baggage of a knowable "Truth" and the presumption of seemingly objective scientific universal knowledge. Instead, he proposes a liberal model for debate.

Herbeck, D.A. 1997. "Policy Debate and the Academe." Perspectives on the Future of the National Debate Tournament. http://www.wfu.edu/organizations/NDT/Articles/herbeck.html (accessed June 10, 2009).

Herbeck argues that debate should reconnect with a more academic mission. The increasing esotericism of debate and the focus on winning decreases debate educational value for Herbeck.

Bellon, J. 2000. "A Research-based Justification for Debate across the Curriculum." *Argumentation & Advocacy* 36, no. 3: 161–75.

Bellon looks at a number of studies considering the role of debate as a cocurricular activity and the benefits of implementing debate in higher-education curricula. The article also lists the benefits of debate for students at all levels.

Making the Case for Debate

A significant portion of the literature on debate is dedicated to extolling its many virtues. Broadly grouped, this scholarship divides along two lines. The first includes research and scholarship that advance the case for the many benefits of debate. One of the most frequently documented benefits is debate's enormous potential as a technology for rehabilitating the public sphere and fostering civic engagement. The second type of research includes a range of empirical studies that provide robust data to validate deeply held beliefs in the merits of a debate education.

Advocacy Research

Freeley, A.J. 1960. "An Anthology of Commentary on Debate." *Speech Teacher* 9, no. 2: 121–26.

Freeley compiles a list of quotations from famous figures as diverse as Aristotle and Hubert Humphrey in support of debate.

Arnold, W.E. 1966. "Debate and the Lawyer." *Journal of the American Forensic Association* 3: 26–28.

This article reports on a study of the legal profession's views on the role and benefits of debate. Arnold found that lawyers overwhelmingly approve of the use of debate as a precursor to a career in the law.

Brigance, W.N. 1968. "The Debate as Training for Citizenship." In *Counterpoint: Debates About Debate*, ed. A.N. Kruger, 17–22. Metuchen, NJ: Scarecrow.

Brigance makes the case for the value of debate for students, particularly in terms of civic education. He argues that debate, in considering many issues and sides, allows students to become effective advocates who are prepared to rigorously test ideas. The article also responds to many of the common complaints about the practice of debate.

Douglas, D. G. 1971. "Toward a Philosophy of Forensic Education." *Journal of the American Forensic Association* 8: 36–41.

Douglas discusses the benefits of debate and forensics in the area of critical thinking. He offers suggestions for making debate participation more effective at training students for interaction in the broader society.

Walwik, T.J., and R.S. Mehrley. 1971. "Intercollegiate Debate—An Intrapersonal View." *Speech Teacher* 20, no. 3: 192–94.

Walwik and Mehrley challenge the view that debate exists for the purpose of training students to be effective advocates in the public sphere. Instead, they argue that debate teaches debaters more effective decision-making skills.

English, W.B. 1972. "A Philosophy for Intercollegiate Debate." *Communicator* 3, no. 2: 19–21.
English defends intercollegiate "national" debate programs as a sound educational practice. He is particularly concerned about changes in the structure of debate tournaments and argues that both regional and national travel are vital to debate.

McBath, J.H. 1984. "Rationale for Forensics." In *American Forensics in Perspective: Papers from the Second National Conference on Forensics*, ed. Donn Parson, 5–11. Annandale, VA: Speech Communication Association.
This report summarizes the work of the 1984 forensics conference and offers educational and societal justifications for forensics programs generally.

Colbert, K., and T. Biggers. 1985. "Why Should We Support Debate." *Journal of the American Forensic Association* 21, no. 3: 237–40.
This essay outlines three educational benefits of debate participation: communication skills, critical thinking, and professional training. The article reviews literature that supports these arguments.

Dauber, C. 1989. "Debate as Empowerment." *Argumentation and Advocacy* 25, no. 4: 205–7.
Dauber discusses the value of academic debate in the context of presidential debates. She argues that debate is a tool of empowerment in an increasingly technical society. While acknowledging faults in contemporary practice, the virtues of empowerment lead her to conclude that debate is worth preserving.

Cross, F. 1996. "The NDT and Me." *Argumentation & Advocacy* 32, no. 3: 151–52.
Cross discusses his career in the National Debate Tournament and how the experience has positively benefited him in his life.

Zompetti, J.P. 2006. "The Role of Advocacy in Civil Society." *Argumentation* 20, no. 2: 167–83.
Zompetti argues that advocacy can provide the foundation for an effective civil society. He believes that debate can provide training for this type of advocacy.

English, E.; S. Llano; G.R. Mitchell; C.E. Morrison; J. Rief; and C. Woods. 2007. "Debate as a Weapon of Mass Destruction." *Communication & Critical/Cultural Studies* 4, no. 2: 221–25.
This article argues that academic debate is a key tool in dealing with civic controversies, particularly the war on terror. The article chronicles the controversy over debating two sides from the 1954 China topic to the 2007 Weapons of Mass Destruction topic.

Galloway, R. 2007. "Dinner and Conversation at the Argumentative Table: Re-conceptualizing Debate as an Argumentative Dialogue." *Contemporary Argumentation & Debate* 28: 1–19.
Galloway argues for debate conceived as dialogue, particularly in the terms of Bakhtin. The article traces how such a scheme could be implemented.

Empirical Studies

Cripe, N.M. 1959. "A Survey of Debate Programs in Two Hundred and Forty-six American Colleges and Universities." *Speech Teacher* 8, no. 2: 157–60.
This survey asked 246 debate teams for core information about their squads such as number of team members, coaches, travel budget, and so on. Cripe's article summarizes and analyzes the results.

Sikkink, D. 1962. "Evidence on the Both Sides Debate Controversy." *Speech Teacher* 11, no. 1: 51–54.
Sikkink presents an assessment of how debaters' attitudes toward the topic changes over the course of the debate season. The study finds that students who defended only the affirmative were favorably disposed to the resolution while those who defended either the negative side or participated in switch-side contests were less favorably disposed.

Huseman, R.; G. Ware; and C. Gruner. 1972. "Critical Thinking, Reflective Thinking, and the Ability to Organize Ideas: A Multi-variate Approach." *Journal of the American Forensic Association* 9: 261–65.

This study assesses debaters, using a series of tests that measure organizing skill, critical thinking, and reflective thinking. It suggests that the skill of the debater has a relation to their scores on the tests.

McGlone, E.L. 1974. "The Behavioral Effects of Forensics Participation." *Journal of the American Forensic Association* 10: 140–46.

McGlone surveys the field of studies concerning the impact of debate participation on students. He suggests that extant scholarship remains questionable and proposes further experimentation-style studies.

Rothenberg, I.F., and J.S. Berman. 1980. "College Debate and Effective Writing." *Teaching Political Science* 8, no. 1: 21–39.

Rothenberg and Berman conduct an empirical study in which students are evaluated on a speech before and after taking a debate class. The study found significant improvement in organization and development. The authors believe these organizational skills may help increase these students' writing ability.

Hill, B. 1982. "Intercollegiate Debate: Why Do Students Bother?" *Southern Speech Communication Journal* 48, no. 1: 77–88.

Hill reports on his empirical study that surveyed participants in debate to understand why they joined. The most consistently important reason for participation cited was educational needs.

Matlon, R., and L.M. Keele. 1984. "A Survey of Participants in the National Debate Tournament, L947–L980." *Journal of the American Forensic Association* 20: 194–205.

Malton conducted a survey of debaters attending the National Debate Tournament to find out what they were currently doing.

Wood, S.C., and P.A. Rowland-Morin. 1989. "Motivational Tension: Winning Vs Pedagogy in Academic Debate." *National Forensic Journal* 7, no. 2: 81–97.

Wood and Rowland-Morin conducted an empirical study on the reasons why debaters debate. Among other things, the study found that debaters place educational goals ahead of competitive goals.

Chandler, R.C., and J.D. Hobbs. 1991. "The Benefits of Intercollegiate Policy Debate Training to Various Professions." In *Argument in Controversy: Proceedings of the Seventh SCA/AFA Conference on Argumentation*, ed. Donn Parson, 388–90. Annandale, VA: Speech Communication Association.

To answer the question "why encourage students to debate?" Chandler and Hobbs surveyed former debaters about the benefits of the activity. Former debaters' perceptions were largely positive about the role of debate in their education.

Littlefield, R. 1991. "An Assessment of University Administrators: Do They Value Competitive Debate and Individual Events Programs?" *National Forensic Journal* 9, no. 2: 87–96.

Littlefield used surveys to assess administrators' feelings on debate programs. He found that although the number of debate and individual event programs has dropped, a very high percentage of administrators value debate.

Colbert, K.R. 1993. "The Effects of Debate Participation on Argumentativeness and Verbal Aggression." *Communication Education* 42, no. 3: 206–14.

This empirical study measure the effect of policy and value debating on argumentativeness and verbal aggression. Colbert found that policy debating increased argumentativeness and value debate decreased verbal aggression.

Greenstreet, R. 1993. "Academic Debate and Critical Thinking: A Look at the Evidence." *National Forensic Journal* 11, no. 1: 13–28.

Greenstreet questions the empirical evidence used to support the claim that debate increases critical-thinking ability.

Jones, K.T. 1994. "Cerebral Gymnastics 101: Why Do Debaters Debate?" *CEDA Yearbook* 15: 65–75.
    Conducting a survey to understand why debaters participate in the activity, Jones identifies as
    a core motivation "cerebral gymnastics"—that is, the desire to be intellectually stimulated.
Allen, M.; S. Berkowitz; and A. Louden. 1999. "A Meta-analysis of the Impact of Forensics and
    Communication Education on Critical Thinking." *Communication Education* 48: 18–30.
    This study considers the empirical evidence of communication education on critical-thinking
    skills. While a wide range of communication training methods enhances critical thinking, the
    authors conclude that forensic participation maximizes critical thinking to the greatest degree.
Williams, D.E.; B.R. McGee; and D.S. Worth. 2001. "University Student Perceptions of the Ef-
    ficacy of Debate Participation: An Empirical Investigation." *Argumentation and Advocacy* 37,
    no. 4: 198–209.
    This study surveys current debaters' views on debate. It found, among other things, that most
    debaters believe the activity fosters analytical skills. At the same time, participants identified
    several downsides, including time demands, trade-offs with academic work, and a negative
    affect on health.
Manchester, B.B., and S.A. Friedley. 2003. "Revisiting Male/Female Participation and Success in
    Forensics: Has Time Changed the Playing Field?" *National Forensic Journal* 21, no. 2: 20–35.
    The authors use a series of empirical methods to examine the level of participation of females
    in forensics. While the authors recognize some gains in participation since 1985, they conclude
    that parity remains elusive.
Rogers, J.E. 2005. "Graduate School, Professional, and Life Choices: An Outcome Assessment
    Confirmation Study Measuring Positive Student Outcomes Beyond Student Experiences for
    Participants in Competitive Intercollegiate Forensics." *Contemporary Argumentation & Debate*
    26: 13–40.
    Rogers performed two studies, which suggest that debaters received numerous benefits from
    having debated. The benefits extend through debaters' graduate education.

Contesting Debate

Debate is certainly debatable, and the substantial body of scholarship that preserves these controversies is robust, complex, and deeply revealing of the pivotal
moments of intellectual fervor. We learn a great deal about the health, vitality,
and future direction of institutions through the study of their controversies, and
debate is no exception. The contest over the merits of "debating both sides" is
long and ongoing. So too have been the jeremiads that appear at regular inter-
vals bemoaning the pending collapse of intercollegiate debate. Disputes have
ranged from discreet methodological differences over best practices to the much
larger questions about epistemology and pedagogy.

Thonssen, L. 1939. "The Social Values of Discussion and Debate." *Quarterly Journal of Speech* 25,
    no. 1: 113–17.
    Thonssen argues
    that debate and discussion should be seen as a unit. He believes there exists a danger that the
    competitive elements of debate will overwhelm its educational potential.
Baccus, J.H. 1941. "Should Tournament Debating Be Discontinued—No." *Western Speech* 5, no. 3:
    7–21.
    In response to criticisms of tournament debating (also switch-side debating), Baccus defends the
    tournament format. He argues that the pedagogical benefits of debating, including learning how
    to defend arguments that are against one's "convictions" is a worthwhile educational activity.

Baird, A.C. 1955. "The College Debater and the Red China Issue." *Central States Speech Journal* 6, no. 2: 5–7.
  Baird defends the 1954 China topic against its critics. He argues that the issue is not "already settled" and that debate on the issues is valuable.
Cripe, N.M. 1957. "Debating Both Sides in Tournaments Is Ethical." *Speech Teacher* 6, no. 3: 209–12.
  Cripe defends debating two sides, particularly against the criticism of Murphy. Cripe argues that debating both sides is a test of ideas rather than convictions.
Murphy, R. 1957. "The Ethics of Debating Both Sides." *Speech Teacher* 6, no. 1: 1–9.
  Murphy argues that switch-side debating is problematic because it forces debaters to argue against their convictions. He presents and then responds to many common objections to his argument.
Dell, G.W. 1958. "In Defense of Debating Both Sides." *Speech Teacher* 7, no. 1: 31–34.
  Dell also defends debating both sides against the attack of Richard Murphy. He argues that debate does not require students to believe in their arguments and that this practice is in fact ethical.
Ehninger, D. 1958. "The Debate About Debating." *Quarterly Journal of Speech* 44, no. 2: 128–36.
  This article reviews the controversy about debating both sides and debate as a game. Ehninger argues that the main problem stems from considering debate as a game and argues against this view.
Nobles, W.S. 1958. "Tournament Debating and Rhetoric." *Western Speech* 22, no. 4: 206–10.
  Nobles believes that tournament debating encourages only a limited set of rhetorical practices that do not effectively prepare students to be effective advocates.
Smith, R. 1959. "The NFL: A Perversion of Values." *Central States Speech Journal* 11, no. 1: 7–10.
  Smith believes the National Forensic League focuses too much on winning to the exclusion of other elements of debate.
Clevenger, T. 1960. "Toward a Point of View for Contest Debate." *Central States Speech Journal* 12, no. 1: 21–26.
  Clevenger argues that critics of debate succeed because they attack debate for failing to realize its perceived virtues, such as fostering "civic training" and teaching public speaking. This is a problem for the image of debate because these goals are not often realized in practice. Rather, Clevenger argues, debate educators should focus on the analytical skills that debate can provide.
Windes, R.R. Jr. 1960. "Competitive Debating: The Speech Program, the Individual, and Society." *Speech Teacher* 9, no. 2: 99–108.
  Windes argues that competitive tournament-style debating encourages good debate practices. Most of the article is addressed at challenging the claim that public debates are a better model for debate.
Klopf, D.W., and J.C. McCroskey. 1964. "Debating Both Sides Ethical." *Central States Speech Journal* 15: 36–39.
  Klopf argues that the debate over "two-sided" debate is finished. Presenting a survey of debate coaches, he concludes that coaches overwhelmingly support the pedagogical benefits of switch sides.
Brockriede, W. 1970. "College Debate and the Reality Gap." *Speaker and Gavel* 7, no. 3: 71–76.
  Brockriede outlines the growing divergence between collegiate debate and public discourse, both because debate has become more insular and public speech has become less rigorous. He considers the implications of this "gap" and suggests remedies to close it.
Ritter, K. 1976. "Debate as an Instrument for Democracy." *Speaker and Gavel* 8, no. 3: 41–43.
  Ritter replies to Schunk's criticism of his argument that debate should shift to a more public model.
Rickert, W.E. 1978. "Debate Poesis." *Journal of the American Forensic Association* 14: 141–43.

Rickert argues that fast technical debate is poetry and as such should be acknowledged as valuable despite its limited audience.

Morello, J.T. 1980. "Intercollegiate Debate: Proposals for a Struggling Activity." *Speaker and Gavel* 17, no. 2: 103–7.
Morello suggests that changes in the debating season, the National Debate Tournament, tournament format, and debate topic could foster a shift from rapid-fire delivery.

Hollihan, T.A., and P. Riley. 1987. "Academic Debate and Democracy: A Clash of Ideologies." *Proceedings of the Fifth SCA/AFA Conference on Argumentation*, eds. Joseph W. Wenzel, et al. Annandale VA: Speech Communication Association 399–404..
Hollihan and Riley argue that the current debate paradigm is antidemocratic insofar as it privileges expert knowledge and is inaccessible to the average citizen.

Rowland, R.C., and S. Deatherage. 1988. "The Crisis in Policy Debate." *Journal of the American Forensic Association* 24: 246–50.
Rowland and Deatherage argue that current practices in debate such as the fast rate of delivery are decreasing participation. They suggest that judges should develop enforcement norms to counter such developments.

Herbeck, D.A. 1989. "Is It Too Late to Save Policy Debate?" Paper presented at the 75th Annual Meeting of the Speech Communication Association, San Francisco, CA, November 18–21.
Herbeck argues that many of the problems faced by the National Debate Tournament, including declining participation, are a result of lack of intellectual leadership. Herbeck argues for rebalancing the activity by focusing on its educational, rather than competitive, aspects.

Panetta, E.M. 1990. "A Rationale for Developing a Nationally Competitive National Debate Tournament Oriented Program." *Argumentation and Advocacy* 27, no. 2: 68–77.
Panetta defends the current model of National Debate Tournament debate. He argues that debate's technical aspects prepare students for a future increasingly defined by specialized professions.

Morello, J.T. 1991. "Policy Implementation: The Virtual Disappearance of an Issue in NDT Debate." Paper presented at the Annual Meeting of the Speech Communication Association. http://eric.ed.gov:80/ERICDocs/data/ericdocs2sql/content_storage_01/0000019b/80/23/cd/ad.pdf (accessed June 28, 2009).
Morello outlines several aspects of policy debate that do not correlate with experiences outside of debate. He proposes changes in the activity to make it more in line with its purported educational goals.

Muir, S.A. 1993. "A Defense of the Ethics of Contemporary Debate." *Philosophy & Rhetoric* 26, no. 4: 277–95.
Muir offers a defense of the debate community's deployment of switch-side debate. He argues that switch-side debate teaches students to appreciate a multiplicity of viewpoints, which supports tolerance over dogmatism.

Balthrop, B. 1996. "The NDT and Intercollegiate Debate." *Argumentation & Advocacy* 32, no. 3: 154–59.
Balthrop focuses on the importance of the National Debate Tournament and the role of debate in civic life. However, he cites issues facing both the academic community and the broader society.

Morello, J.T. 1997. "The Future of the National Debate Tournament." *Perspectives on the Future of the National Debate Tournament*. http://groups.wfu.edu/NDT/Articles/morello.html (accessed June 25, 2009).
Morello outlines several trends that are undermining National Debate Tournament debate.

Mitchell, G.R. 1998. "Pedagogical Possibilities for Argumentative Agency in Academic Debate." *Argumentation and Advocacy* 35, no. 2: 41–61.
Mitchell argues that debate should interact more with the public sphere by supporting public debate and outreach as well as opening up room for public advocacy in contest rounds.

Hicks, D., and R.W. Greene. 2000. "Debating Both Sides: Argument Pedagogy and the Production of the Deliberative Citizen." In *Argument at Century's End: Reflecting on the Past and Envisioning the Future*, ed. T. Hollihan, 300–307. Annandale, VA: National Communication Association.

Hicks and Greene argue that the debates over "debating both sides" are important to understanding the function of debate.

Mitchell, G.R. 2000. "Simulated Public Argument as a Pedagogical Play on Worlds." *Argumentation and Advocacy* 36, no. 3: 134–50.

Juxtaposed to his earlier advocacy for opening the contest round, Mitchell identifies several concerns about using debate in the classroom. He proposes role-play exercises as a way to capture the benefits of debate without the potential downsides.

Greene, R.W., and D. Hicks. 2005. "Lost Convictions." *Cultural Studies* 19, no. 1: 100–126.

In a more developed formulation of their conference paper (1999), Greene and Hicks argue that debating both sides contributed to cold war liberalism because it eliminated the role of conviction in decision making.

Harrigan, C. 2008. "Against Dogmatism: A Continued Defense of Switch Side Debate." *Contemporary Argumentation and Debate* 29: 37–66.

In the most recent entry into the switch-side debate controversy, the author argues that switching sides is a remedy for intolerance and absolutism.

Innovation and Change

Although the basic format of a contest round has remained relatively static for more than 100 years, it is incorrect to conclude that intercollegiate debate is a stable, fixed, and unchanging institution. A distinctive and vibrant area of scholarship centers on proposals for innovation and change. The selections below demonstrate some of the ways in which innovation and change are at the center of the debate conversation.

Baird, A.C. 1923. "Shall American Universities Adopt the British System of Debating?" *Quarterly Journal of Speech Education* 9, no. 3: 215–22.

In this article, Baird argues against the growing trend of American universities to adopt the "British" style of debating (parliamentary debate). He argues that the American system of debating both sides is more rigorous, while acknowledging that the British approach has some merit (i.e., style).

Gray, J.S. 1926. "The Oregon Plan of Debating." *Quarterly Journal of Speech Education* 12, no. 2: 175–80.

Gray outlines the new method of debate that he planned to implement at the University of Oregon—"no-decision" debate—meaning there is neither a winner nor a loser. Gray's premise is that debate is plagued by an inflated importance on winning and a lack of objectivity among judges. One of the innovations in this plan is the use of cross-examination.

Parker, D.R. 1932. "The Use of Cross-examination in Debate." *Quarterly Journal of Speech* 18, no. 1: 97–102.

Parker proposes that debates should be structured more heavily around cross-examination. He suggests that the shift will increase audience attendance at debates as well as teach debaters valuable skills.

Rahskopf, H.G. 1932. "Questions of Facts vs. Questions of Policy." *Quarterly Journal of Speech* 18, no. 1: 60–70.

Rahskopf believes that questions of policy rather than questions of fact should be used for debate resolutions. He argues that questions of fact create ambiguities that prevent effective debating.

Hance, K.G. 1939. "The Dialectic Method in Debate." *Quarterly Journal of Speech* 25, no. 2: 243–48.

Hance argues for the use of cross-examination in debate. In this article he provides guidelines and instruction on how cross-examination could be improved drawing upon classical rhetorical theory.

Murphy, R. 1942. "Flexible Debate Topics." *Quarterly Journal of Speech* 28, no. 2: 160–64.

Murphy argues that the resolution should comprise of a subject area rather than a particular proposition. He believes such an approach would provide substantially more affirmative flexibility and thus prevent debates from becoming repetitive.

Directors of Forensics Big Ten Conference, 1954. "The Forum." *Quarterly Journal of Speech* 40, no. 4: 434–39.

This article is a letter to the journal arguing in favor of debate and tournament-style practice. While the letter notes some areas of improvement, the directors advocate the continued development of the tournament debating system.

Fuge, L.H., and R.P. Newman. 1956. "Cross-Examination in Academic Debating." *Speech Teacher* 5, no. 1: 66–70.

Fuge and Newman make the case for including cross-examination in the debate format. They argue that cross-examination increases audience interest and makes debaters quicker on their feet.

Goodnight, G.T. 1981. "The Re-Union of Argumentation and Debate Theory. In *Dimensions of Argument*, ed. G. Ziegelmueller and J. Rhodes, pp. 415–32. Annandale, VA: Speech Communication Association.

Goodnight attempts to reconnect argumentation theory and debate. He considers ways in which both the judge and the debater can implement more theoretically consistent positions. Goodnight argues that debate theory and argumentation can cross-pollinate.

Kay, J. 1983. "Rapprochement of World 1 and World 2: Discovering the Ties Between Practical Discourse and Forensics." In *Argument in Transition: Proceedings of the Third Summer Conference on Argumentation*, ed. D. Zarefsky, M.O. Sillars and J. Rhodes, 927–37. Annandale, VA: Speech Communication Association.

Kay argues that individual events provide too sterile an environment to be effective at teaching real-world argument skills. Instead, he proposes that individual events be modeled on real-world analogues such as presenting a bill before Congress.

Historical Perspective on Intercollegiate Debate

History matters, and the case for understanding debate's contemporary circumstances through historical perspective is well presented in the keynote address with which this volume begins. On this count, William Keith's *Democracy as Deliberation* is an invaluable contribution to historical studies of debate in the United States. While many unpublished histories that focus on individual college-debate programs are in circulation among particular campus audiences, a modest but valuable collection of published literature exists. Looking toward the future, this remains an area of research poised for growth.

Emerson, J.G. 1931. "The Old Debating Society." *Quarterly Journal of Speech* 17, no. 3: 362–75.

Emerson's article chronicles the development of literary and debate societies in American universities, and laments the decline of these groups and their loss of popularity.

Nichols, E.R. 1936. "A Historical Sketch of Intercollegiate Debating: I." *Quarterly Journal of Speech* 22, no. 2: 213–20.

Nichols offers a brief history of debate from the 4th century B.C.E. Greek tradition of argumentation to 1897.

Nichols, E.R. 1936. "A Historical Sketch of Intercollegiate Debating: II." *Quarterly Journal of Speech* 22, no. 4: 591–602.

Nichols offers a brief history of debate from 1900 to 1910.

Nichols, E.R. 1937. "A Historical Sketch of Intercollegiate Debating: III." *Quarterly Journal of Speech* 23, no. 2: 259–78.

Nichols offers a brief history of debate from 1913 to 1923.

Hopkins, A.A. 1944. "Conserving the Fundamental Values in Debating." *Southern Speech Journal* 10, no. 2: 25–28.

Hopkins describes the state of the University of Florida debate team before World War II, and outlines some practices that make for a better debate program.

Windes, R.R. 1961. *Championship Debating—West Point National Debate Tournament, Final-Round Debates and Critiques*. Portland, ME: J. Weston Walch.

Select transcripts and critiques from National Debate Tournament final rounds from 1949 to 1960.

Kruger, A.N.; R.R. Windes; and West Point National Debate. 1967. *Championship Debating, Volume II: West Point National Debate Tournament, Final-Round Debates and Critiques, 1961–66*. Portland, ME: J. Weston Walch.

Transcripts and critiques of National Debate Tournament final rounds from 1961 to 1966.

Cheshier, D.M.; L.L. Cowperthwaite; A.C. Baird; and University of Iowa. 1993. *On the Side of Truth : A Century of Intercollegiate Debate: Remembrances of A. Craig Baird*. Iowa City: University of Iowa, A. Craig Baird Debate Forum.

This book chronicles the history and legacy of A. Craig Baird at the University of Iowa and in his role in the development of intercollegiate debate.

AFA Policy Debate Caucus. 1994. "Report of the Working Committee from the Quail Roost Conference on Assessment of Professional Activities of Directors of Debate." *Forensic of Pi Kappa Delta* 79 (Winter): 19–25.

Report of the 1994 development conference concerning the requirements for professional advancement for directors of debate.

Hynes, T.J. 1996. "Fifty Years of the National Debate Tournament." *Argumentation and Advocacy* 32, no. 3: 158–61.

Hynes reflects on his own career as a debater in the National Debate Tournament (NDT). He makes the case for the value of the NDT and academic debate.

Zarefsky, D. 1996. "Reflections on the NDT at 50." *Argumentation and Advocacy* 32, no. 3: 153–55.

Zarefsky wishes the National Debate Tournament a happy 50th birthday and discusses its role as a symbol of what is best about the debate community.

Ziegelmueller, G. 1996. "The National Debate Tournament: Through a Half-century of Argument." *Argumentation and Advocacy* 32, no. 3: 143–52.

Presents a history and rationale for the National Debate Tournament from its inception in 1947.

Fine, G.A. 2001. *Gifted Tongues High School Debate and Adolescent Culture*. Princeton, NJ: Princeton University Press.

Fine's book is a thorough sociological inquiry into American high-school debate in the 1990s. Written for a nondebating audience, the book explores the culture of competitive debate.

Atchison, J., and E.M. Panetta. 2008. "Intercollegiate Debate and Speech Communication: Historical Developments and Issues for the Future." In *The Sage Handbook of Rhetorical Studies*, ed. A.A. Lunsford, K.H. Wilson, and R.A. Eberly, 317–34. Los Angeles, CA: Sage.

Atchison and Panetta trace the history of American intercollegiate debate. They further consider the benefits and issues with the development of debate and offer suggestions for pedagogical improvement.

Appendix II: Guide to Debate Organizations on the Web

Anjali Vats, Washington Debate Coalition, Seattle and University of Puget Sound

INTERNATIONAL DEBATE ORGANIZATIONS

Asian Debating Web Site
http://asiandebating.blogspot.com
The Asian Debating Web site provides information about debate across the world, with an emphasis on countries in Asia and the Middle East.

Bangladesh Debating Council
http://debatebangladesh.tripod.com
The Bangladesh debating council (BDC) is the national debating body for English debate in Bangladesh. Its objective is to build national-level debating talents for global debating challenges. The BDC is affiliated with the World Universities Debating Council, the Asian Universities Debating Council, and the World Schools Debating Council.

Benjamin Franklin Transatlantic Fellows Initiative
http://blogs.bftf.org
The Benjamin Franklin Transatlantic Fellows Initiative (BFTF) provides a summer reunion and conference at American University in Bulgaria. Participants in the BFTF take part in opportunities designed to foster relationships among youth from Eurasia, Europe, and America, advance principles of freedom, and build cooperation. The inspiration for the BFTF is American statesman and diplomat Benjamin Franklin who prized religious tolerance over intolerance and social mobility over class privilege, and firmly believed in free speech. The BFTF seeks to build an environment that encourages individual expression, communications, and information sharing in an effort to advance positive relationships among ethnic, religious, and national groups.

Canadian University Society for Intercollegiate Debate
http://www.cusid.ca
The Canadian University Society for Intercollegiate Debate (CUSID) is a national organization that governs and represents university debating in Canada. CUSID sanctions several official tournaments, including various regional championships, the British Parliamentary Championships, the National Championships, and the North American Championships in conjunction with the

American Parliamentary Debate Association. Its membership comprises debating clubs, sanctioned by their respective universities, from across Canada.

Committee on International Discussion and Debate
http://groups.wfu.edu/debate/International%20Debates/cidd.html
The Committee on International Discussion and Debate, formed by the Speech Communication Association (now the National Communication Association; NCA) in 1929, formulates policy and administrative guidelines for NCA-sponsored international student-exchange debates. These international student-exchange debates have included students from Great Britain, Australia, New Zealand, Russia, Japan, and the Philippines, among others.

Debate Association
http://www.debates.org.sg
Debate Association is a nonprofit volunteer-run organization that aims to develop, nurture, and promote debating in Singapore. Together with volunteers, it reaches out to those who have not yet discovered debating, and to those who already love the activity. Debate Association helps schools, teachers, coaches, and students by organizing competitions, running training programs and camps, and providing resources. Debate Association also works with partners from all industries who are interested in using debate as a means to achieve their objectives.

Debaters' Council (Sri Lanka)
http://thedebaterscouncil.blogspot.com
The Debaters' Council is an organization made up of past school and university-level debaters in Sri Lanka. It has selected the Sri Lanka schools' debating team for the World Schools Debating Championships from 2007 to 2010. The council also conducts free workshops and adjudication services for member schools.

Debating Society of Pakistan
http://pakistandebatingsociety.com
The Debating Society of Pakistan (DSP) is a registered nonprofit organization that promotes educational activity through debates in Pakistan. It trains youth in the art of convincing, opens minds, encourages tolerance, and teaches the importance of teamwork. DSP holds three tournaments at the national level and sends the Pakistan National Team to the World Championships each year.

English-Speaking Union Center
http://www.esu.org/page.asp?p=1646
The English-Speaking Union (ESU) Centre for Speech and Debate coordinates the ESU's work in persuasive spoken English, and is the world leader in providing English-language support for the use of debate and extended speech in an educational context. It also provides debate training to teachers and students in the United Kingdom and abroad through a range of programs, including Discover Your Voice, Debate Academy, the Speech and Debate Squad, and British-Debate.com. The ESU has also run the U.K. and U.S. annual debate exchange since 1922, and selects and coaches the England Schools debating team. The ESU supports debate programs in Scotland, Malaysia, and Argentina, among others.

Hong Kong Parliamentary Debating Society
http://www.hkpds.org/index.html
The Hong Kong Parliamentary Debating Society is composed of members of the English debating teams of the Chinese University of Hong Kong and the University of Hong Kong. The society aims to improve the standard of Hong Kong's performance at the international competitions, thereby promoting Hong Kong both as a community rich in debating talent and a city with the highest educational standards.

International Debate Education Association
http://www.idebate.org/about/index.php
The International Debate Education Association (IDEA) develops, organizes, and promotes debate and debate-related activities in communities throughout the world. Established in 1999 to coordinate pilot debate programs initiated by the Open Society Institute, IDEA acts as an independent membership organization of national debate clubs, associations, programs, and individuals who share a common purpose: to promote mutual understanding and democracy globally by supporting discussion and active citizenship locally.

International Forensics Association
http://www.brookdale.cc.nj.us/pages/505.asp
The International Forensics Association (IFA) promotes the diversity of forensic competition in countries around the world. Typically, up to 35 colleges and universities participate in IFA-sponsored tournaments each year. To date, the highlight of each season has included an international tournament held annually in a different country. The IFA is committed to offering students a chance

not only to participate in a highly competitive tournament but also to experience new surroundings and cultural differences, view architectural treasures, and take advantage of opportunities to expand their appreciation of the arts.

International Public Debate Association
http://www.uamont.edu/ipda/mission.html
The International Public Debate Association (IPDA) promotes an alternative debate format that emphasizes real-world, audience-centered delivery. It is dedicated to serving the needs of traditional and nontraditional students of debate, including nonnative English speakers, forensic educators, and the global forensics community.

Iraq Debate
http://www.iraqdebate.org
Iraq Debate is an initiative to support debate in all universities and schools interested in debate. It aims to teach students to express themselves and develop democratic institutions.

Israel Debating Society
http://israeldebate.com/index.php
The Israel Debating Society is a volunteer-run organization that supports debate leagues in Hebrew and English. Israeli national teams have participated in the European Debating Championships, the World Individual Debating and Public Speaking Championships, the Asper Cup, and the World Schools Debating Championships. The Israel Debating Society also participates in International Debate Education Association workshops in Eastern and Central Europe. The Israel Debating Society is currently seeking to provide more teacher training for debate in Hebrew, English, and Arabic; develop its Web site; update its debate handbook; hire a fundraiser; and produce Hebrew debate training videos.

Japan Debate Association
http://japan-debate-association.org
The Japan Debate Association (JDA) was inaugurated in March 1986 with the goal of promoting debate activities and developing debate skills in Japan. The JDA aims to help Japan maintain its role in the international arena by training advocates who can communicate the nation's positions and promote debate activities and exchange of information throughout society.

L.N. Birla Memorial Debate (India)

http://www.birlahighschool.com/lnbirladebate/concept.htm

The L.N. Birla Memorial Debate was instituted in 1994 to honor industrialist and philanthropist L.N. Birla. From 1994 to 1999 it was an annual interschool competition. It became so successful, however, that it became a national event that includes colleges as well as high schools.

National English Debating Competition (China)

http://www.chinadebate.org

The Foreign Language, Teaching and Research Press National English Debating Competition is the only nationwide English debating event in China The tournament, which is conducted in English, attracts the best and brightest students from over 100 Chinese universities. Competitors have gone on to participate in major regional and international events, including the Asian University Debating Championships, the Australasian Debating Championships, and the World Universities Debating Championships.

Paragon Academy (Korea)

http://speakerspoint.com/blog/about/

Paragon Academy, a special learning center based in Seoul, South Korea, specializes in improving the communication skills of young students seeking to adapt to a globalized world. It focuses on public speaking, essay writing, debating, college applications consulting, and more.

QatarDebate

http://www.qatardebate.org

QatarDebate, a member of Qatar Foundation, is a civic engagement initiative that aims to develop and support the standard of open discussion and debate among students and young people in Qatar and the broader Arab World. Its mission is to foster a culture of discussion and debate, and in doing so, create the leaders of tomorrow. Since 2007, over 3,000 students have participated in QatarDebate's annual workshops, and the organization now has a presence in over 30 schools and universities in Qatar. QatarDebate currently works with students in secondary schools (12+) and universities in Qatar, and in 2009 began incorporating preparatory school students into its programs.

Verbattle (India)
http://www.verbattle.com

Verbattle, established in 2005, has been reaching out to school children in the form of Verbattle Junior and to college youth as Verbattle Senior—two major debate competitions that can easily be considered the biggest intellectual event for children and youth in the state of Karnataka. Verbattle aims to grow into a national event and ultimately into a global opportunity for the exchange of opinions.

NATIONAL AND REGIONAL DEBATE ASSOCIATIONS

American Debate Association
http://www.umw.edu/cas/debate/ada/default.php

The American Debate Association (ADA), founded in 1985, is committed to balancing the educational and competitive goals of policy debate in an atmosphere that expands opportunities for participation in the activity at the college level.

American Forensic Association
http://www.americanforensics.org

The American Forensic Association (AFA) promotes argument and advocacy, and supports professions whose activities support its credo. Key components of the AFA credo include a belief in the power of individuals to participate in shaping their world through the human capacity of language, faith in argument, and reason as a means of empowerment, and appreciation for the place of argument and advocacy in preparing students, through classrooms, forums, and competition, for participation in their world through the power of expression. The AFA is also the chartering organization of the National Debate Tournament.

American Parliamentary Debate Association
http://www.apdaweb.org

The American Parliamentary Debate Association is the oldest parliamentary debate association in the United States and its membership includes dozens of colleges and universities.

California Community College Forensics Association
http://www.cccfa.net

The California Community College Forensics Association sponsors the annual California State Championship Forensics Tournament, promotes competitive forensics activities, and provides educational, professional, and leadership experience in the field of speech communication.

Council of Forensics Organizations

http://cas.bethel.edu/dept/comm/cofo/index.html

The Council of Forensics Organization (COFO) was created after the second national developmental conference on forensics, held in Evanston, Illinois, in 1984. COFO aims to increase dialogue between forensic organizations such as the Cross Examination Debate Association, the American Forensic Association, and the National Forensics Association.

Cross Examination Debate Association

http://cedadebate.org

Founded in 1971 as the Southwest Cross Examination Debate Association, the Cross Examination Debate Association (CEDA) is now the primary national association promoting policy topic intercollegiate academic debate. In cooperation with the National Debate Tournament Committee and the American Debate Association, CEDA formulates the annual intercollegiate policy-debate topic used in tournament competition throughout the nation.

CEDA also acts as a tournament-sanctioning agent, providing through its constitution and by-laws a framework for normalizing tournament practices and procedures. Throughout the tournament season, CEDA calculates the National Sweepstakes Standings, the national and regional rankings of member institutions based on compiled tournament results. The association also hosts an annual National Championship Tournament that brings together over 200 individual debate teams from across the nation.

National Catholic Forensics League

http://www.ncfl.org

The National Catholic Forensic League is dedicated to supporting high-school speech and debate activities for public, private, and parochial high schools in the United States and Canada. It hosts the Grand National Tournament annually in May.

National Christian College Forensics Association

http://cas.bethel.edu/dept/comm/nccfi/index.html

The National Christian College Forensics Association sponsors the National Christian College Forensics Invitational, a forensics tournament for schools in the Council of Christian Colleges and Universities, as well as other like-minded schools.

National Christian Forensics and Communications Association

http://www.ncfca.org

The National Christian Forensics and Communications Association (NCFCA) believes that "formal speech and debate can provide a means for home-schooled students to learn and exercise analytical and oratorical skills, addressing life issues from a Biblical world view in a manner that glorifies God." To provide these opportunities, the NCFCA facilitates qualifying tournaments throughout the country and an annual national tournament.

National Communication Association

http://www.natcom.org

The National Communication Association (NCA) is the largest and oldest national organization dedicated to communication scholarship and education. Its goal is to enhance the research, teaching, and service produced by its members on topics of both intellectual and social significance. The NCA's argumentation and forensics division invites submission of thematic panels, discussion panels, and individual papers for competitive review. It welcomes panels, programs, and papers promoting the understanding of argumentation theory, argumentation criticism, and forensic pedagogy, and encourages programs featuring innovative formats as well as papers relating to a given year's convention theme.

National Debate Coaches Association

http://debatecoaches.org

The National Debate Coaches Association (NDCA) is devoted to providing resources for a variety of high-school debate events, including policy, Lincoln–Douglas, Student Congress, and extemporaneous speaking. The NDCA offers curriculum support as well as timely articles and blogs devoted to addressing important issues in the debate community. The NDCA also hosts a national championship tournament in the spring.

National Debate Tournament

http://groups.wfu.edu/NDT/

The National Debate Tournament (NDT) aims to encourage the growth of programs for excellence in forensics education in institutions of higher education in the United States. The NDT is committed to providing opportunities for quality debate to students of all institutions of higher education by maximizing the number and geographic representation of participating schools, encouraging the highest standards of debate excellence by maximizing the competitive quality of participating schools, and encouraging the highest standards of educational excellence by conducting a tournament consistent with the educational objectives of intercollegiate forensics competition. The American Forensic Association is the chartering organization of the NDT.

National Education Debate Association
http://cstl-cla.semo.edu/Underberg/neda
The National Education Debate Association (NEDA) believes that debate should be a practical educational experience and that performance by participants should reflect the stylistic and analytical skills that would be rewarded in typical public forums (i.e., courts, Congress, the classroom, civic gatherings, etc.). To facilitate this mission, NEDA hosts a variety of tournament events open to students and directors willing to abide by and enforce standards of ethical, responsible, humane, and communicative advocacy. NEDA tournaments are viewed as an extension of the speech classroom.

National Federation of State High School Associations
http://www.nfhs.org/speechdebate.aspx
The National Federation of State High School Associations, Speech, Debate and Theatre Association (NFHS SDTA) is a professional organization specifically for directors and coaches of high-school speech, debate, and theatre programs. It serves its members by providing leadership for the administration of education-based interscholastic activities that support academic achievement, good citizenship, and equitable opportunities. The NFHS SDTA also offers many other educational services that are available to anyone, regardless of membership in the organization.

National Forensics Association
http://cas.bethel.edu/dept/comm/nfa/
The National Forensics Association (NFA) is an intercollegiate forensics association devoted to individual events and Lincoln–Douglas debate. It is affiliated with the American Forensic Association, an umbrella group of organizations interested in the promotion of intercollegiate speech and debate.

National Forensic League
http://www.nflonline.org/Main/HomePage
The National Forensic League (NFL) believes that all students should be empowered to become effective communicators, ethical individuals, critical thinkers, and leaders in a democratic society. It exists to promote secondary-school speech and debate activities and interscholastic competition as a means to de-

velop a student's lifelong skills and values, and to increase the public's awareness of the value of speech, debate, and communication education.

National Parliamentary Debate Association
http://www.bethel.edu/Majors/Communication/npda/home.html
The National Parliamentary Debate Association (NPDA) is an intercollegiate debate association whose member schools engage in two-on-two debate, with the resolutions, or topics, changing for each round of competition. Each year, between 200 and 250 schools attend at least one parliamentary debate tournament sponsored by NPDA member schools.

URBAN DEBATE ORGANIZATIONS
Atlanta Urban Debate League
http://audl.wordpress.com
The Atlanta Urban Debate League is a partnership effort between Georgia State University, Emory University, and the Atlanta Public School System to promote debate as a tool for empowering urban and rural youth living in America's most socioeconomically challenged communities. In the spirit of preparing future leaders who can both engage their communities and successfully advocate for their needs, it seeks to extend the benefits of debate and advocacy training to traditionally underserved student and teacher populations.

Associated Leaders of Urban Debate
http://www.debateleaders.org/root/NEWwelcome.shtml
The Associated Leaders of Urban Debate (ALOUD) represents a global network of partner programs transforming the lives of young people through debate. ALOUD promotes youth expression as a vehicle for urban education reform and civic participation.

Austin Urban Debate League
http://www.debateleaders.org/root/Debate_in_your_community.shtml
The Austin Urban Debate League (AUDL) creates a vibrant and competitive debate community open to all students in the Austin, Texas, metropolitan area. In 2004 the league had an initial roster of 14 high schools, located in the Austin Independent School District and neighboring districts of Del Valle and San Marcos. The AUDL is a leader in digital debate and has partnered with Texas State University and the University of Texas.

Baltimore Urban Debate League
http://www.budl.org
The Baltimore Urban Debate League enriches the academic experience of students from Baltimore City's public elementary, middle, and high schools through participation in team policy debate. Through debate, students become engaged learners, critical thinkers, and citizens and leaders who are effective advocates for themselves and their communities.

Boston Urban Debate League
http://www.bostondebate.org
The Boston Urban Debate League (BDL) was founded in 2005 and aims to provide high-school students with an engaging educational opportunity that actively cultivates social and academic skills. BDL initiatives include citywide tournaments, after-school programs, a summer debate institute, coach training, and professional development. The BDL is also developing and implementing debate-across-the-curriculum programs.

Columbus Urban Debate League
http://www.debateleaders.org/root/Debate_in_your_community.shtml
The Columbus (Ohio) Urban Debate League was founded in 2006 in partnership with Capital University and the local school district.

DEBATE-Kansas City
http://www.debatekansascity.org
Since 1998, DEBATE-Kansas City has engaged over 1,300 middle- and high-school students in policy-debate competition. The program's growth, popularity, and reputation are due to the dedication and commitment of its teachers, students, staff, volunteers, and community partners. DEBATE-Kansas City's urban debate programs improve standardized test scores and grade point averages. They help students to develop higher self-esteem as well as reduce student's risky behaviors and increase their desire to graduate and attend college.

District of Columbia Urban Debate League
http://www.dcdebate.org
The District of Columbia Urban Debate League (DCUDL) is part of a national movement that seeks to bring the opportunities and benefits of debate to the underserved urban students of America. Specifically, the DCUDL is dedicated to expanding the opportunities for the young people of the District of Columbia to develop reading, writing, and speaking skills through intellectual competi-

tion, and to become confident, articulate citizens and authentic leaders of their communities.

Duval County Urban Debate League
http://www.dudl.org
The Duval County Urban Debate League (DUDL) is the first for-profit school-system partnership in the ALOUD network. The DUDL is supported by the Blacksonville Community Network (BCN), a social marketing firm that advocates the use of technology to promote positive change and social responsibility in business and in the nonprofit sector. BCN provides digital media, consulting, and interactive strategies to brand nontraditional programs and campaigns to a number of Fortune 500 companies.

Houston Urban Debate League
http://houstonurbandebateleague.org
The Houston Urban Debate League (HUDL) builds, supports, and sustains programs in Houston's public schools to make policy debate an educational resource available to all students. The HUDL builds public–private partnerships that enhance the investment of school districts in debate activities by providing business and community finance, mentoring, communication, and facilities to restore policy debate in all of Houston's public high schools.

IMPACT Alabama
http://www.impactalabama.org/spfhome.php
The SpeakFirst program at IMPACT Alabama enriches the academic experience of gifted students from Birmingham's public high schools through participation in an "all-star" debate team. This highly collaborative initiative addresses a wide array of needs created by the deficit of opportunities and resources in their local communities, including one-on-one tutoring and mentoring, college admissions and financial aid guidance, standardized test preparation, youth development activities, and summer internships for the debaters.

IMPACT Coalition
http://www.impactcoalition.org
The Improving Mentoring Practices and Communication Techniques (IMPACT) Coalition is a mentoring and educational development organization that expands opportunities for urban students, schools, and organizational partners by providing debate training, literacy assistance, curricula, and mentoring services to develop informed, concerned citizens. IMPACT

advocates debate as a key to success in building healthier communities and tomorrow's leaders.

Jersey Urban Debate League

http://www.judl.org

The Jersey Urban Debate League is dedicated to offering students in urban middle schools and high schools in New Jersey the opportunity to engage in competitive academic debate and to providing them with the intellectual and argumentative tools necessary for success.

Miami Dade Urban Debate League

http://debate.miami.edu

The Miami Dade Urban Debate League is one of the fastest-growing urban debate leagues in the nation, with 18 high schools and 14 middle schools participating in the league in 2009, and new schools and students being added at each tournament. Founded by the National Debate Project, the program represents a partnership between the Miami-Dade school district, friends of Miami Urban Debate, and the University of Miami.

Milwaukee Debate League

http://debatemilwaukee.org

The Milwaukee Debate League (MDL) is an urban education program that utilizes competitive, policy debate in an effort to promote equity in education in urban areas. The MDL is a program born of the partnership between the National Debate Project and the Einhorn Family Charitable Trust. As part of the national urban debate league movement, the MDL enables urban schools, which often have not had the necessary resources, to start debate teams and compete on a regular basis so that students can continually sharpen their skills. .

National Association for Urban Debate Leagues

http://urbandebate.org/index.htm

The National Association for Urban Debate Leagues is a national organization that facilitates participation in organized debate activities for as many urban students as possible. NAUDL achieves its mission by building urban debate leagues (UDLs) in new cities, strengthening UDLs that are struggling, expanding the scope and quality of debate coaching and instruction, and connecting existing UDLs through networking events and services.

New Haven Urban Debate League

http://www.udlnewhaven.com

The New Haven Urban Debate League (NHUDL) aims to teach students critical-thinking and public-speaking skills; offer them opportunities to engage in independent research of current events, philosophy, government, and economics; and nurture student self-confidence. The NHUDL is administered by Yale University students and strives to build a supportive student, parent, and coaching community between NHUDL schools and Yale. NAUDL achieves its mission by building urban debate leagues (UDLs) in new cities, strengthening UDLs that are struggling, expanding the scope and quality of debate coaching and instruction, and connecting existing UDLs through networking events and services.

Rhode Island Urban Debate League

http://swearercenter.brown.edu/riudl

The Rhode Island Urban Debate League (RIUDL) offers Rhode Island high-school students opportunities to participate in policy debate by recruiting and training coaches and volunteer coaching assistants, hosting tournaments, and sponsoring a public debate program. Through these actions, the RIUDL aims to enhance students' academic backgrounds, foster their leadership skills, and stimulate their interest in current policy issues.

Seattle Debate Foundation

http://seattledebate.org

The Seattle Debate Foundation (SDF) is a social-justice organization committed to the critical literacy and empowerment of urban youth through debate education. The SDF supports debate through the Seattle and Tacoma urban debate leagues. It partners with public schools, colleges and universities, community centers, and youth-empowerment organizations to create competitive, sustainable debate teams and debating opportunities that can unite the community.

Southern California Urban Debate League

http://communications.fullerton.edu/forensics/SCUDL.htm

The Southern California Urban Debate League (SCUDL) partners high-school students with collegiate speech and debate competitors to develop the skills required to compete in interscholastic debate competitions. Students learn to research, speak, think critically, and advocate on important topics. Each year, scores of SCUDL students attend several tournaments on campuses such as University of Southern California; California State University (CSU), Long Beach; Cypress Community College; and CSU-Fullerton.

SpeakFirst

http://www.impactalabama.org

SpeakFirst's mission is to enrich the academic experience of gifted students from Birmingham's public high schools through participation on an "all-star" debate team. Starting with a select group of incoming high-school freshmen, this highly collaborative initiative addresses a full array of needs in ways proven to be of great academic and civic value. The debate training provided by SpeakFirst develops students' critical-thinking, presentation, and public-speaking skills. SpeakFirst is one of three signature initiatives of IMPACT Alabama. IMPACT Alabama presents a vision of Alabama in which its young citizens understand, appreciate, and engage actively in civic and public life, contributing their diverse talents to solve local and state problems, influencing public policy, voting, and pursuing the common good.

Tacoma Urban Debate League

http://www.seattledebate.org

The Tacoma Urban Debate League (TUDL) is an ALOUD partner. Founded by the Seattle Debate Foundation through partnerships with the Comcast Foundation, University of Puget Sound, the HERO Initiative at the College Success Foundation, Hip Hop Congress, and Free Ya Mind, Inc., TUDL started with three debate programs at Foss, Lincoln, and Mount Tahoma.

Urban Debate League of the Twin Cities

http://www.umpds.org/udl

The Urban Debate League of the Twin Cities (UDLTS) exists to improve urban public education by empowering students to become engaged learners, critical thinkers, and active citizens who are effective advocates for themselves and their communities. In support of this mission, the UDLTS increases public awareness of the organization's goals and objectives; makes decisions based on the best interests of the students and communities it serves; provides quality, challenging instruction and debate opportunities in safe, supportive environments; maintains relationships with officials from the government, the media, the advocacy community, business, foundations, and schools; and partners with community leaders, teachers, and college coaches to provide instruction and mentoring opportunities for student participants.

POLICY DEBATE RESOURCES
3NR.com
http://www.the3nr.com

3NR.com is a collaboration between three debate coaches—Scott Phillips, Roy Levkovitz, and Bill Batterman—whose goal is to make a positive contribution to the high-school debate community's marketplace of ideas. 3NR.com is frequently updated with content that high-school debaters, judges, and coaches will find interesting and thought-provoking in equal parts. In particular, the site administrators seek to spark discussions and debates about a wide range of issues that are important to the high-school debate community.

Cross-X.com
http://www.cross-x.com

Cross-X.com provides evidence for policy debaters as well as forums for discussion of topic-related issues, debate camps, and tournament debating, among other activities. It also provides forums for discussion of other types of debate including Public Forum, Student Congress, Lincoln–Douglas, and Parliamentary Debate.

Debate Across the Curriculum
http://www.budl.org/content/debate-across-curriculum

Debate Across the Curriculum (DAC) is a global movement to include debate as a pedagogical tool for classroom instruction. While debate has long flourished as an extracurricular competitive activity, and debate has been formally taught as a class itself, the DAC movement emphasizes the long-standing tradition of using debate as a vehicle for teaching a wide range of subjects, from English literature to American government—even to subjects like math or biology.

Debate Central
http://debate-central.ncpa.org

Debate Central is an online resource created and maintained by the National Center for Policy Analysis for high-school students researching the high-school policy debate topic. It includes such materials as an analysis of the high-school policy-debate topic and an "Ask the Experts" section for questions related to the topic.

Debatepedia
http://wiki.idebate.org/index.php/Welcome_to_Debatepedia!

Debatepedia is "the Wikipedia of pros and cons." Its mission is to "clarify public debates and improve decision-making globally." Debatepedia is a project of the International Debate Education Association. It utilizes the same wiki technology powering Wikipedia to engage citizen-editors in clarifying public debates by centralizing them into a single pro/con encyclopedia, encouraging better and more informed decision making, and enhancing the workings of democratic institutions. Debatepedia is endorsed by the National Forensic League.

Global Debate Blog
http://globaldebateblog.blogspot.com
The Global Debate Blog features news about debating both in competitive and educational contexts. It is affiliated with Debate Central.

Infinite Prep
http://www.infiniteprep.com
Infinite Prep is dedicated to democratizing the debate community by providing free and low-cost research resources to debaters. It also features a blog that includes free daily evidence as well as information about debate tournaments across the country.

National Debate Project
http://www.nationaldebateproject.org
The National Debate Project (NDP) believes that the acquisition of debate and other civic advocacy skills is central to building a functioning democracy. In the spirit of preparing future leaders who can both engage their communities and successfully advocate for their needs, the NDP seeks to extend the benefits of debate and advocacy training to traditionally underserved student and teacher populations. The NDP also institutionalizes a collaborative infrastructure to facilitate the use of debate and discussion as a catalyst for educational reform.

Planet Debate
http://www.planetdebate.com/
Planet Debate provides curricular resources, topic lectures, and an evidence database for policy debaters and coaches from some of the best-known debate coaches in the country. It also provides support for Lincoln–Douglas, Public Forum, and extemporaneous debate.

Washington Debate Coalition
http://www.washingtondebate.org
The Washington Debate Coalition (WDC) is an educational development or-

ganization that seeks to expand opportunities for students to engage in all forms of speech, debate, and dialogue, with an emphasis on policy debate, in the state of Washington. The WDC advocates and promotes all forms of speech, debate, and dialogue as means of encouraging informed citizen participation in civil society and enhancing critical-thinking skills.

West Coast Debate
http://www.wcdebate.com
West Coast Debate (WCD) provides handbooks, textbooks, and other curricular resources for policy debate, Lincoln–Douglas debate, and individual events.

Women's Debate Institute
http://www.womensdebateinstitute.org/about.html
The Women's Debate Institute provides young women with the opportunity to be part of a strong community of women who love debate. It also offers young women intensive instruction from top-level debate coaches and national debate champions.

ALTERNATIVE MODELS OF DEBATE
Aspen Institute
http://www.aspeninstitute.org
The Aspen Institute aims to foster values-based leadership, encouraging individuals to reflect on the ideals and ideas that define a good society, and to provide a neutral and balanced venue for discussing and acting on critical issues. It accomplishes its goals in four ways (1) seminars on what participants think makes a good society; (2) young leadership fellowships around the globe; (3) policy programs that serve as nonpartisan forums for analysis; and (4) public conferences and events that create a commons for people to share ideas.

Bella Abzug Leadership Institute
http://www.abzuginstitute.org
The Bella Abzug Leadership Institute (BALI) utilizes the signature leadership skills of the late New York representative Bella S. Abzug (1920–98) to mentor and train high-school and college-age women and help develop the confidence and skills they need to be effective, dynamic, and visionary leaders as well as active and creative participants in civic, political, corporate, and community life.

Commission on Presidential Debates
http://www.debates.org
The Commission on Presidential Debates (CPD) was established in 1987 to ensure that debates, as a permanent part of every general election, provide the best possible information to viewers and listeners. Its primary purpose is to sponsor and produce debates for U.S. presidential and vice-presidential candidates and to undertake research and educational activities relating to the debates. The organization, which is a nonprofit, nonpartisan corporation, sponsored all of the presidential debates in 1988, 1992, 1996, 2000, and 2004. To meet its ongoing goal of educating voters, the CPD is engaged in various activities beyond producing and sponsoring the presidential debates. Further, the CPD provides technical assistance to emerging democracies and others interested in establishing debate traditions in their countries. Finally, the CPD coordinates post-debate symposia and research after many of its presidential forums.

The Debaters
http://www.cbc.ca/thedebaters
The Debaters is a weekly Canadian comedy radio program devoted to contesting various news and social topics. In the style of *Whose Line Is It Anyway*, the debaters are awarded points for their arguments and jokes before the audience ultimately determines the winner of the debate.

Debate Solutions
http://www.debatesolutions.com/home.php
Debate Solutions (DS) is an organization that provides support for program development, policy analysis, and skills coaching for students and professionals. DS has been facilitating public debates involving college debaters and the Environmental Protection Agency. It is also working on a debate initiative for historically black colleges and universities.

Democracy Prep Charter School
http://www.democracyprep.org
Democracy Prep is a public charter school in Central Harlem. Its mission is to prepare responsible citizen-scholars in grades 6–12 for success in the college of their choice and a life of active citizenship with a simple philosophy: Work Hard. Go to College. Change the World!

IDebate

http://www.idebate.ncpa.org/about

IDebate is a five-day leadership development camp that trains high-school students in strategic thinking, planning, communication, teamwork, and persuasion. Throughout the program, students are taught to practice their new skills through debate about current issues. They also receive practical training in the art of persuasion, gain in-depth knowledge of various public issues, gather valuable team experiences, and develop relationships with other up-and-coming leaders. IDebate was developed under the leadership of General Tommy Franks in partnership with the National Center for Policy Analysis and Oklahoma Christian University.

Intelligence^2 Debates

http://intelligencesquaredus.org

Intelligence Squared US is a television program, also broadcast on National Public Radio, featuring Oxford-style debates on significant and timely public policy issues. Previous debaters have included Eliot Spitzer, Fareed Zakaria, and John MacArthur. Intelligence Squared US aims to raise the level of public discourse on challenging issues and provide a new forum for intelligent discussion, grounded in facts and informed by reasoned analysis. It also empowers audience members to both ask questions and vote at the end of each debate.

Malcolm X Prison Debate Project

http://malcolmxdebates.org

The Malcolm X Prison Debate Project is a New York-based organization that seeks to empower incarcerated youth and reduce reentry into the system by supporting the establishment of debate programs in youth incarceration centers.

National Center for Policy Analysis

http://www.ncpa.org

The National Center for Policy Analysis (NCPA) is a nonprofit, nonpartisan public policy research organization, established in 1983. The NCPA's goal is to develop and promote private alternatives to government regulation and control, solving problems by relying on the strength of the competitive, entrepreneurial private sector. The NCPA sponsors two debate-related programs, IDebate and Debate Central. IDebate and Debate Central are separately listed in this directory.

National Coalition for Dialogue and Deliberation

http://www.thataway.org

The National Coalition for Dialogue and Deliberation (NCDD) provides infrastructure needed to increase both the individual and collective impact of those attempting to give individuals a voice. NCDD's mission is to bring together and support people, organizations, and resources in ways that expand the power of discussion to benefit society.

National Public Policy Forum (NPPF)

http://www.nppf.net

The National Public Policy Forum (NPPF), sponsored by the law firm of Bickel & Brewer, hosts a debate tournament open to all high-school students whether or not their school has a debate team (but only one team per school may compete). The topic of the debate is based on the current National Forensic League Policy/Team Debate topic but the actual form of debate is unique and distinct from public forum or policy. The competition is judged on factors including, but not limited to, well-founded arguments, effective communication, and grammar. All teams in the top sixteen receive cash prizes and the grand prize winner receives $10,000.

Opposing Views

http://www.opposingviews.com

Opposing Views helps citizens uncover all sides of issues by offering expert debates on significant political, social, health, money, and religion questions. Its point/counterpoint format gives each expert a chance to state his or her information and opinions on an issue. The other side then has the opportunity to object by identifying flaws in the information and opinions, and presenting the opposing side of the argument.

Perspectives Debate

http://www.perspectivesdebate.org

Perspectives Debate is a Philadelphia-based nonprofit organization that promotes youth debate education. Students who debate achieve dramatically increased reading-comprehension, critical-thinking, and public-speaking skills. In the process, debate becomes a forum to foster youth achievement and civic responsibility. Perspectives Debate is helping schools provide curricular and out-of-school-hour debate programs and offering students meaningful enrichment opportunities.